Montazeri

The Life and Thought of Iran's Revolutionary Ayatollah

By the time of his death in 2009, the Grand Ayatollah Montazeri was lauded as the spiritual leader of the Green Movement in Iran. From the 1960's, when he supported Ayatollah Khomeini's opposition to the Shah, Montazeri's life reflected the crucial political shifts within the country. In this book, Sussan Siavoshi presents both the historical context and Montazeri's own political and intellectual journey. Siavoshi highlights how Montazeri, originally a student of Khomeini, became one of the key figures during the revolution of 1978–79. She furthermore analyzes his subsequent writings, explaining how he went from trusted advisor to and nominated successor of Khomeini to an outspoken critic of the Islamic Republic. Examining Montazeri's political thought and practice as well as the historical context, Siavoshi's book is vital for those interested in post-revolutionary Iran and the phenomenon of political Islam.

SUSSAN SIAVOSHI is the Cox Chapman Professor of Political Science at Trinity University, Texas. Born and raised in Iran, she is the author of numerous articles on the politics of post-revolutionary Iran and Shii religious discourse, as well as the book *Liberal Nationalism in Iran: The Failure of a Movement*.

Montazeri

The Life and Thought of Iran's Revolutionary Ayatollah

SUSSAN SIAVOSHI

Trinity University, Texas

CAMBRIDGE
UNIVERSITY PRESS

CAMBRIDGE
UNIVERSITY PRESS

University Printing House, Cambridge CB2 8BS, United Kingdom

One Liberty Plaza, 20th Floor, New York, NY 10006, USA

477 Williamstown Road, Port Melbourne, VIC 3207, Australia

4843/24, 2nd Floor, Ansari Road, Daryaganj, Delhi - 110002, India

79 Anson Road, #06-04/06, Singapore 079906

Cambridge University Press is part of the University of Cambridge.

It furthers the University's mission by disseminating knowledge in the pursuit of education, learning, and research at the highest international levels of excellence.

www.cambridge.org
Information on this title: www.cambridge.org/9781107146310
DOI: 10.1017/9781316536568

© Sussan Siavoshi 2017

First published 2017

Printed in the United Kingdom by Clays, St Ives plc

A catalogue record for this publication is available from the British Library

ISBN 978-1-107-14631-0 Hardback
ISBN 978-1-316-50946-3 Paperback

For my sister and niece, Shirin and Niki

Contents

Figures

Acknowledgments

Many people helped me to write this book. I am grateful to all.

I am especially thankful for the immense support of two of Montazeri's students and family friends: Mohsen Kadivar and Emaddedin Baghi. Kadivar graciously and patiently responded to my many questions in several long conversations about the intellectual and personal life of his mentor and made the writing of this book a much richer experience for me. In my correspondence with Baghi, he too generously shared his personal stories, which helped me understand why Montazeri had such loyal and dedicated followers. I am also thankful to Montazeri's children, Sa'ide and Ahmad, for responding to my questions about their father and their family lives. John Lambert, who met Montazeri on a couple of occasions, once as a free American official and once as a hostage, opened yet another door toward understanding the character of my subject.

I would also like to thank several colleagues – Victoria Aarons, Mehrzad Boroujerdi, Houchang Chehabi, and Michael Fischer from MIT – for reading and commenting on parts of the manuscript. My especial thanks go to Shahrough Akhavi, who read several drafts of my initial proposal and encouraged me to think and rethink about the what, how, and why of this book.

At this end, from Trinity University Library, I thank Pat Ullman, who helped me locate pictures for the book, and Maria McWilliams, who speedily obtained all the inter-library materials I needed. Many members of the Political Science Department – my department – patiently listened to my periodic anxious remarks. David Crockett, the Chair, and Arleen Harrison, our office manager, were particularly indulgent. I am also thankful to then Trinity Vice President of Academic Affairs, Michael Fischer, for his encouragement.

I would be remiss if I left out the anonymous reviewers of the manuscript – their comments and questions helped me greatly.

Several people at Cambridge University Press should be thanked. William Hammell, my very encouraging first managing editor, his successor, Maria Marsh, who saw this project to the end, Tim West, the very competent copy editor, and Sarah Lambert, my project manager.

I reserve my greatest and most heartfelt thanks for Charles Talbot, my friend and companion. He read and reread drafts of this book, edited them all, and made many insightful substantive comments. He was thorough, meticulous, and unrelenting. I will not forget his ever-encouraging words during periods of self-doubt and panic. Without Charles, I would have been lost.

Introduction

Early on December 20, 2009, the Grand Ayatollah Hossein Ali Montazeri drew his last breath at the age of eighty-seven. The world noticed his passing, and long obituaries appeared in the *Guardian*, the *New York Times*, *Le Monde*, and *Pravda*, and on the websites of the BBC and Al Jazeera, recounting his life and his place in the history of the Islamic Republic. In these high-praise remembrances, Montazeri was described as "the most knowledgeable religious scholar in Iran" and "an opposition hero for his principled approach to government," and was saluted for his "unwavering commitment to universal human rights." However, Iranians, inside and outside Iran, had a mixed reaction to his death. To his supporters, who mourned his passing by pouring en masse into the streets, Montazeri was considered the spiritual leader of the 2009 popular protest of the Green Movement, a man who symbolized hope for Islam and for a gentler Islamic Republic. Some of his detractors acknowledged his death, and a few of his accomplishments. The Supreme Leader of the Islamic Republic, Ali Khamenei, issued a statement that was a mixture of praise for Montazeri as a *faqih* (expert in Islamic jurisprudence) and of regret for his "failure":

We are informed that the illustrious scholar Mr. Haj Sheikh Hosein-Ali Montazeri has bid Farewell to this mortal coil and has hastened to the afterlife. He was an eminent scholar and an illustrious thinker and many students benefited from him. Much of his life was spent in the service of Late Imam Khomeini; he engaged in many jihads and endured much scorn in these endeavors. Towards the end of the Imam's life, he failed a difficult and momentous test. I beg the almighty God to envelope him with his mercy and love and to absolve him by accepting the inflictions he endured in this world, as his penance. I send condolences to his honorable wife and children and I pray for divine mercy and absolution for him.[1]

Khamenei's reference to failure related to Montazeri's stand against the mass executions of political prisoners in 1988 and critique of the

1

prolongation of the war between Iran and Iraq. These "failures" led to his dismissal in early 1989.

If the supreme leader of the Islamic Republic praised Montazeri's earlier life and criticized him for his later actions, an earlier foe, Reza Pahlavi, the exiled son of the deposed monarch Mohammad Reza Pahlavi, did the reverse in his own statement, suggesting:

> On the one hand, Ayatollah Montazeri had a vital role in establishing "*velayat-e faqih*," [the guardianship of the Islamic jurist, or the office of the Supreme Leader of the Islamic Republic] the bloodiest and most backward regime in the long history of our country... However, during the last two decades, Mr. Montazeri gradually took a different position from the regime he helped found. He criticized the motives of the leaders of the regime in their continuance of the war with Iraq, and towards the end of the war he condemned the brutal carnage of thousands of Iranian youths... The political life of Ayatollah Montazeri illustrates the possibility of the transition of mind and manner... Let us hope that his generation and his fellow clergymen choose to follow the path that the late Ayatollah Montazeri decisively did.[2]

And then there were those who had no kind words to say about him. Coming from opposite sides of the political spectrum, some were ardent supporters of the Islamic Republic and others, mostly exiled Iranians, were its fiercest critics.

The ongoing and conflicting views about Montazeri demand an investigation into his life as a political actor and a religious scholar. Why did he become a revolutionary and how did he contribute to the creation of the Islamic Republic? Why did he reach the second-highest political position and what did he do in that position? And finally, why did he turn into a critic of not only the behavior but also the character of the governing system? At the base of these questions is the matter of his personality. Was he a heroic and principled man, a man moved to action by his sense of justice and enduring faith, as his supporters would contend? Or was he an opportunist whose fall from power and turn into a dissident was the result of his miscalculation and his naïveté, as his detractors claim? Or was he a man who, in his interaction with diverse forces of a turbulent period, had certain flaws, made some mistakes, but is still worthy of praise?

Montazeri's faith in Islam was his everlasting companion from childhood to death; it was also the primary force that informed his political actions. Hence, along with questions about his life as a political actor are inquiries about his status as a religion man. How did he rise from a humble beginning and move up to the highest ranks within the clerical establishment? How did his faith inform his view of his world, and how in turn did his lived experience change his approach to religious rules? How successful was he, as a jurisprudent, in responding to the needs of contemporary Muslims? And finally, what did he leave behind as a religious legacy?

By answering these questions about a single political ayatollah, this book contributes to the broader debate on whether religion (in this case, Islam), especially if it insists on having a robust public presence, is compatible with democracy and modernity.

Montazeri in the Literature

The overwhelming majority of the scholarly works on the Iranian revolution and its aftermath have focused on the general cultural, institutional, and structural factors. But the peculiarity of Iranian experience cannot be explained solely through an analysis of macro-systemic factors; there were specific individuals whose characters, thoughts, and actions deserve a thorough attention. There have been few studies of the key individuals who led the revolution, who won the battle over the shape of the post-revolutionary state, and who actually established that state. Works on such figures in Persian generally belong in the category of hagiography, while biographies or semi-biographies in English are rare. They include Baqer Moin's 1999 biography of Ayatollah Khomeini; Saeed Barzin's 1992 political biography of Mehdi Bazargan, the first prime minister of the Islamic Republic; and Mahmood T. Davari's 2005 work on Morteza Motahhari, one of the Islamic Republic's theoreticians. But there is a need for many more.

In addition, there are very few works in English whose main focus is Montazeri himself. As I was finishing the final draft of this manuscript in the spring of 2015, Ulrich von Schwerin published his *The Dissident Mullah: Ayatollah Montazeri and the Struggle for Reform in Revolutionary Iran*.[3] This is a good source of information in English about Montazeri's political positions, particularly in the post-revolution period. The other major pieces centered on him, mostly on his thought, are Shahrough Akhavi, "The Thought and Role of Ayatollah Hossein Ali Montazeri in the Politics of Post-1979 Iran";[4] Genevieve Abdo,

"Re-thinking the Islamic Republic: A 'Conversation' with Ayatollah Hossein Ali Montazeri";[5] Babak Rahimi, "Democratic Authority, Public Islam, and Shii Jurisprudence in Iran and Iraq: Hussain Ali Montazeri and Ali Sistani";[6] and a 2003 interview with Montazeri about women by Golbarg Bashi.[7] There is also one attempt to approach Montazeri's actions, particularly his defiance of the post-revolutionary state, from a psychoanalytical perspective in Kambiz Behi's article, "The 'Real' in Resistance: Transgression of Law as Ethical Act."[8] Despite their contributions, none of these works provides a complete view of the man, his life, or his thought. As an intellectual biography, this book goes deeper in its analysis of Montazeri from the beginning of his life to its end.

The Biographical Approach

The primary goal of this biography is to see as much as we can of a religious man who became a major political figure. His prominence in the public arena brought him renown in a way that his life as a clerical scholar alone never could have done. It also brought him controversy, scorn, and hostility, with serious consequences. Yet much of his contribution to the public realm came about through writings and rulings as a Source of Emulation after he lost political power and retreated to his seminary in Qom. The reader may find aspects of his behavior and the evolution of his thinking invite analysis and speculation about the intrinsic nature of the man himself. That, however, is not the primary focus of this study. It is rather to see the unfolding of a life in its engagement with forces outside of itself.

Years ago, the historian Oscar Handlin said: "The proper subject of biography is not the complete person or the complete society, but the point at which the two interact. There the situation and the individual illuminate one another."[9] Handlin's assertion sums up the approach of this biography, a study that focuses on Montazeri's interactions with his sociopolitical and cultural environments, first as a child and a young seminary student, then as a scholar, a teacher, a revolutionary political leader, and eventually a vocal political dissident. He was sometimes the bearer and enabler of conventions of his environments, and sometimes their agitator. On many occasions, and for a large part of his life, Montazeri was a product of and remained loyal to the seminary environment and the ideas, goals, and methods of its established authorities. His early treatment of Baha'is, his initial preference for the notion of "human responsibility" over "human rights," and his everlastingly static approach to women are examples that point to Montazeri as the bearer of the conventions of the traditional seminary system. On the other hand, in his long-lasting political defiance against the post-revolution's centers of power, he challenged many of the established norms, including the authoritarian institutions of the Islamic Republic. On these occasions, Montazeri's actions and discourse shook the ideological conventions of the Islamic Republic, and therefore contributed to the system's vulnerabilities. Did his effort amount to any meaningful change?

Disciplinary studies of leaders in social sciences have largely been placed in the context of "structure versus agency," where the proponents of each school make systematic efforts to prove the supremacy of one over the other in explaining social and political developments. Structuralists take the role of systemic macro-concepts, such as sector, class, and economy, as sufficient explanatory factors, ignoring the role of individual players, while voluntarists highlight the choices made by key actors.[10] My use of the notions of "bearer" and "shaker/agitator" is not meant to be parallel with those of "structure" and "agency," with their implied causal arrow and positivistic expectation. The approach of this biography is hermeneutic, and its intent is to understand a major figure and his actions within a concrete environment rather than to create law-like generalizations. But, through unfolding the life experience of Montazeri, this book also contribute to the general debate on secularism, public religion, and modernity.

The Contour of the Debate on Secularism and Public Religion

The rise of political Islam or Islamism, whose first dramatic manifestation was the 1979 Iranian revolution, was a challenge for the academic community. At the time, the dominant analytical framework for explaining the present and predicting the future of the non-Western societies was provided by the modernization paradigm, whereby the European process of socioeconomic development was the only "natural" and progressive model for the rest of the globe. Part of this historical trajectory was steady secularization of societies, a process which involved a complex but closely related set of structural, epistemic, and ideological changes, resulting in the fading of religious sentiments and the expulsion of religious institutions from public space.[11] In a nutshell, the more modern a society becomes, the greater its distance from religion.

Along with the structural movement of societies from a pre-modern to a modern era comes a transformation of the individual. The passive/reactive, static, religious, superstitious, closed-minded, backward-looking, and fatalistic traditional person gives way to the active, tolerant, autonomous, open-minded, forward-looking, and optimistic modern individual.[12] The transformation of the traditional person, the natural subject of an authoritarian regime, into a modern individual comes with the gift of agency, making the latter a good fit for democracy.

The general outline of the modernization narrative informed the study of all transitional societies for decades. But the Iranian revolution created a major challenge for the supporters of the narrative, due to the explosive appearance of religion in public space. To explain this revolution, two separate strands of analysis developed in the 1980's. One sought the causes of the revolution in socioeconomic and political factors and viewed Islam primarily as a discursive vessel through which the genuine demands, grievances, and frustrations of a developing society were expressed.[13] Implicit in these studies was a lack of importance for religion as a force affecting the process of modernization.

The second strand of analysis, which did situate religion at its center, treated the revolution as a reactionary response against the dynamic of modernization, an expression of a desire to retreat to an earlier golden time.[14] In keeping with this analysis of the revolution was the depiction of its winners. Ayatollah Khomeini and his followers, including Montazeri, who demanded the insertion of relgion into politics, were often described as fundamentalist, other-worldly men whose dream was to take Iran back to the seventh century. When they called for social justice and criticized the West, capitalism, colonialism, or occupation (concerns that, when voiced by the secular left, were labelled progressive and modern), this too was considered traditionalist and regressive.[15] The violence during and after the revolution was accordingly often blamed on the authoritarian nature of Islam and the fanaticism of its followers.[16] Moreover, the logic of modernization theories in general, and of the secularization thesis in particular, suggested that there would be little hope for a democratic transition of the political system so long as Islam played a prominent role in Iranian politics.

The increasing intrusion of religious groups and organizations into the public space was not limited to Iran or the rest of the Islamic world, however, as the cases of the Solidarity in Poland and the Moral Majority in the United States exemplified. This global surge forced a re-examination of the established model of modernization and the axiomatic notion that in modern societies the secularization trend is irreversible. The first major challenge to the classical secularization thesis appeared in José Casanova's 1994 book, *Public Religions in the Modern World*, and has continued since. Casanova criticized the thesis for its undifferentiated approach and offered an analytical framework that divided the process of secularization into three parts: secularization as religious decline, secularization as differentiation of secular and religious spheres, and secularization as privatization of religion.[17] He argued further that only the first two are essential elements of the process of secularization and that the negation of the third, de-privatization of religion, does not necessarily refute the process of secularization nor hinder modernity.[18] Using a series of empirical cases where *collusion* rather than *collision* had defined the relationship between religiosity and secularism, Casanova challenged the binary approach of the secularization thesis and argued that the boundaries between religiosity and secularism can be diffused rather than concise.[19]

The "post"-modernization literature also dealt with the question of democracy. In his 1993 book on *The Third Wave: Democracy in the Late Twentieth Century*, Samuel Huntington called this wave "overwhelmingly a Catholic wave," and highlighted the role of religion in promoting democracy in East Asia, Europe, and Latin America.[20] For Huntington, however, the positive role of public religion in supporting democracy applied only to Christianity. As far as Islam was considered, Huntington, following the lead of Orientalists such as Bernard Lewis, held the religion responsible for "the failure of democracy in much of the Muslim world."[21]

Huntington's position on the role of Islam in the Middle East did not remain unanswered. One of the counterarguments was presented by Asef Bayat in his work on what he calls "post-Islamism." Starting with a study of the Iranian reformist discourse of the early 1990's and extending it later to other parts of the Muslim world, Asef demonstrated cases where political Islam reinvented itself both as a discourse and in practice so that it could accommodate modernity and democracy.[22]

The works of scholars such as Casanova and Bayat may have bruised the original secularization thesis but they did not fatally wound it, as its major tenets, particularly in regard to Islam, have remained robust. A case in point is Iran, where there is an ongoing and heated discussion among the native intellectuals about the place of faith in the modern world. On one side, some ardent secularists, such as Javad Tabatabai, Mohammad Reza Nikfar, Aramesh Doustar, and Mehdi Khalaji, insist that there is no room for Islam in the public sphere. Tabatabai argues that the project of breathing modernity into Shii religion is futile because reason, or the core of modernity, is absent from the Shii theological, philosophical, and legal framework.[23] Nikfar shows his attachment to the undifferentiated view of the process of secularization by considering it to involve a comprehensive trend of cultural, social, and political changes and the establishment of their respective institutions.[24] He further contends that by its very essence, Islam is violent and authoritarian, and until it is chained/tamed it cannot be reconciled with the requirements of a secular, modern, and democratic society.[25] Aramesh Doustar argues that religion stupefies people and creates an unthinking and irrational culture, and therefore its presence in the modern public sphere is unwarranted.[26] Not as radical as Doustar, Mehdi Khalaji still takes the epistemic notion of the secular as a point of departure and argues that Islamic rationality is fundamentally different from modern reason and is incapable of finding solutions to the problems of the modern world. He thus concludes that the effort of those who wish to reconcile the two is doomed to failure. Islamic thought, in particular Islamic law in any of its versions, can never accommodate modernity.[27]

It should be mentioned that the dichotomous vision of the world is not exclusive to these secular writers and is mirrored in the views of supporters of a hegemonic control of the public space by religion, such as Ayatollahs Mohammad Taqi Mesbah Yazdi and Abdollah Javadi Amoli. To them, too, religiosity and secularity *collide* rather than *collude*.

The argument on the other side of the debate, one which is mostly populated by religious reformists, rejects the dualistic approach to Islam and insists that new readings of the religion demonstrate its compatibility with modernity.[28] Along the same lines, a reformist position is that Islam has a right to the public sphere and that its presence is in fact beneficial for modern societies. The reformists see in Islam the capacity to promote inclusion, tolerance of otherness, and support of equal citizenship rights. That said, the overwhelming majority of these religious reformers, including some of Montazeri's own students, argue for a separation of the state from religious institutions.[29] Montazeri does not share the idea of such a separation, but his thought and life experience anticipate and complicate the key questions of this ongoing debate on the problematic of public religion in the modern world.

A Note on Sources

A significant portion of this book relies on Montazeri's own writings on politics, philosophy, and jurisprudence, his memoirs, the collection of his numerous essays, interviews, and public statements, and his "self-critical" responses to fourteen questions posed by his youngest son, Sa'id. In addition to his own writings, there are several books and essays written by his followers and supporters who knew him closely, including a two-volume biography by Mustafa Izadi. The lengthy book of his own memoirs is a product of hours of conversations with a couple of his supporters, which took place during the period from his fall from official power to 1997, when he was put under house arrest.

Half of the *Memoirs* consists of written official and non-official documents and letters, and the other half contains Montazeri's own recollections. These recollections not only provide valuable information about controversial events in contemporary Iranian history, but open a precious window into his personality. As significant as Montazeri's recollections in his memoirs and elsewhere are for this book, heavy reliance on them comes with its perils. Memoirs and autobiographies need to be treated with caution and even skepticism. How much of what Montazeri said about events, about his own motivations and behaviors, about other people – both friends and foes – was truthful? How much did he hide, and how much did he highlight unduly? What were his intentions as he told us his story, and to what extent did the intentionality and purposefulness of his memoirs interfere with their accuracy?

Another challenge in using memoirs as a source of information is the problem of remembering, particularly of the distant past. In his 1932 pioneering study of remembrance, Frederic Bartlett elaborated on the concept in a way that reveals this challenge to the use of memoirs as sources of information. He wrote: "Remembering is not the re-excitation of innumerable fixed, lifeless and fragmentary traces. It is an imaginative reconstruction, or construction, built out of the relation of our attitude towards a whole active mass of organized past reactions or experiences . . . It is thus hardly ever really exact . . . and it is not at all important that it should be."[30] In the case of this biography, the exactness of Montazeri's recollection does matter, as we require an accurate depiction of a life that has become the subject of so much controversy. It matters whether Montazeri's observations of and disappointment in the record of the Islamic Republic, and his more recent sensibilities, affected his reconstruction of the past and his own earlier behavior. Montazeri's *Memoirs* contain recollections about disputed events, and his interpretation/imagining may have been tainted by his changed position regarding major matters such as the war, the treatment of prisoners, and relations with the West. Therefore, it is imperative to corroborate his accounts. Where I rely on the *Memoirs* without providing other, independent sources, I do so in the following manners: as a source for informing the reader about Montazeri's *opinions* regarding matters or events, rather than an authoritative source of information about controversial matters; and where the *Memoirs* include official documents. These latter are identified with numbers in the appendices of the *Memoirs*.

In other cases, in addition to Montazeri's recollections of events, I have used *reconstructions* of the same events from the memoirs, recollections, and journals of other highly placed individuals, particularly those whose accounts differ from Montazeri's. The memoirs and recollections of the following political figures are among the sources I have consulted: Ali Akbar Hashemi Rafsanjani (1934–2017), the former two-term president of the Islamic Republic; Mohammad Mohammadi-Gilani (1928–2014), a member of the Assembly of Experts and the judge of Tehran's Islamic Revolutionary Court from 1980 to 1985; Ayatollah Mohammad Reza Mahdavi Kani (1931–2014), the former head of the Assembly of Experts; Mohammad Rayshahri (1946–), the Minister of Information/Intelligence from 1984 to 1989; Sadeq Khalkhali (1926–2003), the first head of the Revolutionary Courts;

and Khomeini's son Ahmad (1945–95). I have studied the two book-length and one essay-long critique of Montazeri's memoirs by three conservative figures, as well as Montazeri's supporters' responses to these critiques. I also had the opportunity to have e-mail correspondence with two of Montazeri's children, Ahmad and Sa'ide, and with Emaddedin Baghi, a journalist and human rights activist who is one of Montazeri's admirers and a close friend of his family. Finally, I conducted both personal and phone interviews with Mohsen Kadivar, one of Montazeri's most influential students.

There are archival materials available online, as well as newspaper reports and journal essays, regarding both the pre- and post-revolutionary events and Montazeri's place in that context. A good number of Montazeri's statements, proclamations, and decrees were published in newspapers while he was in power. These sources have been useful for checking some of Montazeri's own narratives about the disputed events, as well as those of his detractors and supporters.

If Montazeri's memoirs – along with others' – provide useful information for chronicling the events of his life and the dynamic of his multiple environments, his jurisprudential, semi-jurisprudential, theological, and ontological writings constitute the core of two chapters of this book, one on his political theory, and the other on his approach to human rights. *Mabani Fiqhi-ye Hokumat-e Eslami* (The Jurisprudential Foundation of Islamic State), a subject of Chapter 5, is the most comprehensive document on the ideas of a respected Shi-ite source of emulation on the political setup of an Islamic polity. His revised positions regarding the rule of the jurisprudent are gathered in *Hokumat-e Dini va Huqquq-e Ensan* (Religious Government and the Rights of Human) and in two earlier essays: one on "Velayat-e Faqih va Qanoun-e Assasi" (The Rule of Jurist and the Constitution) and one on "Hokumat-e Mardomi va Qanoun-e Asassi" (Democratic Rule and the Constitution). Here, one can see the development of his thoughts on the subject of *velayat-e faqih* and the shifting focus from the rule of a religious jurist to the rights of subjects/citizens. These publications, along with *Mojazatha-ye Eslami va Huqquq-e Bashar* (Islamic Penal Codes and Human Rights) and *Resaleh-e Huqquq* (Treatise on Rights), as well his position on gender, which appeared in both scattered and focused manner in several of his writings, are all indispensable for understanding Montazeri's bifurcated positions. They are also a key to the debate about the relevance of jurisprudence to the private and public lives of contemporary Muslims.

A Note on Translation and Transliteration

The translation from Persian of all the direct quotes, most of which are from Montazeri's writings, is mine. Even though I have tried to capture the "feel" of these quotes, as the old saying goes, "something always gets lost in translation." In this case, Montazeri's words, tone, rhythm, idioms, use of the vernacular, and particularly his wit have been compromised. Hence, it will be difficult for the English reader to fully appreciate aspects of his character, his humility, his occasional sarcasm, and his open and unadorned narrative.

This biography follows a transliteration formula that provides the closest Persian pronunciations of Persian words. That formula has been applied also to Arabic words that are widely used by Persian-speaking Iranians, except in rare cases where a particular transliteration seems to have already found deep roots. When transliterations occur in the text, as they often do for the names of most important offices and titles, I provide a translation with the first appearance of each. I have also added a glossary at the end of the book to reduce the confusion about transliteration, and more importantly to provide a reference source for technical concepts.

Organization of the Book

The book is divided into two parts. Consisting of four chapters, Part One tells the story of Montazeri's life and deeds within both the pre- and post-revolutionary contexts. Part Two is a hermeneutic study of Montazeri's thought on state–society relations and human rights. The book ends with a chapter on his legacy.

Part One: The Life

Montazeri's identity was closely linked to his experience as a religious teacher/scholar of the *howzeh*. Even though he was most at home in that environment, the peculiar financial, educational, and politi-cal characteristics of the seminary presented him also with challenges. Understanding how he managed to navigate his way in that setting sheds light on his personality and anticipates his behavior as a revolutionary, a statesman, and finally a dissident. That is the task of Chapter 1, "Life in the Seminary: The Making of a Religious Scholar."

Montazeri was in his forties when he became involved in oppositional political activities, which raises the question of why it took him this long to do so. The first part of Chapter 2, "The Birth of a Revolutionary," suggests an answer through a glance at the political dynamic of Iran in the 1950's and 60's and the role of the *howzeh* during that period. Once he appears on the political scene, though, he never leaves, making the rest of the chapter all his own. Here, we see how Montazeri's prison experiences, his extended periods of internal exile in remote and "alien" parts of Iran, and his reactions to these experiences contributed to his development as a revolutionary activist, one who had few rivals among the clergy. The last part of the chapter provides an answer to the question of why, despite all his dedication, Montazeri's public visibility appeared dimmer than that of many others in the immediate aftermath of the collapse of the Pahlavi regime.

Montazeri's contribution to building the religious state, his rise to the second-most important political position in the Islamic Republic, his gradual disillusionment with the Islamic Republic, and his fall from power are matters covered by Chapter 3, "The Post-revolutionary State and Montazeri: The Bearer, the Agitator." The questions of how and why he changed from being an ardent supporter of the Islamic Republic to its critic will be explored through an analysis of his ideas, actions, and personality traits in the context of power politics, competition, and the insecurity of a young and revolutionary state. It is also in this chapter that we witness the start of an agonizing tension within Montazeri between the dictate of his "logocentric" religious training on the one hand, and his "existential" experience on the other, leading to his effort to reconcile traditional jurisprudence to the requirements of the modern age.[31]

Chapter 4, "Life of a Dissident," tells the story of a man who received harsh treatment by a determined state but never yielded. The chapter starts with an elaboration on the expanding and hostile attempt to assassinate Montazeri's character by his detractors, and the development of a counternarrative to preserve his integrity by his supporters. Montazeri left the defense of his character and his legacy mostly to his followers, but did not remain silent on institutional transformations, governmental policies, or the state's meddling with the process of choosing the highest religious authority, the Supreme Source of Emulation. Here, again, we witness the playing out of his character as he continued his criticism of state, despite house arrest, threats against his life, and vandalism of his property. Along with his concrete criticism of the behavior of the leaders of the Islamic Republic came a series of jurisprudential writings and rulings on politics and human rights. These later writings offered many Muslim Iranians with a hope for a guide to reconciling modernity with their faith.

Part Two: The Thought

Chapter 5, "State–Society Relations," traces the development of Montazeri's views on politics from his early positions in the pre-revolutionary period to his final rulings shortly before his passing. Montazeri began as a strong supporter of an elitist political system led by a wise religious jurist. The first part of the chapter is an elaboration on his theory of government during the infancy years of the Islamic Republic. Toward the end of his life, Montazeri took an important leap and bowed down to the will of the people as the source of legitimacy of the state. People not only became but remained the final arbiter of the fate of the state, even if they rejected the Islamic laws as the guiding light of the government. Montazeri's empowerment of the people was explicitly connected to his emphasis on justice. Not so explicit was the connection between granting people's political sovereignty and his reflection on human reason. A brief section of the chapter explains the two key concepts of justice and reason.

Chapter 6 is on human rights. The relationship between the Islamic Republic and the advocates of the Universal Declaration of Human Rights (UDHR) has been always fraught with tension. Part of the reason for this is the conflict between some Islamic laws and the articles of the UDHR. As a jurisprudent, Montazeri had to deal with this tension. His responses are the focus of this chapter. Following a brief elaboration on the history of the UDHR, it discusses the debate on human rights in Iran by elaborating on the key points made by both the detractors and supporters of the declaration. Where was Montazeri's place in this debate? His multipronged approach to human rights in the field of the Islamic penal code, the space of privacy, the right of prisoners, and the civil rights of the Baha'is provide the answer to this question. In all these areas, Montazeri made significant changes, either jurisprudential or practical, in the direction of closing the gap between his opinions and those of the supporters of the UDHR. One of the areas of human rights where Montazeri's position remained most unmoved, however, was gender. Looking back at his ontological and epistemological views helps us understand the root cause of his fervently conservative views on women.

Conclusion

The final chapter is on the political and religious legacies of Montazeri. As this biography testifies, his record is a contested one. His critics in the Islamic Republic have spent a good deal of energy trying to discredit him by attacking his character, ridiculing his political acumen, and dismissing his religious significance. There are also those on the outside who would fault him for his views on women and/or for his resistance to going further in reforming/discarding Shii jurisprudence. But then there are those who not only defend his legacies but attempt to build on them. A small part of this chapter focuses on their voices. A treatment of Montazeri's legacy would be incomplete without mentioning his significance for the debate about secularism, modernity, and religion. And that is where the book ends.

Notes

1 http://farsi.khamenei.ir/message-content?id=8534.
2 http://rezapahlavi.org/en/2009/12/21/statement-of-reza-pahlavi-of-iran-on-the-passing-of-grand-ayatollah-montazeri/.
3 Ulrich von Schwerin, *The Dissident Mullah: Ayatollah Montazeri and the Struggle for Reform in Revolutionary Iran* (London: I.B. Tauris, 2015).
4 Shahrough Akhavi, "The Thought and Role of Ayatollah Hossein Ali Montazeri in the Politics of Post-1979 Iran," *Iranian Studies* 41, no. 5 (2008): 645–66.
5 Genevieve Abdo, "Re-thinking the Islamic Republic: A 'Conversation' with Ayatollah Hossein Ali Montazeri," *Middle East Journal* 55, no. 1 (2001): 9–24.
6 Babak Rahimi, "Democratic Authority, Public Islam, and Shi'i Jurisprudence in Iran and Iraq: Hussain Ali Montazeri and Ali Sistani," *International Political Science Review* 33.2 (2012): 193–208.
7 Golbarg Bashi, "The Question of Women: Interview with Ayatollah Montazeri," *Iranian.com* (2006), at http://iranian.com/Bashi/2006/March/Montazeri/index.html.

8 Kambiz Behi, "The 'Real' in Resistance: Transgression of Law as Ethical Act," *Unbound* 4, no. 30 (2008): 30–50.

9 Oscar Handlin, *Truth in History* (Cambridge, MA: Belknap Press, 1979): 276.

10 For an analysis of structure versus agent, see Gabriel Almond and Stephen Genco, "Clouds, Clocks, and the Study of Politics," *World Politics* 29 (1977): 489–522; Pierre Bourdieu, *Outline of a Theory of Practice* (Cambridge: Cambridge University Press, 1977): Anthony Giddens, *The Constitution of Society: Outline of a Theory of Structuralism* (Cambridge: Polity Press, 1984); and William Sewell, "A Theory of Structure: Duality, Agency, and Transformation," *American Journal of Sociology* 98 (1992): 1–29.

11 Peter Berger, *The Sacred Canopy: Elements of a Sociological Theory of Religion* (New York: Anchor Books, 1990/1967).

12 For a neat classification of these attributes, see Daniel Lerner, *The Passing of Traditional Society* (New York: Free Press, 1958), 44–6.

13 Some of the well-known and early representatives of this broad and varied approach are Ervand Abrahamian, *Iran between Two Revolutions* (Princeton, NJ: Princeton University Press, 1982); Homa Katousian, *The Political Economy of Modern Iran* (London: Macmillan, 1981); and Hossein Bashiriyeh, *The State and Social Revolution in Iran* (New York: St. Martin Press, 1983). I put Nikki Keddie, *Roots of Revolutions: An Interpretive History of Modern Iran* (New Haven, CT: Yale University Press, 1981) within this strand even though the book engages religion, as a revolutionary force, in much larger scale than other studies within this group.

14 See Farhang Rajaee, *Islamic Values and World View: Khomeini on Man, the State and International Politics* (Lanham, MD: University Press of America, 1983) and Said Arjomand, "Traditionalism in Twentieth Century Iran," in *From Nationalism to Revolutionary Islam* (Albany, NY: SUNY Press, 1984): 196–232. One exception within this strand is Roy Parviz Mottahedeh, *The Mantle of the Prophet* (New York: Simon and Shuster, 1985). Even though the focus of Mottahedeh's book is not the revolution, its treatment of Islam and the Muslim clergy anticipates a much more nuanced approach to modernity and tradition.

15 Arjomand, "Traditionalism in Twentieth Century Iran," 223–4.

16 With some revisions of its classical form, Orientalism also came to the aid of the modernization paradigm. Its classic version attributed submissiveness to authority as a part of the essence of Islam. With the rise of political Islam, a new Orientalism was developed where the emphasis was put on the importance of martyrdom, especially for the Shiis, thus substituting the idea of *submissiveness* with *resistance* to authority. See

Martin Kramer, ed. *Shi'ism, Resistance and Revolution* (Boulder, CO: Westview Press, 1987). For a brief account of neo-orientalism, see Yahya Sadowski, "The New Orientalism and the Democracy Debate," *Middle East Report* 183 (July–August 1993): 14–21.

17 Jose Casanova, *Public Religions in the Modern World* (Chicago, IL: Chicago University Press, 1994).

18 Casanova's position was criticized not only by the supporters of the original secularization thesis but also by those who saw his revisions as inadequate or unsuccessful. Among the latter, the most influential was Talal Asad, *Formations of the Seuclar* (Stanford, CA: Stanford University Press, 2003), 181–3.

19 Jose Casanova, "Public Religions Revisited," in *Religion: Beyond the Concept*, Hent de Vries, ed. (New York: Fordham University Press, 2008), 104–5.

20 Samuel Huntington, *The Third Wave: Democracy in the Late Twentieth Century* (Norman, OK: University of Oklahoma Press, 1993), 73–84.

21 See Samuel Huntington, *The Clash of Civilization and the Remaking of the World Order* (New York: Penguin Books, 1996), 29.

22 Asef Bayat, *Post Islamism: The Changing Faces of Political Islam* (New York: Oxford University Press, 2013).

23 For a recent elaboration on Tabatabai's approach to religion and reason, and a critique of it, see Mehrzad Boroujerdi and Alireza Shomali, "The Unfolding of Unreason: Javad Tabatabai's Idea of Political Decline in Iran," *Iranian Studies* 48, no. 6 (2015): 949–65.

24 See a 2015 lecture by Mohammad Nikfar at https://www.youtube.com/watch?v=S3jhPkb6yg4.

25 Mohammad Reza Nikfar, "Elahiyat-e Shekanjeh," at http://www.nilgoon.org/archive/mohammadrezanikfar/pdfs/Nikfar_Theology_of_Torture.pdf.

26 Aramesh Doustar, *Emtena'-e Tafakor dar Farhang-e Dini* [Abstention from Reflection in a Religious Culture] (Paris: Khavaran Publication, 2004).

27 See Mehdi Khalaji's criticism of Ahmad Qabel and his religious view of reason in Ahmad Qabel, *Shari'at-e Aqlani* [The Reasoned Islamic Laws] (2013), at www.ghabel.net. For his views on democracy and his critique of religious reformists, see https://www.youtube.com/watch?v=E4_dD4FzEzc.

28 An elaboration of both the conservatives' and the reformists' arguments will appear in several segments of Part Two of this book.

29 For more on the reformist discourse on separation of state and religion, see Naser Ghobadzadeh, *Religious Secularity* (New York: Oxford University Press, 2014).

30 Frederic C. Bartlett, *Remembering: A Study in Experimental and Social Psychology* (Cambridge: Cambridge University Press, 1954), 213.
31 For an analysis of logocentrism and its replacement with an approach that involves the whole complexity of human existence, see Mohammad Arkoun, *The Unthought in Contemporary Islamic Thought* (London: Saqi Press, 2002).

PART ONE

The Life

1 | *Life in the Seminary*

The Making of a Religious Scholar

Montazeri was born in 1922 in Najafabad, a small agricultural town about thirty kilometers from the city of Isfahan. The founding of Najafabad is shrouded by myths and legends, giving the town a peculiarly religious aura. These birth legends trace the history of Najafabad to the period of the Safavid Empire (1501–1722), specifically to the time of the great sixteenth-century leader Shah Abbas and his court architect, the renowned scholar Shaykh Baha'ad-Din al Amili, known as Shaykh Baha'i (1547–1621). According to one of the stories, a caravan carrying an annual treasure from Isfahan to Najaf, a city under the control of the rival Ottoman Empire, came to rest at what is now the town hall of Najafabad. When the time came to move on, the camels refused to stand up and the trip was halted. Shaykh Baha'i interpreted the event as a divine sign and convinced the king to construct a new and divinely inspired town using the treasure that had been intended for Najaf.[1]

Najafabad was constructed during the reign of Shah Abbas with the aesthetic and architectural sensibilities of the Safavid era. The inspiration for its urban planning was the design of the new Isfahan, with its famous straight and tree-lined main street, Chahar Bagh, and its extensive complex of gardens. It is believed that Shaykh Baha'i himself designed the gardenlike town, meeting the challenge of the aridity of the site through the construction of a series of *qanats*, or deep well networks. When the town was built, it had a large number of vast beautiful gardens and orchards that stretched for miles and produced some of the best peaches and pomegranates of the province.[2]

From its beginning until the mid twentieth century, farming was the major occupation of Najafabad's inhabitants. Men worked in their own small fields and orchards or acted as agricultural workers for wealthier farmers, and women wove carpets at home to provide another source of income. The social life of the town centered around religion, and in the evenings people frequently gathered in mosques or houses of the devout to listen to preachers and to the recitation of the holy book, Quran. Najafabad was a town where simplicity in lifestyle and piety were accorded the highest value, a place marked by its social stability, if not rigidity. This was the environment in which Montazeri's character was formed.

Hossein Ali Montazeri was the first child of a typical and average Najafabadi family.[3] His pious mother, Shah Baygom Sobhani, was the one who first exposed the little boy to the religious life of the town. She frequently took him to religious events, where they would sit among other women and children and listen to a preacher, who would remind them of the suffering of religious holy men and women, prompting them to shed tears and make vows in their names. His introduction to the Quran, however, was the work of his father. A self-taught man with a passion for the Quran, Haj Ali became the young son's first teacher. He knew most of the Quran by heart and would recite it to his son and others, who often gathered in his house or in a nearby mosque after dusk.

Montazeri's father also introduced the little boy to the harsh realities of labor. The small orchard and few sheep that the family owned were not enough to make an adequate living, and Haj Ali had to go to town regularly to find work in construction.[4] He was a hard-working and honest man who expected his children, particularly Hossein Ali, to follow his lead. Montazeri recalled certain moments of his father's strict manners with his characteristic humor:

In the orchard I was my father's helper, but I was a child, hungry and tired. One day when hunger and exhaustion got the best of me I started to whine. My father told me to stop complaining, and warned me that if I continued he would first cut my head off, then give me a good beating, and at last expel me from the garden. I was scared by my father's threats but was also wondering how he could punish me in the order that he put forth.[5]

Like other children of his background, Hossein Ali was sent at an early age to a *maktab* (elementary religious school).[6] For centuries, until the end of the nineteenth and the beginning of the twentieth centuries, *makateb* (*maktab*, sing.) were the only centers for elementary and intermediary education in Iran.[7] Financially independent of the state, most of these local schools relied on the contributions of wealthy individuals and the religious establishment. But, despite their decentralized nature, they all had a similar curriculum: children learned how to read and write by studying the Quran and classical books by famous Persian poets, such as the thirteenth-century Sa'adi.[8]

It took time for the *maktab* to yield its primacy to the emerging state-run secular schools in the twentieth century. For decades into that century, *maktab* remained the predominant place to receive basic and rudimentary education for village and small-town children.[9] Hossein Ali briefly attended a state-run non-religious school, but that experience was a painful one; the only memory he shared in his memoirs about this experience was of his teacher's harsh methods and use of corporal punishment.[10] In less than six months, he left the secular school and returned to the *maktab*, where he felt comfortable and at home. For the rest of his life, religious centers of learning were the sites that provided him with his strongest anchor.

Montazeri's first major mentor, besides his father, was a well-liked and enthusiastic Najafabadi clergyman, Sheikh Ahmad Hojjaji. There was a widespread joke that if Hojjaji's breath touched a child, that child was bound (or doomed) to become a religious student.[11] In the case of Montazeri, the joke became a reality. He described his first encounter with Hojjaji:

I was five or six years old when one day as I was herding a few sheep in the garden, he [Hojajji] walked into the orchard and asked for my father. I ran to my father and told him that a man who has something on his head (I did not know the word for turban at that time) is here to see you.[12]

This "strange-looking" guest would be a great influence on his life. Hojjaji was somewhat different from many other clergymen in his simple lifestyle, his closeness to ordinary people, and his plan to educate the children of meager means, and these qualities made a lasting impression on the young Montazeri.[13] In the early twentieth century, Iranian villages, particularly the remote ones, suffered from a high rate of illiteracy. Hojjaji's plan for educating young village boys was to provide them with opportunities to attend *maktab* for a couple of years, then to go back to their villages not as full-fledged teachers but as a religious and literary resource for their communities. This was his solution to the problem of "brain drain" in remote areas. In his experience, those villagers who had a longer stay in town and a more advanced degree of education would rarely go back home.[14] But for Montazeri's future, Hojjaji had a much higher ambition. He saw in this pupil a potential for greater learning and thus helped him to attend the seminary in Isfahan, where he himself taught.

Shii *Madreseh* and *Howzeh*

Major centers of religious education in places such as Najaf, Isfahan, and Qom have several schools for higher religious education, called *madreseh*.[15] A collection of these schools in each of the cities is under the supervision of a center called *howzeh-e elmieh*. By the 1979 revolution, and despite its periodic eclipses, Qom was the most bustling of Shii *howzeh*, attracting students not only from different regions of Iran but also from the outside regions. Qom was also where Montazeri received most of his education.

Michael Fischer's *Iran: From Religious Dispute to Revolution* gives a breakdown of 6414 religious students in the 1975 Qom *howzeh* based on their ethnic/regional backgrounds.[16] The largest number of students came from the Iranian province of Azarbaijan, trailed by students from Iraq. Due to the paucity of data, Fischer's studies of the socioeconomic backgrounds of these students were limited to a small sample from one of the schools in Qom, *Madreseh* Golpaygani. Based on this sample, at least half of the students came from farming and rural backgrounds, while the rest were predominantly from clerical, merchant, and shopkeeper backgrounds. This pattern likely pertained to most of the religious educational institutions in Iran.

In some ways, the social structure of the *howzeh* reflected the broader national one. There were children of the well-to-do, those who could provide for themselves through the money sent by their family. Of those who came from poorer backgrounds, there were some, Montazeri among them, whose talents and intelligence were recognized by their mentors and were thus invited to join the seminary. For these students, the invitation did not guarantee a comfortable life, and even though some did eventually secure some stipends from one or another mentor or from the director of the *howzeh*, most suffered frequently from lack of rudimentary sustenance. Still, the talented among them were better off than the last group of students, the poor in livelihood and average in talent; to feed themselves, members of this last group had to find jobs outside the seminary.[17]

Despite the economic disparity and the display of contempt, competition, and ill will by some, many students developed a sense of comradery, of belonging to a distinct community. They lived together in the same quarters, observed more or less the same dress code, and practiced the same daily rituals. Soon after his entering into the seminary, Montazeri, like any other student, learned the *howzeh*'s vocabulary and code of conduct. He was expected to spend most of his time there, study hard, and have infrequent contact with the outside world, except during summer recess. Part of the ethical lessons of the *howzeh* was what he had already learned at home: one should not sin, look at unrelated women, or listen to music. The whole reason to be at the *howzeh*, he was told, was to learn.

There is a paucity of detailed and personal accounts of life in the seminary around the time that Montazeri entered the *howzeh*.[18] Montazeri's own recollections are sketchy and incomplete. But there are a few autobiographies by seminary students from earlier times that shed partial light on the lives of their twentieth-century counterparts. The recollections by Aqa Najafi Quchani (1875–1943) of his student years, *Siahat-e Sharq va Gharb*, is one example. Quchani is astonishingly open about the life and education of a student from a poor rural background.[19] Like Montazeri, he was placed in a religious school by his father in the care of a trusted friend, but in Quchani's case this friend exploited him by forcing him to cook and clean, leaving little time for his studies.[20] Quchani's eventual freedom from this unscrupulous man did not guarantee a smoother path, but his thirst for knowledge and his restless soul took him from one seminary to another, first in his home province of Khorasan, next in Yazd, then in Isfahan, and finally in Najaf in Iraq. In Najaf, he found his ideal mentor in Akhound Khorasani, the famous nineteenth-century Shii scholar. Throughout this journey, Quchani encountered greedy and opportunistic mentors, lived in small dark *howzeh* residences, experienced constant hunger often bordering on starvation, and had to deal with the pettiness of other students. It is not easy to know whether he exaggerated the degree of pain, anguish, and danger that confronted young and poor seminary students. What is clear is the drive and perseverance of adept and intelligent students, particularly of children of poor background, whose only opportunity to learn was to join a *howzeh* and find mentors who would care to teach them well.

Some of Quchani's characterization of the life of a young student also appears, in a much more sketchy fashion, in the memoirs of some high clergy closer in age to Montazeri. Ayatollah Mohammad Reza

Mahdavi Kani (1931–2014), for example, draws a relatively vivid picture of the physical space and economic situation of the students of the Qom seminary, specifically those who had to reside in the living quarters provided by the *madreseh*. From his description of the bare, damp, and dark *hojrehs* (the living quarters) to the lack of clean water, meager sustenance, and hunger, Mahdavi Kani's recollections of his student days are not too different from Quchani's.[21] Montazeri's depiction of student life in his memoirs also follows the same pattern, even though it does not betray the same degree of harshness.

Montazeri's Years in Isfahan

It was Hojjaji who convinced Hossein Ali's father to send the twelve-year-old boy to seminary, first in Isfahan, then in Qom. Hojjaji's assessment of his pupil was correct: Montazeri became one of the most knowledgeable Shii jurisprudents in contemporary Iran, even though his early educational experience was fraught with difficulty. Lacking the protection of his family and the coziness of a small town, the young Montazeri was left to fend for himself in the unfamiliar city of Isfahan. In his memoirs, he recounts plainly how his first roommate in one of Isfahan's seminaries not only exploited him by demanding he cook and clean but also frequently abused him verbally and, on at least one occasion, slapped him.[22] Some of these experiences brought Hossein Ali to the verge of quitting seminary education altogether, but the presence of a few caring teachers provided enough moral support and intellectual incentive for him to stay.

The more serious and prolonged difficulty in Montazeri's quest for education was poverty, his constant companion even after he became a teacher. It was the financial hardship that cut short his first attempt, at the age of thirteen, to study in Qom, Iran's highest center for religious learning. After only ten months in Qom, and despite his success in receiving a small stipend from Ayatollah Abdol Karim Haeri, the powerful director of the Qom seminary system, Montazeri realized that he would not be able to live on what he had and therefore returned to Isfahan. At least in Isfahan, unlike in faraway Qom, he was able to frequently travel to his hometown to visit his parents and collect some meager provisions to sustain him for a few days. Traveling back and forth from Najafabad to Isfahan was itself an ordeal, since his family's poor financial circumstances often forced him to walk the entire distance. It would take him several hours of vigorous walking to make the long journey.[23] He frequently had a few companions whose poverty forced them to do the same.

The financial difficulties of religious students were caused by two factors. One was the policies of the leadership of Isfahan's *howzeh*. As everywhere else in Iran, the funding of Isfahan's *howzeh* came from two sources: *awqhaf* (religious endowments) and *sahm-e emam* (a form of religious tithe). The first were donations, usually of land, for specific purposes. The second consisted of half of *khums*, a religious tax that itself amounted to one-fifth of every Muslim's annual income (after expenses). The amount of *sahm-e emam* each institution received depended on the prominence of the *marja' taqlid* (source of emulation) connected to that particular seminary. These "sources of emulation" were learned interpreters of Islamic laws who were able to gather a sizable number of followers. Originally, there were numerous sources of emulation scattered across several seminaries around the country. In time, the number shrank, leaving only a few highly regarded clergy to bear the title. In addition to the number of their followers, a source of emulation had to be recognized by several other *marja' taqlid*.

The prominence of a source of emulation depended upon the number of his followers: those who requested and then received his guidance. In return, these followers would send their *sahm-e emam* to their *marja'*, supplying him with financial power. Usually, the leadership of the seminaries distributed some of the *sahm-e emam* among their students in the form of monthly stipends. The complaint of Montazeri and other students was that most, if not all of the *sahm-e emam* collected by Isfahan's seminary system was sent to Najaf, at that time the center of the Shii religious establishment, leaving very little in the way of stipends for the seminary students.

The other source of difficulty was the financial, institutional, and cultural impact of the rapid secularization of the educational system during Reza Shah's reign.[24] In the early 1930's Reza Shah (1878–1944), the founder of the Pahlavi dynasty (1925–78), initiated a policy of swift secularization of the educational system with a devastating result on the power of the *howzeh*. By the time Montazeri started his seminary education, the effects of Reza Shah's educational policies were already being felt in the seminaries throughout Iran. In 1934 the parliament passed laws that put severe limitations on religious funding and on the autonomy of the clergy to manage their endowment.[25] These restrictive laws also affected the amount of money available to the directors of seminaries to spend on students' stipends and instructors' salaries. And, of course, it was always the poorer seminarians, including Montazeri, who suffered most.

Adding to the financial challenges was the state's intrusion into other areas of traditional power of the religious establishment. After a brief period of relative peace (1921–25) between the state and the clergy, the newly crowned Reza Shah began to neutralize independent and powerful economic, cultural, and political forces, including the clerical establishment, in pursuit of his dual goal of modernization of the country and consolidation of his own power.[26] The time Montazeri spent in Isfahan's seminaries (1936–41) fell outside the period of détente between the crown and the mosque. During these years, state authorities frequently harassed and humiliated seminarians, causing many to leave the *howzeh*. From 1930 until the abdication of Reza Shah in 1941, the number of seminary students steadily decreased, as did the number of mentors and the availability of books and other necessary supplies.[27] There were times when these pressures seemed almost unbearable for Montazeri, yet he remained in the Isfahan *howzeh* for over five years.

Alongside the difficulties, there were pleasant aspects that made life for Montazeri more bearable. One of his live-in schools was the famous Madrasah Chahar-Bagh, a magnificent early eighteenth-century building constructed during the reign of the last Safavid king, Shah Soltan Hossein. With its beautiful tiled façade, open courtyard, shady trees, potted flowers, and flowing water channel, the building was a feast for the eye and nourishment for the soul. Another school, where Montazeri spent most of his time as a student, was Jaddeh Bozorg, a graceful old building constructed by the order of the grandmother of Safavid king, Shah Abbas II, in the mid seventeenth century. Montazeri lived with a roommate in a *hojreh* (living quarter) tucked in a wall of the courtyard.[28] He started each day at dawn with meditative morning prayers, during which he savored the beauty of the garden. Peaceful, quiet, and spiritual, the dawn rituals in that setting prepared him for the day of study. He then would go to a lecture session, followed by discussions of the lessons with his roommate. These practices in a pleasant physical surrounding enriched his otherwise difficult life.[29] In that environment, Montazeri developed his lifelong habit of reading, reflecting, and writing.

Theoretically, students were provided with a freer educational experience in religious seminaries than in secular schools at that time.[30]

Within the limit of what seminaries offered, students were free to choose their own teachers and decide on their subjects of study. With no set curriculum, these schools were open to both the talented and the mediocre, as each, within the limit of his ability, could go as far as he wished. However, such freedom came with a cost: without an institutionalized advising system, students were left to their own devices to judge which educational path they should follow. In his memoirs, Montazeri often lamented the wastefulness and inefficiency of the educational system he experienced in his childhood and youth, where students, with no systematic guidance, had to navigate the courses and texts on their own. If a young scholar were lucky, some informal advising might come his way, courtesy of his chosen mentor. As for Montazeri, proper and informed advice came sporadically, by chance and not by design. Overall, he seemed to be one of the luckier ones, not only because he studied subjects in the sequences that were intended, but also because his deficiencies, such as a lack of knowledge in mathematics, were recognized by his mentors, who partially remedied them by sending him to the appropriate instructors.[31]

Despite the lack of systematic guidance, there was still a general plan of study, with lower- and upper-level categories. Traditional seminary education involved three cycles: *muqaddamat* (introduction), *sath* (intermediate), and *dars-e kharej* (highest level), each of which lasted about four years. In the first level, students learned the basic skills, or the preliminaries, to prepare for the second level, with its focus on "subject matter." The preliminaries consisted of *elm-e sarf* (etymology and derivation), *elm-e nahv* (syntax), and *bayan va ma'ani* (rhetoric). Most of the materials for this introductory level were in set texts, and no matter where students received their education, they would study more or less the same books. *Manteqh* (logic), *usul-e fiqh* (principles of jurisprudence), and *fiqh* (jurisprudence), with their associated texts, constituted the core of the curriculum at the second level. The focus of the last level, *dars-e kharej*, was on jurisprudence. In addition, at this level there were electives such as lessons in ethics, philosophy, and interpretation of the Quran.[32]

None of these levels exposed students to subject matters such as history, modern economy, or politics that would create an intellectual bridge to the outside world. In general, the students focused on a famous text by reading and listening to repetitious materials, a practice that involved very little, if any, intellectual rigor. These materials would be reproduced by the students once they themselves became teachers.

In theory, the system was supposed to allow students to question and argue with their instructors in order to reach a new level of understanding. In practice, most teachers discouraged serious give-and-take with students; instead, they appealed to authoritative *sanad* or proof (reference to Quran, and the authoritative dissemination of sayings attributed to the Prophet and the Infallible Imams) as the final word. Often, those who did allow a more free-flowing discussion were themselves limited by a long tradition of previously accepted and authoritative rulings that confounded any genuine and creative argumentation in the classroom.

Montazeri was a product of this educational system, though at times he challenged his teachers. In his memoirs, Montazeri describes with his characteristic bluntness the pedagogical method of many of his mentors, some of whom come across as pedantic, boring, or incomprehensibly jargonistic. Montazeri, inquisitive by nature and rash by temperament, had a hard time restraining himself from asking many questions, and thus frequently incurred the wrath or at least the annoyance of many of his teachers. In one particular instance, when he persisted in investigating the authenticity of a "proof," his teacher Sayyed Mehdi Hejazi threw his praying beads at him and scolded him for his temerity in challenging a religious authority such as the powerful seventeenth-century conservative Allameh Baqer Majlisi.[33] This episode embarrassed and saddened Montazeri, and made him promise himself never to stifle his own students' inquisitiveness. As noted by his students, he delivered on that promise.[34]

Montazeri was still a student in the intermediate level in Isfahan's seminary when he started to teach his own lower-level courses. He found teaching useful; it allowed him to consider matters more carefully and eased him into higher-level learning. At the age of nineteen, and after years of residence in Isfahan's seminaries, Montazeri left Isfahan in pursuit of a more rigorous course of study in the Qom *howzeh*.

Qom's *Howzeh-ye Elmieh*

Qom, a dusty city ninety miles south of Tehran, was not unfamiliar to Montazeri. In 1935, he had travelled to Qom to study, but his financial difficulties cut his stay short. His second trip, in 1941, proved to be much more lasting. He was excited by the higher degree of vibrancy in the Qom seminaries, where both the instructors and the students came from far-flung places.

As the burial site of Fatemah, sister of the eighth Shii Imam, Qom carried a long history of religious importance. The Safavid kings, as well as the Qajar dynasty (1785–1925), contributed to its centrality as a place of religious learning. However, and coinciding with the decline of the Qajars' power by the end of the nineteenth century, the city and its religious seminaries lost most of their vitality. No longer a central place for education, Qom lost the competition in attracting the most talented to other seminaries, particulary Najaf, which was the residence of major sources of emulation. Not long into the twentieth century, however, Qom's *howzeh* found another opportunity to rise when the prominent clergyman, Sheikh Abdolkarim Haeri (1859–1937), immigrated to the city in 1922.

Born in a small village in Yazd, Haeri spent many decades in the seminaries of Najaf, Samara, and Karbala before moving back to Iran and residing in Arak, a town eighty miles west of Qom, in 1914. His reputation as a man of learning and his effective management style made Arak a magnet for many students. During one brief visit to Qom, he was invited by the city's religious leaders to move there and revive its atrophied seminaries. Haeri agreed, and when he moved to the city, so did many of his influential followers. The congregation of these religious learned men in Qom enabled Haeri quickly to establish a *howzeh-ye elmieh*.

Another factor that helped Haeri in making Qom an important center of Shii learning was the complete collapse of the Ottoman Empire after World War I and the loss of Iraq to the victorious British forces. In the early 1920's, many religious figures in Najaf opposed Britain's attempt to restructure Iraq's political system. Not willing to give in to or compromise with the opposition, the British occupying forces expelled a number of Najaf's major clergymen of Iranian origin. Scattered all around Iran, some of these prominent religious men ended up in Qom.[35] In a span of only a few years, Qom became a thriving educational center, the residence of many influential religious teachers.[36] By the time Montazeri arrived at Qom, its *howzeh-ye elmieh* was the most important of its kind. But politically, it was weak in its dealings with Reza Shah, who was determined to curb the power of the clergy. Even though there was sporadic public resistance on the part of the clergy to Reza Shah's continuous encroachment, none really succeeded in turning the tide. To the contrary, many members of the clergy and their establishments became targets of the wrath of the state and were subsequently punished. Ayatollah Haeri, the leader of Qom's seminary system, calculated the risk of challenging the state and decided to take a quietist approach.[37] The decision proved to be prudent, since the Qom religious center suffered less than many others.

Haeri died in 1937, and with his death the *howzeh* lost an able leader, a man known for both his pragmatism and his administrative skills. Since no one person was able to fill his shoes, the leadership of the seminary system became, for the next nine years, the collective responsibility of three ayatollahs, none of whom enjoyed Haeri's administrative talents or his ability to protect the *howzeh* from the increasing encroachment of the state. No one knows what would have happened to the *howzeh* if Reza Shah, who was sent into exile by the occupying Allied forces in 1941, had remained in power. But his abdication provided a respite for the religious establishment. His successor, the young Mohammad Reza Shah, despite his desire to continue his father's policies, was inexperienced and tentative. So for the time being he chose a cautious path and reduced the state's interference in the affairs of the religious centers. The relative withdrawal of the state allowed the clergy to slowly regain some of their past influence and expand their domain of authority. Nowhere was this trend more evident than in the increasing number of clergy and religious students, a notable reversal of the trend that had characterized the *howzeh*'s population during the 1930's and early 40's.[38]

In addition to the changes occasioned by the relative and temporary retreat of the state from religious affairs, there were internal changes that helped the *howzeh* to grow stronger. After years of fragmented leadership in Qom, another able leader, Ayatollah Hossein Borujerdi Tabataba'i (1875–1961), emerged as the director of the *howzeh*. His influence was doubly asserted in 1946 when he also became the Supreme or General Source of Emulation for the global Shii community. In 1946, the position of *marja'-e taqlid-e tamm* (Supreme/General Source of Emulation) was still a relatively new phenomenon for the Shiis. For most of its history, the theoretical obstacles of the Shii religious sect had made the emergence of one person as the *marja'-e taqlid-e tamm* very challenging, if not impossible. But a combination of socioeconomic and political factors in the nineteenth century facilitated the rise of one clergyman above all others.[39] Like many newly created positions, this office suffered from a lack of proper institution-alization, and on occasions disputes arose about who should hold it.[40] But once Borujerdi became the Supreme *Marja'*, he remained the undis-puted religious leader until his death in 1961.[41]

Like Haeri, Borujerdi proved to be a savvy administrator. Soon after his arrival in Qom, he rationalized the collection of private donations, which put not only the seminary system but the whole city of Qom in a much better financial position. He also revitalized the seminaries and increased the student body. Borujerdi was like the founder of the *howzeh* in other ways as well. He accepted the invitation extended to him by several ayatollahs and moved to Qom in December 1944. Even though he had been a resident of the small town of Borujerd (around 150 miles west of Qom), his reputation as a pious and learned *faqih* had already gone beyond his hometown, and he was accepted as the general *marja' taqlid* of western and southwestern Iran and of parts of the northeastern province of Khorasan.[42]

Following the style of Haeri, Borujerdi decided not to get involved in political disputes with the state. His primary and lasting goal was to create and maintain a flourishing and prosperous *howzeh*, and in his view any serious and overt political entanglement with the state would compromise his plans.[43] His outward political passivity, however, hid his overall political nature. He did his utmost to influence the elec-tion of certain favored candidates to the Majlis (Iranian parliament) and engaged in quiet bargaining with the state over many issues of interest to the *howzeh*. His political style and his decision to make the *howzeh* safe and thriving bore a good measure of success; he was able to raise money for the construction of new mosques and hospitals, and increased the stipends of the religious students. When he first arrived at Qom, the number of religious students was by some accounts about eight hundred and by others about twenty-five hundred; by the time of his death, that number had reached a high of six thousand.[44]

Another area where Borujerdi had a level of success was in reduc-ing tension between the Shii and Sunni communities. He supported a newly formed organization, *Dar-al Taqrib Baynal Mazaheb Al-Islamiya*, which was established by a group of Shii and Sunni scholars to bring the two religious communities closer together.[45] The creation of Israel and the Arab defeat in the 1948 war caused not only the Arab Muslims but many others to think about the Islamic world's sources of vulnerability. Borujerdi believed that the rift between the Sunnis and the Shiis was a serious contributing factor to the Muslims' increasing loss of collective power. He was also dismayed about the religious gap between the two sects, and believed that making sound religious judgment required considering and analyzing both Shii and Sunni sources. Borujerdi's approach to Sunnis and his political and intellectual interest in uniting the two major sects of Islam greatly influenced Hossein Ali Montazeri, who found in Borujerdi his scholarly role model.

Montazeri's Years in Qom

In the 1940's, Qom had several schools, the oldest and most prestigious of which was the Fayziyeh. As a newcomer, however, Montazeri took up residence in a minor school, Haj Molla Sadeq, where he was soon offered, and accepted, the turban. To become a *mo'amem* (turbaned) is a major event for a seminarian: it signifies a life commitment to seeking religious knowledge.

After being turbaned, the excited and anxious Montazeri moved to the prestigious Fayziyeh seminary. Students of the school came from different walks of life: some were well to do, some had families with scholarly and educated backgrounds, and some, like Montazeri, had neither of these support systems. There was also competition among students from different regions of Iran. Several regions were perceived as more prestigious and had more representatives in the seminaries than the others. Despite the egalitarian aspects of the *howzeh*, some of its members were not above bragging about their talent or flaunting their family or regional background. Outward manifestations of a few of these differences were seen in the way students and mentors dressed and talked. Some always appeared in ironed shirts, neat turbans, and clean shoes, and displayed refinement in the manner of their speech. Even though Montazeri was somewhat at a disadvantage in all the social and regional categories, he soon excelled in learning, and some of the most influential seminary teachers, such as Hossein Tabataba'i Borujerdi, Ayatollah Ruhollah Khomeini (1902–89), and Allameh Mohammad Hossein Tabataba'i (1903–81), took notice of him.

Montazeri also struck up a deep and close friendship with a man who became an important theoretician of the Islamic Republic, a future Ayatollah, Morteza Motahhari (1920–79). A few years older than Montazeri, Motahhari, born in Fariman, was from a clerical family in Mashhad, the provisional capital of Khorasan in northeastern Iran. It was Motahhari who convinced Montazeri to move from his place of residence in the Mulla Sadeq seminary to Fayziyeh seminary, where Motahhari lived and where the two became *ham-mobahess* (discussion partners) for the next eleven years. Despite their different emphases – Montazeri focused predominantly on jurisprudence, while Motahhari gravitated toward philosophy – they spent hours discussing and reflecting on religious matters.[46] They also had many light-hearted moments, making fun of and playing tricks on one another. As inseparable friends and companions, they shared their meager incomes and often went to bed half hungry. Still, the two had distinct temperaments. Montazeri was rash and exuberant, while Motahhari was cautious and restrained. In class, Montazeri was always full of questions, some important and some mundane, while Motahhari's interventions and questions were infrequent and meant to be deep.[47] These differences in character appeared most starkly during the decade prior to the overthrow of Pahlavi's regime: Montazeri threw himself with abandon into the center of revolutionary activities, while Motahhari remained, for most of the decade, at the margins of such activities. Still, the years that the two friends spent together in Qom were the most exciting and carefree in Montazeri's life.

When Motahhari was assassinated in May 1979, a deeply affected Montazeri remembered his companion with these words:

One of the participants in a small class taught by Ayatollah Haj Sayyed Mohammad Mohaqeq, known as Damad, was a man older than I by a few years. He suggested that we become discussion-partners. I first showed him a cold shoulder, but increasingly our affection for each other grew ... This young, smart, talented, persevering, ethical, and religiously observant man was the deceased Ayatollah Haj Sheikh Morteza Motahhari ... Despite our financial hardship we took joy and comfort in studying, discussing, and attending educational circles, especially the class on ethics taught by the Grand Ayatollah Khomeini ... [Our shared educational and devotional experience] lasted for ten years until Ayatollah Motahhari who was no longer able to afford the hardship of living at Qom went to Tehran.[48]

Motahhari's move to Tehran separated the two friends in more ways than one. Motahhari became a university professor and met and engaged with more diverse groups of people than the Qom seminary had offered either him or Montazeri. It was in this new environment that he realized the attraction of Marxism for socially conscious Muslim youth. Hence, it became a major part of his calling to update Islamic thought and philosophy in order to reduce the potency of Marxism in pulling away young Muslims from religion. The move to Tehran, and his exposure to new ideas and new conversations – particularly with men such as Ali Shari'ati and Mehdi Bazargan – separated him from the intellectually closed world of the *howzeh*. It took many more years before Montazeri was thrust into the more vibrant and diverse intellectual and political environments where he too could see the world differently and altered his writings accordingly. That lack of prior engagement with this vibrant Tehran circle was probably one major reason for many younger revolutionaries, particularly religiously oriented university students, not taking notice of Montazeri, a man whose revolutionary activities, as we will see in Chapter 2, surpassed those of most others.

Marriage and Children

Montazeri married when he was still Motahhari's roommate. According to Montazeri, Motahhari suggested that the two friends marry at the same time. In 1942, when both were attending a summer session in Isfahan, Motahhari brought up the question of marriage and eventually convinced his friend that staying single was not the right move for young men. Montazeri remembered their conversation in his memoirs:

He then said: "Let's get back to Qom as married men." I pointed out our difficult financial circumstances. But, he said that God is the Provider. Eventually, one Friday morning at school I conducted *tafa'ol* (consulting the Quran to get clues as to the soundness of decisions) . . . The Quran chapters that opened up to us were quite encouraging. So, we both left Qom, I went to Najafabad and the late Motahhari went to Mashhad both with the intention of getting married. I fulfilled my promise but he, giving me some excuses, came back as a bachelor.[49]

Montazeri entered an arranged marriage, as was the norm. His wife, Khadijeh (Mahsoltan) Rabbani, was a daughter of a Najafabadi artisan. Based on the available evidence, including their children's recollections, the marriage was a good and loving one. Montazeri did not talk much about his wife, however. He belonged to a generation of clergy where wives were relegated to the private domain and were neither participants in the public sphere nor the subjects of public conversation. In particular, the expression of love and affection toward wives was to remain exclusively private, never to be heard by others.[50] If there was ever a need to mention their wives, they would to refer to them as "family" or "home." Montazeri mentioned his wife's presence on rare occasions, once referring to a day when Hashemi Rafsanjani, another clergyman and the future president of the Islamic Republic, came to visit him in the small town of Khalkhal, where he was exiled. Montazeri recalled that visit:

One day I with *family* [my emphasis] and children were going to wash some clothes, but since it was not easy to do so at home we went to a stream that was a bit far from our house. *Family* was washing and I was rinsing and spreading the clothes to dry. Incidentally on that day Mr. Hashemi who had come to pay us a visit...found us at the river, and as soon he saw us he said to me [jokingly]: "Well, well! Now you have stooped to washing clothes?"[51]

In some of the videos on Montazeri's life, we see him going to the kitchen and making himself tea or washing his socks and spreading them to dry. These little episodes might not tell us much about the relationship between Montazeri and his wife, but they provide a glimpse into his behavior at home. The only other mention of Montazeri's attitude toward his wife comes from his children. According to Sa'ide, Montazeri's youngest daughter, her father was most respectful of his wife and advised his children to always pay the greatest homage to their mother, to obey her, and to privilege her directives over his own. Even on his deathbed, according to Sa'ide, his last advice to his children was for them to take good care of their mother and to make sure that she took her medications on time.[52] Again, what these little anecdotes tell us about Montazeri is that he was decent and kind. His overall views on the status of women in general, however, must have been reflected in his relationship to his wife. In his approach to the status of women, he was and remained a conservative clergyman.

Montazeri and his wife had seven children: three sons, Mohammad-Ali, always referred to as Mohammad (b. 1944–d. 1981), Ahmad (1955–), and Sa'id (1962–); and four daughters, Esmat (1947–), Ashraf (1951–), Tahereh (1960–), and Sa'ide (1968–). Their firstborn son, Mohammad, had a passionate and volatile character, and of all their children was the most widely known. Montazeri had high hopes for him even before he was born. Reportedly, during his wife's pregnancy both Montazeri and his own grandmother had dreams of Mohammad, which they interpreted as omens of a lofty and pious place for the unborn child. As was the tradition in clerical families, Montazeri's first son followed his father's path, studied religion, and achieved clerical status. Mohammad also became a revolutionary around the time that his father started his political activities, but he surpassed Montazeri in his passion for the revolution. He, along with seventy-one other members of the newly formed political party Jomhuri-ye Eslami, was killed when a powerful bomb exploded at the party headquarters in 1981.

Montazeri spoke highly of his son's dedication to revolution, his preference for humble living, and his quickness of mind.[53] He also recalled his son's sufferings when he was tortured by the Savak, the pre-revolution secret police, and of course mourned his passing as a father would.[54] Nonetheless, he also worried about his son's behavior. Mohammad carried a true revolutionary spirit, which was not extinguished with the Islamic Republic. He was in favor of a permanent revolution, or so it seemed at the beginning, and thus publicly expressed his suspicion of the creeping institutionalization of revolutionary power. Among his frequent targets of attack was Ayatollah Mohammad Beheshti, one of the most powerful men in the early days of the revolution.[55] Mohammad's fervor for keeping the revolutionary fire alive led him into trouble with the law and earned him the nickname "Mamad Ringo" (Mamad is an informal version of Mohammad and Ringo was in reference to a well-known character in a series of Spaghetti Western films).[56]

A famous episode that shed light on Mohammad's character took place in June 1979, when he and a large number of younger revolutionaries decided to fly to Libya to attend its Independence Day. Most of the group carried neither passport nor visa, and were therefore prevented from taking off by the airport police, which was under the control of the moderate administration of Prime Minister Mehdi Bazargan. There is some confusion as to what happened next and who masterminded the whole plan, but most of the group, including Mohammad, decided to sit on the airport runway to disrupt the flight schedules.[57] The widely publicized affair finally pushed Montazeri, who was caught between his familial loyalty and his public responsibilities, to make an open statement calling his son psychologically unstable. He also demanded legal accountability on the part of individuals who were involved in this incident, including his own son, if he happened to be guilty.[58] Later, in his memoirs, he said that while he understood his son's viewpoint, he considered his way of addressing issues counterproductive.[59] The statement was later used by his detractors in their attempts to discredit him, and haunted his reputation as a father for years.

None of Montazeri's other children followed the model set by their maverick brother. Ahmad, the second son, studied engineering and lived in Tehran. In many clerical families, only the firstborn sons are obliged to follow their fathers' path and become seminarians. But after the death of his older brother, Ahmad answered his father's call to go back to Qom and enter the seminary. Now in clerical garb, Ahmad became the spokesperson for and manager of the household. The death of Montazeri in 2009 made his second son the head of the family and the bearer of his legacy. Since then, Ahmad has taken a clear and critical stand against the behavior of the Islamic Republic and has been arrested several times for taking these positions. In one such arrest, he was put in solitary confinement for almost a year.[60] In his principles and beliefs, Ahmad is indeed his father's son, and he carries his legacy faithfully.[61]

Besides Ahmad, the only other child of Montazeri with a university education is his youngest daughter, Sa'ide. She got her master's degree in Persian language and literature from Azad University in Tehran. In pursuing her higher secular education away from Qom, Sa'ide received nothing but support from her father.[62] As the youngest child, she also enjoyed a greater share of her father's affection.[63] The rest of Montazeri's children have modest or little formal and secular education; they all gravitated toward seminary learning. The war with Iraq (1980–88) interrupted the education of Montazeri's third son Sa'id, as he volunteered to go to war. When he returned from the war zone as a wounded veteran, Sa'id entered the seminary and studied with his father. He is now an outspoken human rights activist and a critic of the regime. He was also the son who posed fourteen questions to his father, leading him to respond in a self-critical manner. These questions and answers were published as a book titled *Enteqad az Khod: Ebrat va Vasiyat* (Self-Criticism: Lessons and Last Will).[64]

Of Montazeri's four daughters, Ashraf and Sa'ide are publicly and politically active. Ashraf is the wife of Sayyed Hadi Hashemi, the controversial chief of staff of Montazeri's office, and has a Facebook page where she writes about her observations on sociopolitical developments in Iran. She also publishes critical essays in different venues,

particularly in *Jaras*, a reformist news and commentary Internet site
based outside Iran. Sa'ide is an active web blogger. In their public statements, they all write of their father with affection and respect. Traditional in his approach to family life, Montazeri is praised by his children as a kind and convivial father.[65] They also testified to Montazeri's
tolerant attitude. For example, years ago, when Mohammad Montazeri
was asked about his disagreement with his father about his methods,
he replied: "in our household democracy reigns and we [children and
father] are free to disagree with each other."[66] But Montazeri's con-
viviality and tolerance did not prevent his children from considering
him a father with authority. When I asked Sa'ide what she thought
was her father's greatest lesson for his children, she responded that it
was his insistence on living a just life and tolerating the perils that it
entailed.[67] Such a description of Montazeri's attitude toward life was
corroborated by Emad Baghi, a friend of Montazeri's youngest son.
He remembered one episode in particular when he felt in danger due
to the harassment he received from some governmental officials who,
allegedly by the order of Khomeini, banned one of his books in 1986.
Montazeri called Baghi in for a visit, told him that a principled life is
full of perils, but also asked him to persevere in leading such a life. His
kindness and support touched the young man deeply.[68]

Marriage and family life took Montazeri out of the residential environment of the seminary, which was reserved for only single students.
But his residence in a modest house outside the *howzeh* interrupted
neither his studies nor his relationship with his peers and his mentors.
With them, Montazeri had an unbroken and lasting bound.

Mentors

Motahhari was Montazeri's closest friend during the course of his education in Qom, but there were others, mentors and role models alike,
with whom Montazeri struck up meaningful relationships. In addition
to his fondness for his childhood mentor, Ayatollah Hojjaji, Montazeri
spoke affectionately of two of his later teachers, Ayatollahs Khomeini
and Borujerdi.

Montazeri's first encounter with Khomeini was in his popular class
on ethics, a course that was open to people from outside the seminary. Khomeini's position as a *howzeh* instructor was a complicated
one, at least while Ayatollah Borujerdi was alive. Khomeini was one

of the few teachers who, despite the disapproval of the director of the *howzeh*, took the risks associated with teaching the controversial fields of philosophy and mysticism. He taught a select group of students some of the important texts of mysticism, such as *al-Asfar al-Arba'eh* (Four Journeys), the magnum opus of the seventeenth-century Shii philosopher Molla Sadra. He kept his classes on philosophy and mysticism small for two reasons: first, his belief that only the best and the brightest of students can access the true meaning of the difficult subject matter; and second, his awareness of the long history of opposition to teaching philosophy, particularly mysticism, in many of Iran's seminaries. The fact that he allowed both Montazeri and Motahhari into his select group testifies to Khomeini's high regard for them. The two friends also attended Khomeini's class on *Sharh-e Manzumeh*, a philosophical text by Haj Mollah Hadi Sabzevari, a nineteenth-century teacher who was inspired by Molla Sadra's mystical writings. These classes were demanding, and both Montazeri and Motahhari had to spend hours reading and discussing the lessons, whose obscure meanings frustrated them. There were times when they seriously thought about quitting the lessons, but they persevered, in no small measure due to their respect for Khomeini.

The two friends had a close relationship with Khomeini; they not only talked to him in the classroom, but also had long discussions in less formal settings about a range of issues, including the politics of the *howzeh*, as well as of the country. Even though they treated Khomeini with utmost respect, there were still lighter moments when they would joke with this serious man and make him laugh. Khomeini, in turn, considered them the fruits of his life. When Motahhari was assassinated, Khomeini released a heartfelt statement, addressing not only Motahhari's unique Islamic credentials but also his own affection for him, calling him his dear son, a part of the achievement of his life, a part of his soul.[69] There is no doubt that Khomeini's outpouring of grief for Motahhari was rooted in their mentor–pupil relationship in Qom. Such a close connection also existed between Khomeini and Montazeri at that time, a closeness that, though shattered dramatically at the end of Khomeini's life, lasted for a long time. Khomeini trusted Montazeri and considered him one of his best students, with a vast energy and a hunger for learning.

Montazeri's relationship with his main mentor, Borujerdi, remained warm to the end. He knew Borujerdi even before he met him through the latter's commentaries on one of the most influential Shii texts, *al-Urwah al-Wuthqa*.[70] Both Montazeri and Motahhari regarded the book highly and were determined to meet its influential commentator. Montazeri traveled to Borujerd to attend Borujerdi's lectures in the summer of 1943 and was instantly taken by him, and became an eager proponent for his resettlement in Qom.

When Borujerdi moved to Qom, Montazeri took his classes and, inspired by his lectures, soon began to write each evening from memory what he had heard during the day. With the permission of his teacher, these nocturnal writings became the basis of two edited books: *Nahayat-al Usul* and *Salat*.[71] Of course, the process did not always go as smoothly as Montazeri wished. Borujerdi was a cautious man, and leaving the note-taking to Montazeri (who admittedly never took notes during lectures) made him anxious. So he would periodically ask Montazeri to submit these drafts in order to make sure that they were in fact a faithful reflection of his own ideas. According to Montazeri, Borujerdi was pleasantly surprised by the care and accuracy that had gone into their writing. He was also impressed by Montazeri's own commentaries and questions in the margins.

On the whole, however, Borujerdi was ambivalent toward the publication of his lectures by Montazeri, and was worried about his own reputation and the reaction that the book might receive from prominent ayatollahs in Najaf. So, one day, when Montazeri was in the publishing house working on the last part of one of these books, a friend of Borujerdi, who also happened to be his lawyer, asked Montazeri to halt the publication but promised him that the Ayatollah would pay all the costs of publication to date. The disappointed Montazeri rushed to Borujerdi's house and requested a meeting. Once the meeting was granted, he, with his characteristic bluntness and perseverance, put pressure on the Ayatollah and eventually got his permission to move ahead with the book's publication, a permission Borujerdi rarely granted to anyone.[72]

Whether Montazeri's recollection corresponds faithfully to what actually happened between the two men, the fact remains that Borujerdi considered him one of his favorite students and appointed him as his representatives on several occasions, and Montazeri stayed loyal to his principal mentor to the end. When tensions were brewing in the seminary, and even on those occasions when Montazeri found himself drawn to the points of views of Borujerdi's critics, he did not leave

Borujerdi's side. The *howzeh* was not a harmonious place; there were disagreements, frustrations, and even competition, which would sometimes lead to crisis.

Politics of the *Howzeh*

Even though Borujerdi was the clear leader of the *howzeh*, his policies did not always go unchallenged by some of the other influential seminarians, especially Khomeini. There were several reasons for the tension between these two men, one of which involved national politics and the proper role of the *ulema* in relation to the state: Khomeini was in favor of a more activist approach to national politics, while Borujerdi preferred a quietist method.

But there were also internal matters that caused tensions among seminarians. Despite Borujerdi's many successes in running the *howzeh*, several persistent problems made a few of the senior lecturers, including Khomeini, impatient. Borujerdi himself shared some of these concerns, particularly in the area of curriculum.[73] In fact, Borujerdi assigned a task force – a *hey'at-e hakemeh* (governing council), whose members included Khomeini and Morteza Haeri, son of the founder of the Qom seminary – to devise a reform plan to systematize the educational and financial aspects of the seminary.[74] Even though they were not members of the council, Montazeri and Motahhari were also involved in the discussion of such reforms.[75]

Many instructors focused on the role and purpose of the curriculum and argued that religious education must address the concerns of contemporary society, particularly those of the younger generation. They found a curriculum dominated by grammar and abstract logic deficient, and argued for the inclusion of courses on history, geography, and sciences, as well as foreign languages. But the implementation of a comprehensive reform project was not just a matter of the will of the instructors or the director of the seminary; it also involved people from outside. The explicit or implicit approval of the new initiatives by the people who financed the seminaries – those who paid their *sahm-e emam* to the *howzeh*– was of great consequence. Many of these contributors were against some of the reforms, particularly the inclusion of foreign languages such as English, thinking they would corrupt and contaminate the purity of Islam and the *howzeh*, and they succeeded in preventing the reformers from making headway in all but a few

areas.[76] The reformers did manage to set up a system of examination
that would provide certain standards for gauging learning and thus
rationalize or systematize the judgment about whether students should
move from lower levels to upper ones. Ultimately, though, no matter
how modest or radical these reforms were, most of them were shelved
and not revived until the revolution.

The matters that damaged the relationship between Borujerdi and
some of the *hey'at-e hakemeh* members, such as Khomeini and Haeri,
were not primarily curricular in nature, but administrative and man-
agerial. Khomeini and Haeri had come up with a series of recom-
mendations that would curb Borujerdi's administrative and financial
decision-making power by transferring some of it to several new committees. The angry Borujerdi refused to give his consent and virtually banished Khomeini from his office. It was then that Montazeri,
who had remained out of the discussion on financial aspects, made an
attempt to mediate. Unlike his friend Motahhari, who was never close
to Borujerdi and had raised his suspicion and anger over his alleged
involvement in the internal "coup," Montazeri remained close to both
Borujerdi and Khomeini. In a shuttle diplomacy, Montazeri went back
and forth between the two men. In particular, he tried to convince Borujerdi that the idea of a collective decision-making body should be taken
not as a challenge to Borujerdi's personal status and effectiveness but
as a positive step toward institutionalization or rationalization of the
seminary administration.[77]

The mediation was not very successful, however, and even though
Borujerdi and Khomeini became cordial toward each other, the warmth
of their earlier relationship was gone forever. Another life was also
deeply affected by this episode: that of Motahhari. Borujerdi never forgave Montazeri's close friend for what he considered a betrayal. Partly
due to this strife, and partly to his own financial difficulties, Motahhari left Qom for Tehran sometime between 1952 and 1953.[78] Montazeri, on the other hand, remained in Qom as a trusted follower of
Borujerdi.

Montazeri: The Teacher

Montazeri began teaching when he was still an intermediary-level student in Isfahan. But his reputation as an influential teacher rose only
after he received the permission for *ejtehad* and became worthy of the

title *Hojjat-ol-Islam ol Moslemin*.[79] Montazeri became a *mojtahed* (the practitioner of *ejtehad*) in 1949, when he was just twenty-seven. In Shii Islam, the right to *ejtehad* is conferred on aspirants when they complete all three levels of the *howzeh*'s curriculum and publish a prominent text with their own independent commentaries. Permission can also be granted in a de facto manner, such as when the *marja' taqlid* chooses the aspiring mojtahed to be his local representative in charge of collecting religious donations on his behalf. In the case of Montazeri, he earned the status in both ways: through publication of his commentaries on Borujerdi's lessons, and through his appointment as Borujerdi's sole representative in Najafabad and Isfahan in 1955.

Once a *mojtahed* Montazeri's status as a teacher and the number of his students began to rise. Among his students were some of the future leaders of the Islamic Republic, most notably Ali Khamenei (the current Supreme Leader) and Ali Akbar Hashemi Rafsanjani (the two-time President of the Islamic Republic). Montazeri taught a variety of subjects, philosophy and ethics among them, but his reputation as a great teacher was primarily due to his lessons on jurisprudence. This was particularly the case during the pre-revolutionary period.[80]

Montazeri's pedagogical approach combined those of his main mentors with some innovations of his own. In seminaries, there was no set teaching method, but since its rise under the leadership of Haeri, Qom's *howzeh* had tried two schools of pedagogy, particularly at the highest-level courses. These were the Samara school and the Najaf school, both named after centers of learning in Iraq.[81] The younger and less durable of the two, the Samara school, was introduced and established in Qom by Ayatollah Haeri. Haeri himself was a product of that pedagogical style and had studied with its founder, Ayatollah Mirza Mohammad Hassan Shirazi (ca. 1814–96), in Samara. But after Haeri's death, the Najaf school began to assert itself in the seminary, and with some modification it became the dominant school during Borujerdi's tenure.

The Najaf school was structured around lectures by the instructors: the emphasis was on the end result – the solution of a particular problem, rather than the method for obtaining that solution. On the other hand, and in theory at least, the Samara pedagogical approach was student-centered and skill- or process-oriented. It followed a Socratic method: one or a few students would take a position on an issue, and other students and the instructor would challenge that position. The first student(s) would have then have an opportunity to respond. In this model, the instructor would usually finish the lesson by assessing the discussion and drawing conclusions.

In addition to the student-oriented format, the Samara school focused on teaching certain skills that theoretically would allow students to become independent scholars. In reality, however, due to the early stages of students' educational background, a product of an intellectually stagnated approach, the give and take remained within a very limited and repetitive confine.

As Borujerdi's long-term student, Montazeri leaned more toward Najaf's pedagogical system, even though his style was not totally unresponsive to the principles that underpinned Samara's approach.[82] Borujerdi's method consisted of a couple of steps: (1) a description of the problem – the subject matter of his investigation; and (2) an appeal to different authoritative sources, starting with the Quran, followed by the Prophet's *hadith*, and then the sayings of the twelve Imams. In order to use the last two sources, Borujerdi would compare interpretation of a large number of not only Shii but also Sunni *ravat* (narrators of the sayings and deeds of the Prophet) from various historical periods. Montazeri followed this model in his jurisprudential teaching.

If Borujerdi was Montazeri's main guide in teaching jurisprudence, Khomeini was his model in how to teach courses in philosophy and mysticism. Montazeri always admired Khomeini as a mentor, and for years attended his classes on ethics, principles of jurisprudence, and philosophy. Khomeini attracted students' attention by not speaking of the subject matter in an abstract or exclusively textual and static manner, but instead analyzing issues dynamically, placing them in a concrete context.[83] Montazeri, for one, found Khomeini's style clear, his narrative free of jargon, and his argument compelling.[84]

Despite his attentiveness to his mentors' methods, certain aspects of Montazeri's teaching were unique to him. In a pedagogical system where oral lecture was the norm, Montazeri was one of the first teachers to provide his students with his own written lecture notes. He would choose a large number of interpretations from diverse religious scholars of what would be the focus of the lesson and then summarize them for students in written form, providing them with "a literature review" a day ahead of each class session. That gave his pupils a chance to read the next day's lesson and prepare questions and comments ahead of time. He would then incorporate many of his students' comments and questions in the next written lesson, which he would once again distribute among them prior to class. At the end of each lesson, Montazeri interjected his own position on and interpretation of the subject.[85]

Even though Montazeri was more partial to the Najaf school, emphasizing the previously mentioned method of "problem-solving" rather than teaching skills, he did provide opportunities for his students to discuss the subject matters of his lessons based on their own reflections. In the eyes of many of his students, his encouraging style played a crucial role in their becoming independent religious thinkers.[86] In answer to a reporter's question about what religious and political differences he might detect in the beliefs of his new students compared to his past experiences, Montazeri responded:

Based on their degree of talents, efforts, and perseverance each of my students have their own unique point of view. They come and learn the method of inquiry from their teacher and then develop their own independent views of science, politics, society, and culture. Insisting on their own beliefs about these matters is their right.[87]

This question was asked of him in 2007 when some of his younger students – those who became part of the political and religious reformist movement, such as Mohsen Kadivar – had already in private challenged a few of his positions on sociopolitical issues.[88]

Montazeri: The Scholar

High-ranking clergy are expected to be not only esteemed teachers but also active religious scholars and to publish treatises on established fields of jurisprudence, philosophy, theology, and ethics. A large number of the published treatises of most traditional seminary scholars are a product of their class lectures, written either by themselves or by their students. As a student, Montazeri followed this pattern: his first writings were based on the notes, and his own commentaries, on the oral lessons of his main mentor, Borujerdi. Several of his published works, including his influential *Nahayat-ol Usul*, which includes Borujerdi's main opinions on jurisprudence, belong to this category.[89] When Montazeri began to write his own independent jurisprudential treatises, he used Borujerdi as a model, adopting his primarily *naqli* (textual, emphasizing the Quran and the *hadith* as the primary sources for derivation of rules) rather than *aqli* (rational, emphasizing human reason for the derivation of rules) approach. That somewhat changed in the writing of his later years.

Montazeri's treatises can be divided into three subject matters: theosophy and epistemology; *fiqh/usul-e fiqh* (jurisprudence/principle of jurisprudence); and "semi"-jurisprudential.[90] His theosophical and epistemological treatises consist of writings that focus on proofs of the existence of an all-powerful deity and His plans for humans,[91] the necessity of religion for humans' felicity and the role of ethics in their lives,[92] the corresponding necessity and proof of prophecy,[93] and the proof of the coming of the Twelfth Imam.[94] His six-volume commentaries on *Nahjol-Balagheh* (a compilation of decrees, advice, and other sayings attributed to Ali, the son-in-law of the Prophet Mohammad and the first Shii Imam) also focus primarily on philosophical and theological questions provoked by the sermons of Imam Ali.[95]

In general, though, Montazeri's philosophical and theological writings were not the ones that made him an influential religious scholar, and ultimately a grand ayatollah. There are generally three factors that determine the status of the high clergy and make a few of them grand ayatollahs. These are the number of high-quality students who seek them as teachers, the amount of *sahm-e emam* they receive from their followers, and the quality and quantity of their writings. Regarding this last factor, the writing of juridical/jurisprudential treatises, especially a *resaleh 'amalieh* (practical treatise), is the necessary component for achieving the status of grand ayatollah. Unlike his friend Motahhari, whose major works were on theological and epistemological matters, Montazeri's philosophical treatises were relatively few and for the most part ignored by other scholars. Instead, true to his position as a *faqih*, jurisprudence constitutes the main corpus of his writings.[96]

Juridical writings are usually divided into two categories: *fatva'i* (decreed) and *estedlali* (argued/derived). The first are decrees by the *faqih* and are themselves of two kinds: *resaleh 'amalieh* and *estefta'at* (requests for decrees). The former consist of rules that provide guidance for one's followers. These are usually commentaries on a significant treatise of a prominent and earlier source of emulation, and are normally required of men of the cloth who wish to be considered an established source of emulation. A large number of them concern rituals of cleanliness and rules for prayers and fasting, along with social and economic interactions among people. The *estefta'at* are answers to specific questions posed by one's followers when they confront new circumstances for which the practical treatises have not provided an answer. For instance, a Muslim male who lives abroad might ask his source of emulation about what to do when in an official meeting a woman participant extends her hand in greeting, expecting him to shake it. The traditional juridical rulings have always forbidden bodily contact between unrelated males and females. But in this case – a Muslim living abroad – refusal to shake might be considered rude and offensive. Not being able to decide on one's own, the Muslim man requests his source of emulation for a ruling about the proper religious behavior. The guide will provide an answer. But neither in a "practical treatise" nor in "answers to questions" is a *faqih* required to provide a reason for his judgment; hence the title, "decreed ruling."

In contrast, *fiqh-e estedlali* demand proof and argumentation as a method for deriving laws. To do this, a Shii jurist relies on four sources: (1) the Book (Quran), (2) the *hadith* (the sayings and practice of the Prophet and the Infallible Imams), (3) consensus, and (4) reason. As a rule, and for centuries, these inferences have been overwhelmingly based on the first two sources, with human reason pushed to the background.[97]

Montazeri's legal writings encompass both *fatva'i* and *estedlali* treatises. He wrote a practical treatise, in 1983, which sealed his qualifications as a source of emulation, and prepared him to become the successor to Khomeini as the Supreme Leader. His answers to the inquires of his followers are submitted in three volumes of *estefsa'at*, as well as in volumes of *Pasokh be Porseshha-ye Dini* (Response to Religious Questions).[98] It is in this genre of writing that Montazeri's role as the bearer of centuries-old conventions becomes most obvious.

Respected clergy should also issue treatises in the area of *fiqh-e estedlali* in order to seal their positions within the seminary circles. Many of Montazeri's writings belong to this category.[99] The most famous and politically significant of these writings are his treatises on Islamic government. His earlier ideas on an Islamic state are reflected in a multivolume book, *Mabani Fiqhi-ye Hokumat-e Eslami* (The Juridical Foundations of Islamic Government).[100] Based on a four-year series of lectures in Arabic to his students in *dars-e kharej*, this book is the most comprehensive treatment of the Islamic government. Though Khomeini's treatise on Islamic government received all the attention among observers of Iranian politics and has been most analyzed by Western scholars, only in Montazeri's can one see detailed descriptions of the structure, functions, and institutions of the state under the control of the *faqih*.

In his later years Montazeri wrote several other treatises on state–society relations. These treatises – the focus of Chapters Five and Six of this biography – reveal Montazeri's movement from a static and authoritarian position to a more dynamic and egalitarian one.[101] They were also responsible for his growing reputation outside the confines of seminary circles as the most significant reformist among the high clergy.[102] The significance of Montazeri's last writings was in his increasing emphasis on justice and human reason as the source of lawmaking, an important departure from his long-standing method of extensive reliance on historical and traditionally authoritative *ravayat*.[103]

Most people inside and outside of Iran know or have heard of Montazeri as primarily a religious political actor, a man who helped and later hindered the post-revolution regime to gain power/legitimacy, but it is only through knowing his life as a teacher and a scholar that one can fully appreciate the reasons for his political acts.

Notes

1 Muhammed Ali Sultani Najafabadi, *Tazkireh Shu'ara-yi Najafabad* [Biography of Poets of Najababad] (Isfahan: 1975).
2 For a description of the physical characteristics of Najafabad in the mid nineteenth century by an eyewitness, see the Persian translation of Heinrich Brugsch's travelogue *Safari be Darbare-ye Soltan-e Sahebqaran*, trans. Mohammad Hossein Kord-Bacheh (Tehran: Etela'at Press, 2010), 358–62.
3 His parents had two other sons and two daughters. Montazeri also had three younger half-brothers. When his mother died in 1972, his father married again, and these three children were the product of that late marriage. Correspondence with Sa'ide Montazeri, December 17, 2012.
4 See Mostafa Izadi, *Faqih-e Aliqadr* [The Exalted Jurist] (Tehran: Soroush Publications, 1982), 28–30.
5 See the collected volume of Montazeri's lessons in ethics in Mojtaba Lotfi, ed., *Faraz va Foroud Nafs: Darsha-yi az Akhlaq* [Ascension and Fall of Soul: Lessons in Ethics] (Tehran: Kavir Publications, 2010), 22–3.
6 Hossein Ali Montazeri, *Khaterat* (from now on referred to as *Memoirs*) (Los Angeles, CA: Sherkat Ketab Corp., 2001), 10.
7 For a brief article on *maktab* and its structure and rituals, see Ebrahim Khalil Misaqi Mamaqani, "Sayri dar Adab-e Maktabkhaneh" [A View

on the Manners of Maktabkhaneh], *Honar va Mardom*, nos. 165–6 (1956): 104–8.

8 See Reza Arasteh, *Education and Social Awakening in Iran, 1850–1968* (Leiden: Brill, 1962), 6–8.

9 In fact, despite restrictive policies passed in 1925 regarding the opening up of new *makateb*, the number of *maktab* students continued to rise until reaching its peak in 1935, after which a steady decline made *maktab* a rare institution. See David Menashri, *Education and the Making of Modern Iran* (Ithaca, NY: Cornell University Press, 1992), 101–2.

10 Montazeri, *Memoirs*, 10.

11 Ibid., 14.

12 Ibid., 15.

13 Montazeri's praise for Hojjaji's unadorned lifestyle, his sense of humor, and his approach to education in comparison to some others' was taken by Montazeri's critics, such as Badamchian, as indicative of Montazeri's simple-mindedness and as an implied insult to other clergymen. See Asadollah Badamchian, *Khaterat-e Montazeri va Naqd-e Ān* [Montazeri's Memoirs and Its Critique] (Tehran: Andisheh Nab, 2007), 46–7.

14 Montazeri, *Memoirs*, 14–15.

15 For a description of the earliest Islamic *madreseh*, the Sunni eleventh-century *nezamieh*, see George Makdisi, "Muslim Institutions of Learning in Eleventh Century Baghdad," *Bulletin of the School of Oriental and African Studies*, 24, no. 1 (1961): 1–56.

16 Michael Fischer, *Iran: From Religious Dispute to Revolution* (Cambridge, MA: Harvard University Press, 1980): 78–80.

17 This social structure traces back to the time of Safavid dynasty. For a description of the Safavid social configuration of the *howzeh*, see Ali Akhzari and Ali Akbar Kajbaf, "Structure and Social System of the Clergy in Safavid Era," *Interdisciplinary Journal of Contemporary Research in Business* 4, no. 11 (2013): 216–23.

18 One of the best accounts in English of the life of a seminary student can be found in Roy Mottahedeh's *The Mantle of the Prophet*. In addition to the primary focus of the book, the life of a young seminarian in the mid to late twentieth century, Mottahedeh tells us about the seminary experiences of others, including the seventeenth-century Sayyed Nematollah Jazayeri and the late nineteenth–early twentieth-century Ahmad Kasravi. See Mottahedeh, *The Mantle of the Prophet*, 94–109.

19 There is an interesting analysis of Quchani's memoirs by Michael Fischer, who interprets them as a lighthearted and satirical autobiography written from the point of view of a person who, even though loyal to the clerical establishment, did not restrain himself from mocking some

of its "excesses and naïve practitioners." See Fischer, "Portrait of a Molla: The Autobiography and bildungsroman of Agha Najafi Quchani (1875–1943)," *Persica* (1982): 223–57.

20 Aqa Najafi Quchani, *Siahat-e Sharq va Gharb* [Journey to East and West] (Qom: Afarinesh Press, 1998), 29–41.

21 Mohammad Reza Mahdavi Kani, *Memoirs*, ed. Gholam Reza Khajeh Sarvi (Tehran: Islamic Revolution Document Center, 2006), 44–6.

22 Montazeri, *Memoirs*, 13.

23 Emaddedin Baghi, *Vaqe'iyat-ha va Qezavat-ha* [Truths and Judgments] (1998). On Montazeri's website, this book appears without the name of the author. His authorship of the book is now public knowledge, however.

24 See Rudi Matthee, "Transforming Dangerous Nomads into Useful Artisans, Technicians, Agriculturists: Education in the Reza Shah Period," *Iranian Studies*, 26, no. 3/4 (1993): 313–36. Despite the emphasis of the first part of the title, about transformation of nomad, the article gives a very clear account of the objectives of Reza Shah' educational policies.

25 Shahrough Akhavi, *Religion and Politics in Contemporary Iran* (Albany, NY: SUNY Press, 1980), 56–9.

26 See Nikki Keddie, *Modern Iran: Roots and Results of Revolution* (New Haven, CT: Yale University Press, 2006), 80–8.

27 For the statistics on the yearly decrease of number of students, see Menashri, *Education*, 102. See Montazeri, *Memoirs* on the difficult life of the *howzeh* community during this period.

28 Here, as in most religious schools, each student had not only a *ham-hojreh* (roommate) but also a *ham-mobahess* (discussion partner). In many cases, the two were the same person.

29 Montazeri never talked about this aspect of his life, but in some of his writings, particularly in *Az Aghaz ta Anjam: Goftegooye Do Daneshjoo* [From Beginning to End: The Conversation of Two University Students] (Tehran: Sarayi Press, 2003), he makes his points about the existence of God as the creator of the universe by using the metaphor of a beautiful garden with flowing water and shady trees, a description very similar to those of the gardens of his childhood seminaries.

30 See Fischer, *Iran*, 61.

31 Montazeri, *Memoirs*, 16–21.

32 For a more detailed description of courses of study in traditional seminaries, see Fischer, *Iran*, 247–8.

33 Allameh Mohammad Baqir Majlesi was a powerful religious figure of the Safavid era. He was a proponent of Akhbari school of Shii *fiqh*, a school that privileged the authority of *hadith* and tradition over human reason and thus was critical of *ejtehad* (independent judgment). The

rival school in the Shii *fiqh* was the school of Usuli, which respected reason and independent judgment as one way to reach legal rulings.

34 Personal interview with Mohsen Kadivar, summer 2013. There is other evidence of this attitude. For an example where the interlocutor not only challenged Montazeri but insulted him and his profession, see Hossein Mirmobini, "Written Debates with Shi'i Leader 'Ayatollah' Montazeri," in *Persian Cultural Review* (Sacramento, CA, 2006). Even though Montazeri's responses might not have been satisfactory in their substance, his openness to criticism is evident.

35 Akhavi, *Religion and Politics*, 28.

36 Ibid., 27–28 and Fischer, *Iran*, 109–12.

37 The only policy that Haeri deemed as unacceptable, and thus raised an objection to, was the policy of forced unveiling adopted in 1936. See Hamid Algar's article on Haeri at http://www.iranica.com/articles/haeri.

38 The overall number of *tollab* (*talabeh*, sing.: religious student) in Iran declined from 5532 in 1929/30 to 784 in 1941/42. The jump in the number of students after Reza Shah's abdication is evident in the data related to the year 1946/47, when 3057 *tollab* were studying in the seminaries. See Menashri, *Education*, 102.

39 For the emergence of such a figure in the person of Shaykh Morteza Ansari in Najaf and the role of followers (*muqaleds*) in the same, see Abbas Amanat, "In Between the Madrasa and the Marketplace: The Designation of Clerical Leadership in Modern Shi'ism," in *Authority and Political Culture in Shi'ism*, ed. Said Amir Arjomand, (Albany, NY: SUNY Press, 1988), 98–132. Amanat argues, however, that the first explicit assignment of the title of *marja' taqlid tamm* to Ansari seems to have been in sources from the twentieth century rather than the nineteenth, casting doubt on the assumption of the timing of the emergence of the Supreme Source of Emulation. See 101–2.

40 In choosing the proper person for the office, in addition to the usual problem associated with lack of institutionalization there has been the challenge of regional competition between clergy residing in Iraq and Iran.

41 The emergence of the position of Sole Source of Emulation, however, did not eliminate the existence of local sources. The latter retained local authority among their followers.

42 Hamid Algar, "Borujerdi, Hosayn Tabataba'i," in *Encyclopaedia Iranica*, vol. 4, fasc. 4, 376–9.

43 There was one occasion when Borujerdi's dissatisfactions with policies of the state were made public: his objection to a 1959 land reform bill. According to Shahrough Akhavi, this marked a break in the

cooperation between Borujerdi and the Shah in public policy. See Akhavi, *Religion and Politics*, 91.

44 Montazeri, *Memoirs*, 37; Algar, "Borujerdi, Hosayn Tabataba'i."

45 See Morteza Motahhari, *Takamol-e Ejtemah* [The Evolution of Society] (Tehran: Tavakol Publications, 1993), 204–5.

46 See Mahmood T. Davari, *The Political Thought of Ayatullah Murtaza Mutahhari* (Oxon: Routledge, 2005), 16.

47 Montazeri, *Memoirs*, 34–5.

48 Ibid., app. 2, 442–3.

49 Ibid., 31.

50 There is a most curious exception to this rule, and that is the publication of Khomeini's love letter to his wife while he was in Beirut, Lebanon and on his way to the annual *Hajj*. In that letter, Khomeini spoke of the physical beauty of his wife and his love for her. He also mentioned how much he missed her and wished that she were there so that they could enjoy the beauty of the Mediterranean site together. See Ruhollah Khomeini, *Sahifeh Imam Khomeini* (Tehran: Moasesseh Tanzim va Nashr-e Asar-e Imam Khomeini, 1999), 1:2. The translated version of the letter can be found at http://statics.ml.imam-khomeini.ir/en/File/NewsAttachment/2014/1695-Sahifeh-ye%20Imam-Vol%201.pdf.

51 Montazeri, *Memoirs*, 170.

52 E-mail correspondence with Sa'ide Montazeri, December 2012.

53 Montazeri, *Memoirs*, 142, 213.

54 Ibid., 182–3.

55 The relationship between Beheshti and Mohammad Montazeri was patched up later when Mohammad, after many reckless incidences, reconciled himself with the power establishment and became a member of the newly founded Islamic Republic Party, headed by Beheshti. They both lost their lives in the same explosion.

56 Manouchehr Mahjoobi, the founder of the weekly *Ahangar*, is believed to have been the person who first used this name to refer to Mohammad.

57 For a detailed description of the trip to Libya episode, see http://tarikhirani.ir/fa/files/14/bodyView/146/%D8%B3%D9%81%D8%B1.%D8%B5%D8%A7%D8%AF%D8%B1%DA%A9%D9%86%D9%86%D8%AF%DA%AF%D8%A7%D9%86.%D8%A7%D9%86%D9%82%D9%84%D8%A7%D8%A8.%D8%A8%D9%87.%D9%84%DB%8C%D8%A8%DB%8C%D8%9B.%D8%A7%D8%B3%D9%84%D8%AD%D9%87.%D8%A8%D9%87%E2%80%8C%D8%AC%D8%A7%DB%8C.%DA%AF%D8%B0%D8%B1%D9%86%D8%A7%D9%85%D9%87.html.

58 See Montazeri's written statement at http://davodabadi.blogfa.com/post-298.aspx.

59 Montazeri, *Memoirs*, 249–50.

60 See http://www.rahesabz.net/story/7949/.

61 Ahmad Montazeri's admiration for his father's attributes and his own desire to adopt them were in plain evidence in his response to my questions in a series of e-mail correspondence (spring of 2013). He thought of his father as honest (in both action and speech), respectful of others' opinions, and tolerant of his detractors.

62 Correspondence with Sa'ide Montazeri, December 2012.

63 E-mail correspondence with Ahmad Montazeri, May 4, 2013.

64 Hossein Ali Montazeri, *Enteqad az Khod: Ebrat va Vasiyat* [Self-Criticism: Lessons and Last Will], ed. Sa'id Montazeri (2009), at https://amontazeri.com/ayatollah/censure/336.

65 On most evenings, according to Ahmad, Montazeri would gather the children and play word puzzles. Being a devout religious man, he would include Quranic verses in playing the game.

66 See the text of the interview with Mohammad Montazeri in *Enqelab-e Eslami*, October 10, 1979, 3.

67 Correspondence with Sa'ide Montazeri, December 2012.

68 E-mail correspondence with Baghi, July 25, 2015.

69 See http://www.youtube.com/watch?v=IzFvxn4NjVQ.

70 This book of rules contains answers to more than 3000 questions. It was authored by Sayyed Mohammad Kazem Tabataba'i, a late nineteenth- and early twentieth-century jurisprudent. Writing commentaries on this book is considered an important scholarly endeavor.

71 *Nahayat-al Usul* became one of the most important references on the principles of jurisprudence.

72 Montazeri, *Memoirs*, 48–9.

73 One of the areas that Borujerdi was quite concerned about was textbooks. He believed that the available texts were too bloated with repetitive commentaries and were in desperate need of a proper editing system.

74 See an interview with one of the members of the governing council, Ayatollah Soltani Tabataba'i, in *Majalleh-e Howzeh*, nos. 43–4 at http://www.hawzah.net/fa/magazine/magart/4518/4546/32765.

75 In 1962, Motahhari contributed an essay to a volume by several religious reformers occasioned by the death of Ayatollah Borujerdi. The essay specifically addressed his view of the problems that had plagued the seminaries and their sources. See Morteza Motahhari, "The Fundamental Problem in the Clerical Establishment," trans. Farhad Arshad,

in Linda S. Walbridge, ed., *The Most Learned of the Shi'a* (New York: Oxford University Press, 2001), 161–82.

76 Motahhari referred to this problem – the financial dependence of the *howzeh* on *sahm-e emam* – as the principal source of the stagnation of Islamic studies. See Motahhari, "The Fundamental Problem." In his memoirs, Montazeri addresses this problem, but only briefly.

77 A brief but revealing description of the tension between Khomeini and Borujerdi with regard to the governance of the seminary and Montazeri's attempt to mediate used to be found on the website of Ayatollah Mohammad Javad Alavi Borujerdi, a relative of the Grand Ayatollah Borujerdi, at http://www.alaviboroujerdi.com/Default.aspx?tabid=81&articleType=ArticleView&articleId=303 (last accessed May 2015).

78 See Davari, *The Political Thought*, 29–32.

79 There are several steps in the ladder of prominence that separate one clergyman from another in terms of degree of knowledge and scholarly influence. There is no written or clear criterion for assigning these titles, but over the years an informal standard has been set. The title *hojjat-ol-Islam* is assigned to students who attend the highest-level classes (*dars-e kharej*). *Hojjat-ol-Islam ol Moslemin* is assigned to those who have received permission to engage in limited *ejtehad* (i.e., *ejtehad-e mote-jazzi*). The title of ayatollah is suitable for a person who has reached the stage of engaging in *ejtehad-e motlaq*.

80 Years later, particularly after his fall from official power, Montazeri became more involved in teaching philosophy. He started teaching his family *Manzumeh Hekmat* (Philosophical System) in 1998, soon after he was put under house arrest, and continued until his death in 2009.

81 For a comparative analysis of the jurisprudential approach of the two schools, as well as what came to be known as School of Qom, see Sayyed Mostafa Mohaqqeq Damad, "Tahavolat-e Ejtehad Shii: Sayr-e Tarikhi, Howzeh-ha, Shiveh-ha (2)" [The Evolution of Shii *Ejtehad*: Historical Background, *Howzehs*, Methods (2)], *Tahqigat-e Huqquqi*, 46 (2007–08): 7–44.

82 See Sayyed Mohammad Ali Ayazi, "Negahi be Maktab-e Ejtehadi Aya-tollah Montazeri: Mabani va Raveshha" [A Look at Ayatollah Montazeri's School of Ijtehad: Foundation and Methods], at http://www.rahesabz.net/print/48191.

83 Many former students of Khomeini praised his teaching. For a sample of such praise, see http://www.hawzah.net/fa/MagArt.html?MagazineArticleID=19650&MagazineNumberID=3705.

84 Montazeri, *Memoirs*, 32–3. The description of Khomeini's style of teaching by Montazeri and other students is not reflected in Khomeini's

biography by Baqer Moin. Moin assigns three adjectives to Khome-ini's pedagogy: autocratic, decisive, and self-righteous. See Baqer Moin, *Khomeini: Life of the Ayatollah* (New York: St. Martin Press, 1999), 37. These qualities were certainly not the ones that made Montazeri admire Khomeini's teaching.

85 Personal interview with Mohsen Kadivar, June 2012.

86 From a secular point of view, the reference to "independent thinker" here might seem suspect due to the limited framework of the discussion (limited to a Shii world view). Even though this might be a legitimate criticism, the point is to highlight Montazeri's treatment of students: his trust in their capacity to reflect.

87 Hossein Ali Montazeri, *Didgahha* [Points of View] (Qom, 2002), vol. 3, 167–8.

88 For example, Kadivar asked Montazeri to make a judgment regarding the conflict between the traditional jurisprudence and a few of the articles of the UDHR. According to Kadivar, Montazeri, due to his status as a traditional jurist, could not resolve the conflict, but encouraged his student to find the resolution by pursuing a new line of jurisprudential argument. See Mohsen Kadivar, *Dar Mahzar-e Faqih-e Azadeh: Ostad Ayatollah-ol-Ozma Montazeri* [In the Presence of the Liberated Jurist: the Mentor Grand Ayatollah Montazeri] (2014), 37–8, at http://kadivar.com/wp-content/uploads/2014/02/%D8%AF%D8%B1-%D9%85%D8%AD%D8%B6%D8%B1-%D9%81%D9%82%DB%8C%D9%87-%D8%A2%D8%B2%D8%A7%D8%AF%D9%87.pdf.

89 The importance of this publication lies in its use as a principal source of reference for Borujerdi's ideas on jurisprudence by a large number of Shii jurisprudents. The first and incomplete version of *Nahayat-ol Usul*, on principles of Shii jurisprudence, was first published in 1955; a two-volume edition was published in 1994. *Al-Badr-ol Zaher*, on Friday and travelers' prayer rituals, was first published in 1959 and has been reprinted twice.

90 In addition to his scholarly treatises, Montazeri has other writings, mainly in response to questions posed by people close to him. These writings for the most part are his responses to the charges waged against him after his fall from official power in 1988. For a complete list of Montazeri's writings that includes both scholarly and non-specialized writings, see the sections on books on Montazeri's official website: https://amontazeri.com/book.

91 See Montazeri, *Az Aghaz ta Anjam*, 3rd ed. This is a relatively short piece, in the form of a dialogue between two university students. He wrote it while in prison in the 1970's.

92 Montazeri, *Eslam Din-e Fetrat* [Islam: The Religion for Human Essence] (Tehran: Sayeh Publications, 2006).

93 Montazeri, *Mabaniye Nazari-ye Nabovvat* [The Theoretical Foundation of Prophecy] (Qom: Arghavan-e Danesh Publications, 2008).

94 Montazeri, *Mo'ud-e Adyan* [The Promise of Religions] (Tehran: Kherad Ava Publications, 2005).

95 Montazeri, *Dars-ha'i az Nahj-ol Balagheh* [Lessons from Nahj-ol Balagheh], ed. Emaddedin Baghi (Tehran and Qom: Sarayi Press, 2001).

96 It should be mentioned that due to their over-reliance on the *naqli* (traditional) approach at the expense of the *aqli* (rational) approach, jurisprudential writings have rarely been judged as intellectually worthy endeavors by people outside the seminary circles. This could explain why Montazeri, until his last few treatises, was rarely included in the list of religious thinkers, as a *thinker*, or studied by either Iranian or Western scholars.

97 For a brief treatment of reason in the history of Shii jurisprudence, see Roy Parviz Mottahedeh's introduction to Muhammad Baqir as-Sadr, *Lessons in Jurisprudence* (Oxford: Oneworld, 2003), 1–34.

98 *Resaleh-e Estefta'at*, vols. 1 and 2 (Tehran: Sayeh Publications, 2005), vol. 3 (Qom: Arghavan Danesh Publications, 2009). *Pasokh be Porseshha-ye Dini* primarily addresses theology issues, rather than providing answers to practical problems. The questions asked and responded to in this volume are a mixture of theological, historical, and political ones. Montazeri for the most part doesn't give simple decrees but uses arguments (*estedlal*) for his answers here.

99 For a complete list of such writings, all of them in Arabic, consult the section on books on Montazeri's official website: https://amontazeri .com/book.

100 The original Arabic version was published in four volumes, three of them in 1988, the last in 1990. The Persian translation of these volumes appeared in the period between 1990 and 2007, issued in Qom by Sarayi Publications.

101 These writings are halfway between treatises written only for specialists in the field and ones written for the wider non-specialist audience. They have argumentation but are simplified for a lay audience. They are also written in Persian.

102 *Hokumat-e Dini va Huqquq Ensan* [Islamic Government and Human Rights] (Tehran: Sarayi Press, 2008); *Resaleh Huqquq* [Treatise on Rights], 4th ed. (Tehran: Sara-i Publications, 2005); *Mojazatha-ye Eslami va Huqquq-e Bashar* [Human Rights and Islamic Penal Code] (Qom: Arghavan-e Danesh, 2008).

103 In Islamic legal theory, there is an increasing emphasis on the "spirit of the law" as opposed to "the letter of the law" so that Islamic law can function in the contemporary context. One of the legitimizing factors for this shift of emphasis is the concept of *maslaha*, which refers to the well-being of an individual or a community. This concept has allowed law makers to ignore some of the authoritative *ravayat* or even Quranic directives in the name of the welfare of the community. Even though *maslaha* has been used by both authoritarian and liberal Muslim jurists, this shift has provided the opportunity for reformers to highlight the importance of human reason. For a good overview of the use of *maslaha* in Islamic legal theory, see Felicitas Opwis, "Islamic Law and Legal Change: The Concept of *Maslaha* in Classical and Contemporary Islamic Legal Theory," in *Shari'a: Islamic Law in the Contemporary Context*, eds. Abbas Amanat and Frank Griffel (Stanford, CA: Stanford University Press, 2007), 62–81. For a reflection on how the shift to the "spirit of the law" provides opportunities for reformist Muslim jurists to push for the rights of citizens in facing the modern state (precisely what Montazeri did in his latest writings), see Roy Mottahedeh's "Afterword" in Amanat and Griffel, *Shari'a*, 178–82.

2 | The Birth of a Revolutionary

Though Montazeri had painted a grim picture of the Iranian state's harsh treatment of the clerics, neither he nor the majority of clerics engaged in acts of political opposition during his student years.[1] It was only in the 1960's that an influential segment of the clergy, which then included a middle-aged Montazeri, rose up and challenged the Pahlavi regime. In the course of his unrelenting political activities, Montazeri experienced banishment and exile, as well as incarceration and torture. The resolve and endurance that he demonstrated during these hard times leaves us with the question of why, after so many years in the seminary, he waited until his early forties to engage in national politics.

The National Political Context of the 1950's: The Role of the Clergy

From 1949 to 1953, under the leadership of Mohammad Mossadeq (1882–1967), Iran experienced four years of vibrant yet erratic political liberalization when multiple new groups and organizations – leftist, rightist, nationalist, communist, democratic, liberal, and conservative – entered the public sphere. The most important of these were the nationalist and mostly liberal National Front, which followed Mossadeq's lead, and the communist Tudeh Party, which took an ambivalent view of him. But this period came to an abrupt end in August 1953 with a British- and American-assisted coup d'etat that toppled the Mossadeq administration. Under the leadership of the Grand Ayatollah Sayyed Hossein Borujerdi, the *howzeh* instructors, including Khomeini and Montazeri, neither participated in nor supported the popular movement. In fact, the clerical establishment breathed a sigh of relief when Mossadeq fell and the Shah was reinstated on his throne. The attitude of the clerical establishment toward the nationalist movement was partially the result of its distaste for the communist and Soviet-reliant Tudeh Party, a well-organized force with an inconsistent approach to the nationalist movement. Sporadic as it was, the support of the Tudeh Party for Mossadeq provided the enemies of his administration with an opportunity to portray the communists as the real holders of power. The fear of a possible Tudeh Party takeover and the perceived indifference of the secular Mossadeq to religious concerns contributed to the distrust that the clergy felt toward the nationalist movement.

There were two major exceptions to the clergy's overall political passivity: one a force headed by Ayatollah Abolqasem Kashani (1882–1962), the other an organization founded by Navvab Safavi (1923–55), a Qom seminary student.[2] But neither convinced Montazeri or high-ranking clergy to defy Borujerdi and join forces with them. In the early days of the nationalist movement, Kashani lent his support to Mossadeq, and he and his followers became part of the National Front. But soon religious and personal differences between the two men put a strain on the alliance.[3] Eventually, the unhappy alliance ended in a total break up and Kashani mobilized opposition to the embattled prime minister from supporters in the urban lower and lower-middle classes and in some quarters of the Bazaar. His forces played a crucial role in overthrowing Mossadeq's administration.

The site of Kashani's political activities was Tehran rather than Qom, and his relationship with the director of the *howzeh* was restrained. Despite the tension between his principal mentor and Kashani, Montazeri liked Kashani and found in him a kindred spirit, a plain-speaking man with unpretentious manners. But in the end, when he had to choose between the quietist Borujerdi and the activist Kashani, he, along with most others in the Qom seminaries, remained loyal to the director of the *howzeh*.[4]

The other politically active force that challenged Borujerdi's authority was led by a young cleric named Mojtaba Navvab Safavi (1923–56), the founder of the *Fada'iyan-e Eslam* (the Devotees of Islam) organization.[5] The *Fada'iyan-e Eslam* consisted of a number of radical and mostly young Qom seminary students and some of Tehran's lower classes. The main goal of Navvab Safavi and his followers was to reverse what they saw as an increasing secularization of the state by any means, including assassination of their political and ideological opponents. Not surprisingly, Borujerdi had no patience for such radical methods, and his relationship with Navvab Safavi was even more tense than with Kashani. On his part, Navvab Safavi publicly questioned the quietist leadership of the *howzeh* and incited some of the younger religious students to do the same.[6] But his radical approach and his organization's attempt to destabilize the establishment of the *howzeh* isolated him and his followers from the majority of the clerical establishment. According to Montazeri, even Khomeini, who had sympathies for the ideals of the group, was dismayed by their tactics and their efforts to disturb the order of the *howzeh*.[7] At the end, neither Kashani nor Navvab Safavi proved to be a match for the quietist Borujerdi. During the turbulent years of the early 1950's the religious establishment remained politically aloof.

The Post-coup Period and State–Society Relations: Early 1950's to Early 1960's

After the coup, the Pahlavi regime quickly suppressed the Tudeh Party and neutralized the supporters of Mossadeq, and seemed to have consolidated its power. But the calm did not last long, as a series of socioeconomic and political problems challenged the stability of Pahlavi regime by the end of 1950's. Exacerbating the internal crisis was the pressure on the Shah from outside, primarily from the United States.[8]

Feeling the heat from both internal and external forces, the Shah tried to respond. He first fiddled with the idea of creating a two-party system from the top down in 1958, hoping to satisfy the US and silence political criticism at home. But the 1960 rigged parliamentary elections in favor of the two state-sponsored parties, which virtually excluded all other candidates, backfired and led to a popular protest. The state retreated and declared the elections void, but popular dissatisfaction with the government did not subside. The Shah then chose Ali Amini, a favorite of the United States, as his prime minister, and allowed him to form an administration with plans to initiate reforms, including an extensive land redistribution.

The internal crisis and the external pressure also provided an opportunity for hitherto suppressed political forces to resurface. After almost a decade of inactivity, the leaders of the National Front, this time without Mossadeq, who was under house arrest, revived the umbrella organization. The Bazaar, the Organization of University Students, and other professional associations were also activated. Iran seemed to be on the cusp of another major sociopolitical change, and all these groups looked to the secular and liberal National Front for leadership.[9] For the most part, the influential leaders within the National Front opted for legal and gradual opening of the system, a strategy that did not succeed in extracting concessions from the state and instead led to the disillusionment of many politically conscious Iranians.[10] The people in turn started to look in another direction for new strategy and leadership. It is with this background that the politicization of the *howzeh* and of Montazeri can be understood.

Khomeini's Leadership and Montazeri's Political Awakening

The death of the Grand Ayatollah Borujerdi in 1961 was a harbinger of change in the *howzeh*. His absence opened the door for those clergy who believed in an active role for religion in politics. Khomeini was the leader of this group, and Montazeri followed him. Until this point, Montazeri, loyal to Borujerdi, had held back from activities against the state. Accordingly, his minimal contact with state officials took place within the established rules. For instance, when Montazeri wanted to lobby against the confiscation of a religious building in Najafabad by the education ministry, he, as Borujerdi's representative, met with Prime Minister Manouchehr Eqbal (1957–60), who was on his official trip to Najafabad. His audience with Eqbal was successful and the confiscation was halted.[11] The only episode of confrontation between Montazeri and the state occurred in 1955, when he was summoned by the governor of Isfahan Province and questioned about anti-Baha'i activities.[12] Otherwise, there is no evidence of entanglement between Montazeri and the state.

Two reasons account for Montazeri's lack of political activism. One was his personal loyalty to Borujerdi, who was not only his source of emulation and his primary mentor but also his authority in political matters. Personal attachment, though, tells only part of the story. After all, Montazeri was temperamentally capable of standing his ground and speaking to power when he truly believed in a cause. The other reason was the attitude of the clerical community, a community with which Montazeri deeply identified. From the early 1940's to the early 1960's, the clerical establishment, which was predominantly concerned with the perceived power of the Baha'is, and later with that of the Tudeh Party, did not see the Pahlavi regime as the primary enemy. The lack of interest of the *howzeh* in state politics in the first few years of Mohammad Reza Shah's rule was welcomed by the Shah, and he in turn did not intrude in the affairs of the *howzeh* the way his father had done. In fact, the Shah and the religious establishment found allies in one another in opposing the Tudeh Party, and the Shah was willing, on occasion, to go along with the clergy's attempt to attack the Baha'i temples.[13]

The state's policies in the 1960's and the passing of Borujerdi set the stage for a different relationship between the Pahlavi regime and the *howzeh*. After Borujerdi, there was no consensus in the Shii establishment about who should become the Supreme or General Source of Emulation. In Najaf, two ayatollahs, Sayyed Mohsin Hakim and Abolqasem Khoei, were the most likely candidates, while the contenders in Iran included several others: Mohammad Kazem Shari'atmadari, Mohammad Reza Golpaygani, and Shahabeddin Mar'ashi Najafi. The fifty-nine-year-old Khomeini was not only junior to all the contenders, but he had yet to publish a practical treatise (*resale 'amaliyeh*), which was a precondition for becoming a *marja'*.[14] Still, he had a great appeal for many younger clergy and students, such as Montazeri, as a result of both his religious knowledge and his ideas for the reform of the seminary.[15] These young clergymen were also attracted to Khomeini's assertiveness, a quality that set him apart from Borujerdi in his approach to the state. It was these same supporters, most significantly Montazeri, who worked to get Khomeini's practical treatise published and therefore helped him to reach the status of a source of emulation.

In addition to Khomeini's personal influence, another major factor that contributed to clerical political activism was the state's intended policies, which were easily construed as provocations to the religious establishment. Mohammad Reza Shah's first confrontation with the clergy was indirect, however. In October 1962, the cabinet of the newly appointed and loyal prime minister, Asadollah Alam, presented a bill to the parliament regarding local council elections that contained articles bound to provoke the clergy. Two aspects were especially disconcerting: one was the extension of voting rights to women; the other was the provision that the elected candidates could take their oath of office on *any* holy book rather than exclusively on the Quran. Even though the clergy as a whole protested the bill, it was Khomeini who took the most assertive line in opposing it. After two months of agitation in Qom's *howzeh*, which spread to many parts of the country thanks to the mobilizational ability of Khomeini and his close followers, including Montazeri, the bill was repealed.[16] The success of this campaign substantially increased Khomeini's political influence, not only in the *howzeh*, but also among the conservative Bazaar merchants. They started to channel their *sahm-e emam* to him, thus smoothing his way to eventually becoming a serious candidate for the position of the Supreme Source of Emulation. Now the *howzeh* had a leader who was able to challenge an increasingly assertive Shah.

In March of the following year, the Shah himself introduced a more ambitious six-point plan, first referred to as the "White Revolution" and later as the "Shah's and People's Revolution." He intended to gain legitimacy for the plan, which included articles on women's right to vote and a land-reform provision, through a popular referendum. Even though the clergy found the plan distasteful, they disagreed among themselves as to how they should challenge it. Some focused their objection directly on the substance of the program, particularly the articles on land reform and women's suffrage, while others, including Khomeini, directed their opposition more toward procedure.

According to Montazeri, Khomeini believed that with the exception of voting rights for women, the articles of the proposed six points of the White Revolution, including land reform, eradication of illiteracy, and provision of medical care for poor villagers, were in harmony with Islamic justice, and therefore opposing them would not be the appropriate method for challenging the state.[17] He attacked instead the use of a referendum as a tactic to short-circuit the appropriate parliamentary process, calling it a *bed'at* (an arbitrary revision of established and authoritative readings of laws). Khomeini further argued that the use of an unlawful referendum could provide a precedent for carrying out sinister goals such as eradicating religion from public life and establishing monarchical absolutism.[18] He therefore boycotted the referendum and asked his followers to do the same.

Khomeini's clear and direct stand against the regime landed him first in jail and then in exile in Turkey and, eventually, Iraq. His first incarceration on June 3, 1963 sparked a nationwide protest that was brutally suppressed by the state across three days. Khomeini was kept in jail for two months, and then under house arrest in Tehran until April 1964. Once back in Qom, he gave one of his most fiery speeches condemning the parliament's approval of a capitulatory bill that gave US military advisers immunity from Iranian laws.[19] In the same speech, he called for action and criticized the quietist clergy. In less than ten days, Khomeini was arrested and sent into exile in Turkey.

After the bloody suppression of the uprising in 1963, the public space for debate and demonstrations became critically narrow due to the state's increasing power and its ability to control civil society. Economic growth, the result of the impressive increase of oil revenue, and the regime's increasing intolerance for even mild political resistance coopted many and forced others to withdraw from politics altogether. The few who did not withdraw reached the conclusion that guerilla warfare was the only effective way to challenge the regime. Mostly young activists, they formed several guerilla organizations, two of which became especially prominent: *Sazman Cherikha-ye Fada'i Khalq-e Iran* (Organization of Iranian People's Fadaii Guerrillas, or OIPFG), a Marxist-Leninist organization; and *Sazman Mojahedin-e Khalq-e Iran* (People's Mojahedin Organization of Iran), a religious organization with leftist programs. There were also other religious organizations with a militant outlook, such as *Jam'iyat Mo'talefeh*, which represented the *Bazaaris* and supported Khomeini. *Jam'iyat Mo'talefeh* came to the conclusion that working within the system with reformist intent was useless, and consequently added a military branch for the purpose of assassinating the state's "anti-Islamic" officials.[20]

A different strategy was taken in the *howzeh* by men such as Montazeri. Even though they believed that the time for reform was over and that nothing more could be expected from the Pahlavi regime, they were still not convinced that violence or guerilla tactics, at least by religious teachers, would be an effective means to bring about the desired change. In his memoirs, in answer to a question about whether he endorsed the method of armed struggle during the revolution, Montazeri responded that he did, but only in special circumstances. He also disapproved of what he considered rash actions by some of the guerrillas.[21] For Montazeri, cultural and educational work had to precede revolutionary moves. Once people's minds were awakened to the power of Islam, they would be ready to throw themselves, body and soul, into the revolutionary praxis.

In the early 1960's, there was not yet any hint that the activist clergy intended to topple the secular regime and turn Iran into a religious state. At that time, Khomeini, Montazeri, and most other clergymen called for preservation of the traditional social authority of the clergy, and spoke against the expansion of state control in areas that concerned them. However, as the Iranian state became increasingly powerful and oppressive, shrinking the space for negotiation, Montazeri and other supporters of Khomeini began to formulate, first privately and later publicly, a new language for dismantling the Pahlavi state.

Montazeri and Political Resistance

The imprisonment and exile of his mentor shook Montazeri profoundly. To him, the state's treatment of Khomeini was not only an attack on a beloved and admired teacher, but an attempt to undermine the sanctity of religious offices and sources of emulation, and he could no longer remain silent. From then on, Montazeri became a consummate political actor as well as a political broker. His first move after he heard about Khomeini's arrest and incarceration was to organize a sit-in at Najafabad's Bazaar Mosque, in which both local sources of emulation and merchants from the Bazaar participated. According to Montazeri, he ended the sit-in only after Ayatollah Shari'atmadari informed him of an ongoing delicate negotiation with the regime and a possible deal for releasing Khomeini. In the meantime, the fear that Khomeini might be executed mobilized the clergy to do what they could to prevent it. They hoped that a constitutional law intended to grant immunity from prosecution to the recognized sources of emulation would pertain to Khomeini. Thus, Khomeini needed to be acknowledged by the highest sources of emulation as one of them. Four major sources of emulation, including Shari'atmadari, made public proclamations in which they referred to Khomeini as a grand ayatollah, and those proclamations saved Khomeini from a possible death sentence.

As a junior clergyman, Montazeri did his part to mobilize the seminarians for the campaign to get Khomeini released. He traveled from Najafabad to Qom and then on to Tehran, gathering as many signatures for recognition of Khomeini as a source of emulation as he could. And this was not the only time that he contributed to Khomeini's rise in his religious position. Years later, it was again him who played an enthusiastic role in elevating Khomeini, this time to the position of the Supreme Source of Emulation.[22]

In 1965, Khomeini had been allowed to move from Turkey to Iraq, from where he sent a letter to Montazeri, appointing him as his own political deputy, with total authority in Iran. This is what Montazeri tells us in his memoirs, but he destroyed the newly received letter when Savak arrested him and no trace of it remains. Most of Montazeri's detractors now question the existence of such a letter.[23] Another letter by Khomeini does exist, however, that designates Montazeri as his representative in Iran with total authority over religious matters, especially in the collecting and spending of Khomeini's portion of *sahm-e emam*.[24] Despite the claim of Montazeri's later detractors, it is not implausible that Khomeini had indeed chosen Montazeri to lead an oppositional movement in his absence, a responsibility that Montazeri took seriously. Now a resistant leader on his own, Montazeri challenged the state through different means: he organized meetings of oppositional clergy, wrote statements, gathered signatures on petitions, gave sermons, and led Friday Prayers. He was one of the first clergy to use the mosque as a space for political discourse, and through his Friday Prayer sermons put both old and new demands/claims on the state.[25]

In Sura 62, the Quran commands believers to put business aside and attend communal prayers on Fridays. A practice that dates back to the time of the Prophet's migration from Mecca to Medina, the communal Friday Prayer requires at least five participants and a leader. Appropriate to the occasion, the sermons are supposed to revolve around matters of communal concerns, making the practice of value for social mobilization. Prior to the revolution, Friday Prayer leaders, particularly in the capital, served the state. But during the revolution, the politically active clergy who understood the potential of the communal prayer for creating a public space began to use the occasion instead to challenge the state. Montazeri was a pioneer among these clergy and led a series of Friday Prayers between 1972 and 1973 that contributed to his troubled relationship with the regime. His unadorned style of oration was popular, particularly in his native town, making Najafabad a troublesome locale.

In these sermons, Montazeri spoke of the responsibility of religious leaders to monitor the government's behavior, criticized the quietist clergy for dereliction of their duty, asserted that political activism was the task not just of the clergy but of every Muslim, and judged the failure to oppose injustice as reprehensible as committing it.[26] Through these contentions, he not only warned the state but put demands on both religious leaders and ordinary Muslims. He asked the state to follow the practical and ethical rules of Islam in all its policies, whether economic, social, political, or cultural. He also demanded of ordinary people and their religious leaders that they act in the service of the Islamic community, even if it required risking their private interests.

Even though he did not overtly ask for a revolutionary overthrow of the Pahlavi state, it was not difficult to read such a demand as the logical conclusion of his position.[27]

The *Shahid-e Javid* Controversy

Obviously, Montazeri's activities were not tolerated by the state. He was watched, arrested, interrogated, incarcerated, and banished several times by the secret police. The charges that the state leveled against him, either in public trials or in secret documents made available after the revolution, were: (1) attempts to incite people by giving sermons, writing proclamations, and organizing politicized Friday Prayers to challenge the state; (2) holding unwavering and "zealous" support for Khomeini both as the Supreme Source of Emulation and as the leader of the Islamic political movement; and (3) attempts to help families of political prisoners, thereby supporting the opposition.[28]

In addition to overt punishment, Savak spread rumors about Montazeri to damage his reputation among the revolutionary clergy.[29] Yet none of these tactics discouraged him, just as imprisonment and banishment did not stop his continuing opposition toward the state.[30] There was one particular occasion when Savak managed to exploit a growing public rift among the clergy in order to weaken the revolutionary potential of the activist clergy, including Montazeri. The publication of a highly controversial book titled *Shahid-e Javid* (The Eternal Martyr), written in 1970 by Ne'matollah Salehi Najafabadi (1923–2006), a seminarian, provided the opportunity. The controversy surrounding the book was in its depiction of Imam Hossein, the third Shii Imam, and his reason for waging his last battle in Karbala against the forces of Mo'avieh, the founder of the Ummayed dynasty.[31] Besides the Prophet Mohammad and Ali, the first Infallible Imam, Hossein is the most revered Shii saint. Each year during the tenth and eleventh days of Mohharam, the first month of the Islamic calendar, Shii sites witness the most intense outpouring of emotions by millions in commemoration of Hossein's martyrdom. The traditional Shii interpretation of the battle of Karbala, where Hossein, his followers, and many members of his family were killed, is that Imam Hossein had foreknowledge of the outcome and that his purpose in engaging in a losing battle was only to expose the injustice of Mo'avieh and not to establish a just Islamic state. According to the Shiis, Mo'avieh had usurped the position of successor to the Prophet Mohammad from his rightful heir, his grandson, and therefore he and his successors were illegitimate rulers.

Salehi Najafabadi argued in *Shahid-e Javid* that when Imam Hossein embarked on his journey to challenge the rule of Mo'avieh, he in fact did not *know* that he would be killed in Karbala. Salehi did not deny Hossein's foreknowledge of his martyrdom but contended that his knowledge was general rather specific. This meant, Salehi argued, that Imam Hossein had the following priorities when he waged his battle against the usurpers: first, to achieve a military victory over Mo'avieh's army; second, to reach a temporary truce if unable to prevail in the battle; and third, to achieve martyrdom only if neither victory nor truce were possible.[32]

This revisionist interpretation was a tremendous boost for a revolutionary religious discourse, positioning Imam Hossein as a role model for toppling the Pahlavi regime, and was therefore welcomed by the activist clergy. The political message of Najafabdadi's book was that Hossein's actions should be emulated by anyone who lives under a similar illegitimate and unjust ruler. Montazeri and Ali Meshkini, another religious teacher, wrote forewards to the book and praised it for its revolutionary message and for its scholarship.[33]

But not everyone was happy with these revisionist ideas. The standard interpretation considered the events in Karbala and Hossein's martyrdom to be a unique historical occurrence, which could not be reproduced by ordinary people and consequently could not be taken as a precedent for contemporary uprisings. The conservative clergy therefore vehemently opposed the new interpretation in their sermons, essays, and books, and condemned Salehi Najafabadi and his approach. One of the most extensive challenges appeared in *Shahid-e Agah* (The Aware Martyr), authored by Ayatollah Lotfollah Golpaygani. He criticized Salehi for denying Imam Hossein his foreknowledge, and thus for questioning a major principle of Shii faith and the basis of Shii identity.[34] He also contended that such an interpretation would help colonialists and their local agents take advantage of the confusion among Muslims. He feared the consequences would include the straying away of Muslim youth from religion and the weakening of Islamic societies; he also forbade (declared it as *haram*) his followers to read the book.

Golpaygani was right in at least one sense: Savak did its best to increase dissension among the clergy drawing away some religious students from political activism by keeping the controversy alive. Savak hoped to exploit a dilemma inherent in Salehi's book. If one were to deny Hossein's foreknowledge of his martyrdom and therefore regard him as a man with a temporal political goal, would that result in a heretical questioning of his sacred nature?[35] Indeed, some began to doubt their revolutionary activities, fearing that by modeling Imam Hossein as a warrior with temporal goals, they would do harm to religion, and therefore withdrew from political opposition to the state.[36]

A separate matter that added still more fuel to this controversy was the disagreement among clergy about who should replace Ayatollah Hakim (d. 1970) as the Supreme Source of Emulation. The choice for some, particularly for the traditional *howzeh* clergy, was the politically quietist Ayatollah Abolqasm Khoei (1899–1992). The politically active clergy, and particularly Montazeri, on the other hand, were strongly committed to the revolutionary Ayatollah Khomeini as the candidate for the position. Each group used Salehi's book to strengthen the position of their favorite candidate. The most critical period of controversy occurred when Ayatollah Abolhassan Shamsabadi, Ayatollah Khoei's representative in Isfahan and a fierce critic of Salehi for writing *Shahid-e Javid*, and of Montazeri for endorsing it, was assassinated in 1976 by a group of young men closely associated with Mehdi Hashemi, the younger brother of one of Montazeri's sons-in-law.[37] In the early 1970's, Mehdi Hashemi founded a group called "Amr-e be Ma'rouf and Nayi az Monkar," which came to be known as *Hadafiha*. The goal of the group was to purify the society by violent means, including the assassination of "sinners" such as owners of houses of prostitution. The group also had a dim view of conservative clergy, with their focus on rituals of mourning, and thus saw them as a greater enemy than the Pahlavi regime.[38] The assassination of Shamsabadi infuriated the traditional clergy and the followers of the murdered ayatollah. Some of them accused Montazeri, who was in prison at the time, of knowing about the murder plot. The Savak fueled this suspicion further.[39] But, though Montazeri had no love for Shamsabadi and his conservative colleagues, there was no evidence that he had any prior knowledge of the assassination plot.[40]

Despite some initial and tactical gain by Savak, particularly over the death of Ayatollah Shamsabadi, the secret police failed in ensuring any long-term gain from the controversy over *Shadid Javid*. Soon the number of people joining the ranks of political activists began to rise, and

Savak turned to harsher means to rein in the opposition. Montazeri experienced his own share of the heavy hand of the secret police and was sent to prison and exile several times. His first trial and incarceration were in connection to his membership of an ill-fated organization.

Montazeri and Organizational Attempts

Montazeri was one of the founders of two organizations in the 1960's. The first, *Jame'eh-ye Modarasin-e Howzeh-ye Elmieh-ye Qom* (Society of Qom Seminary Scholars or SQSS), was formed by a few junior and like-minded seminary instructors in 1961. According to Montazeri, the original idea of the founders of SQSS was to provide opportunities to discuss *howzeh* matters as a group and to have a systematic channel of communication with the high clergy. The goals consisted of six educational, cultural, and political objectives, among them reforming the seminary's curriculum, providing more opportunities for research in Islamic fields, and combating "oppressors by defending the rights of the oppressed."[41] Except for this last point, there seemed to be nothing in the six-point program that suggested any hint of oppositional activities. But during the events surrounding the controversial bill on local council elections in 1962, the SQSS became a valuable tool for the combative clergy to use to spread their messages around the country and to mobilize support for political action. The members of the SQSS, particularly Montazeri, threw themselves into their new but unofficial charge to oppose the bill. The clerics' success in defeating the local council bill boosted their confidence and prepared them for an even more aggressive campaign against the upcoming referendum on the White Revolution. Montazeri was one of the members of SQSS who traveled from Qom to Isfahan and Najafabad in an attempt to garner support for the boycott of the referendum.

The SQSS, however, was a public organization, and its activities were visible. As the relationship between the state and the seminary became more tense and confrontational, Montazeri and others realized that if they wished to continue, they had to come up with another type of organization, a secret one. In the fall of 1963, Montazeri and ten other *howzeh* instructors (including many future leaders of the Islamic Republic, such as Ali Khamenei, Ali-Akbar Hashemi Rafsanjani, and Mohammad Taqi Mesbah Yazdi) established a clandestine group, "the Assembly of Eleven," for the purpose of organizing and drafting a program of action.[42] Excited by the prospect of serious and secret activities, these relatively young men got to work: they met, discussed strategies, and wrote a constitution. But fate was not on their side.

In 1966, security forces raided the bookstore of Ahmad Azari Qomi, one of the founders of the Assembly of Eleven, and came across a handwritten copy of the organization's constitution. Among the articles of the constitution were provisions for creating secret cells, aliases for the members to protect their identities, and the means to challenge the legal system of the state in case any of its members got arrested. The discovery of the constitution led to one of the several times that Montazeri was arrested and put in jail. It also ended Montazeri's attempt at building oppositional organizations. For the rest of his period as a revolutionary activist, Montazeri challenged the state without having organizational support.

Montazeri in Prison

In addition to a short detention in 1963, Montazeri was arrested and imprisoned four times. The first of his incarcerations, and probably the most difficult psychologically, happened on March 21, 1966, the day Iranians celebrate the beginning of a new Persian year. On the same day, and before Montazeri's arrest, his son Mohammad was taken to jail. Mohammad had become politicized in the early 1960's, as had many young and religiously oriented Iranians. But he was a distinct activist: he was strict, puritanical, single-minded, and relentless in his pursuit of mobilizing the *howzeh* against the Pahlavi regime. Montazeri recalled his son's fierce and determined efforts in gathering signatures for various petitions as Mohammad compelled or sometimes intimidated even the most reluctant clergy into signing.[43] It was on one such occasion that Mohammad got arrested in Qom in 1966. The secret police then went to Montazeri's house, questioned him about his son's activities, and took him, too, as a prisoner, later charging and trying him for his membership in the "Assembly of Eleven."

Father and son were soon transferred to Qezel Qal'eh prison, a fortress-like building in Tehran. Qezel Qal'eh, originally built as a weapons depot, was turned into a prison by Taymour Bakhtiar, the first head of the Savak, in order to detain the opponents of the Pahlavi regime following the 1953 coup. Like many other prisons, Qezel Qal'eh consisted of different wards and cells for solitary and common confinement. Montazeri and his son were put in separate cells, and even though Montazeri was not treated lightly, the harshness of his experience paled in comparison to what his son went through. Mohammad was severely tortured day after day, and though Montazeri did not personally witness the most brutal treatment, he heard about all of it. On one occasion, through a door left ajar, he had a glimpse of his son's torment. Mohammad himself, in a letter of defense addressed to the military tribunal in charge of his trial, detailed the torture he endured for sixteen consecutive days. He was repeatedly beaten and slapped on his eardrum, he was deprived of sleep, and he received frequent lashes with a plastic-covered metal cable, among other things. One of the most vivid and horrifying methods of torture involved placing his naked buttocks against a hot metal heater, which caused multiple burns and blisters.[44] In his memoirs, Montazeri remembered his son's reaction to his treatment at the hands of his torturers when they made him sit on the hot furnace: "[my son] shouted the name of the 'Imam of Time' while his tormentor cursed the 'Imam of Time.' Mohammad told me that he then recited a verse of the Quran which made him feel less pain."[45] Eventually, Mohammad was put on trial and sentenced to three years in jail.

Charged for his involvement in the activities of the "Assembly of Eleven," Montazeri himself underwent a trial and was sentenced to an eighteen-month prison term. Rumors of torture inflicted on him and his prison-mate and political colleague, Abdol-Rahim Rabbani Shirazi, mobilized the *howzeh* to come to their rescue. The seminarians wrote letters, made public proclamations, and held private meetings with officials of the state. Even Grand Ayatollah Hakim in Najaf became involved: in a meeting with the Iranian ambassador to Iraq, he expressed his dismay and urged a speedy release of the two men.[46] From within the prison, Montazeri and Rabbani also wrote open letters about their own harsh treatment and that of Montazeri's son, addressed to the military prosecutors and copied not only to high clergy but also to the United Nations Commission on Human Rights. All these activities eventually led to the early release of Montazeri and his friend; Montazeri's son however, stayed in jail and suffered further brutality. The treatment of Mohammad had an indelible impact on Montazeri; it shaped his views on the treatment of political prisoners and on the practice of incarcerating people for political reasons.[47]

This prison experience was followed by three more. In 1967, following a secret trip to Najaf to consult with Khomeini about the future of the religious resistance movement, Montazeri was arrested at the border as he was trying to sneak back into Iran. He was sent to Qezel Qal'eh prison, this time for five months. Soon after his release, he was once again arrested and put on trial in a military court for "antistate activities." Charged with inciting disorder and conspiracy against the Pahlavi regime, Montazeri was initially sentenced to a three-year term, which was subsequently reduced to a year and a half. He was sent to Qasr, another prison, this one built during the Reza Shah's reign.[48]

Montazeri's fourth and longest experience with jail was in July 1975, when he was arrested apparently as a result of confessions made by Ahmad Mohadess, a junior clergyman. According to Montazeri, Mohadess, probably under duress, had told the authorities that Montazeri wanted to introduce him to armed guerrilla groups. At that time, Montazeri was in internal exile in Saqez, a small town in the Kurdish and Sunni areas of Iran. The Savak agents stormed into his residence in the middle of the night and took him to Tehran. Despite the official charge, this arrest was probably more a result of a protest by religious students in Qom commemorating the 1963 rebellion. Savak used the occasion to round up many activist clergymen, including Montazeri, from around the country. He was sentenced to ten years, taken to the Evin prison, and kept in solitary confinement for about six months before being transferred to the common ward. Unlike the others, which were all located in the southern part of Tehran, this new prison was situated in the north of the city, not far from some of the most manicured spaces of the capital. It was a heavily secured prison with separate wards for solitary and common confinement. Throughout the 1970's, the Evin prison was under the control of Savak and was crowded with political dissidents.

If the incarceration and torture of his son made Montazeri's first imprisonment the most wrenching psychologically, the abuse during his last prison term, especially in its first six months, was the most difficult to endure physically. During the interrogation sessions he was beaten on the soles of his feet with a metal lash and slapped on the face, once so hard that his ear became infected and his hearing was permanently impaired.[49] He also developed a palsy-like condition that remained with him throughout the rest of his life. Apart from being maltreated, Montazeri was required to do various chores, as were all prisoners. Inmates took turns cooking and cleaning dishes, washing floors, cleaning bathrooms, and washing clothes.[50] In a sense, Montazeri and prisoners like him had to perform functions that outside the prison were done ordinarily by their wives, daughters, or maids. It was a strange and difficult time for political prisoners, but for Montazeri life in captivity was a mixed experience.

Life in Prison

What Montazeri recounted of his experiences with his interrogators and fellow inmates was not a picture of an unmitigated horror, as one usually encounters in prison memoirs, such as the one by Ashraf Dehqani, a female member of the communist guerrilla group *Cherikha-ye Fada'i-ye Khalq-e Iran*.[51] A prisoner in the Pahalvi era, Dehqani told stories of relentless torture, humiliation, and occasional rape. While Montazeri did recount the cruelty that his captors inflicted on him and other prisoners, he also remembered some of the people who incarcerated him, including Savak agents, as having some traces of humanity. For example, he spoke of one of his prison wardens as a relatively mellow man who agreed to transfer him from his assigned ward to the one he requested so that he could be close to his son.[52] He also humanized some of his oppressors as he told of a funny, rather ironic episode related to one of his arrests:

They [Savak agents] arrested me and Mr. Rabbani – in those days whenever something happened they would come for the two of us – Anyhow, that time in the middle of the night they arrested us and took us to Qezel Qal'eh. Actually they first took us to the Evin prison. But at that time Evin was not yet well equipped so its administrators told the agents to transfer us to Qezel Qal'eh. Somewhere half way to our destination and in the middle of the night an interesting thing happened. The Savak agents who were driving us spotted a screaming girl being pulled by some men in the street. The agents stopped the car and got out to find out what all the commotion was about. They soon discovered that on her way to her grandmother's house the girl had been grabbed by these thugs. So, the agents saved the girl, put her into a taxi, and sent her home while forcing the thugs to give them their names and addresses so that they would be arrested later and put on trial. These Savakis were very happy that they had rescued a victim from a potentially devastating fate and were saying that it was God's will that they should pass through the town and save the girl.[53]

With some of his fellow prisoners, particularly from the rank of clerics, Montazeri developed a sustaining camaraderie. A number of clerics with whom he shared prison experiences became prominent figures in the Islamic Republic: Mahmud Taleqani (1911–79), Mohammad Reza Mahdavi Kani (1931–2014), Ali Akbar Hashemi Rafsanjani (1934–2017), and Mohammad Baqer Mohiyeddin Anvari (1926–2012). All of these clerics were active in the opposition, and all were arrested for reasons similar to the ones that jailed Montazeri. After a period in solitary confinement, Montazeri was put in the same ward with his clerical peers. They had all been tortured or abused – some were limping, some couldn't sit, and some had visible signs of maltreatment – but the opportunity to be together eased their pain. In fact, Montazeri recalled some very joyous times with his prison-mates. In reminiscing about those occasions, he said, "We were very happy when we saw each other, we felt as though we were set free. I can't tell you how much fun we had that [first] evening. We all shared stories; Mr. Anvari was especially funny, he made us laugh so hard that our stomachs hurt."[54]

There were other occasions that Montazeri remembered fondly: "One time we decided that we should each choose a poem and recite it as if we were singers. We had made singing mandatory for everyone and expected to have some fun. Mr. Taleqani sang very badly, I, too was very mediocre, but it was Mr. Hashemi who would win the award for the worst singer."[55]

No doubt having like-minded friends in prison helped all these men cope with the hardships. Montazeri's ability to make light of his difficulties is not just manifested in his own memoirs but also attested to by other people. For example, Ali Motahhari, the son of Morteza Motahhari, Montazeri's closest friend in the *howzeh*, recalled that "whenever Ayatollah Montazeri was released from prison he came directly to our house, cheerful and smiling and without any mention of his hardship in prison. He then usually greeted us, the children, in English and asked us how much English we had learned."[56]

But lighthearted moments were not all that these prisoners experienced together. As soon as there were several clergy together, Montazeri and Taleqani turned their ward into a classroom and organized two different high-level religious lessons. Montazeri was also adamant in his decision to lead Friday Prayers for the purpose of addressing political issues. Worried about the risks associated with communal political expression in jail, some advised him against it. But Montazeri, who, according to Rafsanjani, stubbornly insisted, got his way in setting up these prayer sessions. As predicted by his friends, the warden soon put a stop to the practice.[57]

Contrary to what one might expect, Montazeri, a man of limited exposure to the world, found his prison experience mentally invigorating, because so many of the prisoners belonged to the intellectual class. By his own admission, the students of the *howzeh* had little access to sources of knowledge beyond traditional religious writings. Montazeri himself was a product of that limiting educational system, but once imprisoned he found himself in conversation with men who opened his mind to new intellectual perspectives. During his time in Qezel Qal'eh, he met and conversed with political prisoners of different ideological persuasions, such as the secular nationalist Dariush Foruhar (1928–98), the communist Ali Khavari (1928–), and the religious layman and National Front activist Habibollah Payman (1935–).

In jail, he also read books that were not available to him at the *howzeh* and started to learn English from Payman, his fellow prisoner. Despite all these encounters, one should not conclude that prison profoundly changed Montazeri's intellectual outlook. His discussions with people from outside the *howzeh* circles were too brief and sporadic to have any profound impact; he remained loyal to his traditional training in some fundamental ways. Still, these encounters, particularly with the younger leftists, caused Montazeri to start thinking of a language that would engage the younger generation in a dialogue on religion and would hopefully convince them of its "truth." *Az Aqaz ta Anjam: Monazereh Do Daneshjoo* (From Beginning to End: Debate between Two University Students), which tells of a conversation between two university students, one a believer and the other an atheist, was a book that Montazeri conceived in prison. Written in a clear manner, it tells a story that ends with the atheist acknowledging the truth of God. His hope was that such a book would engage leftist youths.

Prison brought Montazeri in contact with the members of guerrilla groups. Some of these encounters were tense and unpleasant, for reasons that were both theological and personal. In his last period of incarceration in Evin, Montazeri met members of the *Mojahedin-e Khalq* and learned about the Marxist *Cherikha-ye Fada'i Khalq*. The *Mojahedin-e Khalq* was one of two main Iranian groups formed after the defeat of the reformist forces in the early 1960's. Three of its six original founders were former members of the Liberation Movement, an organization affiliated with the reformist National Front, but with distinct religious tendencies. These three men came to the conclusion that the methods of reformist organizations had run their course and that armed struggle was the only reliable way to confront an oppressive regime.[58] The proliferation of groups committed to armed struggle in Latin America, Palestine, and Algeria had influenced young Iranians, particularly university students, to form these guerrilla organizations.[59] But the emphasis on guerrilla warfare was alien and distasteful to the reformists, and the relationship between them and the guerrilla organizations was an uneasy one. For Montazeri and his fellow clerics, it was not the dispute over methods of struggle but that over ideology that caused the most tension with the *Mojahedin-e Khalq*. Even though *Mojahedin-e Khalq* shared with the politically active clergy a belief in Islam and a dedication to opposing the Pahlavi regime, they parted ways on some major issues.

Mojahedin-e Khalq was an anticlerical organization, even though its attitude toward the clergy was not clearly hostile until the early 1980's.[60] Like followers of Christian Liberation Theology in Latin America, the members of *Mojahedin-e Khalq* were partial to a Marxist approach in analyzing socioeconomic factors, especially the problems of poverty and discrimination. But as religious believers, they needed to reconcile their faith with this materialist approach to the problems of their society. That they did by calling for a *"jam'eh-ye bi tabaqeh-e tohidi"* (monotheistic classless society) through a new interpretation of the sacred texts. The interpretation that they were seeking would be scientific, contemporary, revolutionary, and able to mobilize support to overthrow the forces of oppression.[61]

By calling for a new hermeneutic, these young men challenged what they considered the outdated educational system of the *howzeh* and its related hierarchy. In their demand for change, they went far beyond the reforms suggested by seminarians such as Motahhari and Montazeri. Theirs were not suggestions for reform but demands for a revolution of the Islamic education.

The radical approach of the *Mojahedin-e Khalq* made both the conservative and reformist clergy uneasy. The seminarians were also concerned about the organization's turn to Marxism, fearing that, even if it were only used to analyze temporal socioeconomic issues, it would endanger faith in Islam, particularly among young people. Their fear

was not without foundation. In 1975, a group within the organization rejected religion and declared themselves Marxist-Leninists, creating a schism that split the organization into two separate bodies.[62]
The new formation followed Marx in his opinion that religion served
as an opiate for the masses and not as a useful tool in the struggle for liberation.[63] Even though many members of the *Mojahedin-e
Khalq* remained loyal to their religious beliefs, in the eyes of men like
Montazeri this schism made even these members suspect because of the
lingering tension in their ideology between faith in God and attraction
to Marxism.

The split within the organization took place when Montazeri was
imprisoned in Evin. One learns from Montazeri's memoirs that during this time he had no contact with the Marxist wing but had irri-
tating encounters with members who were still faithful to Islam. He
found them arrogant, condescending, disrespectful of the authority of
the sources of emulations, and susceptible to falling astray of Islam.
He particularly took offense at their "cavalier attitude" toward rituals of purification, which were so important to clerics in general and
Montazeri in particular.[64]

According to traditional Muslims, individuals who do not believe in
God are impure not only in their thoughts but also in their bodies, due
to their different cleaning practices.[65] Therefore, there were and are
strict rules to avoid contamination caused by sharing the same uten-
sils, cleaning oneself in the same water, and buying food made by the
"infidels," among other things.[66] In prison, Montazeri and his peers
complained about the lax attitude (or the indifference) of the members
of *Mojahedin-e Khalq* in observing rules of purity as they continued to
socialize with the Marxists. Apparently to annoy Montazeri and other
clerics, some of these members made deliberate public display of the
violation of the purification codes, and even on occasion sabotaged
the efforts of the clergy to keep their tools and food separate. Unable
to persuade them to stay away from the Marxists, in late spring of
1976, from within the walls of the prison Montazeri and other clergy,
including Taleqani, Mahdavi Kani, and Rafsanjani, reached a "public
decision," or according to some made an oral religious decree, asking
the *Mojahedin-e Khalq* to separate themselves from the Marxists, not
only ideologically but physically.[67] Predictably, these young men did
not receive the directive kindly, and their relationship with the clergy
deteriorated.

Despite his irritation, Montazeri's attitude toward the *Mojahedin-e Khalq* was tolerant and civil. In his memoirs, Ahmad Ahmad, one of the former members of the organization who was in the same ward as Montazeri in the Evin prison, recalls him with these words:

Mr. Montazeri had a down to earth and honest character and that was why sometimes people wanted to talk to him to feel good. He spoke with them with his sweet Najafabadi accent. He was very hard on himself but was very tolerant toward others. He would always respond to questions even to the irrelevant ones with patience and good humor ... Even though he was physically tired and weak he would never allow others to take care of his chores ... he was obsessed with cleanliness. He would wash his own cloths and spread then on a rope in the prison cell. Once I asked him about why he rewashed his wet cloths when they brushed against the wall? He gave me a very good response. He said "do you want to know what Islam has to say about this or what Montazeri's reasoning is?" I told him that I wished to know the answer to both. He then said: "Islam does not require you to do this, [what I do] then is my own problem. So don't use me as a model."[68]

Montazeri's portrayal of the members of the *Mojahedin-e Khalq* was neither flattering nor hostile. He criticized them for their weaknesses but acknowledged the role they played in the revolutionary process. He also protected the families of imprisoned *Mojahedin-e Khalq* by distributing funds among them – this was one of the Savak charges against him. Moreover, it was Montazeri who in the early 1970's pleaded with the exiled Khomeini to lend his voice in preventing the planned executions of many members of the *Mojahedin-e Khalq* by the Pahlavi regime.[69]

Prison taught Montazeri many things, about his peers, other prisoners, and wardens, and about himself. He reflected on his years in prison this way:

In my view, during the Shah's period, prison was similar to a classroom. Anyone who wished to become skilled and more mature should go to prison where one has the opportunity to see and to converse with many people, an opportunity which for many does not exist outside the prison walls. In jail one can exchange ideas, can argue, and has the opportunity to encounter people with different temperaments. Also, in prison one can know one's essence. There are some people who after a couple of threats or lashes would confess to everything, and, then there are those who [due to these threats or abuses] develop resistance like fortified steel. Prison takes fear away from a human being.[70]

Years of Exile

In addition to imprisonment, the state sentenced Montazeri to several internal exiles in order to further curb his political activities. His first exile followed his release from his second prison term. Considered a security threat in the politically volatile city of Qom during the upcoming coronation of Mohammad Reza Shah in 1967, Montazeri, with no credible charge brought against him, was sentenced to three months of banishment to Masjid Soleyman, a semi-arid town in Khuzestan province. Masjid Soleyman, the first oil-producing town in Iran, had two parts. One consisted of residences belonging to the people associated with the oil industry. This segment of the city was architecturally modern, with buildings equipped with up-to-date amenities. The other part of the city was older, traditional, and basically neglected. When Montazeri arrived in Masjid Soleyman, it had already lost its prominence and its prosperous section was on a path of decline. But he was respectfully received by the governor of the town, and was taken to the house of a prominent member of the clergy, who was the religious figure for the oil industry employees and who resided in the oil-related section of the town. Montazeri's comments on his first exile were very much in keeping with his recollections of his jail times: he gave a fair share to both good and bad, in regard to both people he encountered and things that happened to him. An amusing exchange with two military policemen, who were escorting him on the train from Qom to Masjid Soleyman, sheds light on how some of these young men, themselves of peasant origins, were socialized in the military, as well as on Montazeri's propensity to speak his mind:

During the trip the military policemen treated me very harshly. I tried to convince them to let me out of the train during the prayer time, but I did not succeed. So I had to perform my ablution in the train's bathroom. Even there they did not leave me alone and stood guard with their guns by the bathroom door. During the trip we sometimes quarreled. One of them once said: "Sir, you use the soil and water of this country so why don't you pray for the Imperial Majesty?" I replied: "Are the soil and water of this country the property of the Imperial Majesty?" and he said: "Yes, they are." And then I said: "Well if you tell me that security [the stability of his regime] is his business, that I can comprehend, but owning its water and soil?!"[71]

After his release from his first exile, Montazeri ignored the ban on his travel to Qom and went to the city, only to be escorted out by security forces and sent to his hometown of Najafabad, where he arrived in January 1968. During his stay in Najafabad, Montazeri made a secret trip to Karbala and Najaf to see Khomeini. That trip cost him another jail period. Soon after his release from his third incarceration, he was sent to Najafabad at the end of spring 1970 and forbidden to leave. This banishment was due to his having signed a letter of protest against the American investment in Iran, and also to his effort to secure Khomeini the position of the Supreme Source of Emulation after the death of Ayatollah Hakim.

During his exile, or forced residence, in Najafabad, Montazeri led an active life – he taught, wrote, and gave sermons. And it was during this period that he gave the previously mentioned famous set of Friday Prayers and that the controversy over the book *Shahid-e Javid* reached its peak. Historically, the quietist strand in Shii Islam has been nourished by the story of the occultation of Mahdi and his eventual second coming. Shiis believe that Mahdi, the Twelfth Imam and the last male descendent of the Prophet Mohammad through the line of his daughter Fatima and his son-in-law and cousin Ali, had gone into occultation at a young age but would return to deliver the world from injustice at some point in the future. For many, the implication of this story is that no one can construct a just government prior to the second coming of the Mahdi, and therefore one should endure life under the control of unjust rulers. Like most committed revolutionaries, Montazeri was trying to deconstruct this narrative and shift the emphasis from the story of Mahdi to the story of the martyrdom of Imam Hossein in Karbala and his brave war against an unjust power, all for the sake of bringing a just order. Montazeri's goal was to use the battle of Karbala and its potent emotional impact as a mobilizing tool for revolutionary action during his Friday sermons.

Montazeri was removed from Najafabad to yet another location in 1973. The excuse for this exile was his alleged involvement with the activities of a religious group, called Abuzar, centered in the city of Nahavand in the province of Hamadan. The Abuzar group consisted mostly of young religious laymen who had decided that the best way to fight the regime was through guerrilla activities. They were soon discovered by the Savak; many of them were arrested, and the group itself was disbanded by the end of 1972. Their connection with Qom's *howzeh* was through not Montazeri but Ayatollah Rabbani Shirazi, Montazeri's close political associate. So, in his letter of protest against his exile sentence, Montazeri implied that the real reason for his sentence lay elsewhere. He defended himself by declaring that all his activities were legal under the provisions of the Iranian constitution.

Predictably, he did not succeed in having his sentence overturned – a fate he shared with two dozen other clergymen who were rounded up at the same time and sentenced to exile in different parts of the country. He was sent to Tabas, a desert town in the eastern province of Khorasan. The arid and hot town was chosen to keep Montazeri away from the center of activities, but the authorities failed to isolate him entirely. According to official documents, during his stay in Tabas he was visited by many who traveled from faraway places to see him. He also remained abreast of events in the *howzeh*, particularly the still-raging controversy over Salehi Najafabdai's book, as well as the hostility of a group of seminarians called *velayati* against Ali Shari'ati. A religious but lay Sorbonne-educated political activist, Shari'ati's oratory and writing skills had captured the imagination of thousands of religious university students. His criticism of the traditional approach to Shii doctrines led some – mostly a group called *velayati* – to accuse him of spreading Wahhabism. Here, Savak found another opportunity, similar to the one provided by the controversy over the *Shahid-e Javid*, to exploit a religious rift. Savak imprisoned Shari'ati in September 1973, then published the transcript of parts of his interrogation in which he spoke of his anticlerical activities.[72] Many clergy rejoiced at the imprisonment of the famous orator, but Montazeri was not among them. Four days after Shari'ati's detention, Montazeri wrote a letter addressed to the high clergy in Qom attacking the *velayati* group for spreading lies and baseless accusations, which he asserted would only benefit their mutual enemies.[73] At the end, he called upon the high clergy to interfere and provide opportunities for scientific debate when confronted with a controversial thesis, lest feuds and factionalism destroy the religious community. The letter was disseminated by one of Montazeri's students: Ali Khamenei, the future Supreme Leader of the Islamic Republic.[74]

As a matter of practice, authorities did not keep exiled individuals in any one area for long, fearing that they might forge ties with the locals. In the case of Montazeri, they were frustrated with his quickly rising popularity among the townspeople, particularly the downtrodden, who were attracted to his message of justice, and therefore decided to move him at the end of summer 1974 from Tabas to yet another peripheral town: Khalkhal.[75]

The topography and climate of Khalkhal, a mountainous and cold area in Eastern Azarbaijan province, could not have been more different than the flat, dry, desert climate of Tabas, but the two were equally forbidding. This time, the state authorities had better success in confining Montazeri. Azarbaijan was the province where the politically cautious and non-confrontational Ayatollah Kazem Shari'atmadari enjoyed strong support among the local clergy, who might otherwise have been Montazeri's conduit to the ordinary people. Moreover, Montazeri's unfamiliarity with Azari, the language of the province, further limited his effort to communicate. He tried in vain to mobilize the population, but the odds were against him.

After only five months in Khalkhal, upon the urging of the local authorities, who did not wish to be bothered by his presence, Montazeri was moved once more, this time to Saqez, a Kurdish town with a Sunni majority population. Saqez was probably chosen because the officers at the headquarters of Savak believed that the Shii cleric would not be able to get along with the Sunni population and would therefore be ineffective. Still, the local Savak feared his influence on the people and requested that headquarters restrict the number of his visitors from outside the province.[76] Life was tough for Montazeri during this last period of exile. He was tired of the inconstancies of his life; he had no roots and no place to cling to. The cold weather, the lack of clean water, and his general isolation from most of his family and from the center of political activities made Montazeri's experience a challenging one. He remembered his time in Saqez with very little of his characteristic cheerfulness. Nonetheless, he at times did engage the Sunni clergy, sometimes arguing about their different interpretations of Islam's history.

Montazeri's exiles took him to remote and unfamiliar areas of the country. During these trying times, he did what he could to mobilize the locals, but his success was modest at best. He was moved from one place to another before he could forge lasting relations, and he was sent to places where he either did not speak the local language or did not share the local religious views. Unlike in his periods in prison, and despite the fact that he was not physically abused, he often felt lonely and depressed.

His last period of exile ended in 1975, when the Savak rounded up a score of clergy from around the country and sent them to jail on the occasion of the commemoration of the June 1963 uprising and its bloody suppression.[77] These commemorations went beyond the walls of the seminary and took on the character of public protest. The reasons for the intensity of this year's events in comparison to previous ones lie in a series of state decisions, including the changing of the calendar from Islamic to pre-Islamic, the creation of a one-party system, and the more rigorous observance of a 1967 Family Protection Act, which the clergy saw as an affront to their own Islamic family laws. From Najaf, Khomeini wrote a number of proclamations against the regime's policies, particularly the one-party system and the demand for universal party membership.[78] Frightened by the intensity of the protest against these policies, the Savak was moved to act.

The Revolutionary Period: 1977–79

Montazeri was freed in November 1978, three years into his ten-year sentence. He was not the only one: Taleqani was also freed, while many of their other prison companions had been already sent home. Once out, Montazeri found himself in the midst of a political environment embroiled in a major revolution. The years between 1963 and 1975 had been a good period for the Pahlavi regime. The security apparatus of the state had been successful in crushing the major guerrilla organizations. Thanks to a huge increase in the price of oil, Iran had experienced a few years of very rapid economic growth. Oppositional actions were sporadic, and mass mobilization still lay in the future. Mohammad Reza Shah was feeling confident about his control of the home front and his ability to project his influence outside Iran's borders. By the mid1970's, Iran had one of the largest armies in the region and was considered the keeper of regional stability by the Nixon administration.

But by 1975, there were signs of potentially critical problems confronting the state.[79] Corruption and nepotism had profoundly infected the state, and rapid growth and ambitious planning had created economic bottlenecks and uneven development. In addition, a global recession and the subsequent fall of oil prices had put a damper on the economy. In the United States, Jimmy Carter, the Democratic Party nominee, who had made the promotion of human rights an important part of his foreign policy platform, was elected president in 1976. The Shah, a supporter of the candidacy of the incumbent Republican Gerald Ford, was worried how Carter's declared policies might affect the Pahlavi regime, with its abysmal record on human rights. Despite his veneer of strength, the Shah never felt completely secure in his power, particularly in his relationship with the United States. The memory of his return to Iran after the coup of 1953 and the role of the United States in that period led to his exaggerated view of the influence of foreign powers on Iranian politics. He was also sick with cancer and wished a smooth transition of power to his son once he was gone. The combination of these factors led him to decide on a liberalization policy after years of holding a harsh grip over the political landscape.

The first phase of a two-year revolutionary period began in May 1977. It continued well into the fall, with a series of open letters written primarily by secular intellectuals, most of whom were adherents of Mossadeq's liberal vision for Iran. Their reformist demands included a return to the constitution, elimination of all repressive and arbitrary tools and institutions, and protection of freedom of expression.[80] The letter-writing campaign led to the revival of reform-oriented old political organizations and the creation of some new ones. For most of this reformist phase, the political activities were confined to indoor sites, but toward its end it spilled out into the street and gave start to a second phase. The state was not ready for street demonstrations and suppressed them by the use of force. Yet the decision not to torture those arrested or to send them to military courts emboldened the protest movement.

During the first phase of the protests until January 1978, most of the leaders of the opposition were secular intellectuals, and their demands on the state did not exceed what might be achieved through reforms. Montazeri and many other political activists associated with the *howzeh* were in prison at this time and consequently unable to play a part in these events. But Khomeini, in exile abroad, was not so constricted, and in September 1977 he sent a message to his religious followers, urging them to do their part, to start writing letters, and to "declare the crimes of the Shah to the world."[81]

In January 1978, an insulting article, written about Khomeini by a pseudonymous author, appeared in *Ettela'at*, one of two major daily papers in Iran. It attacked Khomeini personally, as well as his family background, and accused him of being an agent of "old colonialism," meaning that of Britain. The article infuriated the clerical community, and a number of grand ayatollahs, including Shari'atmaderi, demanded a retraction and called for a peaceful protest in Qom. The police interfered, and more than a dozen protesters were killed. From then on, calls for reform were overwhelmed by radical and revolutionary voices. Khomeini – with his uncompromising stands and his demand for the overthrow of the regime – emerged as the distinct leader of the movement. Inevitably, Khomeini's leadership brought with it an emphasis on Islam and Islamic political discourse. The regime's policy toward this development was inconsistent, vacillating between suppression and concession.

The combination of carrot and stick proved to be an ineffective approach; one part emboldened the opposition and the other fueled its anger. Meanwhile, unresolved economic problems contributed to the revolutionary fervor. By the time Montazeri was freed, there was already a dramatic shift in the balance of power from the state to the revolutionary forces led by Khomeini. Huge street demonstrations were now part of the daily life of Iranian cities, and strikes by workers in key industries, including the oil industry, put additional pressure on the state. After a period of vacillation, the Shah, in a last desperate attempt to save his throne, entered into a negotiation with some of the National Front leaders. But no one among the National Front leaders except Shapur Bakhtiar was willing to take his offer of the prime ministership.[82] Bakhtiar accepted on the condition that the Shah would depart from Iran; he did not, however, ask for the abdication of the embattled monarch. He put in place a series of reforms, dissolved Savak, released political prisoners, and began a review of foreign contracts. But from the point of view of the revolutionaries, all of this was too little, too late. On January 12, less than a week into Bakhtiar's prime ministership, Khomeini declared the establishment of a body, the Revolutionary Council, to run the affairs of the revolution. One of the most important tasks of the Revolutionary Council was to prepare the ground for the creation of a provisional government. For their safety, the names of the council members (which included Morteza Motahhari, Mohammad Reza Mahdavi Kani, Ali Khamenei, Mahmud Taleqani, Mohammad Besheshti, and Ali Akbar Hashemi Rafsnajani) were kept secret. Most of these men were already members of the non-secretive organization *Jame'eh-ye Rohaniyat-e Mobaraz* (Society of Combatant Clergy, SCC), which was founded in Tehran in 1977 to organize and sponsor the religious opposition.

The Shah departed Iran in January, and Khomeini, despite the initial but unsuccessful effort of Bakhtiar to block his return, triumphantly entered Iran on February 1, 1979. Within a few days, Khomeini declared publicly the formation of the Provisional Revolutionary Government, headed by Mehdi Bazargan, one of the leaders of the Liberation Movement. With this declaration, Iran entered into a brief phase of dual sovereignty and witnessed the revolutionary forces and the government of Bakhtiar competing to secure the loyalty of different branches of the military, a crucial factor in this contest. The last phase of the revolution involved intense clashes between the revolutionary forces (including guerrilla groups) and troops loyal to the Shah's appointed government, which ended in victory on the part of the revolutionaries. On February 11, 1979, the Pahlavi state fell.

Montazeri and the Triumph of the Revolution

One of Montazeri's first acts after his release from prison was to visit Khomeini, who was living in Paris following his expulsion from Najaf by the Iraqi government in October 1978.[83] Over a decade since his last visit with Khomeini, the reunion was an emotional boost for Montazeri, who found himself once again in the presence of his mentor. The circumstances were different and unfamiliar, however. When Montazeri arrived in Paris, he found his teacher surrounded by nonclerics. Ebrahim Yazdi, a member of the Liberation Movement and Khomeini's translator and chief of staff, seemed to be his closest confidant and advisor. Along with Yazdi, the public face of Khomeini's entourage included Hassan Bani Sadr, the future president of the Islamic Republic, and Sadeq Qotbzadeh, the future foreign minister and head of the national radio and television system of the Islamic Republic. According to Montazeri, the major preoccupation of Khomeini and his advisers at that time was the creation of a parallel government to compete with the one currently in place. The appointment of Mehdi Bazargan as the head of the Provisional Government was already agreed upon, and it seemed that members of his cabinet had also been chosen and that all had given their consent. There was one exception, however, and that was Karim Sanjabi, a prominent member of the National Front, who had yet to agree to fill the post of the minister of foreign affairs. According to Montazeri, Khomeini asked him to help secure the consent of Sanjabi in joining Bazargan's administration.

Once back in Iran, Montazeri's time was filled with many different activities. Every day he had meetings with a large number of people who had come to Qom either to pay their respects or to request his help. As one of Khomeini's major representatives in Iran, Montazeri received and distributed a significant part of the funds that came from Khomeini's religious and political followers. In addition, he spent some of his time giving interviews and delivering sermons to the public. On special occasions, he would travel to Tehran to be part of the bigger and more rapidly unfolding revolutionary play. One of his final acts prior to the collapse of the old regime was to write a long and emotional open letter to the members of the armed forces. In that letter, he appealed to their sense of nationalism and religiosity, and wrote of his hope for a civilian/military unity that could bring about a just government under the leadership of Ayatollah Khomeini.

When Khomeini had returned and the eyes of the world were focused on Iran, Montazeri was in a peculiar place. He was not a member of the powerful Revolutionary Council. He contended that he did not wish to become a member because all of the council's business was conducted in Tehran, and commuting to the capital on a regular basis was hard on him, still frail from prison. Whether Montazeri was included in the Welcome Committee organized for Khomeini's return to Iran is not certain.[84] In any case, he was not the one who accompanied Motahhari when the latter entered the plane to greet Khomeini at the highly symbolic moment of his arrival in Tehran. At this time, the most visible personalities among the revolutionaries were clergymen such as Ayatollahs Taleqani, Motahhari, and Beheshti and laymen such as Hassan Bani-Sadr, Sadeq Qotbzadeh, and Ebrahim Yazdi.[85] Most of these men, with the exception of Taleqani, had not been as involved in the process of revolution for as long or as intensely as Montazeri had been. Motahhari, for example, started his earnest participation only in 1977.[86] The same can be said about Beheshti. Why then should Montazeri's public visibility, particularly outside Iran, have appeared dimmer than that of others at this time?

Men such as Qotbzadeh, Yazdi, and Bani Sadr were in Paris with Khomeini and were his connection to the rest of the world, particularly to the progressive segments of the West. It was important to present the revolutionary movement to the people outside Iran as a just struggle against an unjust rule, and these men, with their linguistic ability, were fit for the job. What explains the visibility of clergymen such as Motahhari and Beheshti is their active engagement with the revolutionary process in its crucial last year. Ironically, Montazeri, whose revolutionary record eclipsed that of Beheshti or even Motahhari, had been in prison for prolonged periods of time and had missed a great deal of the preparations for the revolution during its final year.

Another factor that sheds some light on this question is Montazeri's absence from the vibrant religious intellectual circles of Tehran. For at least a decade before the revolution, several lay and clerical teachers and professionals, including Motahhari, had created circles of intellectual gatherings and organized lecture series engaging the younger generation of Iranians – particularly the university students. The involvement of Ali Shari'ati added dynamism to this process and invited others to engage more seriously with the modern Western intellectual tradition. These circles not only presented men such as Motahhari as the intellectual leaders to religiously oriented, educated Iranians but also created a political affinity among these clerical leaders, who naturally sought one another's advice about revolutionary strategies.[87] Montazeri was not a part of this Tehrani circle. He belonged to the traditional *howzeh*, and as soon as he was freed from jail, he left Tehran for Qom and abandoned most of the activities in the capital to these men.

Montazeri's personality and appearance must be mentioned as factors that contributed to this neglect. His strong Najafabadi rural accent, his short stature, his down-to-earth manners, his unrestrained passion and impatience, some of which will appear more vividly in the later chapters, led to a portrayal of Montazeri as a man not of the same caliber as the serious and dignified Khomeini, Taleqani, or Beheshti. His tolerance, combined with his unadorned manners, gave many the liberty not only to be comfortable with him but to laugh at his expense. For example, in his memoirs about his prison experience, Rafsanjani recounts a story about a comedic play based on one of Montazeri's prison Friday Prayer sermons, designed and performed by Hassan Lahouti. Rafsanjani recalls that even though the comic aspect of the play was included at Montazeri's expense, the latter took it with good humor.[88] In the eyes of many in a revolutionary situation, that aspect of his character made him less than a model of a revolutionary leader.

All these factors together may have contributed to the inattention to his role as a revolutionary actor or religious thinker in the early (and some not-so-early) studies of the revolution. This scant attention is particularly noteworthy in the academic works where religion and religious actors were a primary focus of study.[89]

Despite all these issues, Montazeri was indeed an influential revolutionary actor. For many of the revolutionary clerics, and in the absence of Khomeini, he was their protector and their leader.[90] In fact, on occasion his influence superseded that of the other powerful men who surrounded Khomeini. An example of this involves Bakhtiar, the sitting prime minister. Soon after the Shah's departure from Iran, Bakhtiar offered to go to Paris and meet with Khomeini. Mottahari and Beheshti, among others, were in favor of the visit. But Montazeri convinced Khomeini not to meet with Bakhtiar before the latter resigned from his post, arguing that the balance of power was already in favor of the revolutionaries and that any conciliatory gesture toward the officials of the dying Pahlavi regime would only help the latter. Khomeini was convinced and the meeting was cancelled.[91] Also, together with Motahhari, Montazeri was the one who made decisions about Khomeini's place of residence and his security apparatus during the days before the old regime had collapsed.

How then should we judge Montazeri's importance as a revolutionary? No one disputes that between 1963 and 1978 Montazeri dedicated his life to the revolution. Where there is disagreement it is in the judgment about his significance for the revolution. In contemporary Iran, there are two contradictory narratives about Montazeri's role, one presented by his later detractors and one by his supporters and defenders. Detractors, such as Asadollah Badamchian, argue that the naïve Montazeri was neither an important player nor a serious confidant of Khomeini.[92] These critics conclude that Montazeri played no more than a peripheral role compared to the key players, such as the intellectually superior Motahhari, the suave and sophisticated Beheshti, and the politically skilled Hashemi Rafsanjani. Of course, this judgment, or at least its public expression, developed only after Montazeri was ousted from his position as Successor to Khomeini in 1989; prior to that, many of the same detractors had praised him for his unique service to Khomeini and to the revolution. In his book, *Faqih-e Aliqadr* (The Exalted Jurist), Mostafa Izadi has collected a series of the accolades showered on Montazeri when he was a favorite son of the revolution.[93] For example, the current Supreme Leader, Ali Khamenei, once considered Montazeri an essential figure at the center of the revolution, a man whose knowledge and courageous personality made his contributions unique. Mohammad Emami Kashani, a member of the conservative Guardian Council, argued that Montazeri's simplicity in speech and lifestyle veiled his political astuteness and his ability to mobilize people for political action. Azari Qomi, who himself became a thorn in the side of the Islamic Republic in the mid 1990's, mentioned that from the time Khomeini was first sent to exile, the activist clergy considered him the one who would replace Khomeini should anything happen to him. Similar statements were made by other members of the revolutionary elite.

It is true that no one individual can make or break a movement of such magnitude as the Iranian revolution. But there is no doubt, as Savak documents of the time reveal, that Montazeri was second to none in his dedication to an Islamic revolution. He was a man fully engaged with the rapidly changing political environment of the 1960's–70's, a man who made sacrifices for a cause he believed in, all in the hope of establishing a just Islamic system. It was his revolutionary credentials, along with his jurisprudential knowledge, that made him the contender for the highest position in the post-revolutionary order, i.e., the heir to the Supreme Leader of the Islamic Republic.

Notes

1 Roy Mottahedeh argues that the reasons for clerical political inactions during this period were two: one the disillusionment of people with the heavy-handed method of some activist mollahs; the other the recognition by a large number of clergymen of the fractious nature of the clerical establishment, which was only revealed when the clergy became active during the Constitutional Revolution. Together these two factors made the clergy politically cautious. Mottahedeh, *The Mantle*, 227–8.

2 There were other clergymen, such as Mahmud Taleqani, Mohammad Ali Angaji, and Sayyed Reza Zanjani, who defied Borujerdi and supported Mossadeq, but none of them had the oragnaizational backing enjoyed by Kashani.

3 There are several narratives about which of these two men should bear the primary responsibility for the rift. In the post-revolution Iran, starting with Khomeini, and continuing up to the period of this writing, the religious narrative puts the blame squarely on Mossadeq. Thus, Kashani

is considered the real hero of the nationalization era and Mossadeq is seen as an ultimate traitor. For a detailed treatment of the two men in this narrative, see Farhang Rajaee, "Post-Revolutionary Historiography in Iran," in *Musaddiq, Iranian Nationalism and Oil*, James Bill and W. Roger Louis, eds. (Austin, TX: University of Texas Press, 1988), 118–40. On the other side, supporters of Mossadeq see in Kashani an unreasonable or ambitious man who put impossible demands on Mossadeq. See, for example, Karim Sanjabi's political memoirs, *Omid ha va na-Omidiha* [Hopes and Despairs] (London: Jebheh Melliun Iran, 1989), 123–5. The third narrative, the scholarly approach, does not spare Mossadeq from blame, but still, with the possible exception of Yann Richard's judgment in his chapter in Nikki Keddie, ed., *Religion and Politics in Iran* (New Haven, CT: Yale University Press, 1983), considers Kashani to be the man who did the most damage to the relationship and was most instrumental to the success of the coup. See the works of Richard Cottam, Ervand Abrahamian, Sharough Akhavi, Homa Katouzian, and Fakhreddin Azimi.

4 Based on some evidence, Borujerdi, due to his concern about the Tudeh Party, ultimately supported the coup.

5 For a concise summary of Navvaf Safavi's life and thought, see Sohrab Behdad, "Islamic Utopia in Pre-Revolutionary Iran: Navvab Safavi and the Fada'ian-e Eslam," *Middle Eastern Studies* 33, no. 1 (1997): 40–65.

6 This public rebuke was published in a pamphlet, *Rahnama-ye Haqayeq* [The Guide to Truths] ca. 1950. See Ali Rahnama, *Nirouha-ye Mazhabi dar Bastar-e Harekat-e Nehzat-e Melli* [Religious Forces within the Dynamic of the Nationalist Movement] (Tehran: Gam-e No Press, 2005), 57–9.

7 Montazeri, *Memoirs*, 62. The post-revolution official historiography is silent about the existence of any such tension between Navvab Safavi and the clerical establishment. And as for Khomeini's position toward Navvab Safavi, several clergy, including Ahmad Khomeini and Sadeq Khalkhali, focus on the affinity between the two on the subject of antiregime activities. For more information on this, see the Islamic Revolution Document Center, at http://www.irdc.ir/fa/content/8586/default .aspx.

8 For an informed analysis of Iran–US relations during the reign of Mohammad Reza Pahlavi, see Richard Cottam, *Iran and the United States: A Cold War Case Study* (Pittsburgh, PA: University of Pittsburgh Press, 1988). For the specific period of the early 1960's, see 110–31.

9 Not all of the organizations within the National Front were secular. Some, such as *Nehzat Azadi-ye Iran* (Liberation Movement of Iran), a religious organization founded by Mehdi Bazargan, Mahmood Taleqani,

and Yadollah Sahabi in 1961, had religious tendencies. See Houchang Chehabi, *Iranian Politics and Religious Modernism: Liberation Movement of Iran under Shah and Khomeini* (Ithaca, NY: Cornell University Press, 1990).

10 See Sussan Siavoshi, *Liberal Nationalism in Iran: The Failure of a Movement* (Boulder, CO: Westview Press, 1990), 87–117.

11 This meeting, which Montazeri recalled in his memoirs (83), was used to cast a negative light on his character as one who was not a dedicated revolutionary until later years, by Abbas Salimi Namin in *Pasdasht-e Haqqiqat* [Guarding the Truth] (Tehran: Daftar Motale'at va Tadvin Tarikh Iran, 2000), 40.

12 A subsequent brief but confidential memo from Isfahan's military commander to the Ministry of War mentioned the surveillance of Montazeri's activities in that regard. See Appendix 4 in Montazeri, *Memoirs*, 444.

13 For the role of state security and military organizations in the anti-Baha'i activities, such as the demolition of sections of the Baha'i temple in Tehran, see Erfan Qane'i-Nejad, *Dar Damgah-e Hadeseh: Goftegou-yi ba Parviz Sabeti, Modir-e Amniyat Dakheli-ye Savak* [In the Trap of Events: A Conversation with Parviz Sabeti, The Savak Internal Division Director] (Los Angeles, CA: Sherkat Ketab, 2012), 119–20.

14 Moin, *Khomeini*, 70.

15 For a detailed account of the dynamic of choosing the *marja* and the role of Khomeini's followers in attempting to make him the Supreme Source of Emulation, see Abdolvahab Farani, "Marja'iyat Imam Khomeini," at http://library.tebyan.net/newindex.aspx?pid=102834&ParentID=0& BookID=57298&MetaDataID=13410&Volume=1&PageIndex=0& PersonalID=0&NavigateMode=CommonLibrary&Content=.

16 For an inside account of the movement, see Ali Davani, *Nehzat-e Do Mahe-ye Ruhanyoun –e Iran* [The Two-Month Movement of the Iranian Clergy], 2nd ed. (Tehran: Markaz Asnad-e Eslami, 1998).

17 Montazeri, *Memoirs*, 103–4.

18 Khomeini, *Sahifeh Imam Khomeini*, 1:135–7.

19 Ibid., 415–24.

20 The most well-publicized assassinations by this group was the 1965 fatal shooting of Prime Minister Hassan Ali Mansour. It was the government of Mansour that had presented the bill to parliament to give US advisors legal immunity. This assassination led to the arrest and executions of several of the organization's members.

21 Montazeri, *Memoirs*, 216–17.

22 See Izadi, *Faqih-e Aliqadr*, 49–51. The only person who was unrivaled in his position as Supreme Source of Emulation was Borujerdi.

After his death, there was never a consensus about who was the highest source. However, following the death of Ayatollah Sayyed Mohsen Hakim (1889–1970), who since the passing of Borujerdi had been considered by many to be the Supreme *Marja'*, Montazeri and Abdolrahim Rabbani Shirazi were the first among their peers to write an open letter recommending Khomeini for this highest religious position. Their appeal was based not only on Khomeini's traditional qualification as a bearer of Islamic knowledge but also on his courage and ability to safeguard Islam and Muslims.

23 See Badamchian, *Khaterat-e Montazeri*, 298–9. At least one of Montazeri's detractors, who played a crucial role in undermining him, Mohammad Rayshahri, the Minister of Information and General Prosecutor of the Islamic Republic, in a special edition focused on Montazeri in his monthly *Arzeshha*, acknowledged that Montazeri was chosen by Khomeini to be the latter's representative with total authority in Iran while Khomeini was in exile. See Mohammad Rayshahri, "Montazeri: az Owj ta Forud" [Montazeri: The Rise and Fall], *Arzeshha* (January–February 1998): 5.

24 See Montazeri, *Memoirs*, app. 18, 454–5.

25 For an incisive study of claims in the context of contentious politics, see Charles Tilly and Sidney Tarrow, *Contentious Politics* (Boulder, CO: Paradigm Publishers, 2007).

26 For transcripts of these sermons, see Izadi, *Faqih-e Aliqadr*, 113–27.

27 These sermons were given when Khomeini's position on Islam and politics was published in Najaf in a book on *Islamic Government*. Here, Khomeini advocated the establishment of an Islamic state led by a religious jurist.

28 See a copy of the Savak document dated April 5, 1972 in Izadi, *Faqih-e Aliqadr*, 85.

29 For relevant copies of such directives, see ibid., 141, 142, and 146. All of these directives occurred during 1970.

30 Ibid., 147.

31 For a brief but informative description of the meaning and function of Hossein martyrdom see, Hamid Enayat, *Modern Islamic Political Thought* (Austin, TX: University of Texas Press, 1982), 181–94.

32 See Ne'matollah Salehi Najafabadi, *Shahid-e Javid* [The Eternal Martyr], 9th ed. (Qom, 1970), no. D, 158–9.

33 Soon after the beginning of the controversy, Ali Meshkini, who according to Montazeri was pressured, wrote an essay where he took back his praise for the book, but Montazeri remained true to his foreword. Salehi was a childhood friend of Montazeri. They met at the elementary school and became fast friends. They also shared for a while a *hojreh* at

one of the seminaries of Isfahan's *Howzeh*. Their friendship lasted until the death of Salehi in 2006. For more details on their connection, see the following interview with Montazeri: http://www.rahesabz.net/story/ 82455/.

34 Lotfollah Golpaygani, *Shahid-e Agah* (1971), digital version, 13–15, http://toraath.com/index.php?name=Sections&req=viewarticle&artid= 168&page=1.

35 One of the people who wrote a critical piece on the theological aspects of the book was none other than Montazeri's friend, Morteza Motahhari. See his *Hamaseh-ye Hosseini* (The Epic of Hossein).

36 Hojjat-ol Islam Rasoul Ja'afarian, *Jarianha va Sazmanha-ye Siasi-e Iran dar Faseleh Salha-ye 1320–1357* [Iran's Political Movements and Organizations between 1941–1978] (Tehran: Islamic Revolution Document Center, 2006).

37 In the post-revolution official historiography, Shamsabadi is portrayed as a political supporter of Khomeini. See Mohammad Rayshahri, *Memoirs* (Tehran: Islamic Revolution Document Center, 2009), 4:325–7.

38 For a detailed account of Hashemi's activities, see Evan Siegel, "The Case of Mehdi Hashemi," at http://iran.qlineorientalist.com/Articles/ MehdiHashemi/MehdiHashemi.html.

39 In his memoirs, Mahdavi Kani, who was also at the prison, mentions that after the assassination, some of the prison guards, provoked by Savak, would sarcastically but implicitly accused Montazeri of involvement in the murder plot. Mahdavi Kani, *Memoirs*, 144.

40 Years later, after the fall of Montazeri from his official position as the Designated Successor to Khomeini, one of his detractors, Abbas Salimi Namin, in his review of Montazeri's *Memoirs*, and in reference to one of the passages therein, accused him of knowing the motivation and the goal of Mehdi Hashemi's group and of the methods used to kill Shamsabadi. He stopped short of accusing Montazeri of foreknowledge of the plot. See Salimi Namin, *Pasdasht*, 63–4.

41 See a description of some of the articles of the original constitution at: http://www.jameehmodarresin.org/aboutmenufa.html. Later, changes were made to the original version.

42 Hedayatollah Behbudim, *Sharh Esm: Zendeqi-Nameh Ayatollah Sayyed Ali Hosseini Khamenei* [Description of the Name: The Life of Ayatollah Sayyid Ali Hosseini Khamenei] (Tehran: Institution for Political Studies and Research, 2012), 157 and 228.

43 Montazeri, *Memoirs*, 106, 128, and 140

44 See Mohammad's letter at http://www.farsnews.com/newstext.php? nn=13911019000295.

45 Montazeri, *Memoirs*, 183.

46 See a letter from Hakim in Montazeri's *Memoirs*, app. 28, 461.

47 For a Laconian analysis of Montazeri post-revoltuionary resistance to treatment of prisoners, see Behi, "The 'Real' in Resistance."

48 Qasr remained Tehran's main prison until the construction of the Evin prison in the late 1960's.

49 Qodratollah Alikhani, one of Montazeri's prison-mates during his last incarceration, remembers Montazeri receiving severe beatings in Evin prison. See a 2014 interview with Alikhani in the daily *Jomhuri Eslami* at http://noandish.com/fa/news/7478/%D8%AE%D8%A7%D8%B7 %D8%B1%D8%A7%D8%AA-%D8%B9%D9%84%DB%8C%D8 %AE%D8%A7%D9%86%DB%8C-%D8%A7%D8%B2-%D8%B2 %D9%86%D8%AF%D8%A7%D9%86-%D8%B4%D8%A7%D9 %87-%D9%88-%D9%87%D8%A7%D8%B4%D9%85%DB%8C- %D9%88-%D9%85%D9%86%D8%AA%D8%B8%D8%B1%DB %8C.

50 According to Mahdavi Kani, he and other younger imprisoned clergymen, such as Hashemi Rafsanjani, would try to prevent Taleqani and Montazeri, their older inmates, from having to perform these tasks by volunteering to substitute for them. However, Montazeri would insist on doing his share. See Mahdavi Kani, *Memoirs*, 162–3.

51 See Ashraf Dehqani's memoirs of prison in *Hamaseh-e Moqavemat* [The Epic of Resistance], 2nd ed. (London: Cherikha-ye Fada'i Khalq-e Iran Publications, 2004).

52 Montazeri, *Memoirs*, 197.

53 Ibid., 201.

54 Ibid., 207. This night, and Anvari's theatrical talents, had a great impact on these men. In addition to Montazeri, Hashemi Rafsanjani and Mahdavi Kani also recall this evening with fondness and nostalgia. See 'Ali Akbar Hashemi Rafsanjani, *Enqelab va Pirouzi* [Revolution and Triumph], ed. Abbas Bashiri (Tehran: Bureau for Propagation of Revolution's Education, 2009), 56–59 and Mahdavi Kani, *Memoirs*, 156–7.

55 Montazeri, *Memoirs*, 210–11. In his memoirs, Mahdavi Kani also recalls Hashemi's bad vocal performance, which went beyond just one evening. According to Kani, Hashemi would recite Quran every morning, making himself the butt of a joke among some of his prison-mates. See Mahdavi Kani, *Memoirs*, 161.

56 See Ali Motahhari's essay in the daily *Etemad* at http://fararu.com/fa/ news/37120/%D8%AE%D8%A7%D8%B7%D8%B1%D8%A7%D8 %AA-%D8%B9%D9%84%DB%8C-%D9%85%D8%B7%D9%87 %D8%B1%DB%8C-%D8%A7%D8%B2-%D8%A2%DB%8C%D8 %AA-%D8%A7%D9%84%D9%84%D9%87-%D9%85%D9%86 %D8%AA%D8%B8%D8%B1%DB%8C.

57 See Hashemi Rafsanjani, *Enqelab va Pirouzi*, 61.

58 Chehabi, *Iranian Politics and Religious Modernism*, 210–13.

59 See Ervand Abrahamian, *The Iranian Mojahedin* (New Haven, CT: Yale University Press, 1989), 84–7.

60 This anticlerical attitude ultimately led to the bloody confrontation between the *Mojahedin-e Khalq* and the clergy soon after the triumph of the Islamic Revolution and the establishment of the Islamic Republic.

61 For a concise elaboration of the organization's ideology, see Abrahamian, *The Iranian Mojahedin*, 92–104.

62 Mohammad Taqi Shahram, *Bayanieh E'lam-e Mavazeh-e Ideologic Sazman-e Mojahedin-e Khalq-e Iran* [Statement on the Ideological Stands of People's Mojahedin Organization of Iran] at http://www .peykarandeesh.org/PeykarArchive/Mojahedin-ML/bayaniyeh-1354 .html. See in particular 35–43.

63 Ibid.

64 According to many of his friends, including Motahhari, Montazeri was concerned to an obsessive degree about these rituals.

65 Whether People of the Book are also "impure" has been a matter of debate among the sources of emulation. In the past fifty years, more and more have decided that People of the Book should not be considered impure. Montazeri is among them.

66 For a sample of such areas of contamination, see Montazeri, *Estefta'at* (Tehran: Sayeh Publications, 2005), 1:27–8 and 167–9. See also *Estefta'at* (Tehran: Argavan Danesh Publications, 2009), 3:27–31.

67 This decision/decree has been a matter of discussion among both religious and secular revolutionaries. Some have argued that the reason behind it was political, caused by fear over the Marxists' influence on Muslim activists. According to this view, physical separation would reduce the chances of intimate encounters among the two groups and reduce opportunities for such an influence. See the account of Mohammdi Gorgani, a close associate of Talaqani, in *Tarikh-e Irani* at http:// tarikhirani.ir/fa/news/4/bodyView/1289/0/%D8%B1%D9%88%D8 %A7%DB%8C%D8%AA.%D9%85%D8%AD%D9%85%D8%AF %DB%8C.%DA%AF%D8%B1%DA%AF%D8%A7%D9%86%DB %8C.%D8%A7%D8%B2.%D9%81%D8%AA%D9%88%D8%A7 %DB%8C.%D9%86%D8%AC%D8%B3.%D8%A8%D9%88%D8 %AF%D9%86.%DA%A9%D9%85%D9%88%D9%86%DB%8C %D8%B3%D8%AA%E2%80%8C%D9%87%D8%A7.%D8%AF %D8%B1.%D8%B2%D9%86%D8%AF%D8%A7%D9%86.html. Montazeri, on the other hand, gives a different reason for the decision, informed by his traditional religious view of the ritual of purification. See *Memoirs*, 212–14.

68 Ahmad Ahmad, *Memoirs*, ed. Mohsen Kazemi (Tehran: Sureh Mehr Publications, 2005), 436.

69 Montazeri, *Memoirs*, app. 30, 464.

70 Montazeri, *Memoirs*, 223.

71 Ibid., 143–4.

72 In his studies of the scant Savak documents related to Shari'ati's interrogations, Ali Rahnama makes the point that Shari'ati himself may have wished to highlight his anticlerical writings in order to obscure his antiregime ones. See Ali Rahnama, *An Islamic Utopian: A Political Biography of Ali Shari'ati* (London: I.B. Tauris, 1998), 330–5.

73 Rahnama, *An Islamic Utopian*, p. 336.

74 Izadi, *Faqih-e Aliqadr*, 157–62.

75 For a copy of the Savak document on this subject, see ibid., 168.

76 Ibid., 182–4.

77 See Ali Shirkhani, *Hamase-ye 17 Khordad 1354-e Madrase-yi Fayziyah* [The Epic of Fayziyah Seminary's Uprising of June 7, 1975] (Tehran: Islamic Revolution Document Center, 1998). This book contains interviews with nineteen seminary students who participated in the events.

78 Khomeini, *Sahifeh Imam Khomeini*, 3:76.

79 For a detailed description and analysis of the factors that led to the revolution, see Abrahamian, *Iran between Two Revolutions*; Keddie, *Roots of Revolution*, and Mohsen Milani, *The Making of Iran's Islamic Revolution: From Monarchy to Islamic Republic* (Boulder, CO: Westview Press, 1988).

80 For an account of the events and activists of this period, see Abrahamian, *Iran between Two Revolutions*, 496–506.

81 See the entire message in Monhandes Mehdi Bazargan, *Enqelab Iran dar Do Harekat* [Iranian Revolution in Two Movements] (Tehran: Nehzat Azadi, 1984), 26.

82 As a consequence of his acceptance of the offer from the discredited and weak Shah, Bakhtiar was expelled from the National Front.

83 In a meeting between the Iraqi and Iranian ministers of foreign affairs in the United States, Iran (reportedly) requested that Khomeini be expelled from Najaf.

84 When he was asked what role he played in the formation of the committee, Montazeri gave a vague answer. See Montazeri, *Memoirs*, 241. Others, such as Mahdavi Kani, do not mention Montazeri's name as one of the leaders of the committee. According to Mahdavi Kani, Ayatollah Motahhari was the chair of the committee. See Mahdvai Kani, *Memoirs*, 189–90.

85 In the West, scholarly works on revolutions, such as Nikki Keddie's *Roots of Revolution* and Mohsen Milani's *The Making of Iran's Islamic*

Revolution, paid very little attention, if any, to the role of Montazeri prior to and during the revolution.

86 After his forty-three-day detention related to his participation in the events of the 1963 uprising, Motahhari had very little overt confrontation with the state and instead concentrated on teaching and writing. Between 1964 and 1976, Motahhari followed a cautious path. See Davari, *The Political Thought*, 35–85 and Mahdavi Kani, *Memoirs*, 171.

87 The relationship between Motahhari and Shari'ati, which had an enthusiastic beginning, ended in complete disengagement due to several disagreements. For an informative account of the ups and down of this relationship see Rahnama, *An Islamic Utopian*.

88 'Ali Akbar Hashemi Rafsanjani, *Karnameh va Khaterat of Hashemi Rafsanjani, 1357–58: Enqelab va Pirouzi*, ed. Abbas Bashiri (Tehran: Daftar Nashr Ma'aref Eslami, 2004), 61.

89 For example, in Fischer. *Iran* there is only one mention of Montazeri, while there are nine and eighteen of Motahhari and Taleqani, respectively. Again, in Said Arjomand, *The Turban for the Crown* (New York: Oxford University Press, 1988), Montazeri appears as an independent actor/thinker only once (pp. 167–8). In the few other places where his name is mentioned, it is always in the context of the acts of others. The curious thing is that even in later books, Montazeri has been disregarded as a thinker of the Islamic Republic. For example, in Hamid Dabashi, *The Theology of Discontent* (New York: SUNY Press, 1993), a book devoted to the thinkers whose ideas, in the words of the author, "have shaped the nature and constitution of the Islamic Revolution," the clergymen chosen for inclusion are Motahhari, Taleqani, and – with no surprise – Khomeini. There is no mention of Montazeri even though he not only played a significant role in shaping the constitution of the Islamic Republic but, by the time Dabashi's book was published, had already written the most extensive treatise on Islamic state. One should also mention yet another later book, Vanessa Martin, *Creating an Islamic State: Khomeini and the Making of a New Iran* (London: I. B. Tauris, 2000): Martin includes Motahhari because of his importance as a student of Khomeini, and devotes a whole chapter to his thought, but mentions Montazeri only in passing, in just three sentences.

90 See an interview with Rafsanjani at http://tarikhirani.ir/fa/news/20/ bodyView/774/%D9%86%D8%A7%DA%AF%D9%81%D8%AA %D9%87%E2%80%8C%D9%87%D8%A7%DB%8C.%D9%87 %D8%A7%D8%B4%D9%85%DB%8C.%D8%B1%D9%81%D8 %B3%D9%86%D8%AC%D8%A7%D9%86%DB%8C.%D8%A7 %D8%B2.%D8%B9%D8%B2%D9%84.%D8%A2%DB%8C%D8

%AA%E2%80%8C%D8%A7%D9%84%D9%84%D9%87.%D9
%85%D9%86%D8%AA%D8%B8%D8%B1%DB%8C.html.

91 Montazeri's primay role in this regard is corroborated in Khalkhali's
memoirs. See Sadeq Khalkahli, *Khaterat-e Ayatollah Khalkhali: Avalin
Hakem-e Shar' Dadgaha-ye Enqelab* [The Memoirs of Ayatollah
Khalkahli: The First Religious Judge of the Revolutionary Court]
(Tehran, Sayeh Press, 2005), 270–1.

92 Badamchian, *Khaterat-e Montazeri*, esp. 458–66.

93 Izadi, *Faqih-e Aliqadr*, 335–66.

3 | The Post-revolutionary State and Montazeri

The Bearer, The Agitator

Here I stand, I cannot do otherwise.
Martin Luther

During the 1980's, the Iranians witnessed Montazeri's quick rise and crushing fall from the second-highest position of power in the Islamic Republic. As a part of a greater story of the post-revolution politics, Montazeri's life contained contradictory and puzzling aspects. He started as a genuine revolutionary figure, believing ardently in the total dismantling of the old order. His attitude was, however, deeply informed by his traditional religious training. He thus lent his support to the creation of a novel Islamic political structure that was legitimized only by an authoritarian reading of the Islamic traditions and laws. Within a few years after the establishment of the Islamic Republic, Montazeri found himself caught in a dilemma between his desire to remain the bearer of this political system on the one hand, and the call of his lived experience to challenge the deeds of the same system on the other. This dilemma cost him dearly.

"Explosion of Light!" With these words, Yasser Arafat, the Palestinian leader and Iran's first foreign guest, celebrated the triumph of the revolution. Arafat's words resonated with those who saw in the revolution the power of throwing off an oppressive dark force. To them, the first few months of the "new order," despite the chaos resulting from the collapse of the institutions of the old state, the summary executions of many associates of the Pahlavi regime, and rebellions in the border provinces, were indeed exciting months. The early euphoria over the triumph of the revolution nonetheless hid from the ordinary people the critical challenge faced by the key players: the construction of a new order.

The participation of multiple groups in the revolution greatly contributed to its success in toppling the financially and militarily well-endowed Pahlavi state. But that diversity also created serious complications for a smooth transition to a new order. Distinct groups – whether liberal, socialist, communist, religious, or secular – considered themselves the major owners of the revolution and expected their visions to be included in the design of this new system. A series of power struggles among the former allies and an eventual concentration of power in the hands of the militant clergy resulted from these expectations.

The Post-revolution State and the Fate of the Liberal Reformists

The battle between moderation and radicalism defined the character of political contest in the first few months of post-revolutionary Iran. The Provisional Government and its supporters carried the banner of moderation, while the dominant segment of the Revolutionary Council and its newly organized Islamic Republican Party (IRP), along with most of the religious and secular leftist forces, flew the flag of radicalism. Montazeri belonged to the second group, as he openly criticized the Provisional Government, accusing it of being neither Islamic nor revolutionary.[1] He complained that the government lacked "revolutionary combativeness," that it had failed to purge (or rather, send into retirement with a just pension) a large number of the remnants of the old regime, who were still running the bureaucracy, that it had yet to change the banking laws to make them compatible with Islamic principles, and that it had failed in agricultural and resource preservation. On the other hand, he moderated his criticism by adding that he believed in the sincerity and good will of the government, and appreciated the fact that it had inherited an economically bankrupt and politically chaotic country.[2] Montazeri was not the only critic of Bazargan's government, but his criticism carried particular weight, especially after he became the popular Tehran Friday Prayer leader, with the ear of millions of listeners.

The tension between Montazeri and the Provisional Government extended beyond domestic affairs and included foreign policy disputes. Montazeri's strong support for liberation movements challenged the Provisional Government's approach to foreign policy and affected its ability to normalize relations with many states, particularly the conservative and oil-rich states of the Persian Gulf. The revolutionary rhetoric of Montazeri against the conservative Muslim countries and his passionate support for liberation movements and radical states such as Libya were a cause of tremendous annoyance for Bazargan's government. The Provisional Government was also challenged by other revolutionaries, but Montazeri's fiery language and his position on foreign policy put him among the people it considered most threatening to its policies of moderation. What made his criticism doubly annoying to some of Bazargan's team was their unflattering view of Montazeri, who they considered a simpleton and an intellectual light weight.[3]

The uncontrollable revolutionary fervor and constant interference from competing forces led Bazargan to submit his resignation to Khomeini on several occasions. The ayatollah refused to accept it until the occupation of the American embassy in November 1979, an event Bazargan vehemently opposed. With Bazargan's resignation, the Provisional Government and what remained of a moderate phase of the revolution ended. But defeating the Provisional Government was only one of the post-revolutionary steps in taking control of the state. For the radical/revolutionary segment of the clerical establishment to declare victory, the struggle over the constitution had to be won in its favor, and Montazeri played a pivotal role in that struggle.

The Creation of the New Order: The Referendum and the New Constitution

The event that prepared the way for the adoption of the 1979 constitution was the referendum on the general character of Iran's political system. Based on Khomeini's decision, the referendum gave people only two options: (1) an Islamic republic or (2) a monarchical system. Predictably, the limitation of these options precipitated heated discussion among the ideologically diverse groups and individuals. The dispute over proper wording was finally settled when Khomeini made his famous statement in Tehran in March 1979, shortly after the victory of the revolution. Speaking as the voice of the people, he declared: "What our nation wants is an 'Islamic republic,' not merely a 'republic,' nor a 'democratic republic,' nor a 'democratic Islamic republic.'"[4]

Within a month, a referendum was held, and according to the official statistics more than 98 percent of the voters opted for the Islamic Republic. The outcome of the referendum emboldened the supporters of Khomeini, Montazeri among them, to declare it a mandate for Islam and a vote against the seculars, liberals, and leftists. Pushing for a single ideology, they started to use the famous phrase *vahdat-e kalameh* ("unity of the word") in a narrower sense. In Paris, before the revolution, Khomeini used it to mean a unity of purpose for all forces, whether religious, nationalist, or secular, in the fight against the Shah's regime. The community of revolutionaries based on that early conceptualization was wide and inviting, and included "all the layers of Iranian nation."[5] But after the toppling of the old regime, Khomeini contracted the meaning of "unity of the word" by excising nationalist and secular values and worldviews from it. Montazeri did the same. Belief in Islam, and more specifically in the clerical Islam, was the essential ingredient of the new use of "unity" and was the yardstick that would separate the true revolutionaries from the imposters. The implication was obvious: any deviation and attempt to create a pluralistic discourse and a more inclusive "unity" would signal the role of outsiders and would lead to the betrayal of the revolution.

With the referendum out of the way, national attention shifted to the writing of a constitution for the newly formed Islamic Republic. By the order of Khomeini, starting in January 1979 while he was still in Paris and ending in June 1979, a draft of the future constitution was not only written but had gone through two sets of revisions.[6] None of the revisions provided for the office of *velayat-e faqih*. In retrospect, the last draft was as liberal and democratic as it could possibly have been.[7]

Khomeini neither commented on the June draft nor asked for further revision, but he reserved the right to weigh in during the thirty days that were set aside for public debate.[8] During that time, he did indeed make his views known, as did a large number of religious, secular, and left- and right-leanings groups. Their positions and arguments appeared on a daily basis in newspapers and on radio and television broadcasts. Montazeri offered the most specific and, in retrospect, influential clerical contribution to the debate in a two-part pamphlet, "Collection of Two Messages," suggesting far-reaching revisions to the last draft.[9] His most significant revision proposed investing the ultimate power of the state in the hands of a knowledgeable and just Shii jurist who was also familiar with current events. The general message of the pamphlet was that no article of the constitution should be outside the moral and legal framework created by Shii Islam as interpreted by the clergy. The pamphlet, with its traditional and religiously elitist approach to state–society relations, was widely publicized and found many defenders as well as critics, all of whom wished to influence the formulation of the articles of the constitution.

In addition to the discussion on the substance of the constitution, there was debate over the rules of procedure for changing the draft into an official constitution of the Islamic Republic. In general, the reformist and liberal members of the Revolutionary Council (such as Bazargan) were in favor of convening a large constitutional assembly. Others, including the cleric Hashemi Rafsanjani, argued in favor of submitting the latest draft directly to the public for a vote.[10]

No one side prevailed during the discussion, and members of the Revolutionary Council decided to take the issue to Khomeini. In that meeting, Khomeini gave his consent to Ayatollah Taleqani's suggestion for the formation of a smaller body of experts who could do the job speedily as a compromised solution. An election date for the Assembly for the Final Review of the Constitution (AFRC) was soon set, and ideas started to float around as to who should be nominated for this key task. Khomeini asked Montazeri to leave Qom and run for one of Tehran's seats on the assembly. Montazeri responded to Khomeini's call, became a candidate, won a seat, and left Qom for Tehran.

The AFRC was mostly clerical. Out of seventy-two representatives, only twenty-one were laypeople, including one woman. The assembly was also dominated by members of the newly formed IRP, a party led by Beheshti, Rafsanjani, and Ali Khamenei. There was no representative from the two important guerrilla groups or from the National Front. The overwhelming presence of the clerical rank naturally oriented the revision of the constitution in a direction guided by the principles of Shii Islam. One of the major outcomes of this orientation was the willingness of the majority of the assembly to include the institution of the *velayat-e faqih* in the final draft. However, some clerics, the most influential of whom was Ayatollah Taleqani, worried about the theocratic implication of the office and opposed its inclusion.

In the elections to the AFRC, Montazeri received the largest number of votes after Taleqani and Bani-Sadr, and ahead of Beheshti.[11] Once the assembly was convened, it was Montazeri and not Taleqani who was elected as the Speaker, while Beheshti was elected Deputy Speaker. Hassan Ayat, another strong supporter of the *velayat-e faqih*, was chosen as Secretary. The election of these men to the highest positions of the assembly and their control over setting the agenda and managing the debate further paved the way for the inclusion of the institution of the rule of the Islamic jurist into the final draft.

A decade later, Montazeri's detractors argued that his selection as the chair of the assembly was not due to his leadership abilities but merely a symbolic gesture in recognition of his religious credentials and his revolutionary record. The real power of the chamber was invested in the savvy hands of Beheshti. There is some truth to this assessment, at least if one takes presiding over the sessions as an indication. The first two preliminary sessions of the assembly were run by the oldest member, but out of the following sixty-five sessions, Montazeri presided over fifteen, while Beheshti, at the request of the former, assumed the position of chair for the other fifty, including the one in which the fifth article about the rule of the *vali faqih* was passed.[12] It was Montazeri himself who, after his election to the chair of the assembly, asked Beheshti to preside over the first session, admitting that the latter was more "involved with such matters."[13] The proceedings of the AFRC also hint that Montazeri was not nearly as effective as Beheshti in running sessions or exuding a commanding presence. However, Montazeri showed incredible dedication to his task as a representative of the assembly. He argued passionately about important articles and chastised those who were frequently absent from meetings and did not take such a momentous occasion seriously. He himself spent most of his time at the site of the assembly, ate modest food, and at times slept where he worked.

What some of his detractors failed to acknowledge was Montazeri's contribution in steering the constitution in the direction that it took. Montazeri was a major voice against the preliminary draft, the one that the moderate and liberal forces within the assembly supported as the basis of deliberation, and instead pushed for the inclusion of other "suggestions" that had been presented since June.[14] Concomitant with efforts to dismiss the liberal approach to the constitution was his attempt to undermine the voices that viewed the revolution as a nationalist one, and thus supported exporting it to the Muslim world. In the eighteenth session of the assembly, he said:

Gentlemen should keep in mind that the revolution that occurred in Iran was not a geographical or Iranian revolution. Even though we are Iranians, what was in the slogans of *all* [emphasis is mine] was [a demand for] an Islamic government. Islam is not limited to Iran and our goal is to free all Muslims in all countries from the yoke of despotism and colonialism, and to establish Islamic programs.[15]

In addition to his efforts to marginalize the voices of liberals and nationalists, Montazeri also fought against the influence of the left, particularly of the *Mojahedin-e Khalq,* by advising the assembly members to reject the adjective *towhidi* (a concept popularized by Ali Shari'ati and adopted by the *Mojahedin-e Khalq*) in describing the character of the Islamic regime.[16] The concept of *towhidi,* with its socialist and anti-clerical connotations, was a matter of concern for some time. Equally, however, Montazeri was very receptive to the notion of "Islam as an ideology" (again, an idea popularized by Shari'ati) as the determinant of all aspects of social life, including the political system.[17] He hoped that the use of such language could rally support for *velayat-e faqih* among those who were not keen on clerical rule. In his Octobter 19, 1958 Friday Prayer sermon, he said:

These days there are a lot of noise intended to create a negative atmosphere about the office of *velayat-e faqih* . . . this office is not dictatorial because this nation is committed to the *ideology* [emphasis is mine] of Islam and wishes to have a political system based on Islamic standards. Logically, such a system must be supervised by those who are experts and *ideologues* [emphasis is mine]. This does not mean that a *faqih* will have dictatorial power . . . He is limited by the legal framework set by Islam . . . *Faqih* is not synonymous with clergy, it is possible for someone without the turban to be the *faqih.* The only condition for him is to be an ideologue [have extensive knowledge of Islam and be politically aware].[18]

Not everyone was in favor of the rule of the Islamic jurist. Ayatollah Taleqani, Hassan Bani Sadr, and Rahmatollah Moqaddam Maraghe'i, a representative from Azarbaijan and a man close to the Grand Ayatollah Shari'atmadari, were among its critics. But the opposing representatives were too few to have a winning voice. On the day that the article on the rule of the Islamic jurist was brought before the assembly, only two people were allowed to speak. Beheshti, the powerful vice chair, spoke for the article, and Maraghe'i spoke against it. Eventually, the article passed with the support of fifty-three members. Only eight people cast an opposing vote, while five abstained.[19]

Montazeri's support for the authoritarian article on the rule of jurist did not prevent him from supporting some other articles on the rights of the people. Some of these were social welfare programs such as

Article 29 on the universal right to pension, medical care, unemployment compensation, and so on. On political rights, he was most outspoken on banning torture. Unlike some of his colleagues in the chamber, such as Meshkini, who sanctioned the use of physical force under certain circumstances, Montazeri was uncompromising in his opposition to all forms of torture.[20] He also spoke in favor of the right to assemble and to free speech, and against search and seizure and spying on people. Yet, his support for the freedoms of the people was always limited by his insistence that these freedoms should be in harmony with Islamic principles.

The AFRC finished writing the final draft during the last week of November, and put the draft to a two-day popular referendum on December 1 and 2. It passed. The approved constitution provided for a president, a prime minister, and a national (later Islamic) assembly. It was a bifurcated document, which attempted to reconcile theocratic and authoritarian institutions on the one hand with republican and democratic ones on the other. At the time, Montazeri was happy with the outcome, especially with the prominent role of religion and the inclusion of the office of the Supreme Leader in the constitution. Years later, he expressed some regret that the assembly had not had enough time to study the constitutions of other countries. Yet his regret was most likely the product of his later reevaluation of the constitution and his disillusionment with the actual practices of the Islamic Republic. In fact, during the early days of the revolution, and during meetings of the assembly, he revealed no such misgivings. In an interview with the daily *Kayhan* in July 1979, Montazeri, who attributed the cause of people's revolutionary sacrifices to their religious devotion, criticized the spring draft of the constitution for its contamination with Western ideas.[21] His support for Islamic purity as a guide to designing the constitution was also documented in the proceedings of the Assembly of Experts.[22]

Once the work of the AFRC was over, Montazeri the teacher/scholar prevailed, at least for a time, over Montazeri the politician. In the early winter of 1980, he resigned from his position as the leader of Tehran's Friday Prayers, after having led them for eighteen sessions, and went back to Qom to teach. However, life as he knew it in the 1940's and 50's – a life unencumbered by national politics – was gone forever, and whether he wished it or not, he was drawn into the politics of the post-revolutionary state.

Figure 3.1 Montazeri leading the Tehran Friday Prayer, December 7, 1979. Bettmann/Getty Images

Already, two dramatic events had contributed to the emergence of Montazeri as a prominent national figure and a fitting successor to Khomeini. One was the May 1979 assassination of his influential friend and classmate Morteza Motahhari. If Motahhari had survived, he would have been another likely candidate to succeed Khomeini. The other event was the unexpected death in September 1979 of Ayatollah Taleqani, the first post-revolutionary Friday Prayer leader of Tehran. After his death, Khomeini chose Montazeri to succeed Taleqani as Tehran's Friday Prayer leader, and with that appointment Montazeri found a powerful forum in which to be heard by millions of people who either participated in the prayers or listened on radio and television. His knowledge of jurisprudence, combined with his two prominent positions as Tehran Friday Prayer leader and chairman of the AFRC, put him in the most favorable place to become the next Supreme Leader of the Islamic Republic.

As early as 1980, the domestic and foreign media portrayed Montazeri not only as an influential leader but as "the hope of the nation and the Imam," as the second most important man in Iran, and as the potential successor to Khomeini.[23] Montazeri owed this accolade partially to Khomeini's decision to put him in charge of some sensitive matters. One such matter, which Montazeri shared with another influential ayatollah, and his potential competitor, Ali Meshkini, was the appointment of a cadre of religious judges to run the newly established but chaotically run Islamic court system.[24] Khomeini also assigned to Montazeri the task of selecting Friday Prayer leaders for different regions. Due to the popularity of Friday Prayers among large segments of the population, these leaders could exert significant political power; Montazeri, by having control over their appointments, was able to spread his own influence around the country. Probably the most symbolically important delegation of responsibility was Khomeini's decision to refer his *ehtiyatat* to Montazeri. In Islamic tradition, a source of emulation can refuse to issue a *fatwa* and exercise caution (*ehtiyat*) on a matter that requires ruling, but urge his followers to follow the *fatwa* of another *marja'*. As the leader of the revolution, Khomeini referred many such questions (which later became state laws) to Montazeri. Such referrals were a sign of Khomeini's utmost trust in Montazeri's jurisprudential knowledge and might have also been a sign of his acceptance of Montazeri as his eventual successor. This fact was not lost on other leaders, including presidents, prime ministers, and other officials who sought Montazeri's support for their policies.

The Defeat of the Left and the Ouster of Bani Sadr

The first presidential election on January 24, 1980 led to the overwhelming victory of Abolhassan Bani Sadr, an independent candidate with close ties to Khomeini. Less than two months later, the elections for the first national/Islamic assembly resulted in a chamber dominated by the IRP candidates. With major institutions of the state filled, the Islamic Republic appeared to be well established, but two factors created an extraordinary situation in Iran, consuming the energy and resources of the nation. One was the hostage crisis, which had already begun in November 1979, and the other was the war with Iraq. The power struggles among the officials, particularly between the president on the one hand, and the leaders of the judiciary and legislative bodies on the other, did not help the situation.

Despite his opposition to theocracy, Bani Sadr had enjoyed the support and trust of both Khomeini and his influential son Ahmad since their pre-revolutionary days in Paris.[25] Counting on his strong popular mandate and Khomeini's support, Bani Sadr attempted to make his office the most powerful state institution by reining in others now under the control of the IRP. Unfortunately for him, he sorely underestimated the influence of his opponents, who controlled all other levers of power, including the Islamic Consultative Assembly.

A heterogeneous set of political forces – including the liberal reformist Liberation Movement and the radical *Mojahedin-e Khalq* – saw an ally in Bani Sadr. He and his supporters, despite many of their differences, shared the view that for the revolutionary state to survive it needed the skills of experts and that expertise should be the standard for putting people in positions of responsibility. The other side, labelled as *Maktabi* (i.e. ideological) and represented by Mohammad Ali Raja'i, the IRP hand-pick prime minister, put its emphasis on revolutionary dedication and willingness to sacrifice for the cause. This gap between these two forces was most evident in their approach to the war with Iraq that broke out soon after the presidential election.

Bani Sadr, the commander in chief of the armed forces, saw the role of the regular army as entirely crucial in conducting the war. He insisted on the primacy of a professionally trained army in waging a war, which in his view was a classic state-against-state conflict. His opponents, on the other hand, argued that since Iraq, unlike Iran, had all the help of the technologically and militarily advanced countries, the Revolutionary Guards (IRGC), populated by fighters who were eager to sacrifice themselves for Islam and the revolution, should be at the forefront. Both sides did what they could to get the support of Khomeini and other influential leaders like Montazeri.

In his own memoirs, Bani Sadr claims that he tried and almost succeeded in gaining Montazeri's cooperation in restricting the IRGC and putting the army in the lead in the conduct of the war. But Montazeri, after some hesitation, changed his mind and took the side of the IRGC instead. In Bani Sadr's view, this change of heart harked back to Montazeri's general opportunism.[26] Montazeri did support the IRGC and did push for quick actions in the war zone. Whether his actions were based on opportunism is, of course, open to question. Iran was stalled in the war, and there was a general air of impatience with the country's responses to the Iraqi advances. There was also a widespread mistrust of the army commanders because of their association with the old regime.

The tension between Bani Sadr and Montazeri became public when the latter sent a message to the clergy in Ahvaz, the site of some of the most intense battles. He criticized the lack of speedy action at the war front and implicitly blamed the regular army commanders. Annoyed by this message, Bani Sadr sent his own public message to Montazeri and implicitly accused him of ignorance in his judgment of the battle-fields.[27] Montazeri responded equally sharply by saying that he knew very well about the conditions at the front, since the army's rank-and-file paid him daily visits and informed him about the disastrous ways the commanding officers were handling the situation.[28] Soon after these back-and-forth messages, Iran initiated a few battles, but performed poorly in several of them. The dejected Bani Sadr blamed the clergy, especially Montazeri, for urging premature action on the part of Iranian forces and contributing to their losses. Of course, there were other domestic and international matters that widened the gap between Bani Sadr and his opponents, particularly the leaders of the IRP.

In the meantime, there were almost daily demonstrations in support of Bani Sadr. The IRP leaders countered these demonstrations by mobi-lizing their own followers. Among them were a group of club wield-ers who physically attacked and injured the pro-Bani Sadr demonstra-tors. The ongoing public protests, the constant exchange of accusations between Bani Sadr and his rivals, and the potential instability of the regime eventually led Khomeini to dismiss Bani Sadr as commander in chief and to give his consent to the parliament to vote on Bani Sadr's competency as president, a vote which of course had a foregone con-clusion. At this point, Bani Sadr went into hiding, and in his absence the parliament voted overwhelmingly for his dismissal.

Throughout this turbulent period, and particularly when demon-strations and counterdemonstrations became daily events, Montazeri took the side of Bani Sadr's opponents and criticized the president's supporters.[29] But, unlike some of the other influential clergy, such as Beheshti and Abdol Karim Musavi Ardebili – leaders of the IRP – Montazeri condemned the use of violence by the counterdemonstra-tors.[30] Both Musavi Ardebili and Beheshti had explicitly defended the club wielders by suggesting that their use of physical violence was less of a problem than the lethal effect of the liberal language in the newspa-pers that supported Bani Sadr.[31] Except for his disagreement about the use of violence, Montazeri's support for the anti-Bani Sadr camp was complete.

In an interview following Bani Sadr's dismissal as commander in chief, Montazeri accused him of being self-delusional about his own personal power, the power of his office, and his approach to policies. Bani Sadr's huge election victory, Montazeri suggested, was due not to the candidate's personal charisma but rather to that of Khomeini. He chastised Bani Sadr for giving ammunition to enemies through his critical and accusatory statements about the regime officials, the state of the country, and the use of torture.[32] These statements were made when Montazeri believed that pure faith and sacrifice for that faith would deliver Iran and the rest of the Islamic world. He saw in Bani Sadr a man who, if left in his position of power, would have destroyed the achievements and promises of the revolution. Ironically, less than a decade later, he himself fell victim to similar charges, which led to his own dismissal as the Successor to the Supreme Leader.

With the defeat of Bani Sadr, the opportunity for peaceful political opposition to clerical rule came to an end as the guerrilla groups took to violence. In one of the most spectacular instances of bomb attacks, committed by the *Mojahedin-e Khalq*, more than seventy officials of the Islamic Republic, including Montazeri's son, were killed. That attack, and others that soon followed, took the lives of a president, a prime minister, and a few regional clergy, and led to a period of extreme repression and bloodletting by the state. In the end not only all the armed guerrilla groups but also the non-violent liberal opposition were neutralized.

The Intra-clerical Rivalry and Montazeri

The elimination of the liberals and the leftists did not lead to a period of consensual politics but brought to the surface the fissures within the clerical establishment and its base. The IRP, now in hegemonic power over the state apparatus, was the site of most of the competition between two loosely formed right and left factions, each trying to prevail over the economic, foreign, and cultural policies of the Islamic Republic.

The rightists defended private property and were wary of attempts to confiscate property and to nationalize foreign trade. Within state institutions, Ali Khamenei, who succeeded Bani Sadr as president, carried their voice. The leftists, represented most visibly by Mir Hossein Musavi, the new prime minister, advocated restrictions on accumulation of wealth, and urged nationalization of foreign trade and confiscation of the property of absentee-owners. The conflicting economic

Figure 3.2 Montazeri with the recently elected President Khamenei in Khomeini's residence, March 1982. Kaveh Kazemi/Hulton Archive/Getty Images

positions of the two factions had foreign policy implications. The rightists and their supporters within the traditional merchant class did not wish to create tension within the region, fearing that it would lead to further economic disruption. The leftists were in favor of a foreign policy that would support liberation movements and thus challenge imperialism and its "lackeys," i.e., the conservative Arab leaders of the region. There were also differences between the two factions with regards to cultural policies: the right-leaning faction was concerned with the negative impact of "too much freedom" on Islamic values; the leftists were inclined to allow wider room for cultural expression.[33]

Neither of these two factions could consistently claim Montazeri as one of its own. He gave and withheld his support from one or the other on different matters on different occasions. In the area of foreign policy, considering his view of a continual revolution, his support for liberation movements, and his sharp critique of colonialism, neocolonialism, and conservative Arab countries, he would feel at home with the leftist faction. When it came to domestic politics, he started out as a reliable supporter of the economic policies of the leftist faction but gradually distanced himself from some of its important positions.

In March 18, 1980, the Revolutionary Council passed a three-point measure to distribute certain agricultural land among the landless peasants.[34] The three clerics, Montazeri, Beheshti, and Meshkini, who were chosen by Khomeini to judge its compatibility with Islamic principles approved of the measure, and soon a group of seven-member committees were formed to oversee the implementation of the law in different regions of the country. One point of the measure, *band-e jim*, which limited land ownership to three times what was considered enough to make a living (by the standard of each region) was received with dismay by the conservative clerics. For a while, their criticism was muted due to the revolutionary atmosphere and the fact that the newly approved constitution had emphasized social and economic justice. But a few months later, due partially to the heavy hand of many of the overseeing committees, the voices of dissent became bolder and louder. Some influential and high clergy, such as Ayatollah Golpaygani and Sadeq Rouhani, were at the forefront, attacking *band-e jim*. Eventually, Khomeini gave his consent to shelving the controversial point. Years later, in his memoirs, Montazeri backtracked from his position by denying that he was ever in favor of distribution of legitimately owned land if it was under cultivation by the owner.[35] But the truth is that the law that was passed included that provision and Montazeri must have known about it. In any event, he was blamed for the failure of the program, and the conservatives did not forgive him for it.

As time passed, Montazeri did begin to worry about property confiscation, even that of expatriates, an item that was on the agenda of the leftist government. His argument for halting such confiscations was based on his expressed hope that it might lead to a return of some who had fled the revolution out of fear.

Montazeri's overall economic position was that governments would never be good business managers and that the economy should be left to market forces. He did not deny that governments had the responsibility to provide for the needy, but he thought that they should do so by means of taxes – under certain circumstances as high as 80 percent, on wealth if necessary. He was also in favor of progressive taxation, imposed on wealth rather than on individuals. He supported government's intervention in the unlawful accumulation of wealth by designing appropriate laws and finding mechanisms for their implementation.[36] Still, he was not in favor of a centralized economy,

believing that it would lead to increased corruption, bureaucratization, and wasteful activities. For example, he criticized the decision
of Musavi's government to turn the *Jahad Sazandegi* (reconstruction
crusade) into a centralized ministry. Originally a grassroots decentralized organization, *Jahad Sazandegi* was formed in the early days of the
revolution by a group of young, skilled, and well-educated men and
women to help people in remote rural areas.[37] Montazeri wished to
keep it in its original form.

Montazeri also went against a well-established leftist program: subsidies to consumers. He argued for subsidies to be given to producers,
particularly to farmers. He believed that a policy of strengthening the
agricultural sector was crucial for reducing dependence on the outside
world, as well as for slowing immigration to the cities by the rural population. But his most comprehensive critique of the leftist approach of
Musavi's administration came toward the end of his time as the Designated Successor to Khomeini. In a conversation with Musavi and other
government officials, Montazeri expressed his disapproval of undue
governmental control over the economy and foreign commerce and
advised Musavi to allow a wider participation in economic affairs by
the private sector.[38]

Montazeri's reluctance to give his overall support to either of the factions and his tendency to criticize each with his characteristic bluntness
did not earn him many friends, particularly within the state machinery. During the early 1980's, he began to move away from the harsher
policies of the state and gave a series of speeches in support of a gentler
and more tolerant approach toward society, annoying the authoritarians on both the left and the right.[39] In a meeting with parliamentarians
in 1983, he emphasized freedom of speech for all, including the much
maligned liberals. In a lecture to the members of the IRGC, he warned
against radicalism and the use of force; he said it was not for them to
decide the guilt or innocence of people or to punish them. Finally, in a
speech to the prosecutors, he made an astonishing move away from his
earlier harsh rulings against violators of the laws, such as drug dealers
and hoarders. He likely did so because he had watched in horror as
many of these violators were sent to their deaths. Not ready to question the divinely ordained laws, he came up with another solution. In
his speech, he asked the prosecutors not to create files for the trials
of first-time offenders, and instead to first try the gentler method of
offering them fatherly advice or a stern warning.

All these speeches had the potential to undermine the dominant power of the institutions controlled by one or the other faction. Still, his differences with the leftists were less pronounced than those with the right, and Montazeri found himself on most occasions on their side, particularly in areas of foreign policy. Moreover, many of his loyal followers belonged to the leftist camp.

The Heir Apparent

Montazeri was selected to be the next Supreme Leader by the Assembly of Experts in 1985. According to the constitution, the assembly did not have the right to choose a successor before the current Supreme Leader had died or was dismissed. Montazeri, in a letter to Ayatollah Ali Meshkini, his rumored rival and the Speaker of the Assembly of Experts, said as much. But many leaders, especially the politically savvy Rafsanjani, were concerned that with no designated successor the revolutionary state could face a transitional crisis with unpredictable and possibly destabilizing effects after Khomeini's passing. Given Montazeri's record of political accomplishments before and after the revolution and his jurisprudential credentials, he seemed a good choice. There were other potential contenders, some of them senior ayatollahs whose status as jurisprudents was higher than his. In the same letter to Meshkini, Montazeri himself mentioned that with the availability of so many sources of emulation, it would be inappropriate and insulting to those eminent ayatollahs for him to be chosen as the heir apparent.[40]

Once the matter of his nomination became public, there were direct and indirect objections. In the Assembly of Experts itself, not all members supported him. On the day that the vote was scheduled, twenty-two of the seventy-two assembly members did not show up, a clear sign that many of the absent members opposed the nomination.[41] There was also opposition by clerics outside the assembly, most publicly expressed by Ayatollah Sayyed Sadeq Rouhani, the same man who vehemently fought against *band-e jim*. During one of his class sessions in Qom, Rouhani launched an attack on Montazeri's nomination, arguing that only God and not the Assembly of Experts had the authority to choose the successor, and concluding that the Iranian regime was being un-Islamic.[42] But with the exception of a letter to Montazeri by Ali Meshkini, there was no written expression of reservations about his appointment.

To Montazeri's letter, Ali Meshkini wrote a reply. After paying him some backhanded homage, Meshkini implicitly disputed Montazeri's reluctance to accept the honor by stating that Montazeri himself was involved in setting things in motion for his eventual nomination through the publication of his *resaleh 'amaliye* (a publication necessary for becoming a source of emulation). He also stated that even though the majority of the assembly's members were in favor of his appointment, there were some who had concerns about certain people in Montazeri's office. He ended his letter by warning Montazeri to be careful of his own advisors.[43]

Despite these reservations, Montazeri was well ahead of all the potential candidates in his record of political and revolutionary activities, he had the jurisprudential requirement of being a source of emulation, and he had substantial support among large segments of the population. The more urbane and educated segments did not take him seriously, possibly because he was not part of the pre-revolutionary intellectual religious circles. His simple mannerisms and rural accent had made him a source of jokes among many urban Iranians. But he was the *marja'* for many others, including some state officials. He also enjoyed a widespread support among the lower and lower-middle classes for the same attitudes that left the urbane Iranians unimpressed. His interest in justice and the plight of the downtrodden added to his popularity in these groups, and they enthusiastically welcomed his selection.

In his new position, and with extended authority, Montazeri felt even more responsible for the acts of the state than before. There were three areas in particular – education, liberation movements, and the judicial system – that Montazeri believed were crucial for the viability of a just, Islamic community both inside and outside Iran. Of the three, the educational area was the least controversial. The other two – the cause of liberation movements and his approach to the justice system, particularly in its treatment of political prisoners – proved to be highly divisive.

Reform of Religious Education

The triumph of the revolution and the establishment of the Islamic Republic provided opportunities for the expansion of religious education beyond the wildest dreams of the *howzeh* reformers of the 1950's and 60's. After almost fifty years, the religious establishment once again was in a position to exert control over education. For many politically oriented religious leaders, however, the goal of controlling the educational system was closely associated with the political goal of defeating the secular leftist groups that had great influence in the universities. Soon after the establishment of the Islamic Republic, the policy of purging universities of "Western influences" became a priority, and committees were set up to address changes in order to bring universities in line with religious orthodoxy. Montazeri played his part in this effort by assigning his own representatives to universities. At the same time, he and many other religious leaders knew that making universities more Islamic required a parallel reform of the traditional and parochial system of seminary education. One of the key problems of the seminary education was its outmoded curriculum.

There had been occasional efforts to offer new courses in the *howzeh* prior to the revolution by Motahhari and Beheshti. Dividing his time between Tehran and Qom, Motahhari taught courses on comparative philosophy and history of philosophy in Qom in the early 1970's. And Beheshti, who was one of the founders of a new school in Qom, called *Haqani*, was a pioneer in teaching lessons on Western philosophy and comparative religion. But the existence of such courses did not lead to a systematic reform of the *howzeh*'s curriculum, due partially to a lack of funding for innovation in religious education.

A major factor that allowed the post-revolution educational reformers to succeed in funding their projects was the patronage of the Islamic state, with its vast financial resources. The state could now free the *howzeh* from dependence on the payers of *sahm-e emam* and the strings attached to these contributions. What escaped the attention of some reformers was that the state's financial largess would come with an attempt to take away the traditional independence of religious centers. Montazeri came to realize the negative effect of state patronage once he was ousted from power. In the early years of the revolution, however, he meshed the state's goals in his attempt to rejuvenate religious education.

One initiative that had Montazeri's strong support was the creation of Imam Sadiq University, an institution initially set up to train Islamic diplomats.[44] Its curriculum consisted of modern social science courses such as history, political science, and international relations, as well as classes on theology and other foundational Islamic subjects. The diplomat-in-training was also required to study two foreign languages,

Arabic and either English or French, whose acquisition was specifically justified on the grounds that effectively communicating the religious basis of Islamic diplomacy was paramount. Along the same lines, Montazeri proposed creating Shii educational centers abroad, particularly in African countries such as Kenya, Sierra Leone, and Ghana. Of these three countries, only Sierra Leone had a Muslim majority population, but even there the Shiis constituted a small minority. Montazeri's goal was to provide educational support for native Shiis in the hope of enabling them to introduce this school of faith to non-Shii and non-Muslim populations in the Third World.

Another initiative of Montazeri's was the creation of Sunni seminaries in Iran. Influenced by his main mentor Ayatollah Borujerdi, Montazeri was interested in forging a better relationship with the Sunnis within and outside Iran. He was instrumental in establishing the Grand Islamic Center in Kurdistan, a Sunni-majority area of Iran. Previously, Sunni students had had to go to Egypt, Pakistan, and Saudi Arabia for religious education. Setting up a center in Kurdistan and in other Sunni-majority regions of Iran could potentially reduce the religious and political influences of foreign countries and thus solidify control of the Islamic Republic over its minority Sunnis. In Qom, Montazeri's office created one of the most extensive libraries of its kind, providing necessary resources not only for his own students, but for a large number of foreigners, including a cadre of religious activists connected to liberation movements.

Not all of Montazeri's educational goals were realized. Other influential forces within the religious establishment had different ideas about education and wanted to reduce his influence. His later fall from power provided them with an opportunity to marginalize his role in the educational area. More importantly, many institutions and projects that he had built or carried out were taken over or destroyed by his opponents after he was ousted from his position.[45]

Foreign Policy and Liberation Movements

Soon after the establishment of the new state, two general approaches to foreign policy emerged, each linked to a different understanding of the nature and goal of the revolution. One was based on the belief that this revolution was essentially Islamic and that Iran was the first leg of a wider revolution whose ultimate goal was to liberate the oppressed

Muslim masses everywhere from the yoke of the "global arrogance" and its regional "lackeys." A segment of the elite, among whom were lay religious leftists and radical clergy, supported this characterization and continued to advocate radical changes in the global power structure.

The other approach, a pragmatic one, understood the revolution in nationalist terms, put its emphasis on the interest of Iran as a nation-state, and favored a speedy normalization of relations with other states. The Provisional Government and, for the most part, the Foreign Ministry during the period of Bani Sadr and Ali Khamenei's presidencies followed this line on foreign policy.[46]

Montazeri was a faithful supporter of the first view, and was particularly partial to the cause of liberation movements. His commitment to the emancipation of the "oppressed" was due more to his religious faith and belief in justice than to abstract theories of imperialism. Still, he offered some analysis of colonialism and its antidote in his speeches, written statements, and interviews. The earliest trace of his view of the global structure of domination and subordination can be found in his sermons at Friday Prayers during 1971–72 in Najafabad.[47] There, the gist of his analysis was that subjugation of a large part of the world by a few powerful countries had been a historical norm. And even though the means of control might have varied, the goal was always the same: to appropriate the resources of the weak by the strong. But, he also said, there was another side to the story of colonialism, and that was the story of resistance; whenever the powerless masses mustered resolve and made a mental commitment to regain their dignity, they prevailed over more powerful forces.

However, bringing to life the hidden "will to resist" in the oppressed people of the twentieth century was a more difficult challenge than in the past, Montazeri asserted. New technology for producing and spreading mind-seducing consumer products had helped the imperialists to numb and pacify people of the Third World, particularly its youth. In one Friday Prayer sermon in Najafabad in 1971, he said:

[The West] built Apollo [not with loose and immoral libertarian behavior but] with its science . . . You should know however, that they wish to distract us with these things [dancing, cinema, and television] . . . they don't want us to reach our potential or become aware, lest we fancy progress . . . We [the Muslim world] have oil, we have minerals, we have everything. What we don't have is what Islam has asked for: faith and honor. We have put ourselves at their [the West's, as well as the Soviet Union's] mercy and they, instead of helping us build industry, build "youth palaces," and send us movie stars.[48]

Yet he saw in the victory of the Vietnamese liberation movement over the immensely powerful military of the United States real possibilities for change and a hopeful example for other liberation movements. These latter, Montazeri contended, possessed the same resolve and could mobilize forces to challenge the unjust global power structure. On occasion, Montazeri deemed the Soviet Union a force equally as oppressive as that of the United States, particularly after its invasion of Afghanistan at the end of 1979.[49]

Alliance- and coalition-building were crucial factors in his vision for eliminating international injustice. Smaller and less powerful than colonialists, the liberation movements and a few independent countries like Libya, Algeria, and Syria had the potential to successfully change the balance of power by forging strong alliances. He also saw the victory of the Islamic Revolution as the best gift to the anticolonial forces. The toppling of the most powerful American-dependent regime by a resource-poor population was an inspiration and a model for freedom-seeking movements and their allies in the region.[50] The Islamic Revolution therefore could and must be exported, and the Islamic Republic should speed the process through spiritual and material means. To Montazeri, these were not just empty slogans; he made the cause of liberation movements his own by devoting a significant amount of attention and resources to it.

Montazeri's anticolonial attitude was shaped by his pre-revolution experience: by his objection to American companies' investment in Iran and his conversations with his leftist prison inmates in the 1950's. Nonetheless, the most penetrating influence on him was his son Mohammad's constant passion and loyalty to the cause of liberation movements.[51] During his years of living outside Iran between 1970 and 1977 in Pakistan, Afghanistan, Iraq, Lebanon, Syria, and finally Europe, Mohammad had developed working relations with several separate liberation movements, which he aspired to bring together in a campaign to build a global Islamic state. His most immediate passion was saved for the Palestinian movement, and he did his best to recruit young men from different parts of the region to fight on behalf of the Palestinians. He himself received his training in guerrilla warfare in Lebanon from members of the Fatah, the Palestinian resistance movement.

The revolution brought Mohammad back home and provided him with ample opportunity to pursue his dream. Soon after the establishment of the Islamic Republic, Khomeini ordered the formation of the paramilitary organization of the IRGC to safeguard the achievement of the revolution. The IRGC consisted of several units, one of which was Mohammad's brainchild: the "Unit of Liberation Movements." But Mohammad's impulsive acts, the most dramatic of which was his attempted trip to Libya, alienated the moderate Provisional Government and many of the revolutionary clerics. Even his father publicly criticized him for his lack of respect for order and for his rash methods. But Montazeri's criticism of his son was over his tactics, not his principles; for Montazeri, the justice of Mohammad's cause was all too obvious, and he tried his best to fulfill his son's dream after he was killed.[52]

In 1981, Montazeri organized "Unity Week," intended to bring Sunnis and Shiis closer together.[53] Montazeri was hoping that Unity Week would provide the representatives of the two sects with an opportunity to focus on their commonalities and take steps toward creating strong alliances across the Muslim world. Montazeri also proposed the designation of the birthday of the twelfth Shii Imam, Mahdi, as the "Day of the Oppressed," to remind people of the plight of the downtrodden around the globe and to show Iran's solidarity with liberation movements. Both these initiatives were enthusiastically welcomed by revolutionary leaders, but their execution, especially the liberation of oppressed peoples, was not easily translated into practical foreign policy.

One case where the tension between the pragmatic and the revolutionary approaches caused problems for Montazeri was Afghanistan. In 1979, the Provisional Government supported the Afghan Sunni resistance against the Soviet-backed communist government. But after the collapse of Bazargan's administration in November 1979, the Islamic Republic, or more specifically the Foreign Ministry, changed its strategy in the hope of striking a modus vivendi with the Soviets. Two factors were responsible for this change: (1) Iran's international isolation, which became an acute problem upon the start of the war with the well-armed Iraq and convinced some Iranian power holders to turn toward the Soviet Union for support; and (2) the Soviet invasion of Afghanistan. The invasion ironically led to Iran's practical withdrawal of material support for the majority Sunni resistance movement; the growing involvement of the United States and Saudi Arabia in support of the Sunni *Mojahedin* in Afghanistan had led to that decision.[54] Instead, Iran began a focused support for the minority *Hazari* Shii, and received the benign neglect of the Soviet Union. The weak and divided Shii *Hazari* were hardly a threat to the Soviet Union and thus were useful to the Soviet policy of exploiting the gulf between different religious and ethnic groups in Afghanistan.[55]

Montazeri's office exerted a great deal of control over policies regarding liberation movements, including those in Afghanistan. Even though Montazeri was unhappy about the Foreign Ministry's decision to strike a détente with the Soviet Union, he welcomed the decision to help the *Hazari* movement. To that end, he set up a bank account and asked people to donate money for the cause. He also opened his impressive library in Qom to Afghan religious students. His intention was to support a cadre of future religious leaders who, upon their return, would provide much-needed guidance to Shii communities in Afghanistan. But Montazeri's involvement in the tactical planning and day-to-day business of the resistance movement was minimal; he entrusted that responsibility to Mehdi Hashemi, his son-in-law's brother.

The child of one of Montazeri's teacher, Mehdi Hashemi was born in 1944 in Qahdarijan, near Najafabad. During his years in Isfahan and Qom's *howzehs*, he became politicized. As mentioned earlier, he founded the *Hadafiha* group and was eventually implicated in the murder of a few men and women, including Ayatollah Shamsabadi, and was imprisoned. According to his televised confession in 1986, he made a deal with the Savak and thus escaped the death penalty, but remained a prisoner until the collapse of the Pahlavi regime. After his release, Hashemi found a hospitable environment in which to continue his political activities not only locally but nationally and internationally.[56] For all these activities, he was resented by many, who took their complaints to people in power even before Montazeri was designated as the successor to Khomeini.[57] The same age as Mohammad Montazeri, Mehdi replaced Mohammad, after the latter's death, in the IRGC Unit of Liberation Movements. He shared not only some of Mohammad's temperament but also his dream of unifying liberation movements. Like his predecessor and friend, he viewed the Afghani Shii resistance as only a part of that goal.[58] However, his dream remained just that, due to the long-standing tribal divisions among the Afghan groups and the ongoing internal power struggles within Iran. Hashemi's group supported some factions within the Afghani Shii, while the Foreign Ministry was in favor of others, undermining the hope for the unification of the Shii resistance. There are different accounts as to who deserves the blame for the intensification of rivalries among the Afghan Shiis, which resulted in fraternal bloodletting. In his memoirs, Mohammad Rayshahri, the Minister of Information and a powerful enemy of Montazeri, pointed the finger at Hashemi.[59] Rayshahri's account is based on Hashemi's confessions, made after he was arrested by the Ministry of Information in 1986 and charged with a multitude of crimes.[60] Hashemi confessed that he, in coordination with a foreign country (Libya), had tried to subvert the Islamic Republic Foreign Ministry's efforts to unify the resistance, all for his own benefit. Montazeri, on the other hand, blamed the Foreign Ministry. A few months after Hashemi's arrest, Montazeri wrote a private letter to then President Khamenei, blaming "the kids [the Support Center for Afghanistan Islamic Revolution] in the Foreign Ministry" for sabotaging the plans for unification of the Afghan Shiis.[61] In the same letter, he also handed over the control of Afghanistan policy to Khamenei.

Afghanistan was only one foreign policy issue that caused tension between Montazeri and the rest of the established elite. The more important source of tension lay in the internal dynamic of Lebanese Hezbollah and its impact on the cause of liberation movements. In the early to mid 1980's, the leaders of the newly formed Shii organization of Hezbollah called for the establishment of an Islamic state in Lebanon and looked at Khomeini as its own Supreme Leader. Similar to the Afghanistan case, the policy toward Lebanese resistance movements, i.e. Hezbollah, had been under the general supervision of Montazeri and his office and was carried out by Hashemi. For a time, Hezbollah leaders saw eye to eye with Hashemi in his effort to unite liberation movements across the Middle East in a radical rejection of Israel, the United States, and conservative regional leaders. In time, however, some of the influential leaders of Hezbollah, most importantly Hossein Fadlallah, moved away from part of their past radical slogans. They also dropped the idea of a Lebanese Islamic Republic. In relation to Iran, the now more moderate Fadlallah distanced himself from

Hashemi and other Iranian foreign policy radicals and found new allies in the pragmatists, especially Rafsanjani, the powerful Speaker of the Iranian parliament, the man authorized by Khomeini to be in charge of war efforts. Fadlallah's decision to throw his lot in with the Iranian pragmatists was followed by his acceptance of Rafsanjani's request to free some hostages held by Hezbollah in Lebanon. This allowed for a secret deal between Iran and United States, an exchange of arms for hostages. Two unrelated factors – freedom for some hostages held in Lebanon and the channeling of funds to the Nicaraguan contras – drove the United States into this bargain. For its part, the Islamic Republic wished to get sophisticated arms for its poorly armed troops in a war that was going badly.

The new development in Lebanon undermined Mehdi Hashemi's goals and reduced the power of Montazeri's office in setting policy toward the Lebanese – and, by extension, Palestinian – liberation movements. Set on turning the tide, Hashemi allegedly kidnapped a Syrian diplomat sympathetic to the pragmatists on October 1986 and attempted to sabotage the thawing of Iran's relations with Saudi Arabia.[62] He was arrested on October 12, and was charged with a multitude of offenses against the Islamic Republic. None of this helped Montazeri's hand in the foreign policy domain.

One policy matter caused Montazeri particular unhappiness with the rest of the power elite, namely the secret arms-for-hostages deal (a.k.a., the Iran-contra Affair). He was not among the handful of Iranian leaders who had known about the affair,[63] having learned about it almost a year later from Manouchehr Qorbanifar, one of the main go-betweens for the deal.[64] Montazeri was angry that he was kept in dark about this decision, particularly in light of the fact that his office was actively involved in setting policies regarding groups like Hezbollah. A sensitive matter for Montazeri, once he had found out about the deal, was the involvement of Israel. Montazeri shared the information provided by Qorbanifar with his sons and his son-in-law Hadi, Mehdi's brother. Mehdi, already in prison, found out about the deal and leaked the news to a Lebanese newspaper. The exposure of the secret resulted in a crisis and the deal was halted.

Whether the continuation of the arms-for-hostages deal would have turned the tide of war in favor of Iran or have led Iran and the United States to start putting a painful past behind them is impossible to know. But unquestionably the leak killed any prospect of reconciliation between Iran and the United States. Those who orchestrated the deal on the Iranian side, among whom were Rafsanjani and Khomeini's powerful son Ahmad, probably never forgave Montazeri for the result of this episode. Despite the defeat of the pragmatists in this case, the arrest of Hashemi and the fall-out of the leak led Montazeri's office to lose its influence in foreign policy and its connections with the liberation movements.

The Judicial System and the Fate of Political Prisoners

Montazeri's long-standing interest in the fate of political prisoners was the product of his own experience as a prisoner, as well as his involvement in the judicial system of the Islamic Republic. One of the earliest tasks entrusted to him by Khomeini was to oversee the selection of religious judges for the new Islamic court system. The new court system was largely in shambles as a consequence of the haste to transform it into an Islamic institution. The lack of professional training and the arbitrary decisions of a large number of the newly recruited judges were a source of grievance among the populace and a matter of deep concern for Montazeri. This is how he described the situation:

Judges were provided with very broad but vague directives from the General Prosecutor. They were also quite inexperienced. For example one day, I came across a file where the presiding judge had written at the end of the dossier: "In the Name of God, the Compassionate, the Merciful [and then gave the verdict]: execution." Who was supposed to be executed and for what crime was not spelled out. The judge did not even bother to put the name of the accused on the ruling, only his own signature. Well, with such a ruling one could arrest and execute anybody, randomly. In the early days [of the Islamic Republic] they would arrest people en masse and then there would be demonstrations where certain groups would shout "E'dam Bayad Gardad" [He/She Must Be Executed]! In a nutshell this was the condition of our judicial system in those days.[65]

To reduce the damage, before a cadre of jurists could be trained for the job, Montazeri and Meshkini, who shared the responsibility, sent a twelve-point directive to revolutionary courts all over the country. It demanded courts' strict adherence to legal codes, avoidance of the use of personal vendettas in sentencing, humane and respectful treatment of the arrested, and a clear setting out of division of responsibilities, which would prevent the interference of the IRGC and the police in the affairs of the court.[66]

These instructions were ignored, and from July 1981 to the end of 1982 the situation in courts and in prisons got progressively worse. In a series of bombings in 1981, several dozen Iranian political elites, including a president, a prime minister, several members of parliament, and several high officials of the IRP, including Beheshti, were killed. Mohammad Montazeri was one of the fatalities. The state reacted with a massive suppression of the opposition, targeting in particular the *Mojahedin-e Khalq*, which had claimed responsibility for some of the most spectacular of the bombings. The palpable anger and fear that drove this harsh policy intimidated and silenced its potential critics. But not Montazeri, who became a persistent critical voice against its harshness and excesses. One of his first objections was contained in a long message celebrating the birthday of the Prophet Mohammad during Unity Week in early January 1982. He condemned extremism and "stupid excesses," and demanded that the court system be mindful of unjust treatment of the accused, lest it unwittingly help create a generation of antirevolutionaries.[67]

In another speech on the third anniversary of Khomeini's return to Iran, Montazeri pursued the same theme, this time even more forcefully, and accused some of the "extremist elements" in charge of executing the policy of possibly being the "enemy's fifth column," intent on subverting the just cause of the revolution and paving the way for its destruction.[68] He then advised the officials of the Islamic Republic to adopt a gentler policy toward the opposition so that they could attract rather than alienate non-believers, as well as those deceived by the violent opposition.

These messages annoyed Ayatollah Mohammadi-Gilani, the Evin prison's chief judge, and Asadollah Lajevardi, the notorious head warden of Tehran's prison and the revolution's prosecutor. Lajevardi was renowned for his severity, having put several hundreds of prisoners, if not thousands, to death. He reportedly ordered the policy of postconfession torture on many of the prisoners as a way of "educating the deviants." Montazeri knew about these matters. He met with Khomeini and convinced him to allow an amnesty committee to look into the cases and rein in those responsible for such excesses. A provision that limited the effectiveness of the amnesty committee was the veto power of the men in charge of the prison. Lajevardi used that power and refused to cooperate with the committee, and therefore put himself on a collision course with Montazeri and with the High Judicial Council. He lost that battle and was fired from his job. Lajevardi's dismissal reportedly made Khomeini unhappy but caused many others to breathe a sigh of relief.[69] Subsequent wardens were Montazeri's men, who had a much more humane and relaxed attitude; they made the lives of prisoners less intolerable.[70] The relative calm period did not last long. In 1988, a new crop of wardens took over, and once again mass executions became the norm in prisons.

The reason for this new round of widespread executions was Operation Mersad, a military attack on Iranian forces by the *Mojahedin-e Khalq*. Soon after the armistice with Iraq, Masoud Rajavi, the leader of *Mojahedin-e Khalq*, ordered his armed followers, supported by the Iraqi government, to attack Iran from Iraq, hoping to mobilize Iranian opposition at home and overthrow the Islamic Republic. The operation, which began in late July, lasted only a few days, with a crushing defeat of the *Mojahedin-e Khalq*. It left in its wake weeks of bloodletting in Iran's prisons. Angered by Rajavi's incursion, Khomeini ordered a physical purge of prisoners who still identified with the *Mojahedin-e Khalq* (*sar-e mo'ze*). On July 30, a news blockade in the prisons ended all communication with the outside and set the stage for speedy interrogations followed by executions of scores of political prisoners.[71] Montazeri found the rationale and the extent of the executions unacceptable; he wrote two letters to Khomeini, one on July 31 and the other on August 4. In his memoirs, he recalled how he came to this risky decision:

I felt that this was wrong and decided to write a letter to the Imam [Khomeini]. It happened that Messrs. Sayyed Hadi Hashemi and Qazizadeh were at my house so I consulted with them. They both advised me against it by reasoning that Imam was very angry with the *Monafeqins* ["hypocrites", in reference to *Mojahedin-e Khalq*] and the Mersad episode, and that if I wrote him and objected to the policy he would be annoyed. They soon left the room but I was still anxious. I did my noon and afternoon prayers and then was thinking about my responsibility as the Successor, I have been part of this revolution. If an innocent person gets killed in this Islamic Republic I am responsible for it. I consulted the Quran and the following Sura came to my view as I opened the Book: "They were guided to good words so then they were guided to the right path." After that I sat down and wrote the letter.[72]

The letters he wrote shed light on his reflection on Islamic justice, the responsibility of the Islamic Republic to uphold it, and its failure to do so. Montazeri's son Ahmad, who read the first letter on the night of July 30, also advised his father to reconsider, but Montazeri was too upset about the executions and stuck with his decision. This is how Ahmad remembers his conversation with his father:

At ten p.m. on July 30, I went to my father's room . . . He handed me a written statement. I started to read the letter and was increasingly anxious as I came across phrases such as "the execution of several thousands in a span of a few days." [These words] would be taken as incendiary . . . I told my father: "Sir these things should not be written, it is better that you tell them to Imam Khomeini in person. Please think about the potential perils if the letter falls into the hands of others." With agitation my father responded to my plea by saying: "the blood that is shed unjustly will ruin everything."[73]

But what was really said in these letters? In his first correspondence, Montazeri warned Khomeini of the dire consequences of his severe ruling and of the mistakes and violations that were bound to occur in carrying it out.[74] He argued such violence would not help the goals of the revolution and might well play into the hands of the *Mojahedin-e Khalq* and other antirevolutionary forces and make them attractive alternatives to the Islamic Republic. He also pleaded with Khomeini to spare women, particularly those with children, from execution. Montazeri did not receive an answer to his first letter, so he wrote a second on the cases of prisoners who had been judged and executed unjustly.[75] Soon after sending this second letter, Montazeri received a written response from Ahmad Khomeini relaying a message from his father asking him to stop interfering.[76] Montazeri did not heed the leader's demand.

He was affected by his encounters with the families of prisoners. Day after day, these families, who saw in him their only hope for rescuing their loved ones, gathered at his house and, with tearful eyes, asked for his intervention. The appeals moved him deeply and made him more resolute. Without Khomeini's blessing, Montazeri summoned four men, three from the prosecution office, the fourth a representative of the Ministry of Information, whose decisions had sent hundreds of prisoners to their death. In August 2016, the audio recording of that private meeting became available through Montazeri's official website.

The recording reveals the depth of his anger and frustration. Here are some of his pointed remarks:

In my view the greatest crime against the Islamic Republic for which history will condemn us has been done by you [gentlemen]. Honestly, you will be judged by history as criminals... So many times we raised our voice against executions that were committed during the Shah. [But] How many did the Shah [actually] execute? Let's compare our own with his... Often [these prisoners'] refusal to disown their ideological position [*sar-e mo'ze*] was the result of the harsh behavior of wardens such as Lajevardi... I would have acted the same [as these prisoners] if I were treated as such.[77]

The meeting was for naught, and the executions of prisoners continued. As a last attempt, Montazeri sent the same men a letter with a somewhat different tone from the ones he had addressed to Khomeini. In this one, Montazeri asserted his authority as an Islamic jurist and cited several precedents set by the forgiving behavior of the Prophet and the First Imam when they encountered similar situations. He was hoping that his words would remind these men that if they wished to remain true Muslims they should follow the lead of their Prophet and treat their captives kindly.

He ended his letter with a point that was later used against him by his enemies. He wrote: "*Mojahedin-e Khalq* is not a collection of people, it is a way of thinking and interpretation, it is a kind of reasoning. The response to an incorrect reasoning should be a correct reasoning and not killing. Rather than solving the problem, killing exacerbates it."[78] After Montazeri's dismissal, his detractors used this to accuse Montazeri of being a sympathizer and supporter of the *Mojahedin-e Khalq*.

Was Montazeri's defense of prisoners limited to Muslim prisoners, or did it extend to non-believers, particularly to communists? I posed this question to a follower of Montazeri, a close friend of his son: the political activist and journalist Emaddedin Baghi. He responded by telling two stories.[79] The first was of a private conversation he had had with Montazeri in the early 1980's, when he was charged as Montazeri's representative with visiting and providing cash to the families of prisoners. In answer to his question of whether he should support the families of Muslim prisoners only, or if he could extend a helping hand to non-believers, Montazeri responded that the faith of a prisoner should have no bearing on their just treatment or support for their family.

The other story, which can be accessed on Baghi's website, related to the fate of a communist prisoner who was arrested after the bombings in the summer of 1981. By the order of Montazeri, when his representatives in the prisons were convinced of the man's innocence, they prepared the case for his release.[80] There are former communist prisoners whose memoirs corroborate Baghi's account.[81]

Regardless of which prisoners Montazeri meant to protect and support, the fact remains that his long-lasting and active opposition to the harsh treatment of the incarcerated brought him the wrath of many powerful leaders of the Islamic Republic, including Khomeini.

The Gathering of the Storm

Iranians welcomed the end of the eighth year of bloody war with Iraq in 1988. But once the darkness of war was lifted, the country began to see and assess the damages. A horrific number of dead and injured, bombed-out towns and cities, and ruined infrastructure were only some of the most visible signs of the damage. By February 1989, the time to celebrate the tenth anniversary of the Islamic Revolution, Iran was confronted with runaway inflation, high unemployment, and no real prospect for its youth.

Anniversaries of the revolution were occasions to mobilize support for the Islamic Republic by emphasizing the achievements and victories of the country under the wise stewardship of Khomeini. To mark the tenth – the first post-war – anniversary, huge and costly celebration were planned. It is possible that those who organized the expensive events thought that it would be a good idea to show the war-weary people that the war had not broken the spirit of the country, that the revolution was still alive, and that Iran had come out of the war with dignity and high spirits. Needless to say, Montazeri thought otherwise and shared his view with the nation.

Until then, Montazeri's public critique of the state's behavior, unlike his private correspondences, had remained somewhat mild and was never about the overall record of the revolution. The reactions of the power holders, including Khomeini himself, to Montazeri's points of view were similarly expressed in private meetings or correspondences. But that private mode changed into a public one in a speech Montazeri delivered during the anniversary period in February 1989. There, instead of expressing hopes and celebrating the achievement of the revolution, Montazeri unleashed a devastating critique on the overall performance of the Islamic Republic. Above all, he chastised the state for its unwillingness/inability to end sooner a war that had laid waste to the country. Incensed by the amount of money that went into the anniversary, he called for the occasion to be a time for reflection on mistakes, for atonement, and for asking people's forgiveness:

After ten years we need to examine our record . . . our enemies forced this war on us and in the course of it we lost too many of our precious and valuable young people. Too many cities were laid in ruin. We need to investigate our record to see what our mistakes were and learn not to repeat them. On many occasions we showed obstinacy, shouting slogans that frightened the world. The people of the world thought our only task here in Iran was to kill . . . but we just put our head down and insisted "It is as we say." There is a wiser path, and now that we understand we should confess [our mistakes] to God and to the Iranian nation.[82]

According to Montazeri, even though he was an early supporter of the war and a believer in Iran's right to defend its integrity, he had nonetheless advocated an end to the war once the Iraqi forces were driven out of much of Iran's territory and the country was in a position to negotiate a beneficial conclusion.[83] This was the first time that he publicly criticized the war by pointing out its devastating consequences.

In the same speech, he also criticized press censorship, addressed the harsh treatment of prisoners, and asked for freed prisoners to be welcomed back into the community with Islamic affection. Montazeri's focus on the well-being and freedom of people and his mention of the grave mistakes of the Islamic Republic were a testimony to the distance he had traveled since the early days of the republic, when his discourse emphasized sacrifice, martyrdom, and demand for unconditional support. He regretted the change in the meaning of "unity of the word" from its broader pre-revolutionary definition to its more restricted post-revolutionary one. In the early days of the post-revolutionary period, Montazeri himself was ardently in favor of restricting the meaning when he excluded from the Islamic Iranian community a large group of people. In the forty-third session of the assembly for reviewing the constitution he stated, "[I]t doesn't matter what the nationalists or a few obtuse kids said, they are not part of the Iranian nation."[84] Ten years later, in an interview in response to the question of what he saw as the major causes of the problems faced by the Islamic Republic, he said:

It is true that international pressure and war caused many hardships on the nation and the revolution. But if we could only go back to our pre-revolutionary Islamic and *nationalist* [emphasis is mine] concept of "unity of the word," and would not consider the revolution as exclusive to a partic-ular faction, and would extend our hand to all groups and individuals who believed in the revolution, the Islamic Republic, and its leadership, and would allow them to participate in building the country, then we would surely be able to overcome all our internal and external problems.[85]

Even though it appears that he was affirming what he had earlier declared to the Assembly of Experts (i.e., belief in the "leadership" of the Islamic Republic as a condition of inclusion), it is noteworthy that he now welcomed the "nationalists" (the groups that he had previously excluded from the Iranian nation) not only as part of the community, but as participants in rebuilding the country.

On the eve of the first decade of the revolution, Montazeri's judg-ment of the Islamic Republic's records was in a stark opposition to that of the rest of the elite in their celebratory, if not self-congratulatory, speeches. Whether he was conscious of the enormity of his action, Montazeri did indeed take off the gloves when he publicly confronted the state's deed and direction. Only a few days later, his critical ver-dict on the record of the Islamic Republic encountered severe public reaction.[86]

The first attack came on February 18, in a letter signed by three members of the elite: Mehdi Karrubi, the Speaker of the Parliament; Mehdi Emam Jamarani, a close friend of Ahmad Khomeini; and Hamid Rouhani, Ayatollah Khomeini's official biographer.[87] The letter, sup-posedly a private correspondence, was soon published in several media outlets, including the parliament's official bulletin, which was under the control of Rafsanjani. It targeted Montazeri's character and record, and criticized his family and advisors, including his daughter Ashraf, his son Ahmad, and his son-in-law Hadi Hashemi. The authors chas-tised Montazeri for his unfair criticism of the Islamic Republic, sug-gesting that it would only feed the propaganda machine of its enemies. They complained about his dogged effort to release political prisoners, whom they accused of engaging in terrorist acts after their release. They also attacked his economic position through a cryptic reference to his role in the shelved "*band-e jim*" concerning the previously mentioned and ill-fated land-confiscation policy. The letter ended with a warning to Montazeri to "purify" his office of unsavory characters, lest he do harm to Islam and to the revolution and hence be judged unfit to be the next leader.[88]

Four days later, Khomeini reacted to Montazeri's speech in his public message to the clerical establishment. Apologizing to the families of the martyrs for those critics who belittled the sacrifices of their loved ones, he said that he never regretted for one moment the decision to continue the war. Defending the war by listing its achievements, he told his audience not to forget that it was a mere episode in the unending struggle between right and wrong and that it was the Islamic Republic's duty to fight it.[89] Having framed it in these moral and religious terms, he concluded that the material end result of this particular war was of secondary importance.

Not long after making those remarks, and just four days before dismissing Montazeri, Khomeini sent another message, this time to the war refugees, in which, without naming Montazeri, he targeted him for criticism less ambiguously than in his previous message. He chastised the well-meaning but gullible people who had become the mouthpiece of the liberals and the hypocrites (*Mojahedin-e Khalq*). He hinted ominously to his once dear student that he had signed eternal brotherhood with no one, whatever position they occupied. He concluded by saying that if those who had become pawns in the hand of the enemy did not change their behavior, they would be mercilessly rejected by the people.[90]

Khomeini's accusations compelled Montazeri to write a letter explaining himself and his speech. He disputed the accusation that his words were due to the influence of enemies of the revolution and insisted that he had spoken on the basis of information he received for years from committed people in charge of many of the Islamic Republic's institutions, as well as from ordinary people who had sought his help in addressing the country's problems. He ended by expressing willingness to abide by Khomeini's judgment and keep his peace from then on.[91] But seeking reconciliation and surrendering to the order of the leader was not all that defined the letter. There was also a defiant tone to it that spoke of Montazeri's personality, as well as the agony he was feeling. On the one hand, he was incensed by the misdirection of the system, and couldn't hold his tongue; on the other, he realized that he might have gone too far in provoking his old mentor, who also happened to be the powerful leader of the country.

The conciliatory tone did not help. Four days later, on March 26, Khomeini sent a harsh letter to Montazeri.[92] Here, Khomeini asserted he was convinced that Montazeri would put the fate of the country and its people in the hands of the liberals and the hypocrites. Therefore, he had lost his legitimacy to be the next leader of the Islamic Republic. After dismissing Montazeri as his representative for collecting *sahm-e emam*, he advised him to purge his household of questionable individuals, to refrain from being the mouthpiece of the hypocrites, and to stay away from politics. If he failed to heed this advice, Khomeini threatened to do what his responsibility dictated. The letter was made public almost a decade later, after one of Montazeri's most direct attack on Ali Khamenei, the second Supreme Leader.

There are disagreements as to why Khomeini sent such a harsh message after Montazeri had conveyed his willingness to abide by his directives. According to Ahmad Montazeri, the letter was written not by Khomeini but by his son, Ahmad, who was rumored to have been in control of his father's affairs by then.[93] Not in dispute, though, is the fact that during the time between these two exchanges, an earlier private letter that Montazeri had written to Khomeini protesting the 1988 widespread executions of prisoners was leaked and broadcast by the BBC.[94] Montazeri's nemeses argued that his office leaked the letter in order to tarnish the face of the Islamic Republic. Montazeri's supporters, however, accused his enemies within the regime of having done this to anger Khomeini and to make a reconciliation between the two men impossible. The available evidence does not settle the matter, but the dynamic of the period allows for a probable hypothesis. Considering Montazeri's conciliatory letter, Khomeini's illness, and the prospect therefore of Montazeri's imminent ascendance to the position of Supreme Leader, it seems unlikely that Montazeri or his office would have leaked a letter written months earlier knowing that it inevitably would cause consternation.

Khomeini's harsh letter devastated Montazeri. But once his son had compared its handwriting with that of another letter written by Ahmad Khomeini, he took a sigh of relief that his mentor was not the author of such contempt and hostility.[95] Still, in response, Montazeri tendered his resignation in writing on March 27. He first reminded Khomeini that he had not sought the position of the Successor and that, in fact, he had implored Khomeini and the Assembly of Experts not to offer it to him. He continued that he was not ready for such a responsibility, and requested that Khomeini direct the Assembly of Experts to relieve him from the duty and allow him to return to the seminary as instructor and scholar. In the same letter, he addressed his supporters, asking them to refrain from acting or saying anything in protest. Khomeini "accepted" the resignation on March 28, and stated his belief that Montazeri could be a *faqih* whose views would benefit both the *howzeh* and the state. This was the last time that Khomeini wrote to Montazeri.

The break must have been hard for both men. To Khomeini, Montazeri was one of his two favorite pupils, "the fruit of his life," a man whom he trusted with important missions and responsibilities while in exile. And to Montazeri, Khomeini was a respected and revered mentor, a man who had fought courageously against a powerful state and had prevailed by sheer determination and unshakable faith. They had a long history together, but they also had characteristics that made a decisive break possible. Both men were stubborn. Khomeini believed that his past and present positions should make it clear to everyone that his final decisions were for the good of Islam and the revolution, and therefore must be obeyed. Montazeri, a blunt and argumentative man, was not one to submit to orders if he believed they were harmful to Islam and to the survival of a revolution for which he himself had fought and sacrificed.

There is a telling video shot at the end of 1987, less than three months after Mehdi Hashemi's execution and before Montazeri's ouster, in which both men appear, along with many other members of the political elite, including Rafsanjani and Khamenei. This was occasioned by Khomeini's delivering his revised will for keeping in a safe place, where it was not to be opened until after his death. The frail Khomeini speaks faintly and with an air of exhaustion. Soon after the meeting starts, he looks at Montazeri and asks him to assign two or three people to take the two copies of the will to the designated places. Montazeri, with an air akin to defiance or sarcasm, questions why he should be the one to choose these men, knowing well that he no longer has Khomeini's trust.[96]

Nonetheless, the personal history of the two men should not obscure the role played by some other influential figures in pulling Montazeri down. During his time as the Successor to Khomeini, Montazeri was a thorn in the side of various power holders, including some who had supported his appointment. They all knew that Montazeri could offend with his blunt manner, and while at the beginning they considered his criticisms *neq* (inconsequential nagging), many later came to the conclusion that they might have long-term negative consequence for their own policies and plans. Montazeri spared no one.

Among the powerful men whom he challenged were his three first supporters for the position: Rafsanjani, Khamenei, and Ahmad Khomeini. Rafsanjani was a politically astute man who wielded a great deal of power. Many believed that he was positioning himself to be the real captain of the state behind the figure of the Successor to Khomeini. Montazeri criticized Rafsanjani's performance as the acting commander in chief during the war and found him wanting in that position.[97] His critique of the state irritated Rafsanjani, who expressed his frustration in a circumspect manner in several journal entries. Years later, in an interview in 2011, he talked somewhat more openly about his thought regarding Montazeri's dismissal. Even though he acknowledged the latter's sense of duty, he criticized him for his lack of patience as well as his judgment as a statesman. He faulted him for his rush to go public about state matters, some of them confidential. He also saw Montazeri's ardent support for Mehdi Hashemi as an important factor in alienating a large number of people in power. He described as a flaw Montazeri's stubbornness and lack of interest in following the much repeated advice of statesmen, implying that he was not suited for the leadership of the Islamic Republic.[98] But Rafsanjani never accused Montazeri of opportunism or greed for power.

Montazeri's role in undermining the policy of arms for hostages, albeit indirect, was likely the most damaging factor in his relationship with Rafsanjani. Still, it seems that Rafsanjani did not wish to completely discredit Montazeri. According to many, he was the one who persuaded Khomeini, by begging and crying, not to make public his very harsh first letter of March 26 to Montazeri.

Montazeri's effort to help liberation movements in Afghanistan and, to a lesser degree, Palestine went against the approach of President Khamenei and his close associate Ali Akbar Velayati, the foreign minister. In Khamenei's factional battle with Prime Minister Musavi, Montazeri more often than not supported Musavi. There was also tension between the two men regarding a three-member committee assigned to coordinate the resistance movement in Iraq in 1988.[99] It is hard to know what role Khamenei played in any plot to oust

Montazeri. There is no clear evidence that he had any aspiration to replace Montazeri while the latter was still Khomeini's Designated Successor.

Ahmad Khomeini sought Montazeri's dismissal for his own mixed reasons. He wrote a long letter of complaint to Montazeri a month after the latter had been removed from his position. At the center of his complaint was Montazeri's failure to understand the wisdom of Ayatollah Khomeini and the disrespectful way he challenged the leader of the revolution, to the point that it made his father's "heart to bleed." Ahmad's eventual turn against Montazeri was ostensibly in defense of a revered father, but Montazeri and his supporters had a different view of his motivation. To them, it seemed that he had gradually developed a thirst for power of his own, as his father had become more frail, and that he perhaps wished to control the state, replacing his father as the leader of the revolution. There is no solid evidence that Ahmad had such an ambition, but he did become increasingly active in the political affairs of the country as his father became progressively ill, and he did support Montazeri's dismissal for months before it actually happened.[100] Both Ahmad Khomeini and Ali Khamenei were involved with Rafsanjani in the secret deal with the United States, and they both held Montazeri partly responsible for its unraveling.

Mohammad Rayshahri, the holder of several sensitive positions in the Islamic Republic, also had axes to grind. Montazeri's relentless criticism of the harsh treatment and execution of prisoners and his repeated warning that the powerful Ministry of Information was run by unqualified zealots angered Rayshahri, who, according to Montazeri, was heavily in favor of the executions and wanted to expand his own turf. A contributing factor to Rayshahri's problem with Montazeri might have been personal. According to a widely believed story, Rayshahri pursued Mehdi Hashemi in order to discredit Montazeri so that his own father-in-law, Ayatollah Ali Meshkini, could assume the position of Designated Successor. Rayshahri, predictably, denied the charge.[101]

Montazeri's later position on the IRGC was not appreciated by some of its powerful commanders, such as Mohsen Rezai and Rahim Safavi. After his initial support for the IRGC against the regular army, a cause for Bani Sadr's annoyance with him, Montazeri began to change his thinking as the IRGC exerted its command to the detriment of the regular army. His reevaluation was construed by his detractors as important evidence of Mehdi Hashemi's influence on him. They pointed out that his criticism of the IRGC started when the unit of Liberation Movements of the Guard was eliminated and Hashemi was thrown out of the Guard.[102] Within a year and a half after the war started, the IRGC, which had the support of many powerful officials, took control of the war effort at the expense of the regular army, despite the army's effective performance up to that point.[103] Confident of its support base, the IRGC refused to share power with the army, a refusal which resulted in devastating consequences for some of Iran's major operations. Throughout this period, Montazeri's office was open to many, including frustrated army officers and the rank and file of both the army and the IRGC, who came with complaints about their commanders. The steady expansion of the institutional power of the IRGC ultimately led Montazeri to write Khomeini with a warning against the consequence of giving the IRGC undue power in the war.[104] IRGC leaders and their backers recognized that Montazeri was an impediment to their ambitions and were happy to see him go.

Montazeri continued to have supporters, though. Close to 100 parliamentary representatives were among his backers and followers, as were an undetermined number of members of the IRGC and the army. He was the source of emulation for most of these people. Due to his authority to assign Friday Prayer leaders, Montazeri had a nationwide network of support. His simplicity, his constant public appeal for justice, and his defense of the underdog made him a "man of the people," and attracted many from among the populace. He also drew supporters from the educated middle class. Many of those who had not taken him seriously at the beginning of the revolution came to respect his firmness in trying to challenge some of the harsh policies of the state. But despite his support among these varied groups, Montazeri was in no position to fight back. The constellation of forces against him was too powerful. The men in charge of the machinery of the state and, above all, the charismatic leader had sided against him, ending his career as the second most important official of the Islamic Republic. That end, however, was the beginning of another era of his political life: the life of a relentless dissident.

Notes

1 Interview with Montazeri, *Kayhan*, July 11, 1979, 6.
2 *Kayhan*, May 27, 1979, 6.

3 For example, see Karim Sanjabi's views on Montazeri in his *Omid ha va na-Omidiha*, 372.

4 See the entire speech of Khomeini upon his arrival to Qom from Tehran on March 1, 1979 in Khomeini, *Sahifeh Imam Khomeini*, vol. 6.

5 Khomeini, *Sahifeh Imam Khomeini*, vol. 5, January 21, 1979.

6 For a detailed analysis of the evolution and differences among all these drafts, see Siavush Randjbar Daemi, "Building the Islamic State: The Draft Constitution of 1979 Reconsidered," *Iranian Studies* 46, no. 4 (2013): 641–63.

7 The June draft can be accessed through the official site of Abbas Amir-Entezam, the spokesperson of the Provisional Government, at http://www.iran-amirentezam.com/node/31.

8 Randjbar Daemi, "Building the Islamic State," 652–3.

9 See the text of this pamphlet in Montazeri, *Memoirs*, app. 59, 486–97.

10 Interestingly, Rafsanjani's argument against a constitutional assembly was based on his expressed fear that in the feverish post-revolutionary environment, the overwhelming majority of such an elected assembly would come from the rank of the clerics and that the final draft prepared by such an assembly would be so drastically reactionary that the seculars would "bite their fingers out of regret." See Ezatollah Sahabi, *Nagofteh haye Enqelab va Mabahes-e Bonyadi-i Melli* [The Unsaid of the Revolution and the Fundamental National Issues] (Tehran: Gam-e Nou, 2004), 228–30.

11 Taleqani with 2 016 851 votes, Bani Sadr with 1 713 126 votes, and Montazeri with 1 673 960 votes were the three top vote-getters of the elections. See *Kayhan*, August 11, 1979, 3.

12 See *The Proceedings of the Assembly for the Final Review of the Constitution of the Islamic Republic* (Tehran: Office of Cultural Affairs and Public Relations of the Islamic Consultative Assembly, 1985), vols. 1–3.

13 Ibid., 1:21.

14 Ibid., 1:38.

15 Ibid., 1:450.

16 Ibid., 1:214. The original meaning of *towhid* is "monotheism," the oneness of god. Later, however, it found different connotations in Ali Shari'ati's ideas, the last of which was a "class-less society." See Rahnama, *An Islamic Utopian*, 199 and 285. Shari'ati also uses the term in his criticism of the clerical establishment. The *Mojahedin-e Khalq* adopted it to express similar positions.

17 Ali Shari'ati, "Ma va Iqbal," in *Majmou'eh Asar*, vol. 5 (Tehran: Elham, 1995), 141.

18 *Proceedings of the Assembly*, 1:107.

19 Ibid., 1:384.

20 Ibid., 1:777–8.

21 *Kayhan*, July 11, 1979, 6.

22 See, for example, Montazeri's speech in the thirtieth session of the AFRC, where he criticized those who in his views were enamored with Western ideas of the notion of liberal freedom. *Proceedings of the Assembly*, 1:770.

23 FBIS-MEA, November 15, 1980.

24 Ali Meshkini was the other cleric who wrote a preface to *Shahid-e Javid*, the controversial 1970 book. He was also the father-in-law of Rayshahri, the man who played the most important role in bringing down Mehdi Hashemi.

25 On a few occasions after Bani Sadr's ouster, Khomeini stated that he was not in favor of his presidency. However, some, including Ayatollah Mahdavi Kani, an original member of the Revolutionary Council, argued that Khomeini, despite warnings, strongly supported Bani Sadr's candidacy. Mahdavi Kani, *Memoirs*, 280–4.

26 For Bani Sadr's portrayal of Montazeri as opportunistic and irresponsible, see Hassan Bani Sadr, *My Turn to Speak*, trans. William Ford (Washington, DC: Brassy's US, 1991), 198–201.

27 *Kayhan*, January 3, 1981, 3.

28 Ibid., January 4, 1981, 2.

29 See, for example, his May 1 speech in condemnation of the protest of Mashhad clergy in support of Bani Sadr. FBIS, May 4, 1981.

30 *Kayhan*, February 21, 1981, 9.

31 See Beheshti on this issue in *Kayhan*, February 26, 1981, 16.

32 FBIS-SAS, June 19, 1981. Montazeri's son was part of the committee charged with investigating the charges of torture in prisons. He, along other members of the committee, stated that there was no indication of systematic torture and thus opposed Bani Sadr's allegation. Montazeri chose to believe the report of the committee and of his son.

33 For an elaboration on the factions and their stances in the 1980's, see Maziar Behrooz, "Factionalism in Iran under Khomeini," *Middle Eastern Studies* 27, no. 4 (1991): 597–614.

34 See the text of these measures at http://rc.majlis.ir/fa/law/show/98700.

35 Montazeri, *Memoirs*, 299–300.

36 Ibid., 297–8.

37 In a speech to some of the members of the parliament, he lamented the disappearance of revolutionary simplicity and its replacement with bureaucratization. FBIS, December 18, 1983.

38 Montazeri, *Memoirs*, app. 109, 530–1.

39 These speeches used to be available on YouTube (at http://www.youtube.com/watch?v=OYFNy61x0x4, last accesed May 2015).

Unfortunately, they are no longer available there at the time of publication.

40 Montazeri, *Memoirs*, app. 69, 503–5. In his own memoirs, Mohammad Rayshahri questions Montazeri's sincerity, arguing that Montazeri wrote the letter months after he was already chosen. But that is not exactly true: what Rayshahri is referring to is a meeting of the Assembly of Experts at which the matter was discussed several months before the actual vote – the vote itself took place about two months after Montazeri's September 4 letter.

41 According to Hashemi Rafsanjani, Montazeri's assumption of the position of heir was approved by two-thirds of the members of the assembly. See 'Ali Akbar Hashemi Rafsanjani, *Karnameh va Khaterat of Hashemi Rafsanjani, 1364: Omid va Delvapasi*, ed. Sara Lahuti (Tehran: Daftar Nashr Ma'aref Eslami, 2008), 317.

42 See http://news.bbc.co.uk/2/hi/middle_east/7458709.stm. Rouhani was soon attacked and put under house arrest. According to Montazeri, it was Rayshahri who ordered the assault. Rayshahri is silent about this incident. There were also clerics associated with the Grand Ayatollahs Golpayegani and Khoei who disfavored Montazeri's selection as the successor. See David Menashri, "Iran," *Middle East Contemporary Survey*, 10 (1986), 333.

43 See the text of Meshkini's letter in Montazeri, *Memoirs*, app. 69, 503–5.

44 Many of the Islamic Republic's foreign officials have been educated at Imam Sadiq University.

45 One of the most publicized of these acts was Montazeri's expulsion from the board of trustees of Imam Sadiq University. The man who replaced him and who took credit for the school was Ayatollah Mahdavi Kani.

46 Mehdi Bazargan, *Enqelab Iran dar Do Harekat*, 111.

47 Izadi, *Faqih-e Aliqadr*, 124–6.

48 Ibid., 125.

49 Within a month of the Soviets' invasion of Afghanistan, Montazeri, in a speech to a delegation participating in the World Liberation Movements Conference, said that "in the eyes of Iranians there is no distinction between Eastern and Western imperialists. There is no difference between Soviet Union and the United States." See FBIS, January 11, 1980.

50 FBIS-MEA, December 8, 1980.

51 Ahmad Sadeq Ardestani, *Zendeginameh Hojjat-ol Islam Shahid Mohammad Montazeri* [The Life Story of the Martyr Hojjat-ol Islam Mohammad Montazeri] (Qom: Mohammad, 1982).

52 *Kayhan*, May 21, 1979, 12.

53 The Sunnis and Shiis disagree on the birthday of the Prophet, and therefore each community celebrates a different day. However, the difference
is less than a week, and Montazeri's initiation of Unity Week in 1981
was intended to bridge this gap.

54 Olivier Roy, "Afghanistan: An Islamic War of Resistance," in *Fundamentalism and the State*, M. Marty and R. S. Appleby, eds. (Chicago,
IL: University of Chicago Press, 1993), 490–510.

55 See Robert L. Canfield, "New Trends among the Hazaras: From 'The
Amity of Wolves' to 'The Practice of Brotherhood,'" *Iranian Studies* 37
no. 2 (2004): 241–62.

56 Siegel, "The Case of Mehdi Hashemi."

57 See two of Rafsanjani's 1982 journal entries, one concerning Hashemi's
role in the raging factional fighting in Isfahan and a reference to Montazeri's office (July 19, 130), the other about a complaint raised by the
conservative SIQH regarding Montazeri and his office (September 22,
182).

58 The unit was dissolved and a new council was created by the parliament
at the end of 1982. From then on the affairs of liberation movements
were directed through Montazeri's office.

59 Rayshahri, *Memoirs*, 4:63–4.

60 These confessions were most probably the result of physical and mental
tortures. See Ervand Abrahamian, *Tortured Confessions: Prisons and
Public Recantations in Modern Iran* (Berkeley, CA: University of California Press, 1999): 162–7. See also Ahmad Montazeri's interview in
Jaras: http://www.rahesabz.net/story/89402/.

61 Montazeri, *Memoirs*, app.116, 537.

62 Siegel, "The Case of Mehdi Hashemi."

63 Among them were Rafsanjani, Khamenei, Ahmad Khomeini, and Hassan Rouhani, the man who would later be elected president in 2013.
Khomeini himself approved the deal, but how much of the detail he
was told is not quite clear.

64 When Qorbanifar did not collect the amount he had expected to receive
from Iran, he wrote two letters to Mohsen Kangarloo, the man in
charge of transferring the money, but also sent a copy of each to
Montazeri. See Montazeri, *Memoirs*, 328 and apps. 130 and 131,
555–67.

65 Montazeri, *Memoirs*, 288–9.

66 See the complete list of the twelve directives in Montazeri, *Memoirs*,
app. 64, 260–1.

67 The complete message can be found in FBIS-MEA, January 7, 1982.

68 Ibid., February 1, 1982.

69 'Ali Akbar Hashemi Rafsanjani, *Karnameh va Khaterat of Hashemi Rafsanjani, 1363: Be Su-ye Sarnevesht*, ed. Mohsen Hashemi (Tehran: Daftar Nashr Ma'aref Eslami, 2007).

70 Reza Afshar, *Human Rights in Iran: The Abuse of Cultural Relativism* (Philadelphia, PA: University of Pennsylvania Press, 2001), 104–18.

71 For a detailed description of the 1988 mass executions, see Abrahamian, *Tortured Confessions*, 209–28.

72 Montazeri, *Memoirs*, 353.

73 See Ahmad Montazeri's recollection at http://www.radiofarda.com/content/f7-AhmadMontazeri-over-executions-of-summer-1367/25112818.html.

74 Montazeri, *Memoirs*, app. 153, 353–54.

75 Ibid., app. 154, 354–5. The story of these prisoners was provided to him by a local judge who was disturbed by indiscriminate execution in his province. According to a newly publicized audio tape (see next paragraph), Montazeri said that Khomeini asked him to send the provincial judge to see Khomeini so that he could hear him first hand. According to Montazeri, Ahmad Khomeini prevented a meaningful give and take between the judge and his father. The entire audio tape can be accessed at http://www.bbc.com/persian/iran/2016/08/160809_l47_aud_montazeri_comment_on_executaion.

76 Montazeri, *Memoirs*, app. 156, 358.

77 http://www.bbc.com/persian/iran/2016/08/160809_l47_aud_montazeri_comment_on_executaion.

78 Montazeri, *Memoirs*, app. 155, 355–6.

79 Personal correspondence with Emaddedin Baghi, July 25, 2015.

80 According to Baghi, right before this man was to be set free the prison wardens executed him (http://www.emadbaghi.com/archives/000210php, last accessed October 2015).

81 See, for example, the memoirs of Efat Mahbaz, a female communist and former prisoner, at http://www.rahetudeh.com/rahetude/mataleb/mahbaz/mahbaz2.html.

82 FBIS-NES, February 13, 1989. Another part of this same speech can be accessed in the monthly *Arzeshha*, January–February 1998, 15.

83 Montazeri, *Memoirs*, 329–30. He explains his earlier public silence about the war as being due to his obedience to Khomeini as the leader. There is no independent verification of Montazeri's claim regarding his opposition to the war at an early stage. The only clue that points to his change of position (from an idealistic approach arguing for an invasion of Iraq and the toppling of Saddam, to a more sober and cautious attitude) can be found in two of Rafsanjani's typically cryptic journal entries in 1983, one from May 8, page 74, the other from July 29, page

129. The earliest document that shows Montazeri's support for the end of war is a written letter to Khomeini dated only a few months prior to Iran's acceptance of ceasefire. See Montazeri, *Memoirs*, app. 125, 544–8.

84 *Proceedings of the Assembly*, 2:1183.

85 Montazeri, *Memoirs*, app.162, 611.

86 In fact, the day after Montazeri's speech, Rafsanjani, in an interview with a French newspaper and in response to the tension surrounding Montazeri, stated that there would be no other Successor to Khomeini but "the Grand Ayatollah Montazeri."

87 All three were among the founders of the leftist organization *Majma'eh Rohaniyoun Mobarez*. Years later, however, Rouhani, who had joined the ranks of the conservatives, denied being a founder of the leftist MRM.

88 Montazeri, *Memoirs*, app. 167, 616–23. The tough accusations in the letter prompted an answer from Montazeri and a longer response from his son, Ahmad. See apps. 168 and 171.

89 The achievements that Khomeini listed consisted mostly of symbolic, non-material, and psychological matters, such as the unveiling of the dishonesty and hypocrisy of the superpowers, the strengthening of unity among people, and the teaching of the Muslim community the lesson of standing on their own feet. See Khomeini, *Sahifeh Imam Khomeini*, March 1989.

90 FBIS-NES, March 23, 1989.

91 Montazeri, *Memoirs*, 367–8.

92 See the text of the contested letter in *Arzeshha*, January–February 1998, 18.

93 Ahmad Montazeri contends that the substance of the letter betrays the fact that Khomeini, a learned man, could not have written it. As for the handwriting style, he is convinced that it belongs to Ahmad. For an elaboration on these points, see an interview with Ahmad Montazeri in *Jaras*, January 18, 2015.

94 There is also a story told by Bani Sadr that Montazeri's private letters to Khomeini were sent to Turkey and, through an emissary, to Bani Sadr, with a permission for use at the latter's discretion. See http://enghelabe-eslami.com/component/content/article/19-didgagha/maghalat/4269-2013-09-25-19-34-18.html.

95 Personal correspondence with Ahmad Montazeri.

96 https://www.youtube.com/watch?v=6MRnvzpTbOQ.

97 Montazeri, *Memoirs*, 324–5.

98 http://tarikhirani.ir/fa/news/20/bodyView/774/%D9%86%D8%A7%DA%AF%D9%81%D8%AA%D9%87%E2%80%8C%D9%87

%D8%A7%DB%8C.%D9%87%D8%A7%D8%B4%D9%85%DB
%8C.%D8%B1%D9%81%D8%B3%D9%86%D8%AC%D8%A7
%D9%86%DB%8C.%D8%A7%D8%B2.%D8%B9%D8%B2%D9
%84.%D8%A2%DB%8C%D8%AA%E2%80%8C%D8%A7%D9
%84%D9%84%D9%87.%D9%85%D9%86%D8%AA%D8%B8
%D8%B1%DB%8C.html.

99 Both Montazeri's representative on the committee and Khamenei were fighting over whose approach should prevail. Rafsanjani, in many of his daily journal entries, addresses this tension.

100 Again, Rafsanjani's memoirs, as opaque as they are on these matters, are a good source for getting a sense about Ahmad Khomeini and his positions.

101 See his denial in a televised interview in http://www.monazereh.ir/v-548.htm.

102 Salimi Namin, *Pasdasht*, 103–5. Montazeri's own account is that the Guard was seeking undue power at the expense of the army even though it lacked the latter's expertise. Hashemi Rafsanjani presents a picture that is quite close to Montazeri's claim; see http://www.ensani.ir/fa/content/45727/default.aspx.

103 See Hashemi Rafsanjani's description at http://www.ensani.ir/fa/content/45727/default.aspx.

104 Montazeri, *Memoirs*, app. 127, 549–52.

4 | *Life of a Dissident*

After his dismissal as the Designated Successor, Montazeri went back to what he enjoyed most: teaching and writing, away from the public eye. The state did its own part to make him invisible; by the order of Prime Minister Musavi, Montazeri's pictures were taken down from the walls of public offices and his giant mural images on buildings and billboards were whitewashed. Those in control of the Islamic Republic considered Montazeri a serious threat to the state and to themselves, and all kept a watchful eye on him.

In some respect, his detractors suspected him to be a bigger challenge to the Islamic Republic than he had been to the Pahlavi regime. The pre-revolutionary state had perceived him as a threat primarily due to his association with Khomeini, rather than his personal popularity among the general public. The only region where Montazeri had a truly independent reputation was in the province of Isfahan. Now he was a leader with a high national reputation, a man whose dismissal not only shook Iran but was noticed around the world. Even though his popularity did not match that of the charismatic Khomeini, he was officially the second most important public figure of the Islamic Republic. For that reason, statesmen and state-sanctioned media had paid him their greatest respect and publicly solicited his advice regarding both religious matters and state policies.

Throughout his years as the heir to Khomeini, Montazeri had also developed important supporters and followers in the state machinery and among the general public. He had around 100 supporters among the deputies of the Third Parliament, many of whom were his religious followers. He was the source of emulation for many within the army and the IRGC as well. Despite his appeal to his followers for calm, soon after his dismissal there were demonstrations in his hometown of Najafabad, where a number of people were reportedly killed. It was possible that if Khomeini were to die, a fast-approaching eventuality,

Montazeri's followers and supporters would mobilize their forces and demand his reinstatement, this time not as heir but as actual Supreme Leader. That possibility struck fear in the heart of those who had set the wheels rolling for Montazeri's ouster; they pursued a dual policy of suppressing his supporters and of discrediting the man himself. A large number of his followers within the army and the IRGC officer corps were arrested and charged with spying for the CIA within a month of his dismissal.[1]

The attempt to discredit Montazeri himself was made through the construction of a new narrative about his character and deeds. In building their story, his critics highlighted Montazeri's relationship with two men: Khomeini and Mehdi Hashemi. Montazeri's followers did the same to rehabilitate Montazeri and his record.

The Role of Khomeini

Within a few days after his dismissal, criticisms of Montazeri were aired publicly. The heads of the three branches of government remained silent, but their supportive media did the job. A series of varied editorials from major newspapers associated with the two dominant factions hit the stands.

One of the first editorials on the matter of dismissal and the roles of both Khomeini and Montazeri in the same appeared in the conservative daily *Resalat*, which was under the control of Ayatollah Azari Qomi. The editorial did not openly criticize Montazeri, nor did it directly address his suitability or lack thereof for the office of Supreme Leader. In an utterly religious tone, it interpreted Khomeini's decision to dismiss, and Montazeri's decision to accept, as the fulfillment of both men's duties to God and to Islam. Alluding to Khomeini's now-famous phrase in reference to Montazeri as the "fruit of my life," the editorial compared Khomeini to Abraham and Montazeri to Ishma'el, and rhetorically asked the following questions:

Where else in history but in the life of the prophets has there ever been such greatness when one sacrifices, like Abraham, the product of one's life to one's deity and for the interest of one's religion? Where in history can there be a child with such devotion, who like Ishma'el goes to the altar of love to be sacrificed for the sake of the divine interests of the Muslims, while uttering the beautiful words: "do what God commands"?[2]

Other editorials targeted Montazeri without inhibition and were nei-ther poetic nor circumspect. The daily *Jomhuri Esalmi* compared the character of Khomeini, a leader whose wisdom, foresight, and firmness saved the revolution and its fruits, with that of Montazeri, a gullible man whose naïvité and vulnerability to the state's enemies would have destroyed all the achievements of the revolution had he remained the Successor.[3] Other dailies, such as *Ettela'at*, followed suit. The *Tehran Times*, which had only recently supported Montazeri's criticism of the state, jumped on the bandwagon.

None of these editorials had the emotional and polemical weight of a long, open letter by Khomeini's son Ahmad, dated one month after Montazeri's dismissal. Called the "Chronicle of Suffering," this letter became a model for all subsequent narratives about both Montazeri and the events surrounding his downfall.[4] Ahmad contended that his wise father, despite his love for Montazeri, was never in favor of his appointment as the future leader of the Islamic Republic. His father knew well that his gullible student could be easily manipulated by sin-ister forces, and Montazeri, with his unrelenting defense of the ambi-tious and traitorous Mehdi Hashemi, had proved his mentor right. Still, Khomeini, Ahmad continued, gave him repeated chances to reform himself and his household; it was only after all efforts failed that he made the hard decision to dismiss his dear Montazeri for the sake of the present and future well-being of the Islamic community.

The sharp contrast in the official narrative between the indepen-dence of mind and infinite wisdom of Khomeini on the one hand, and the characteristic lack of judgment and sophistication of Montazeri on the other necessitated an explanation of Khomeini's earlier posi-tion: his lack of public opposition to Montazeri's appointment in 1985. Depending on how Khomeini's silence was interpreted, it could provide or deny legitimacy for any claim that Montazeri might have over future leadership of the state. For Montazeri's foes, Khomeini's harsh letter dated March 26, 1989, in which he professed never to have favored him for the post, was a key piece of evidence.

Khomeini had said the same thing about both Bazargan and Bani Sadr but only after their resignation and dismissal, respectively. In both cases, Rafsanjani, along with others in ranking positions, had recounted Khomeini's support for the appointments of both men, espe-cially for that of Bani Sadr. Moreover, there were rumors that Khomeini had not actually written the harsh letter to Montazeri, or that if he had, it was under the influence of Montazeri's enemies, such as Mohammad Rayshahri, the Minister of Information, and Ahmad Khomeini, with his easy access to his father. So it was crucial for Montazeri's nemeses to find other voices that could corroborate the content of the letter.

The most widely publicized voice of support came from Ayatollah Mohammadi-Gilani, a member of the Assembly of Experts and a man who resented Montazeri's defense of political prisoners while he himself was the Evin prison's head judge. According to him, before Montazeri's nomination got to the point of no return, Mohammadi-Gilani had paid a visit to Khomeini and expressed his reservations about Montazeri. He convinced Khomeini, who shared his own doubts about Montazeri and his associates, to put a stop to the nomination process. Khomeini, the story went, summoned Rafsanjani and told him about his reservations, but Rafsanjani defied Khomeini and went ahead with the plan.[5]

The supporters of Mohammadi-Gilani's account had no explanation for why Rafsanjani would defy Khomeini; they put their emphasis instead on Khomeini's own subsequent silence. They contented that he did not interfere and kept his silence because of his "antiauthoritarian nature" and trust in "his friends" who favored the nomination. To strengthen their argument about Khomeini's lack of further intervention, they pointed out that Montazeri's most "egregious" acts occurred *after* he became the Successor.[6]

Rafsanjani offered a different version of Khomeini's reaction to Montazeri's nomination. He said that even though the leader had expressed reservations about the nomination, his concern was not because he lacked confidence in Montazeri's character and abilities, but instead about the potential reactions of other contenders and their possible machinations to undermine the process and jeopardize the stability of the Islamic Republic.[7]

Montazeri and his supporters also challenged Mohammdi-Gilani's story. One of their points concerned Khomeini's assertive and decisive character. Had he not thought that Montazeri was a suitable candidate for the position, a position that could change the direction of the country, he would certainly have said so and intervened. As for the facts, Montazeri's supporters reminded people that from the early days of the revolution, Khomeini had put Montazeri in charge of many tasks, some of them quite sensitive. He routinely asked Montazeri to act on his behalf and to decide on important religious and political matters.

Khomeini's trust showed that he was not standing in the way of Montazeri's appointment but in fact was grooming him for the job.

The back-and-forth between Montazeri's supporters and detractors about this continued even after Montazeri's death. But the detractors' use of Khomeini's initial position regarding Montazeri's appointment paled in comparison to their utilization of Mehdi Hashemi as a device for discrediting Montazeri.

The Role of Mehdi Hashemi

Few if any of the numerous books, essays, and editorials critical of Montazeri since his dismissal have failed to mention Hashemi's story as a central point. Certain parts of the story, including Montazeri's feelings toward Hashemi and his reaction to his arrest and trial, have never been in dispute. Montazeri trusted and ardently defended Hashemi, the son of one of his mentors, for as long as he could, and in the process of doing so locked horns with many, above all Khomeini. After Hashemi's arrest (see Chapter 3) and Montazeri's initial protests, Khomeini wrote to Montazeri and warned him that due to his association with Mehdi Hashemi, his lofty reputation was in danger, and asked him either to cooperate with the Ministry of Information's efforts to prosecute Hashemi or to remain silent. With a polite tone, Khomeini also criticized Montazeri for his trusting attitude, the lack of protocol shown in his rush to go public without properly judging the information he had received, and his tenderness toward the *Mojahedin-e Khalq*.[8] Montazeri soon responded with his own letter. In it, he addressed not only the Hashemi affair, but also an array of economic, political, and foreign policy issues, including the dismal situations in prisons. His defiance was obvious from the very beginning of the letter. He said:

Based on your gradually [and newly] formed view of me I am either a simpleton, a gullible person whose ideas are developed by the directive of men such as Hashemi...or I am a person who in addition to reading and listening to an array of contradictory accounts, meets every day, for at least two hours, with people from all walks of life including cabinet ministers, parliamentarians, officials from the Revolutionary Guards, the army, the bureaucracy, and the judiciary, not to mention workers, Bazaaris...And therefore have some independence of mind, some autonomous will.[9]

Then he delivered his first punch:

If the first presumption about me is correct then yours and others' praise and support for me is misguided. [And] for the future of this country and the revolution you need to make some serious adjustment . . . that responsibility falls first and foremost on the shoulder of the founder of this revolution, and, do not mind me, I have not one iota of interest in high position. If the second assumption is correct then please entertain the thought that what I am about to say in this letter might be correct.

He then brought up Hashemi's case. He spoke of his trust in him and questioned the motives of the Ministry of Information in its pursuit of Hashemi and other people close to himself, fearing that the arrest was a sinister ploy to create a rift between him and Khomeini. In a particularly sharp paragraph, Montazeri added that the only reason Hashemi was out of favor was because he was not a "*boz-e akhvash*," a stupid person who, like a goat, only shook his head in agreement with whatever he heard.

His strong and unwavering defense of Hashemi, and his refusal to heed several appeals, requests, and warnings by power holders, provided his detractors with the perfect opportunity to attack his character as unsuitable for leadership. Long before Hashemi was arrested, his activities had alarmed such men as Rafsanjani, who reportedly approached Montazeri and offered to give Hashemi a diplomatic position in order to get him out of the country. Montazeri refused to intervene, replying that the decision was Hashemi's and not his.[10] In another reported episode, Ahmad Khomeini and the leftist Musavi Khoiniha, the Islamic Republic prosecutor, paid Montazeri a visit and showed him evidence of Hashemi's pre-revolutionary cooperation with the Savak. Once again, Montazeri was asked to intervene by convincing Hashemi to leave Iran for a position abroad, and again he refused.

At the heart of the controversy over Montazeri's attitude toward Hashemi were Hashemi's character, intentions, and deeds, as well as the fairness of the process by which he was arrested, put on trial, and executed. Was he a traitor intent on sabotaging the revolution and the Islamic Republic, as he was charged, or was he, despite certain character flaws, a dedicated revolutionary and sincere in his devotion to Khomeini? Hashemi's "confessions" portrayed him as a criminal, a murderer, and an ambitious man. He confessed to having been involved in plotting murders, including that of Ayatollah Shamsabadi, prior to the revolution. He confessed that to escape execution he had sold his soul to the devil by becoming a Savak informant.[11] He also confessed

that he had been greedy for power and had wished to reach its pin-
nacle by sabotaging the interest and security of the Islamic Republic.
Finally, he added that he had used the trusting and naïve Ayatollah
Montazeri to accomplish all his sinister goals. Particularly damaging
for Montazeri was Hashemi's statement about his own effort to place
liberals and "hypocrites" in Montazeri's office in order to weaken the
Islamic Republic.[12]

After Hashemi's televised confession and his execution, Montazeri
wrote Khomeini, at last condemning Hashemi and his actions. This
was added to the evidence of Montazeri's unsuitability for leadership,
his critics accusing him of opportunism.[13]

The efforts to use Hashemi's confessions as a weapon to discredit
Montazeri did not go unanswered. The counternarrative to the official
story began with a questioning of the televised confessions. Both pre-
and post-revolutionary states were known for their use of such confessions, and there was little doubt that they were extracted under some
form of torture or deceptive promises.[14] Rejecting the validity of Hah-
semi's public utterances, the counternarrative focused on factional politics and power struggles within the Islamic Republic. In his *Vaqe'iyat-
ha va Qezavat-ha*, which provided the most detailed response to the
accusations made against Montazeri, Emaddedin Baghi conceded that
Hashemi's overbearing character offended and angered many people
and was indeed a problem. But Baghi challenged the portrayal of
Hashemi as a traitor and attributed the hostility toward him to the
internal conflict within the Third Line. A short-lived and obscure faction, the Third Line was founded by Ahmad Khomeini in1980 and
included both Hadi and Mehdi Hashemi as members. Baghi stated
that the conflict within the faction saw Ahmad Khomeini and the
two Hashemi brothers on opposing sides.[15] According to this account,
Ahmad was supportive of Bani Sadr and the *Mojahedin-e Khalq*, while
the Hashemi brothers were critical of both.[16] Baghi also challenged
as fabrication Rayshahri's claims about Hashemi's involvement in the
pre-revolutionary murders, his association with Savak, his plot to sabotage the Islamic Republic, and his undue influence on Montazeri. Baghi
asserted that it was unreasonable to demand Montazeri prematurely
condemn Hashemi, and concluded that no responsible person in Montazeri's position would have done so.

Montazeri's own recounting of his reasons for defending Hashemi
did the most for his case. He did not deny his attachment to Hashemi,

whose fate, arrest, and trial were emotionally and politically devastating to him. He had long trusted Hashemi, thought of him as bright, energetic, a skilled orator, a man whose dedication to the cause of the liberation of oppressed people was undeniable. Because of Hashemi's close friendship with Montazeri's beloved son Mohammad, who was killed, the father felt a special closeness and trust toward Hashemi. Other family connections also stirred his feelings. His household was stunned and saddened by Hashemi's arrest. Hadi, his son-in-law, and Ashraf, Hadi's wife, were particularly affected. Mehdi's elderly mother added to the pressure by repeatedly appealing to him to do whatever was possible to save her son.

But in defending his refusal to cooperate with the state against Hashemi, Montazeri focused on the legal procedures that were used in arresting, charging, and executing Hashemi. In the book *Enteqad-e az Khod* (Self-Criticism), Montazeri's son Sa'id asked his father two questions about Hashemi, one concerning his guilt or innocence, the other the reasons for Montazeri's adamant refusal to condemn him. In response, Montazeri stated:

I have suspended my judgment about all the murders that have been attributed to Mr. Sayyed Mehdi Hashemi and his friends. I cannot, either rationally or legally, form a definite opinion about them because the procedures which were used were [non-transparent], unfair, and politically motivated...as for the reasons for my sensitivity toward the case there were several. One was allowing the Ministry of Information to handle the investigation/interrogation and the creation of a special court just for the sake of trying Hashemi. Another reason was the widespread arrest of several young clergymen and personnel of the Revolutionary Guards, all of whom were under my supervision, right after Hashemi's arrest. These arrests and the subsequent treatment of the detainees convinced me that Hashemi's affair was only a pretext for embarking on a political purge[17]...And, finally, the fact that a court whose prosecutor was Mr. Fallahian, Mr. Rayshahri's replacement as Minister of Information, could not have possibly been objective...No one in charge of [Hashemi's] file was an independent agent, they all had ties to a faction whose animosity toward me and people associated with me became clear years later...These are the reasons for my sensitivity.[18]

Earlier in his memoirs, Montazeri had expressed in clearer terms what he thought of the reliability of Hashemi's forced confessions. But neither Montazeri nor his supporters had the means to disseminate their message. The threat against anyone who would challenge the official story was so real that Baghi's book appeared on Montazeri's website as the work of an anonymous author. Two decades later, when Baghi was arrested, one of the charges against him was the authorship of this book.

Along with the discursive method used to discredit and marginalize Montazeri were actions intended to ensure a smooth succession of power from Khomeini to a next, but different, Supreme Leader.

The Amended Constitution and the Victory of Politics over Religion

In April 1989, soon after the dismissal of Montazeri, a barrage of newspaper articles and editorials urged a speedy revision to the constitution. Along with this public effort were letters to Khomeini by some parliamentarians and members of the Supreme Judiciary Council asking the same.[19] The haste was due to an awareness of Khomeini's imminent death. With his departure, the most important pillar of stability would be lost, and any subsequent attempt to make major changes in the constitution could encounter swift opposition and result in the instability of the Islamic Republic. Therefore, on April 23, Khomeini issued an order for the creation of a twenty-member assembly to amend the constitution. The assembly had members from all major institutions of the state; its charge consisted of eight tasks, including reviews of the executive, judiciary, and legislative branches as well as of the office of the Supreme Leader.

One of the most far-reaching acts of this assembly was the inclusion in the constitution an Expediency Discernment Council of the System (or, in short, the Expediency Council), a newly formed institution whose charge was to adjudicate disputes between the parliament and the Guardian Council. Throughout the 1980's there were intense and frequent fights between the leftist parliament and the conservative Guardian Council. The Guardian Council had the constitutional authority to veto any bill passed by the legislative body on two grounds: the first on the basis of the financial burden of the bill, the second on its incompatibility with Islamic laws. It was the second that became a source of contention. During the tenure of the leftist Prime Minister Mir Hossein Musavi, the parliament had passed several bills, particularly in the area of redistribution of wealth, which the

Guardian Council deemed un-Islamic and therefore vetoed. On occasion, Khomeini had intervened and resolved the issue.

Such an ad hoc solution was not sustainable or desirable, so Khomeini, upon the request of the heads of the three branches of government and his own son, ordered the formation of the Expediency Council in February 1988. The Expediency Council was to make its decision with only one goal in mind: the promotion of the interest of the state, even if it clashed with Islamic laws. Khomeini emphasized this point when he announced, "Gentlemen be aware that the interest of the regime [of the Islamic Republic] is of prime importance and neglecting it sometimes leads to the defeat of dear Islam."[20] With this announcement, he gave power to the *ahkam-e hokumati* (state ordinances) to abrogate any Islamic law if necessary. The creation of the Expediency Council undermined substantially the institutional power of the Guardian Council as the protector of religious laws in politics and in the affairs of the state. Now, with its inclusion in the constitution, the Expediency Council became the permanent and legitimate body to make the final judgment on bills passed by the legislative body.

The trumping of the state's interests over religious laws was potentially problematic for a jurist like Montazeri, who believed that only well-established laws of Islam would protect society against the threat of arbitrariness.[21]

Another ominous sign that the Islamic Republic was on its way to privileging political exigencies over Islamic principles was a suggested change in the qualifications of the Supreme Leader. To the disappointment of many, particularly the high clergy, Khomeini, in his April 29, 1989 letter to the chair of the Assembly of Experts, regarding the qualification of *vali faqih*, wrote: "in this world of politics and deceit we should elect a person who can defend our Islamic dignity. From the beginning I was against making the qualification of 'source of emulation' as a condition for leadership... Being a just *mojtahed* would suffice."[22] The original Article 5 of the 1979 constitution, which combined the religious and political offices of *marja'iyat* and *velayat*, was befitting to Montazeri as Designated Successor to Khomeini. Most of the grand ayatollahs did not have the political records that Montazeri had, and those among the leaders of the Islamic Republic who met the political qualifications could not compete with Montazeri's religious credentials. With the suggested change in the qualifications, the field would become constitutionally open to many.

Khomeini died on June 3, 1989, before the amendments to the constitution were put to a referendum. The power holders of the state decided to keep his death secret for a few hours, until the decision on his replacement was settled in an emergency meeting of the Assembly of Experts. According to Rafsanjani, who chaired that important session, some members did not favor having one person at the helm of the state and wished to discuss the creation of a "leadership council," but they did not prevail.[23] Of the two nominated individuals, one, the Grand Ayatollah Mohammad Reza Golpaygani, secured only fourteen votes of the seventy-four available, while the other, Hojjat-ol-Eslam Ali Khameini, the president of the Islamic Republic, with years of political experience but without *marja'iyat*, received sixty. On June 5, the Assembly of Experts, which also decided to confer the title of ayatollah on Sayyed Ali Khamenei, declared him the Supreme Leader of the Islamic Republic.[24] On July 28, alongside the election of a new president, the referendum on the amendments to the constitution was held. Rafsanjani won the election to presidency, the referendum on the constitutional amendments passed, and the succession crisis that some feared and others hoped for never materialized.

With the separation of religious leadership (*marja'iyat*) from political leadership (*velayat*), an immediate campaign by state authorities got under way to keep the Supreme Source of Emulation in Qom rather than in Najaf. Their choice was the accommodating Ayatollah Mohammad Ali Araki, who sent a warm congratulatory message to Khamenei on his assumption of the office of Supreme Leader. There were of course other qualified ayatollahs – Ayatollahs Golpayegani, Sadeq Rouhani, and Montazeri, all of whom were residents of Qom – but none was as reliable to the state as Ayatollah Araki. While not a favorite of the most influential of the high clergy, Araki nonetheless received a partial consent.[25]

The elevation of Khamenei to the position of Supreme Leader did not receive the blessing of all high clergy, though there was no public statement in opposition to his selection.[26] Montazeri did not publicly oppose the selection of Khamenei, and in fact sent the new Supreme Leader a congratulatory letter. Years later, Montazeri stated that his gesture reflected the insistence of some of his colleagues and his own worries about the potential succession crisis.[27] Rafsanjani gives a different account in his memoirs, where he claims that he sought Montazeri's approval of Khamenei's appointment in exchange for supporting

Montazeri's selection as the Supreme Source of Emulation.[28] But in the same journal entry, Rafsanjani also mentions that he was involved in attempts to make the aged and politically accommodating Ayatollah Mohammad Ali Araki the Supreme Source of Emulation.

Montazeri did not vote for the amended constitution. Besides opposing absolute power for the Supreme Leader, he objected to having an Expediency Council sanctioned by the constitution. His opposition to any constitutional amendment was not surprising. Before he lost his position, he had written to Khomeini about the need for eventual amendments to the constitution but warned that it would be premature to presently start the process.[29]

Ousted from his political position, Montazeri no longer had the same means by which to reach out to the people. Yet he was able to express his views in classes, sermons, treatises, correspondence, and interviews, and he was determined to use them all. For the rest of his life, his actions were those of a dissident outside the formal power structure. On three occasions, the state or its associated vigilante groups reacted sharply to his acts of defiance. Two such incidents, one in 1990 and one in 1993, occurred during Rafsanjani's presidency. Still another, one that resulted in more than five years of house arrest, took place in 1997, under President Khatami's watch. Some of the confrontations between Montazeri and the state were over politics and state–society relations, while others were predominantly over religion, or more specifically over the position of the Supreme Source of Emulation. The first attack on Montazeri, orchestrated by the state in 1990, was closely entangled with the factional politics of the period, with the left and right under the control of the clerical organizations *Jam'eh Rohaniyat Mobarez* (The Society of Combatant Clergy, SCC) and *Majma'eh Rohaniyoun Mobarez* (The Association of Combatant Clergy, ACC), respectively.

The Rise of the Right

When Khomeini was alive, he often took the side of the leftist/statist group, but in general he tried to encourage a balance of power between the two. Lacking the charisma and authority of Khomeini, the new leader, Khamenei, chose another route; he decided to get the support of the right by weakening the leftist forces, many of whom were sympathetic to Montazeri.

In the summer of 1989, Sayyed Abdolkarim Musavi Ardebili, the left-leaning head of the judiciary, was replaced by the conservative Ayatollah Mohammad Yazdi. The conservative Guardian Council interpreted its supervisory role in elections as including the vetting of candidates for both the parliament and the Assembly of Experts.[30] By the end of January 1990, the Assembly of Experts itself decided to change its own bylaws and thus restricted its membership to "individuals who are more reliable."[31] On the overtly punitive side, Khamenei expanded the geographical reach of the Special Court of the Clergy by ordering the creation of new branches under the control of the rightist forces in several regions.[32] All these measures came at the expense of the left-leaning groups.

The Rafsanjani administration's ambitious reconstruction policies, which involved liberalization of the economy and borrowing from foreign sources, further weakened the leftist position. The only important institution that the leftists still controlled was the parliament, and some of its members tried to use its podium to fight back. The first major opportunity came with the trip of Nicolae Ceausescu to Iran in December of 1989, which caused a mini-crisis for the right-leaning Foreign Ministry.[33] Soon after Ceausescu's return to Romania, his rule collapsed and he was executed. Ceausescu's official trip to Iran showed a glaring misreading of the international dynamic within the Soviet bloc by the Islamic Republic and embarrassed its custodians. Even before Ceausescu's execution, more than eighty members of the parliament, many of whom were Montazeri sympathizers, signed a petition and requested the impeachment of Ali Akbar Velayati, Rafsanjani's foreign minister.[34] Criticism of the visit was also made by the media.[35]

Sensing the gathering of a storm, Khamenei gave a speech in which he sharply rebuked the critics and asked everyone to remain faithful to the principle of "unity of the word."[36] Rafsanjani, in his own televised speech, supported Khamenei's "fatherly reprimand" and advised everyone to toe the line.[37] But many parliamentary deputies, the main targets of both speeches, showed their defiance by refusing to sign a parliamentary letter of support for Khamenei's directive.[38]

Along with their attack on foreign policy, some of the leftist members of the parliament, such as the ever controversial Sadeq Khalkhali, targetted the government's new economic policies.[39] Their criticism, however, was quite mild compared to what would soon come from Montazeri. Rafsanjani's decision to borrow from foreign financial institutions was a controversial move for a state that still professed revolutionary values such as "independence from global arrogance" and "support for the downtrodden." Montazeri raised his voice in defense of those values, without which he believed the revolution was for naught. Independence was at their core, and foreign borrowing, in his view, was its antithesis.

It was in the midst of the crisis caused by Ceausescu's trip that Montazeri launched his attack. Starting with a letter addressed to the parliament, followed by a public sermon, and continuing with a speech in his seminary class, all within the span of a week, Montazeri forcefully took the government to task. During his sermon, where a large number of the listeners had come from his hometown of Najafabad, he spoke of how the Pahlavi regime's policy of foreign borrowing, along with its corollary granting of legal immunity to American personnel, had sparked a protest movement under Khomeini's leadership. He argued that adopting this policy would destroy a revolution for which so many people had given their blood; he echoed his pre-revolutionary sermons at the Najafabad Friday Prayers by advising his listeners not to forget their social and Islamic responsibility of "promoting the good and prohibiting the bad."[40] The speech touched upon several sensitive issues, including his own sacrifices for the revolution and the humiliating and harsh treatment he had received in return, and it had all the ingredients to anger the government.

Soon after his speech in seminary, a group of demonstrators congregated in front of his house, chanting slogans such as "Death to Liberals" and "Death to Anti *Velayat-e Faqih*."[41] In their slogans, they also stripped Montazeri of his title of ayatollah. Led by several Friday Prayer leaders, the demonstrations soon spread to Shiraz, Ahvaz, and Shahrud.[42] Two days after his speech, Khamenei appointed Rayshahri, Montazeri's ardent nemesis, as the prosecutor of the Special Court for the Clergy. He ended his letter of appointment with these words: "The violations [by clergy] should be dealt with decisively and in keeping with Islamic laws. It is hoped that – as has already been witnessed from you, that by relying upon God and placing your trust in the judicial justice of Islam – you will accept this grave responsibility."[43]

Emboldened by his appointment, Rayshahri added his own menacing statements. In Isfahan, near Montazeri's birthplace, he attacked him by reminding his audience of the Mehdi Hashemi affair.[44] He used this and other occasions to threaten Montazeri, boasting about having executed fourteen clergy (he called them "pseudo clergy") and disbarred another 286 in Qom alone since the reestablishment of the Special Court of the Clergy.[45] Angered by this cascade of attacks, a group of Montazeri's students and followers wrote to over a dozen institutions and individuals, including the Supreme Leader and the heads of three branches of the government, registering their dismay and demanding an end to threats against Montazeri.[46]

After their projection of force, the state and its supporters eventually slowed the pace of attacks on Montazeri, only to pick it up again a few months later. This time, they spread anti-Montazeri messages through books and essays, starting with the publication of Rayshahri's memoirs in the middle of 1990. Soon thereafter, a two-part article co-authored by two of Montazeri's detractors appeared in the daily *Jomhuri Eslami* on two consecutive days. What distinguished this article from previous ones was its use of Mehdi Hashemi's affair to cast doubt not only on Montazeri's *political* qualifications but also on his *religious* credentials and status as a source of emulation.[47] At the heart of the argument – particularly on the part of one of its authors, Baqer Alavi – was the claim that Montazeri's contradictory reaction to the Hashemi affair demonstrated that he was not only gullible but was also "devoid of all principle of faith and practical piety." This was no ordinary charge. It was one thing to attack Montazeri's political qualifications but quite another to insult him as a source of emulation. Such an act required a response. About ten days later, in consecutive sessions of the parliament, two deputies took the authors to task for their assault on Montazeri's religious credentials.[48]

Montazeri did not publicly react to these painful and personal attacks, but his silence did not extend to social and political matters. At the end of October 1991, Montazeri, prompted by the Madrid Peace Conference on the Israeli-Palestinian conflict, took to the pulpit. He chastised Sunni Muslim leaders for their betrayal of the Palestinians, and then addressed his own Shii colleagues, saying:

Today is the day that silence is a sin. The *howzeh*, the religious scholars, and the sources of emulation should raise their voices...If we can't be of any help and our voice doesn't reach anyone at least by closing our classes and by marching in the street we can make a whimper...We should all declare a general day of mourning."[49]

His students and followers heeded his request and hundreds marched in the streets of Qom in solidarity with the Palestinians. Prior to his speech, the leftist members of parliament had convened an international conference on Palestine on October 19. Knowing Montazeri's deep feeling of responsibility toward the Palestinians, 100 or so deputies went to Qom to brief him about this conference. Rayshahri, who took this event as an objectionable political gesture, ordered one of Montazeri's visitors, Hojjat-ol-Islam Hossein Hashemian, the Deputy Speaker of the Parliament, to appear before the Special Court of the Clergy. He put others on notice.

In response, Morteza Alviri, another member of the parliament, used the assembly's podium to defend Montazeri, Hashemian, and the trip to Qom.[50] He pointed out that Montazeri was one of the highest sources of emulation and that people who visited him did so because they were his religious followers. Alviri defiantly reminded his audience that it was the right of every Muslim to choose their own source of emulation and that for that, one needed no permission. Not surprisingly, Alviri's speech was attacked the next day, in the November 18 editorials of three major conservative dailies: *Kayhan, Resalat,* and *Jomhuri Eslami.* While these editorials criticized Alviri for his entire speech, they reserved their harshest assault for his support of Montazeri.

Alviri's speech also criticized the Guardian Council and warned against the negative consequences of the council's new interpretation of its own power in supervising elections. Predictably, the Guardian Council used its newly acquired power with devastating results for the left when it rejected the qualifications of forty members of the Third Session of Parliament in their bid to run for the Fourth Session.[51] By midsummer 1991, all three branches of the government were securely in the hands of the non-leftist groups. Now Montazeri had even fewer supporters within state institutions.

The factional competition and state policies were only part of what created friction between Montazeri and those in power. By the beginning of 1993, the fate of the office of *marja'iyat* had become the major cause of his troubled relations with the state.

Marja'iyat and its Political Fall-out

The history of the institution of *Marja'iyat-e Tamm* (Supreme Source of Emulation) is fraught with complexity and confusion. As briefly explained in Chapter 1, this position developed late in the nineteenth century but remained a contested office until the 1950's, when

Ayatollah Borujerdi was accepted as the Supreme *Marja'* for all Shiis. Following the 1979 revolution, Ayatollah Khomeini occupied this position. But after his death, given that there were several qualified *marja'*, the office of Supreme Source of Emulation once again became contested. Since this position is vested with unparalleled religious authority, the question of who should be a source of emulation, and more importantly the supreme one, was of prime concern for the state and for Khamenei, who, despite his supreme political position, had not produced a *resale 'amalieh* and carried only the rank of junior clergy.[52] The logic of *velayat-e faqih* is as follows: since religious laws should inform politics, the person most eligible for the political leadership of the community is the one with the greatest religious knowledge, i.e., "the Supreme Source of Emulation." Before his death, Khomeini ordered a change in the qualification of the office, but this change left an unresolved conflict between the theory and the new practice. In the 1990's, the potential of this conflict to disadvantage Khamenei and benefit Montazeri caused fear among Khamenei's supporters.

From August 1992 to December 1994, the Shii community lost three of its major sources of emulation: Ayatollah Khoei in August 1992, Ayatollah Golpayegani in December 1993, and Ayatollah Mohammad Ali Araki in December 1994. Ever since Khamenei's selection as the supreme political leader, his allies had been doing their best to get the consent of the major sources of emulation to select him as the supreme religious authority, and thus to combine the two offices, which had been separated ever since Khomeini's death. The fact that Khamenei did not have the qualifications for the position made the task difficult, especially since the Shii establishment was traditionally autonomous and independent of the state. Most of its members wished to keep it that way. Moreover, the prestige of the religious establishment depended on choosing a Supreme *Marja'* who was a highly regarded religious scholar. Consequently, despite the effort of his political backers in the *howzeh*, Khamenei did not receive the support of many others and thus failed to secure this highest religious office for himself.

At the very least, Khamenei and those associated with him wanted to prevent Montazeri's rise to the position. They worried about unforeseen political consequences if he were to be selected, and were concerned with the efforts of his followers on his behalf. Adding to their consternation, on two occasions, one in 1993 and the other in 1997,

Montazeri pointedly criticized the custodians of the state, and above all Khamenei, for political failures and for meddling in the selection of the highest religious authority. Both speeches resulted in dramatic reactions from the state. He gave the first during the anniversary celebration of the revolution. A month earlier, a group of his supporters had been arrested and jailed, charged with illegal acts in support of Montazeri's *marja'iyat*. Among the charges was the complaint that they had distributed leaflets insulting Khamenei. Two of those arrested, Haj Davood Karimi and Mahmoud Dardkeshan, were veterans of the war and former commanders of the IRGC. Karimi, in particular, had an impeccable background as a war hero. Physically frail as a result of his war wounds, he was rumored to have been tortured by the state for the purpose of extracting a public confession about Montazeri's act of treason.[53]

Angered by these arrests and the reported maltreatment of the men, Montazeri gave a short speech on February 10, reminding the audience of his own and his family's sacrifices for the revolution. He urged people to participate in the celebration marches organized for the anniversary of the revolution as an expression of support for its values, but added that this celebration was not a statement of approval of the men in power: "If I have been quiet thus far, it has been for the sake of protecting the Islamic Revolution. Our situation is like that of those two women who were fighting over the same child, and after the judge ordered the child to be cut in half, the one who was the [real] mother gave up her right for the sake of her child's protection."[54] The inferences could not have been clearer.

It is hard to know for certain whether Montazeri gave this speech hoping that the marches might turn into a rejection of those now in control of the state, but if there was such a hope, as his detractors claimed, it did not materialize. Instead, the regime mobilized forces against him and his office. According to a communiqué released by Montazeri's office, a fabricated version of his speech was distributed among people who were then invited by certain "military organs" to protest against Montazeri in front of his house. The angry demonstrators pulled down the headboard of his office while shouting "Death to Montazeri." The disruption of his class the next day by hundreds of hecklers forced him to stop his lessons for a few weeks, hoping that in time things would calm down. But the greatest attack was yet to come. Three days after his speech, a massive military force destroyed the barricade around his house and office and invaded the Hosseiniyeh Shahid where he held his classes. The soldiers also stormed into his office, his documents' center, and his son-in-law's house, and took away boxes of documents along with money and office and household supplies. The authorities offered no account of these events, but the semi-official media criticized Montazeri for his ill-use of the Judgment of Solomon story, and defended the attacks against him as well deserved.

The reaction to his speech, dramatic as it was, did not lead to the arrest of Montazeri, his son, or his son-in-law.[55] Nonetheless, the deployment of such force against a source of emulation was grave and unprecedented in the Islamic Republic.[56] The din of bulldozers and fire trucks, of sawing into the metal barricade and through doors, and the blackout of a large section of the city for the sake of the operation stunned not just Montazeri's family but the entire neighborhood. He prayed while his wife, children, and grandchildren watched the destruction with terror. The projection of massive force against Montazeri made any public display of support for him close to impossible. According to some reports, however, there were demonstrations in his defense in Najafabad and Isfahan, leading to the arrests of many.[57]

Montazeri made no public statement after the attack, though a few months later he wrote an open letter, apparently not for immediate publication but for posterity.[58] It was left to his son Ahmad to become the spokesman for Montazeri and his household. He held interviews, wrote letters of protest, and responded to the accusations of the semi-official media. His son's emergence as the public persona of Montazeri's household and office was a deliberate decision to send a message that Montazeri was so insulted that he would not engage any further in explaining himself or responding to his attackers. The choice of Ahmad, whose manner of speech was different from that of his father, highlighted Montazeri's own daring and blunt style. The difference was particularly evident in Ahmad's response to questions from a reporter for the official Islamic Republic News Agency (IRNA) about the recent events.[59] Ahmad's answers were generally in tune with his father's, but his choice of words and his manner were studied and cautious. It was probably a wise decision for the time to select him as spokesman.

Another decision Montazeri made in consultation with his son was to replace his chief of staff Hadi Hashemi (his son-in-law and the brother of Mehdi Hashemi) with Sayyed Asghar Nazemzadeh, one of his former students, who had no radical political record. In previous cases the attacks on him and his office relied on such charges as recklessness and having connections with *Mojahedin-e Khalq* and the liberals, charges that always resurrected Mehdi Hashemi or targeted Hadi Hashemi as representative of all that was wrong with Montazeri's office. The ferocity of the latest attack affected Montazeri so profoundly that for the next three years he rarely addressed internal Iranian politics.

After a few months, the controversy died down, and the state kept its distance from him. With the death of Ayatollah Araki, the man whom the Islamic Republic considered its chosen Supreme *Marja'*, concerted efforts to promote Khamenei to the position began in earnest. Two clergymen, Ayatollah Mohammad Yazdi, the Chief of the Judiciary, and Hojjat-ol-Islam Ali Akbar Nateq Nouri, the Speaker of the Parliament, were particularly outspoken in their support for Khamenei's candidacy.[60] In their public statements during Friday Prayers and in other venues they argued that combining *marja'iyat* and political leadership would allow the global Shii community to receive unified religious guidance together with political strength. Several members of the *howzeh*, including some Friday Prayer leaders, also aligned themselves with Khamenei. In the meantime, the Society of Qom Seminary Scholars (SQSS) and Tehran's SCC included Khamenei in their list of acceptable sources of emulation. In addition to that of Khamenei, the SQSS offered six other names, while the SCC offered another two.

The appearance of Khamenei's name in these lists did not lead to automatic support for his assumption of the highest religious position among a large section of the religious establishment, particularly the many high clergy who refused to give their consent. In failing to ensure a clear consensus for Khamenei, his supporters began to backpedal by explaining the historical complexity and the democratic process involved in choosing sources of emulation. In his Friday Prayer sermon in Tehran, Ahmad Jannati, another ally of Khamenei, revealed that there was no consensus among the clergy for choosing one person as the Supreme Source of Emulation, and therefore it would be up to the emulators themselves to follow whomever they might wish.[61]

Montazeri's name did not appear in the published list of the two major and politically conservative clerical organizations, but he did have support in many quarters of the *howzeh* and remained a serious candidate. There were also other clerics who were not mentioned in the official media because of their refusal to lend support to the regime, but who were considered candidates by some Shii clergy residing outside Iran. Such speculations from abroad were broadcast by foreign media outlets and reached the ears of many Iranians who regularly listened to "tabooed" issues from stations such as BBC Persian through their shortwave radios. Unable to cut off access to the outside media, state officials responded by mobilizing a large number of Friday Prayer leaders to attack these speculations in their sermons and speeches around the country. The Supreme Leader himself gave the most important of these speeches on December 14, 1994, less than a month after Araki's death.[62]

Khamenei declared that, despite invitations from prominent people, he had declined to assume the position of Supreme Source of Emulation because of his heavy responsibility as the Supreme Leader.[63] Leaving the door open for the future, however, he added that if there came a time of need for him to shoulder the duty of *marja'iyat*, he would submit. In the same speech, he accused the foreign media of being the mouthpiece for a "Zionist Entity," labeled as "pseudo clergy" those religious men whose names were put forth as candidates, and accused the same men of having connections to the enemies of Islam. He ended this part of his speech with a warning: "The Iranian nation will not forgive traitors."

A few days after Khamenei's speech, Montazeri's lesson was once again disrupted by a mob that vandalized his classroom, referred to him as the "BBC's *marja'*," and called for his execution. Unlike the 1993 attack, this one was unprovoked: Montazeri had not made any speeches or issued any public statements critical of the state. Before Khamenei's speech, though, Montazeri had sent a letter to him through Ayatollah Mo'men, a member of both the Guardian Council and the Assembly of Experts. It was a private, admonitory, and blunt letter. He wrote that breaking the independence of the office of *marja'iyat* was against the interest of Islam and the Shiis, and advised Khamenei – who, Montazeri said, unlike Khomenei did not have the religious qualifications to be both a *marja'* and the *vali* (political leader) – to put a stop to the efforts by government officials to push for a union of the two offices.[64]

This letter aside, Montazeri had decided to keep a low public profile and had advised his office staff not to engage in a campaign on his behalf. Nevertheless, his followers continued to campaign through letters, leaflets, and meetings, particularly in Qom, to keep him in the public eye and to advocate his candidacy as the Supreme Source of Emulation. Fearful of Montazeri's popularity, the regime mobilized its forces to bring the dynamic in his favor to a halt by arresting several of his supporters and threatening many more.[65] There was a definite pattern to the actions and reactions on the part of Montazeri and/or his followers, on the one side, and the government, on the other. The authoritarian state would not tolerate independent critical voices, particularly from someone with such religious weight as Montazeri, and he and his followers were not ready to go silent. Yet the imbalance of power between him and the state almost always resulted in the temporary suppression of Montazeri and his followers.

For the next few years after the subject of *marja'iyat* was put on the back burner, Montazeri devoted most of his time to teaching and writing. Occasionally, he would make verbal or written statements regarding events that occurred outside Iran, such as condemning the ethnic cleansing in Bosnia or the Israeli attack on southern Lebanon. But with the election of the reformist Mohammad Khatami to the presidency in early 1997, and the excitement that it created, Montazeri broke his silence on Iranian politics.

Khatami's Presidency and the Reform Era

Mohammad Khatami won the presidential election in 1997. His victory and the fact that the Supreme Leader Khamenei supported his competitor, Ali Akbar Nateq Nouri, raised questions for students of Iranian politics. How could a regime – regularly referred to in the Western media and in some of its scholarly circles as totalitarian – allow a man whose programs revolved around political development and whose campaign slogans were primarily about freedom, civil society, pluralism, and tolerance to win the election?[66] In Iran itself, the result of the election created unprecedented hope for reform of the system among the winners and confusion and shock among the losers. Part of the surprise for everyone was the large margin of Khatami's victory: he received close to 70 percent of the votes in an election with an 88 percent voter turnout. The election energized a large part of the electorate and allowed a reformist discourse to flourish. There was a proliferation of varied newspapers and journals, and an Islamic feminist movement succeeded in making women and gender issues an important part of the reformist political discourse. The political opening of the Khatami era also brought to the fore a louder voice in support of Montazeri as an exalted religious leader, not only from his ordinary followers, but from some of the reformers in power.

Montazeri watched the rise of the Khatami phenomenon with great interest, as did his followers, who asked for his guidance during the 1997 elections. In response, Montazeri made a public statement in which he first advised the state to conduct a free and fair election and warned against treating the electorate as incapable children, and then addressed the voters and urged them to exercise their own judgment and resist the undue pressure of the propaganda machine.[67] If in the early days of the revolution Montazeri had trusted the state and distrusted people's judgment, in this message he conveyed the opposite sentiment.

After the election, in his letter of congratulations to Khatami, Montazeri expressed his hope that the new president would take the result as it was intended by the electorate: a vote of no confidence in the power establishment and a revolutionary act to compel the state to return to the genuine values of the revolution. He then wished Khatami success in carrying out the difficult job of setting things right, a responsibility entrusted to him by both the people and God.[68] The language of his congratulatory note, particularly his use of the words "revolutionary act," was not taken kindly by the authorities, and later those words were used against him. But, for the moment, Montazeri was obviously pleased with the result of the elections and pinned his hope on Khatami and the reform movement. An explosive sermon in 1997 was the most dramatic indication of his hope.

1997 Sermon and House Arrest

About three months into Khatami's first term, Montazeri gave a sermon on the birthday of Ali, the first Shii Imam, that proved to be his most controversial speech since the establishment of the Islamic Republic. His words were particularly serious not only for their reformist emphasis on the political rights of the people, but for their jurisprudentially framed disapproval of Khamenei and his performance as the Supreme Leader. He started with a mild criticism of Khamenei in which he juxtaposed two models of rule by the *faqih*. In the first and the proper model, the *faqih* would have only general supervisory authority, while in the second, the one presently exercised in the Islamic

Republic, the Supreme Leader presumed to dictate on all matters, large and small.

Montazeri delivered the punch when he revealed the contents of his own private letter to Khamenei upon the death of the Supreme Source of Emulation Ayatollah Araki in December of 1994. In that letter, Montazeri had challenged Khamenei's qualifications for *marja'iyat*. Midway in the sermon, he also mentioned that according to the authoritative *ravayat*, the Islamic political leader had to have the qualifications of an exalted source of emulation. In so many words, by rejecting Khamenei's qualifications as a source of emulation, Montazeri also judged him as unfit to hold the position of Supreme Leader.[69]

Several months later, while he was under house arrest, Montazeri mentioned his reasons for delivering that sermon, among which were the Shii establishment's gradual loss of its historical independence; the undue interference of the state in the religious affairs of Qom, which had endangered the institution of *marja'iyat*; and the obstacles created by some state institutions for Khatami's administration.[70] According to Mohsen Kadivar, the sermon followed a visit from Ayatollah Azari Qomi, a conservative clergy and previous supporter of Khamenei, who provided Montazeri with clear proof that Khamenei, through the SQSS, was planning to assume the role of the Supreme Source of Emulation.[71] Whatever prompted him to give the sermon just then, its tone and part of its substance were no doubt a reflection of Montazeri's trust in the potential for change imbedded in Khatami's era.

Montazeri miscalculated the change in the political atmosphere when, in the same speech, he dismissed the idea that he could be harmed by official media attacks or that he and his supporters would be intimidated by a group of wrong-headed "children." Contrary to his prediction, the reactions of his detractors were harsher than ever. A combination of vigilante groups and uniformed men attacked his office and his school and invaded and vandalized his house. Newspapers and powerful individuals, mostly conservative and ultraconservative, viciously assaulted him verbally. They called him both a simpleton and a symbol of "corruption and irreligiosity," and labelled his household "the second den of spies."[72] Some accused him of having worldly ambitions, and others threatened him with "cutting the head from the body of traitors."[73] A little over two weeks after his sermon, Khamenei gave a speech to a huge gathering of the Basij where he defended his office and attacked Montazeri without uttering his name.

Khamenei used the now familiar insults in referring to Montazeri as a naïve, ignorant, helpless, and impressionable man who unwittingly served as a fifth column for enemies of the Islamic Republic. Returning Montazeri's favor about qualifications for sources of emulation, Khamenei said that to be worthy of the status a source of emulation had to have enough political awareness not to be deceived by the enemy nor to repeat the political analysis of the "Israeli radio." By adding political awareness as a qualification of a *marja'*, Khamenei tried to challenge any claim that Montazeri might have had on the position of Supreme *Marja'iyat*. Finally, Khamenei emphasized the need for "legal actions" against those who "work for the enemy."[74]

By the order of the Islamic Republic High Council of National Security, whose chair was President Khatami, Montazeri was put under house arrest. Even though he was familiar with adversity, this was the first time that the Islamic Republic, his own "child," with the acquiescence, if not outright cooperation, of a reformist government, for which he had high hopes, had officially sentenced him to an undetermined period of house arrest. Years later, toward the end of his home imprisonment, Ali Motahhari, the son of his friend, received permission to visit Montazeri. The first thing the now frail Montazeri said to him was, "Ali, did you see what they have done to me?"[75] This brief utterance summed up all the sadness, frustration, and betrayal that Montazeri must have felt.

Now, for the first time, the harsh letter that Khomeini wrote to Montazeri on March 26, 1989, threatening him with dismissal, was published, providing fuel for a new round of attacks on him. His followers responded with a public letter of their own, protesting the attack on Montazeri's household. Another letter, signed by 385 of the members of Qom's *howzeh*, was sent to the high clergy, decrying Montazeri's sentence. There were also gatherings and strikes in his birthplace, Najafabad. Instead of diminishing him, as Khamenei and others would have liked, the house arrest brought more attention to Montazeri, not only in Iran but also abroad. Meanwhile, the attacks on Montazeri and his character continued. But whereas the earlier castigations of 1989 mocked only his "gullibility" and "naïvité," now he was being charged also with "political shrewdness" and "opportunism."[76]

Was there any truth to the charge of political ambition that his detractors leveled against him? It is likely that Montazeri thought of himself as the best qualified and most deserving person for the office

Figure 4.1 Montazeri with his son and advisor, Ahmad, a day before his release from house arrest, January 29, 2003. AFP/Getty Images

of supreme leadership. It is also probably true that he looked for a particularly opportune time to give his most pointed sermon. It is definitely true that he hoped the election of the reformist Khatami, with his promises of the rule of law, empowerment of the civil society, and expansion of freedom, would shake the power establishment and thus lead to drastic changes in the balance of power within the Islamic Republic. But to argue that his primary motivation in speaking out was a desire for personal power requires more convincing evidence than that provided by his critics, and Montazeri's followers pointed out the paucity of evidence effectively.

His supporters built their counternarrative on the key moments in his political life, one of which happened a few months before his dismissal. Everyone knew that Khomeini was gravely ill at that point and did not have much time to live. If Montazeri were truly power hungry, he would have kept his mouth shut for just a bit longer and would have refrained from criticizing the policies of the regime, particularly toward political prisoners and the war. It was his conscience rather than greed for power, his supporters argued, that guided Montazeri to say what he said and to do what he did. They also challenged the depiction of Montazeri as "shrewd and opportunist" by reminding of his behavior toward Mehdi Hashemi. A shrewd politician, one inclined to change his position opportunistically, would have discontinued his support for the clearly doomed Hashemi long before Montazeri did, and would not have sent such a terse letter to the most powerful leader of the Islamic Republic.

The counterarguments of Montazeri's supporters fell on deaf ears among the accusers, and his house arrest continued. During the five-year confinement, he had face-to-face contact only with his family and close relatives. He was banned from convening classes for religious students and from giving public sermons. Some of his students, such as Kadivar, went to his son's house and through an intercom spoke with him for hours about scholarly as well as political matters. The pupil found his mentor alert, full of mental energy, but also wistful about the restriction put on him to do what he loved to do best: see his students, discuss and argue with them face to face. The restrictions did not, however, extend to written correspondence, and Montazeri, who could not detach himself from politics, reacted to such dramatic events as the gruesome killings of a secular nationalist, Dariush Foruhar, and his wife; the accusations of apostasy leveled against two religious reformers; the bloody suppression of reformist university students; and the attempted assassination of Sa'id Hajjarian, the astute advisor of Khatami. Many sought his opinions about these and other matters, and his responses were publicized by reformist groups, journals, and newspapers. More than a few of these newspapers and their editors paid for the risks they took when their licenses were revoked by the state or they were summoned to court.[77] Of particular significance was the impeachment of Abdollah Nouri, Khatami's popular minister of the interior, by conservative members of the parliament in June 1998. They accused Nouri of undue support for forces loyal to Montazeri and "the gang of Mehdi Hashemi."[78] By a slim margin, the conservatives won a vote of no confidence against Nouri.[79] At the beginning of the third year of Khatmai's presidency, when Nouri had been appointed to his cabinet now as his advisor, they attacked him again. Summoned by the Special Court of the Clergy, Nouri was tried for insults and sins committed by his reformist newspaper, *Khordad*.[80] Among the charges against him was supporting normalizing relations with the United States, a deviation from the Line of the Imam (i.e., Khomeini). Other charges included the political promotion of Montazeri and defending Bazargan's Liberation Movement.[81]

The foreign media also took a renewed interest in Montazeri during his house arrest by soliciting his written responses on varied subjects, particularly political liberties. In the meantime, Montazeri's office created an official website (administered from abroad), an entirely new thing among sources of emulation, and this added a new challenge for the authorities, who were intent on isolating him. Within a month, part of his controversial *Memoirs* appeared on the Internet.[82] The *Memoirs* contained the most comprehensive counternarrative to what had been circulated in Iran by his critics since his fall from official power. Sensing its importance, these critics undertook to rebut the *Memoirs* in several lengthy volumes.[83]

The efforts of Montazeri's supporters to keep his voice heard did not go without additional punishment. His younger son, his grandson, his son-in-law, and more than half of his office staff were arrested on different occasions and charged with various violations. His son Sa'id and his son-in-law Hadi Hashemi were incarcerated for months. Throughout this period, and despite his depressed mood and physical ailments, Montazeri's voice became louder and stronger. The pamphlets "Velayat-e Faqih va Qanoun-e Asassi" (The Rule of Jurist and the Constitution) and "Hokumat Mardomi va Qanoun-e Assasi" (Democratic Rule and the Constitution) were products of that time. During the same period, Montazeri was sowing the seeds of many of his future jurisprudential writings, where he would shift his focus from the duty of people to their rights.

The sustained effort by Montazeri's close followers and some high clergy eventually led to public calls for his release. More than 100 parliamentary deputies signed a letter to Khatami demanding an end to the house arrest. The respected and popular Ayatollah Tahari Esfahani wrote to prominent sources of emulation in Qom pleading with them to act for Montazeri's release. The reformist organization of university students, *Daftar Tahkim-e Vahdat*, sent yet another letter to Khatami urging him to secure Montazeri's freedom. It was Montazeri's serious illness in the last few months of the house arrest that provided the immediate reason for lifting his sentence. Allowing him to die under the condition of house arrest could have turned him into a martyr, creating new headaches for the state. Eventually, despite disagreement among the elite, his house arrest was lifted on January 30, 2003. The frail Montazeri was soon admitted to a hospital in Qom but reportedly was prevented by the city's IRGC from traveling to Tehran for further medical treatment.

He spent the rest of his life living in a modest, unadorned room with a simple twin bed and a desk and chair. He would wake up in the early hours of the day, pray and recite a few verses of the Quran, take a stroll in his small garden, read newspapers, meet with groups of people who came from different parts of the country to visit him, bless little babies by whispering prayers in their ears at the request of their parents, respond to religious questions from his followers, and teach a small group of students. Due to his illness, he later ceased to teach students outside his own family circle, but he continued to convene a class for family members. He especially liked to teach *Nahjol Balagheh*, the religious text of Imam Ali, a revered leader whom he admired greatly and took as his model of justice and simplicity.

Figure 4.2 Montazeri with his loyal pupil, Mohsen Kadivar, on the day of his release from house arrest, January 30, 2003. Atta Kenare/AFP/Getty Images

Montazeri followed the political developments of the last few years of Khatami's presidency with despair and sadness. In response to a letter Khatami sent him toward the end of his second term, Montazeri wrote a harsh reply, addressed not to the president himself but to his office. He rejected Khatami's analysis of what had caused his reform programs to fail. Khatami had attributed the failures to the general culture: a culture beaten down by a long tradition of dictatorial rule, a culture that had made the people passive and in perpetual need of a hero to rescue them from injustice. Whether the culture was as dysfunctional as Khatami assessed, Montazeri replied, the reformists' responsibility was not to enable that culture but to challenge it. Instead of remaining quiet or turning into an apologist for the trustees and bearers of that culture, the president should have taken them to task. He had the support of twenty million voters, who had stood by him and elected him for a second time. In Montazeri's view, the least Khatami should have done in order to preserve his own dignity and retain some hope for the future of the reform movement was first to inform the people of the obstacles put in his path and then resign.[84] The result of his not having done so was that he left the people disillusioned and alienated from politics.

Montazeri's suggestions were reminiscent of his own past behavior when he took powerful forces to task. Despite his failure and the price he had paid, he never gave up on the idea that one should not compromise on principles. Whether Montazeri's assessment of Khatami's performance was correct – and he definitely showed some astuteness in his analysis – his approach was in reality more "passionate and idealistic" than "cool and realistic." It is almost impossible to know what would have happened if Khatami had done at the beginning of his term what Montazeri had expected him to do. Nonetheless, Montazeri's letter to Khatami provides yet another example of his approach to politics and political action.

The Post-reform Period

Montazeri was correct in at least one of his predictions about the outcome of Khatami's administrative style: the disillusionment of the populace with the reformist elite and their record. The next elections brought to power Mahmoud Ahmadinejad, a relatively unknown man whose campaign slogans shifted the emphasis from political openness

Figure 4.3 Montazeri in his study, 2005. Behrouz Mehri/AFP/Getty Images

to justice, virtue, and the well-being of the downtrodden. He mobilized a different segment of Iranians and defeated strong candidates such as Rafsanjani, men who were part of the established elite. A veteran of the war with Iraq, Ahmadinejad's political world was colored by his experiences of those horrible eight years, which made his support of revolutionary sacrifice and martyrdom stronger than before. To him, political development was a luxury of the upper-middle class and the elite, who in their flirtation with the "counter-values" of the colonial West would destroy the genuine principles for which the revolution was fought and won. The language of the early days of the revolution was revived by Ahmadinejad, who reversed the fragile accomplishments of the reform period, which aimed to expand the political space and to normalize relations with the outside world. For the next four years, the reformists watched helplessly as authoritarian and conservative forces gained the upper hand in setting the agenda for domestic and foreign policy.

During this period, Montazeri did not initiate any new criticism of the state. When questioned by foreign media and others, he repeated some of his earlier objections, but said nothing that would invite the state's violent reaction. Yet during the first term of Ahmadinejad's presidency, he wrote some of his most politically relevant and accessible books. The *Treatise on Rights, Religious Government and Rights of*

Humans, and *Islamic Punishment* gave his most extensive and original views on the rights of the people.

Montazeri: The Spiritual Leader of the Green Movement

Prospects for the tenth presidential election of the Islamic Republic in 2009 ignited little if any excitement on the part of the general public. Four candidates passed the vetting process of the Guardian Council: the sitting president, Mahmoud Ahmadinejad; Mohsen Reza'i, a former head of the IRGC and a self-proclaimed independent with ties to some conservative groups; the former Prime Minister of the Islamic Republic, Mir Hossein Musavi; and the former Speaker of the Parliament, Mehdi Karrubi. The latter two belonged to the reformist camp, though neither enjoyed the popularity that Khatami had had twelve years earlier. But the previously lackluster campaign suddenly changed in the last few days before the election, when millions unexpectedly mobilized in support of the reformist candidates, particularly Musavi.

The sudden surge of interest in the election had much to do with the new styles of campaigning. The televised debates attracted millions of viewers, who saw some real disagreement among the candidates, and who particularly appreciated Musavi's criticisms of Ahmadinejad's performance at home and abroad. Soon, green, the adopted color of Musavi's campaign, appeared everywhere in banners, dresses, headbands, bracelets, and makeup, and adorned huge gatherings, particularly in major cities.

The hopes of Musavi's and Karrubi's supporters, whose mobilization gave life to the Green Movement, were dashed when the election officials announced Ahmadinejad the winner. A large number of the voters, who met the announcement with skepticism, took to the street and staged huge peaceful demonstrations, demanding a recount. The Supreme Leader referred the matter to the Guardian Council. The council decided to recount only 10 percent of the cast vote; it then declared that the elections had been conducted fairly. Predictably, the protestors saw the state's response as a mockery of their demands and continued their demonstrations, which rapidly spread to most major cities in Iran. The state used uniformed police as well as plain-clothed club wielders and members of the Basij force to attack the protesters, resulting in scores of deaths.

The demonstrations were ultimately suppressed, but they shook the Islamic Republic to its core. The state employed all its resources – including people at the helms of the various branches of government, the Friday Prayer leaders, and its print, audio, and visual media – to criticize the Green Movement. Mild in tone in the initial phase, the regime's supporters soon became more aggressive; they labeled the movement a *fetneh* (sedition) and called for its decisive uprooting. In the span of a few weeks, the state closed down the newspapers sympathetic to Musavi and Karrubi, jailed many of their advisors and aids, and eventually put both men and their wives under house arrest. Extremist voices not only asked for them to be tried but vaguely suggested execution as the proper punishment.

Not surprisingly, Montazeri, who was following the events, stood up in support of the Green Movement. Before the election, he had advised his followers to vote, and to do so as autonomous agents. But once it became clear that the demand for a recount would not be meaningfully addressed, he began another round of public statements, starting with a response to a question about fraudulent elections. He declared that Islam prohibited fraud and that such an election would take away the legitimacy of a government.[85] He sent a public message to the nation, lamenting the state's willful disregard for the opportunity of forging a trusting relationship with its citizens. Appealing to their faith, Montazeri addressed the security forces and advised them to perform their religious duty by refusing to violate the legitimate rights of the protesters.[86] Might Montazeri then have been thinking about his and Khomeini's pleas to the pre-revolutionary army three decades before not to harm the protestors and to join with the revolutionaries?

This message was not Montazeri's last one to the people, nor was it his last cry against the state's violation of people's rights. Even though a few other high-profile clergy had condemned the suppression of the protesters, none of them had the weight or the symbolic political authority of Montazeri. In the last year of his life, as ill and physically weak as he was, his strong voice continued to denounce the state's oppressive behavior, in the hope of saving the Islamic Republic. Once again – reminiscent of his bold public protest against the treatment of prisoners in 1988 – Montazeri cried out against the arrest, torture, televised confession, and killing of protestors. He disdained in particular the formulaic and forced confessions of the detainees. In his public response to a letter sent to him by 293 intellectuals, journalists, and university professors, he declared that the captains of the state should stop making a mockery of Islamic law or "at least have the courage to declare that this regime is neither a republic nor Islamic."[87]

During the turbulent months prior to Montazeri's death, more and more activists, university students and professors, journalists, and women's groups reached out to him and asked for his continuing support and interventions. Even the reformist presidential candidates and Green Movement leaders, Mir Hossein Musavi and Mehdi Karrubi, asked for his support. He gave them what they asked for, quite graciously, even though when he had been in need, neither of these two men had offered to help or support him. Musavi was the prime minster who ordered Montazeri's pictures to be taken down from the walls of the government offices; worse, Karrubi was one of the three authors of a harsh and condescending letter to him upon his dismissal in 1989. Still, Montazeri saw in them a hope for reforming the Islamic Republic, in which he retained faith despite his profound disappointment with its leaders. He condemned attacks on the Green Movement's leaders, their campaign organizers, and their associated media. He also appealed to the sources of emulation across the country and encouraged them to perform their religious duty of "prohibiting evil" by speaking up against injustice, violation of laws, and suppression of people's rights by the state.[88]

Montazeri's last dramatic stand was in the form of legal rulings, occasioned by five questions put to him by his religious follower and student Mohsen Kadivar.[89] Kadivar first inquired about the consequences of the loss or absence of necessary qualifications, such as justice, honesty, and popular support, in holders of public offices. He then asked about the religious duty of people in response to such a loss. Kadivar's third and fourth questions were more specific, clearly targeting the custodians of the Islamic Republic. In the third, he listed several concrete actions, such as ordering the beating and killing of innocent individuals, "betraying the nation's trust," and "preventing the exercise of the religiously sanctioned right of the true owners of the country to determine the national fate," and asked Montazeri whether these acts would be enough to rule a government unjust. The fourth question concerned a prioritization of values: Could political leaders legitimately sacrifice justice at the altar of "the expedient interest of the regime," and what would be the obligations of the faithful in such a situation? His last question pertained to the definition of tyrants and the fate of tyrannical rule.

In response to the first question, Montazeri ruled that the loss of qualifications could lead to dismissal either automatically or through people's decision. In either case, the dismissed officials would have no legitimate claim to power, and in answer to the second question, if they resisted their dismissal, it would be the *duty* of people to find the least costly and most beneficial means of carrying out the judgment. Montazeri did not elaborate on what was included in the best or least costly manner, but he did not mention any exclusion, including revolution. It is also important to note that here Montazeri freed people of the responsibility to prove their case: instead, it was the duty of the public officials to prove their innocence.

In response to the third question, Montazeri considered all the actions that Kadivar had listed as cardinal sins and stated that whoever committed them had lost the most essential qualification, namely justice. Justice was also the principle that informed his answer to the fourth question, on prioritization of values and goals of the state. For Montazeri, the protection of the state was not the priority; rendering justice and protecting the rights of the people was. In response to the question on tyranny, Montazeri defined it as a purposeful opposition to religious laws, standards of reason, and national covenants, and considered the custodians of the Islamic Republic guilty on all these accounts. He then put a heavy burden on the clergy, asking them to not remain silent in the face of injustice but to fight against tyrannical rule. Probably thinking of his own long and painful battles with two regimes, he told them that fulfilling their promise to God involved embarking on a long journey full of suffering.

In the last month of Montazeri's life, ten members of Iran's Center of Defenders of Human Rights visited him on the Universal Day of Human Rights and presented him with their Human Rights Activist award for 2009–10. The award was given to him not primarily for his jurisprudential scholarship but for his practical efforts, his wholehearted support for the Green Movement and the rights of prisoners, and his protest against the "state's harsh method" in dealing with citizens.[90]

Figure 4.4 Montazeri's funeral procession in Qom, December 21, 2009. AFP/Getty Images

The End of a Life

Four days after his last public statement, on December 20, 2009, Montazeri died. He was mourned by Iranians from many walks of life: religious and non-religious, men and women, young and old. Despite the risks involved in publicly mourning a dissident ayatollah, especially during an already tense time after the 2009 election, many grief-stricken people poured into the streets, calling him the "spiritual father of the Green Movement." Montazeri's popularity, most dramatically manifested during his funeral, showed that the elaborate story used to discredit his character and deeds had not resonated with a large segment of Iranians. For some of these Iranians, Montazeri was their exalted source of emulation, and for all of them he was a model of resistance against injustice – a model worthy of imitation. Montazeri might have found in this passionate display of emotions a gratifying acknowledgment of his life of struggles, defeats, and triumphs.

Notes

1 FBIS-NES, May 16, 1989.
2 *Resalat*, March 29, 1989.

3 *Jomhuri-e Eslami*, March 30, 1989.

4 See the text of the letter republished in *Arzeshha*, January–February 1998, 28–43.

5 See Salimi Namin's reference to Mohammadi-Gilani's memoirs at http://kuku.parsiblog.com/Posts/689/.

6 See the daily *Rajanews* at http://www.rajanews.com/detail.asp?id=47114.

7 Rafsanjani, *Hope and Worries*, 314.

8 Montazeri, *Memoirs*, app. 142, 580–1.

9 See the text of both letters in Montazeri, *Memoirs*, app. 143, 581–94.

10 See Baghi, *Vaqe'iyat-ha va Qezavat-ha*, 235.

11 Some of these televised confessions are available on Youtube. See, e.g., https://www.youtube.com/watch?v=MmRa4z6zA2o, https://www.youtube.com/watch?v=Ck_c9FpoaTg and https://www.youtube.com/watch?v=Dy0TuC2V1oo.

12 See the text of televised confessions in Rayshahri, *Memoirs*, 4:170–82.

13 In his review of Montazeri's *Memoirs*, Salimi Namin gives the most extensive analysis of his letters regarding Hashemi's affairs, and though he does not explicitly call Montazeri an opportunist, the implication is quite clear. Salimi Namin, *Pasdasht*, 55–90.

14 Abrahamian, *Tortured Confessions*.

15 Baghi, *Vaqe'iyat-ha va Qezavat-ha*, ch. 2.

16 This internal disagreement has not been independently verified. But, it is true that Ahmad supported the *Mojahedin-e Khalq* at least for most of the 1979. See his interview and a subsequent open letter by some members of the *Mojahedin-e Khalq* in daily *Ettela'at*, October 16, 1979: 2,4, 9 and October 21, 1979: 9.

17 In this part, Montazeri goes into detail about how many of these men, who had no connection to Hashemi, were tortured by agents of the Ministry of Information so that they would confess their participation in a plot to overthrow the regime.

18 Montazeri, *Enteqad az Khod*, 69–87.

19 There were precious few voices against such a hasty revision. One exception was an editorial in the daily *Ettela'at* on April 22, 1989 warning that amendments to the constitution should not become a pastime in the future and advising the coming generations to refrain from "try[ing] to amend the Constitution as soon as minor political, economic, or ideological difficulties arise."

20 See the edict of February 6, 1988 at http://salmanfarsi.ghasam.ir/fa/news-details/27540/%D8%B3%D8%A7%D9%84%D8%B1%D9%88%D8%B2%D8%AA%D8%B4%DA%A9%DB%8C%D9%84-%D9%85%D8%AC%D9%85%D8%B9-%D8%AA%D8%B4%D8

%AE%DB%8C%D8%B5-%D9%85%D8%B5%D9%84%D8%AD
%D8%AA-%D9%86%D8%B8%D8%A7%D9%85-%D8%A8%D9
%87-%D9%81%D8%B1%D9%85%D8%A7%D9%86-%D8%A7
%D9%85%D8%A7%D9%85-%D8%AE%D9%85%DB%8C%D9
%86%DB%8C-%D8%B1%D9%87-/.

21 Montazeri's argument on the topic of the Expediency Council is more complicated than can be dealt with in this chapter. See Chapter 5 for his views on this and other matters related to good governance.

22 Khomeini, *Sahifeh Imam Khomeini*, vol. 21, April 29, 1989.

23 Apparently, Meshkini, the chair of the assembly, after giving a brief convening speech, did not remain in the chamber to participate in Khamenei's election.

24 'Ali Akbar Hashemi Rafsanjani, *Karnameh va Khaterat of Hashemi Rafsanjani, 1368: Bazsazi va Sazandegi*, ed. Ali Lahuti (Tehran: Daftar Nashr Ma'aref Enqelab, 2012), 149–52.

25 Ibid., 164.

26 The only semi-public opposition to Khamenei's appointment came from a group of parliamentary representatives, labeled by Rafsanjani as "radicals." See Rafsanjani, *Bazsazi va Sazandegi*, 151–2.

27 Montazeri, *Enteqad az Khod*, 128.

28 Rafsanjani, *Bazsazi va Sazandegi*, 162.

29 Montazeri, *Memoirs*, 393–4 and app. 190, 656–7.

30 The Guardian Council's first clear exercise of this new power occurred during the mid-term parliamentary election in January 1990, when it rejected the application of Behzad Nabavi, one of the four Tehran candidates of the leftist factions.

31 Rafsanjani, *Bazsazi va Sazandegi*, 531. It is instructive to see the result of this decision. In the elections for the first regular session of the Assembly of Experts in 1982, out of 168 applicants, only twelve were disqualified by the Guardian Council, while in its second session in 1990, the qualifications of sixty-two out of 180 were rejected.

32 The court, which was initially set up in Tehran, was expanded by ten branches on Khamenei's order. See Mirjam Kunkler, "The Special Court of the Clergy and the Repression of Dissident Clergy in Iran," in *The Rule of Law, Islam, and Constitutional Politics in Egypt and Iran*, Said Arjomand and Nathan Brown, eds. (Albany, NY: SUNY Press, 2013), 57–100.

33 At the time, Iranian diplomacy had had a brief shift toward better relations with the Eastern bloc, and the invitation of Ceausescu was part of that shift. Some, including a large number of the parliamentary representatives, objected not only to the trip but to the idea of a shift of attention toward the Soviets.

34 See the proceedings of the parliament at http://ical.ir/index.php?
option=com_mashrooh&view=session&id=1353&Itemid=38. Before
this, while Ceausescu was in Iran, Sadeq Khalkhali used the parliamentary podium to criticize the Romanian president and his closeness to
Israel and the apartheid South Africa, and to question the wisdom of
the trip. Interestingly, Mehdi Karrubi, the Speaker of the Parliament
and a member of the leftist faction, undermined Khalkhali's speech by
suggesting that it was a personal view and defended the policy of the
officials of the state. See FBIS-NES, December 19, 1989.

35 Two dailies, *Ettala'at* and *Tehran Times*, ran editorials which targeted
the Foreign Ministry.

36 FBIS-NES, December 28, 1989.

37 Ibid.

38 See Rafsanjani, *Bazsazi va Sazandegi*, 488.

39 See Sadeq Khalkhali's pre-agenda speech published in *Jomhuri Eslami*,
December 11, 1989.

40 See the full speech in Montazeri's *Memoirs*, app. 218, 705–10.

41 It was rumored that around the same time, Bazargan and his organization Freedom Movement had convened a congress for the first time and
that the attack on Montazeri was related to his suspected connection
with this movement. See *London Kayhan*, January 11, 1990.

42 By the order of Khomeini, Montazeri was in charge of selecting Friday Prayer leaders. In that capacity, he had created a council under his
own chairmanship to deal with the affairs of Friday Prayer leaders who
exerted political influence in their region – sometimes in harmony and
other times in conflict with other officials of those regions. But now it was
Khamenei who took control of the assignment of Friday Prayer leaders.
He also moved the council, now called the Policy Making Council of Friday Prayers, from Qom to Tehran. Not surprisingly, most of its members
became direct transmitters of state policies in their regions.

43 For the full text of the letter of appointment, see FBIS-NES, January 3,
1990.

44 Without naming him, Rayshahri attacked Montazeri for criticizing the
economic policies of the state and added that those who engaged in that
kind of criticism were knowingly or unknowingly plotting against the
system and would be confronted. FBIS-NES, January 12, 1990.

45 FBIS-NES, January 24, 1990.

46 See the letter and the names of 108 (of a total of 136) signatories in
Montazeri, *Memoirs*, app. 220, 716–18.

47 *Jomhuri Eslami*, August 6, 1990, 10, and August 7, 1990, 11. It was
in the second article, published on August 11, that the author attacked
Montazeri's religious credentials.

48 The deputies were Sadeq Khalkhali and Abdolhassan Haerizadeh. See *Resalat*, August 23, 1990, 5 and August 24, 1990, 5.

49 Montazeri, *Memoirs*, app. 221, 718–20.

50 The entire speech is in the digital library of the Islamic Consultative Assembly and can be found at http://www.ical.ir/index.php?option= com_mashrooh&view=session&id=1587&page=28174&Itemid=38.

51 Of these forty, thirty-seven were left-leaning. See Hadi Sajjadipur, *The Fourth Session of the Islamic Consultative Assembly* (Tehran: Islamic Revolution Document Center, 2009), 64–5.

52 For the importance of *resale 'amalieh* in claiming the position of religious leadership, see Roy Mottahedeh's lecture on "The Quandaries of Emulation: The Theory and Politics of Shii Manuals of Practice," given at the University of Washington. The full text of the lecture can be found at http://depts.washington.edu/nelc/pdf/event_files/ziadeh_series/ Ziadeh2011Booklet_FINAL.pdf.

53 Later, when Karimi died, his funeral was attended by several leaders of the Islamic Republic, but none of them mentioned his association with Montazeri or his arrest and jail sentence in 1993.

54 Montazeri, *Memoirs*, app. 223, 730–1.

55 Montazeri's grandson was temporarily detained, but his detention occurred the previous day during the disruption in Montazeri's lesson.

56 The attacks on other sources of emulation, such as Shari'atmadari and Sadeq Rouhani, were much smaller-scale operations.

57 FBIS-NES, March 31, 1993.

58 Montazeri, *Memoirs*, app. 222, 720–30.

59 Ibid., app. 224, 732–9.

60 See Mohammad Yazdi's Friday Prayer sermon in which he referred to Khamenei as successor to Khomeini both politically and religiously. FBIS-NES, December 9, 1994. See also Nateq Nouri's speech at the memorial service for Ayatollah Araki's in which he, on his own, announced Khamenei to be the *"marja'-e taqlid* of the Shiis of the world." FBIS-NES, December 5, 1994.

61 See the entire sermon in FBIS-NES, December 27, 1994.

62 The speech was broadcast by the Voice of the Islamic Republic. See the entire text on FBIS-NES, December 15, 1994.

63 In the same speech, Khamenei did say that he would be a *marja'* for those outside the country who had invited him to be their source of emulation.

64 Montazeri, *Memoirs*, app. 253, 422–3.

65 Two letters, one by students in Montazeri's jurisprudence class addressed to the leaders of Qom's *howzeh*, the other by a group of university professors, writers, and journalists addressed to President Rafsanjani,

condemned the attack and demanded the protection of Montazeri and his *Bayt* from future attacks.

66 A series of studies with new interpretations of the trajectory of the revolution and the nature of the Islamic Republic were soon published. See, for example, David Menashri, *Post Revolutionary Iran: Religion, Society and Power* (London: Frank Cass, 2001) and Daniel Brumberg, *Reinventing Khomeini: The Struggle for Reform in Iran* (Chicago, IL: University of Chicago Press, 2001).

67 Montazeri, *Memoirs*, app. 251, 774–5.

68 Ibid., app. 252, 775–8.

69 See the entire text of the sermon at https://amontazeri.com/ayatollah/freedom/353, 13–32.

70 Montazeri, *Didgahha*, 1:31–32.

71 Mohsen Kadivar, *Faraz va Foroud Azari Qomi* [The Rise and Fall of Azari Qomi], 12. The electronic version of the book can be found at http://kadivar.com/?cat=1720.

72 "Den of spies" was the term used to refer to the US embassy after it was occupied in 1979. For the use of "second den of spies," see the Basij weekly *Shalamcheh* no. 21, December 1998 (second half of the month of Azar 1376).

73 This threat was by Mohsen Rafiqdoost, an IRGC commander. See *Resalat*, November 26, 1997.

74 The entire speech can be found in *Arzeshha*, the special edition on Montazeri, January–February 1998, 49–51.

75 Beside his family, Montazeri was not allowed to meet with anyone. On rare occasions toward the end of his period of house arrest, the authorities gave permission for a few others to visit him. Ali Motahhari was one such.

76 Montazeri's depiction as such was most clearly elaborated in a booklet published by the Political Bureau of the Office of Representative of the *Faqih* in the IRGC in 1998. See particularly the chapter on "Mr. Montazeri's Shrewdness in Escaping Bottlenecks," at http://www.rasekhoon.net/article/show-23544.aspx.

77 For example, charged with promoting Montazeri, the permission for publication of the weekly *Nameh Ava* and the daily *Khordad* was suspended.

78 See the entire text of the impeachment in Akbar Ganji, ed., *Naqdi bara-ye Tamam-e Fosul* [A Criticism for All Seasons] (Tehran: Tarh-e Nou Press, 1999), 110–238.

79 Out of 265 members present during the impeachment session, 137 cast their vote for no confidence. http://www.khabaronline.ir/detail/370815/Politics/parliament.

80 Islamic Republic News Agency (IRNA), October 3, 1999.
81 Apparently one of the unspoken reasons for Nouri's charge of propagation of Montazeri was that he, as a member of the National Security Council, did not vote in favor of confining Montazeri in his house after the latter's controversial sermon in November 1998. See Ganji, *Naqdi bara-ye Tamam-e Fosul*, 79.
82 Eventually, his website was blocked by Iranian authorities within Iran. But it can be easily accessed outside the country.
83 The authors were Abbas Salimi Namin, the conservative head of the Bureau for Studies and Codification of Iranian History, and Masoud Rezai. Another two reviews were written by Asadollah Badamchian, one of the founders of the conservative party Mo'talefeh and the editor of the right-wing weekly *Shoma*, and Hamid Rouhani, the official biographer of Khomeini and one of the three authors of the harsh letter sent to Montazeri soon before his dismissal.
84 See the text of Montazeri's letter in Montazeri, *Didgahha*, 2:342–5.
85 Montazeri, *Didgahha*, 3:383–4.
86 Ibid., 393–5.
87 Ibid., 424.
88 Ibid., 428.
89 For the complete text of the questions and answers, see ibid., 403–11.
90 Ibid., 476–7.

PART TWO

The Thought

5 | *State–Society Relations*

In his 1979 public message to the AFRC, Montazeri emphasized the Islamic nature of the revolution and criticized the earlier drafts of the constitution for their use of Western political models. Years later, he retreated from many of his earlier positions and adopted concepts that are part of the lexicon of Western political theories. His juridico-political positions evolved steadily from the time of the revolution to the end of his life. How this evolution occured, in what areas it was most significant, and what it might mean for the future of political jurisprudence are some of the key questions that inform the direction of this chapter.

Shii Jurisprudence and Political Thought

The discourse of political guardianship of the religious jurist is exclusive to Shii discourse, with no similar counterpart in Sunni jurisprudence. The Shiis believe that Ali was not only the first religious successor of the Prophet but that he was designated by God to fill the Prophet's position as the ruler of the community of the faithful. By His consent, Ali's right to rule was also extended to his infallible descendants, down to the Twelfth Imam. The belief in both infallibility and the entitlement to leadership of the twelve Imams (i.e., the Imamate) is the basis for the theory of the guardianship of the Islamic jurist.[1]

Historically, the area of guardianship in Shii jurisprudence was limited to *hasbieh* affairs, i.e., administering justice, leading Friday Prayers, collecting religious taxes, and managing the affairs of members of the community who were unable to take care of themselves. Managing the political affairs of the community (i.e., creating and

A version of this chapter first appeared as "The Flock of a Shepherd or the Sovereign Citizen: Ayatollah Montazeri on the Role of the People," *Journal of South Asian and Middle Eastern Studies*, 39, no. 4 (Summer 2016).

preserving order and security, making and implementing public policies, and conducting foreign affairs) was left to the temporal king. It was during the reign of the Safavid that the cleric Mohaqqeq Karaki (d. 1533) presented for the first time the idea of the political rule of the Islamic jurist.[2] It took another three centuries, however, before a Shii theory of political guardianship of the Islamic jurist appeared as a distinct topic in the work of another clergy, Mulla Ahmad Naraqi (d. 1829). Naraqi's interpretation of the responsibilities of the Islamic jurist failed for a long time to get much traction in the religious establishment. Most jurists continued to believe in the traditional separation of the responsibilities of the clergy and the king.[3] Both the dominant and the marginal views were in accord, however, regarding an authoritarian model of state–society relations, in which the ruler would have total control over an obedient community.

In Iran, the paradigmatic shift away from an authoritarian discourse of state–society relations to a democratic one took place around the Constitutional Revolution (1905–11). At the heart of the shift were demands for constitutional restrictions on the power of the king and the inclusion of people as participants in politics. Those advocating democracy were not exclusively secular intellectuals but included such religious thinkers as Mohammad Hossein Naini, who was also convinced that the arbitrary power of a king should be reined in.

Despite his belief in an active political role for the clergy, Naini had more in common with the secular revolutionaries than with Naraqi in his views about the proper structure of the state.[4] Naini emphasized the necessity of a written constitution and the establishment of a parliament to guard against the despotic urges of a king. He believed that Islamic principles of justice, freedom, and equality could be observed within a democratic political structure, and put his seal of approval on principles of equality before the law, popular participation, and the accountability of the ruler.[5] His advocacy of an Islamically legitimate government made no mention of rule by a *faqih*, but it did include the right of the clergy to pass judgment on the compatibility of parliamentary legislation with Islamic laws. At the time of the Constitutional Revolution, the idea of a political guardianship of the Islamic jurist was far removed from the thinking of not only progressive clergy but even conservative and anticonstitutional ones, such as the outspoken Shaykh Fazlollah Nouri.

The change came with Khomeini in the book, *Velayat-e Faqih: Hokumat Eslami*, based on his 1970's lectures in Iraq.[6] A precursor of the change was in another of his books, the 1944 *Kashfol Asrar*, in which he sharply criticized the Pahlavi regime, portraying it as unauthentic and dictatorial.[7] Khomeini lamented that a country in which Islam had already provided rules for all conceivable aspects of governing now borrowed its laws from the West. He argued for the creation of institutions that would guarantee a meaningful advisory role for the Islamic jurists in political affairs. He asked for an assembly of religious jurists that would select the monarch and check his dictatorial tendency, along with a parliament consisting of religious experts, or at least supervised by such experts, that would implement the rules of Islam.[8]

When the political climate changed and the confrontation with the state led to his exile, Khomeini's ideas about the rule of the *faqih* became crystalized in his lectures. He was well aware that there existed little jurisprudential precedent to support his call for rulership of the *faqih* and that he would encounter resistance from a significant segment of the clerical establishment. So he went on the offensive, writing in the introduction to the book version of his lessons that, based on Islamic theology and jurisprudence, the desirability of political rule by Shii jurists was self-evident. This had been obscured, he continued, as a result of the malevolent colonial interference in the affairs of the Islamic world by non-Muslims over centuries.[9] Now was the time, he judged, to redress this wrong by putting the rightful ruler, a knowing and just *faqih*, in control of the state, as God intended. Khomeini did not spell out procedures for instituting a rule of the *faqih*,[10] but with no hesitation he declared that the ruler would be God-designated rather than popularly elected.[11]

Khomeini's ideas and the triumph of the Islamic Revolution inspired other jurists both in and outside Iran to offer their own theories of an Islamic state.[12] In Iran, it was Montazeri who provided the most comprehensive case in support of the guardianship of the *faqih*.

Montazeri's case for the rule of the *faqih* is predicated on the rational argument about the necessity of government. In the absence of laws and their effective implementation, the multiple and at times conflicting desires of people could lead to a chaotic and dangerous situation and would make communal life almost impossible.[13] What form government should take, however, depends on the nature of the people who are in need of it.

Montazeri examines human nature in two of his books: *Az Aghaz ta Anjam* and *Eslam Din-e Fetrat*. In the first, he sees humans as creatures who belong simultaneously in three worlds and play three different functions.[14] At the most basic level, they are biological entities equipped with natural powers to survive. At the next level, the animal world, humans have faculties that bring to their soul higher sensations and emotions, such as love, lust, hate, and friendship, which cause either joy or misery. The last and highest world, that of reason and intellect, belongs exclusively to humans, and only there do they find their true essence *(fetrat)*. In the second book, *Eslam Din-e Fetrat*, Montazeri approaches the soul somewhat differently. Here he speaks of several tendencies within it – *amareh* (lasciviousness), *lavvameh* (conscience/remorsefulness), *molhameh* (revelatory/inspirational), and *motma'neh* (capable of certitude) – all of which are God-given and thus necessary, but not necessarily harmonious. The way to bring them into harmony and to avoid the risk of lowly animal life is to make the higher tendencies, led by reason, dominate the self.[15] With higher faculties in charge of the soul, humans would develop the potential to reach salvation.[16] Yet, due to its imperfection, reason remains only a necessary and not a sufficient component of achieving this goal. (See more on Montazeri's view on reason later in this chapter.)

The imperfection of reason is the result of the imperfection of the human creature. Like most traditional jurists, Montazeri believed that the attributes of each being were closely connected to the nature of that being. God, the Perfect Being, possesses perfect reason, while humans, created and dependent beings, can only reason imperfectly. Considering humans' complex and competing internal powers, along with their God-given free will, it is easy to see how reason can lose control over the lower faculties and how humans can be pulled downward.[17] In His infinite wisdom and generosity, God appointed guides and messengers to reveal His rules and direct humans toward eternal salvation. This view of humans and their essence is at the basis of Montazeri's conception of state. In Hobbesian terms, Montazeri pictures how individuals' selfish and animalistic interests, exacerbated by the natural state of scarcity, dominate and destroy any prospect for a cooperative communal life.[18] To escape the chaos of the state of nature, humans need an enforcer of law and order, whom they should obey. Yet at the same time God has created humans to be free of subjugation and obedience to anyone but Him. The tension between these two ideas – the need for government and the right to be free from subjugation – is too obvious to be shoved aside, so what is to be done? For

Montazeri, as for some others, a God-approved government was the solution.

Montazeri and *Velayat-e Faqih*: Formation of an Idea

Montazeri's earliest exploration of the idea of an Islamic state took place in his discussions with Motahhari during their student years in the quietist period of the *howzeh*. They both favored a state headed by an elected *faqih*, but according to Montazeri, when they shared their views with Khomeini, their most politically inclined mentor, he dismissed the idea.[19] Motahhari soon left Qom for Tehran and kept his belief in an elected *faqih* for the rest of his life. Montazeri, influenced by the ideas of both Khomeini and his primary mentor Borujerdi, dropped his support for election and opted for the divine designation of *vali faqih*.[20]

Montazeri first wrote about the rule of the *faqih* in the early 1950's, in his commentaries on the books of his two mentors, Ayatollah Borujerdi and Ayatollah Khomeini. There, he supported the theoretical foundation for God's designated guardianship of the jurist. Despite their potential revolutionary implications, these jurisprudential writings were academic and abstract, read only by the students of the *howzeh*. In public, and even after the exile of Khomeini and the beginning of the serious and risky phase of his own political activism, Montazeri did not advocate the actual establishment of the rule of jurist. In his criticism of the Pahlavi regime, particularly in his Friday Prayer sermons at Najafabad in the early 1970's, he dropped some hints about the rule of the clergy, but for the most part he only emphasized the state's responsibility to follow Islamic rules.[21] He also suggested that if the state failed in that responsibility, then it would be incumbent upon the people, particularly the clergy, to actively engage in the religious act of "prohibiting evil." His demands at this time were closer to the earlier views of Khomeini in *Kashfol Asrar* than to the latter's position while in Najaf, where he advocated the elimination of monarchy and the establishment of the rule of the *faqih*. Operating within Iran and under the watchful eyes of the secret police, Montazeri did not have the luxury to follow his mentor's lead. As it was, even his milder demands for reform of the state brought him imprisonment and internal exile.

Within a few months after the collapse of the Pahlavi state, Montazeri, now freed from the threat of the secret police and from his own semi self-censorship, wrote a two-part pamphlet called "Collection of Two Messages," in which he proposed the rule of the Islamic jurist. But it was in *The Jurisprudential Foundation of Islamic State* that he developed the concept of *velayat-e faqih* extensively and systematically. He justified his call for theocracy on philosophical grounds.

Collection of Two Messages

In this two-part pamphlet, Montazeri made his call for a designated *faqih* in the following statement:

In the Shii view and on behalf of God, the prophet gave the right to rule to Ali [his son-in-law and the First Imam]...And one after another to Ali's descendants [down to the Twelfth Imam]. Since his occultation, the Twelfth Imam has *designated* [emphasis is mine] the commander of the faithful to be from among those who have certain qualifications.[22]

How such a designated ruler would take control of the state he did not discuss. What he did address was the extent of the ruler's control and his attendant responsibilities. The designated leader would have total control over legislative, judiciary, and executive functions, and would have accountability to God in following the laws of Islam. He remained silent on the question of whether there was any need for human-made institutional mechanisms to check the leader.

Montazeri understood the possible consequences of having power concentrated in the hands of one person. During the debates in the AFRC, he repeatedly warned against the establishment of a strong presidency, citing the danger of falling into yet another dictatorial regime. But his sensitivity applied only to an office whose occupant did not require formal religious or "true" knowledge. Trusting the Socratic dictum that "knowledge is virtue," he, with no hint of irony, pushed for the creation of a powerful office headed by one whose knowledge of Islamic laws would make him a bulwark against the danger of dictatorial rule.

Still, the popular character of the revolution and the call for an exercise of the will of the people were not easily or quickly suppressed. Supporters of popular sovereignty managed to include the language of republicanism and democracy in certain articles of the final constitution. A host of freedoms, along with articles for protection of the people against arbitrary rule, remained in the final draft, and in theory, if not in practice, the *vali faqih* became an "elected" rather than an "Imam-designated" position. Supporters of the office of *vali faqih* did succeed, however, in having the popular vote restricted to the election of an Assembly of Experts, consisting of clergy, who would then select the leader.

Montazeri's two-part pamphlet and his comments during the debates in the assembly testified to his conflicted and confused approach to political institutions. On the one hand, he was an excited revolutionary who wished to replace the oppressive and corrupt institutions of the previous regime with new liberating and just ones; on the other, he was a product of a religious education with an elitist approach to government and a patronizing view of the people. Devoid of administrative experience, he opted for an elitist state, thinking that it would be just and fair. His expansive work on *The Jurisprudential Foundation of Islamic State* was the product of these early years.

The Jurisprudential Foundation of Islamic State

After concluding his work on the constitution, Montazeri left Tehran and resumed his teaching in Qom's *howzeh*. Yet, still excited with ideas about the constitution, he began teaching a five-year *dars-e kharej* on the topic of *velayat-e faqih*. The lessons were collected and published, first in their original Arabic, and later in a Persian translation. They formed a systematic and technical elaboration of the main points of the "Collection of Two Essays," with one notable change regarding the method of selection of the *vali faqih*. Here, he rejected designation in favor of election.

Like most of his other technical writings, Montazeri's analysis in *The Jurisprudential Foundation of Islamic State* was based on four authoritative pillars: the Quran, *hadith*, consensus, and reason. His appeal to reason pertained to the necessity of having government as well as his critique of non-theocratic systems of rule, while the other three authoritative sources fortified his case for the desirability, or rather the necessity, of forming an Islamic government led by a jurist. What made the book a particularly significant contribution to Shii political thought was the vast number of *ravayat* (authoritative interpretations of the sayings and deeds of the Prophet and the twelve Imams) that Montazeri brought to bear, a testimony to his immense command of Islamic jurisprudence.

By the time Montazeri wrote on the rule of jurist, he had already had some exposure to the diverse and contentious discourse about ideal forms of government. The freedom of expression experienced during the first few months of post-revolutionary Iran allowed a diverse conversation about the best form of government, and people from the left and right, conservatives and progressives, made their cases for an ideal polity. These lively debates had the effect of providing a crash course on alternative forms of polity for Montazeri, who, certain about the superiority of the rule of the *faqih*, challenged these other forms of governing. At the beginning of his book, drawing upon Platonic, Aristotelian, and modern ideas of polity, he specified the defects of six types of government: tyranny, constitutional monarchy, aristocracy, oligarchy, party-dictated rule, and democracy.[23] The most notable of his criticisms pertains to democratic rule. His earlier criticism of democracy, presented in his two-part pamphlet, was a standard religious denunciation of the system for its human-centered ideological foundation. Now he cited its failure in its inability to deliver on its promises. Using a leftist critique, he maintained that in Western capitalist countries what passed for people's rule was only a hollow expression of popular will. In reality, the wealthy few, through their control over the means of communication, had been able to manipulate the misinformed masses and manage elections to serve their own interests.[24]

Having dismissed these "defective" forms of government, he shifted his attention to Islamic government, the ideal form of rule, and laid out the goal and the character of the state and the functions of the ruler in one succinct paragraph:

Islamic government is an entity that has the authority to implement divine laws and fulfill the interest of the people in accordance with Islamic standard. The Islamic government is not a dictatorship, and that is why the Islamic ruler is called *emam* [leader], *vali* [governor], and *ra'i* [shepherd]. He is an *emam*, because he is a role model for the society, he is a *vali*, because he administers the affairs of the people, and he is a *ra'i* because he is an ever present protector of people from harm. In our view the ruling position is not one from which the ruler can extract glory or put burden on people; instead we see it as an entity that fulfills the interest of the community, an entity that frees people from the shackles of imitation, customs, and all other [oppressive norms] that have been imposed on them.[25]

The "burden" of responsibility that Montazeri put on the ruler was indeed grave; the leader must see to the "totality of his subjects' well-being," both material and spiritual, this-worldly and other-worldly. In principle, Montazeri's maximalist view of the role of the custodian of the state left no area of human experience outside the domain of his control.

Like other supporters of the rule of jurist, Montazeri looked back to the precedent of the Prophet for a model that a contemporary leader should emulate. He saw the Prophet's "simple life style and his devotion to justice, liberality, equality, and sacrifice" as particularly important for good leadership.[26] Of course, no one in the occultation era could compare with the Prophet, but there were qualities that would make some followers more worthy than others. After presenting numerous *ravayat*, Montazeri identified eight qualifications as undisputed requirements for rulership.[27] They were reason, faith in Islam, knowledge of Islamic jurisprudence, justice, wisdom and skills for administering the state, maleness, and attributes such as piety and lack of envy.[28] For Montazeri, more than anything else, including the institutional makeup of the government, the personal qualities of the leader would guarantee the faithful application of Islamic laws for the good of the community.

Through his emphasis on the qualifications of the leader, Montazeri also found an opportunity to advocate election rather than divine designation as the proper procedure for selecting the *vali faqih*.[29] Unlike Khomeini, who believed designation does not require infallibility, Montazeri argued that infallibility is a precondition for designation, and that it can be determined only by God, the Prophet, and the rightful Imams, not by ordinary humans. Considering the practical impossibility of determining a specific person as God's choice, insistence on designation would amount to giving up on an Islamic government, leaving the community of faithful defenseless. The only alternative would be to elect a leader – by the people – from among all those with the requisite qualifications.

To give his argument for an elected leader a historical weight, Montazeri referred back to the example of the Prophet and the Infallible Imams who, according to the Shiis, had the inherent and divinely ordained right to be the rulers of the community. In practice, however, their right was realized only when people accepted them as rulers and gave their explicit allegiance (*bay'at*). Montazeri related this history to emphasize the point that if the rightful Prophet and the Imams needed the people's concurrence to become political leaders, then popular consent through elections would be necessary – equally, if not more so – in order for any lesser men to be legitimate leaders.[30] He stated that in the Islamic Republic, the terms of the contract between the leader and the people were provided in the constitution of 1979.

The proposal in *The Jurisprudential Foundation* that the leader be chosen by election rather than by designation was not meant to lead to a serious change in state–society relations. Montazeri demanded the electorate choose only from among men with the previously mentioned eight qualifications, severely restricting people's choice. Any major deviation from these standards, he warned, would result in a flawed and illegitimate government.[31] Moreover, he maintained that after a properly conducted election, the people had no right to dismiss or disobey a justly elected leader, as long as he followed the divine laws.[32] In Shii jurisprudence, there are two categories of contract: *'aqd-e lazem* and *'aqd-e jayez*. The former, once put into effect, become irrevocable. The latter can be nullified.[33] Montazeri's idea of the contract in this writing was clearly of the first kind, limiting the role of the people to the extent that the system of election was quite compatible with "the spirit of designation."[34]

Montazeri's ideal system did not materialize. In addition to all the violations of the 1979 constitution itself, now, at the end of the first decade of the Islamic Republic, there were constitutional changes regarding the qualifications of the Supreme Leader, the expansion of his power, the inclusion of the Expediency Council, and the introduction of *akham-e hokumati*, all of which severely undermined, "legally/constitutionally," what Montazeri had in mind. By the end of the 1980's, "raison d'etat" superseded all other concerns and interests.

Having been stripped of his position as the Designated Successor, Montazri had no authority to reverse this trend or affect the actual behavior of the state. But he had time to rethink his views on state–society relations. Toward the end of the first decade after his dismissal, his reflections resulted in two essays: "Velayat-e Faqih va Qanoun-e Asassi" (The Rule of Jurist and the Constitution) (1998) and "Hokumat-e Mardomi va Qanoun-e Asassi" (Democratic Rule and the Constitution) (2000). He wrote these treatises following lively debates over questions about state–society relations, such as the legitimate form of government, the proper place of religion in politics, and the role of the people as participants. Montazeri's writings on these matters were influenced by these debates and in turn gave religious legitimacy for their expansion.

Political Discourses of the 1990's: Clerical Voices

The second half of the 1990's was an intellectually vibrant period in the history of the Islamic Republic, as a group of socially conscious thinkers presented new ideas on constructing relations between religion and politics. From the ranks of the clergy, the philosopher Mohammad Shabestari (1936–) and the jurisprudent Mohsen Kadivar (1959) were two of the best-known participants of this movement.[35] They challenged in particular the officially sanctioned understanding of the *velayat-e faqih*. An older clergyman, Ayatollah Mehdi Haeri Yazdi (1923–1999), also contributed. Such reformist ideas provoked reactions from supporters of the theocratic rule of the *vali faqih*, among whom the most influential were Ayatollahs Abdollah Javadi Amoli and Mohammad Taqi Mesbah Yazdi.

The Reformist Discourse

Mohammad Mojtahed Shabestari[36]
Shabestari's contribution to religious reformist discourse, with its spillover into politics, was grounded in hermeneutics. He argued that readers always bring certain preconceived ideas or prior knowledge into their interpretation of a text.[37] The further removed an interpreter is from the time and culture of the author, the greater her difficulties in reaching the true meaning of the text. According to Shabestari, this long-standing problem has been always dealt with in one of two ways: either by clinging to the surface, the literal reading of the text, or by allowing one's interest to dictate a subjective meaning. Both these methods are destined never to disclose the essential message of the text, leaving it forever hidden.[38]

Shabestari believed that both the interpreter and her audience should engage the text continuously so that it could develop into a living agent and reveal its own true meaning.[39] He thus judged the static and too-literal interpretative method of the traditional school of jurisprudence as faulty. He also questioned the validity of the elitist practice of the traditional school and called for a process of interpretation that was more democratic, one that included the audience in the act of discovering the textual meaning.[40] The political implication of this epistemological approach was significant; it would not only undermine the textual interpretation in support of the rule of the *vali faqih*, but could also lead to an empowerment of the people as political participants.

Shabestari did not just hint at this political implication; he directly tackled politics in his *Hermeneutic* and later in his *Naqdi bar Qaraat Rasmi az Din*. There, he divided the political discourse of the 1990's into three distinct categories, explained each, and found the middle one most satisfactory.[41] The first belonged to the theocrats, who took the Prophet's rule as the political model appropriate for all times. The third was that of the secularists, who offered a model of government in which religion was absent not only in the institutions of the state but also in its moral compass. The middle category, the one approved by Shabestari, was based on the argument that belief in certain general religious values was necessary for good governance, and that the state, in choosing its policies, should remain faithful to those values. Nonetheless, the form taken by the institutions of the state, according to Shabestari, could be open to change. He found erroneous the contention that democracy by its nature shuns divine values and laws, and argued that such a claim would elevate democracy to an ideology rather than treat it as a method of governing. The only principles underlying a democratic rule – the absolute equality of individuals before laws, regardless of sex, race, and class – are consistent with Islamic values, if not with its established laws. For Shabestari, therefore, there was no reason for a religious state such as the Islamic Republic to resist the calls for adopting a democratic system of government.[42]

Mohsen Kadivar[43]

Like Montazeri's, but unlike Shabestari's, Kadivar's interest and approach were predominantly jurisprudential and deeply steeped in Islamic legal studies. Despite their differences in method, Kadivar shared Shabestari's concern about the dictatorial tendencies within the Islamic Republic and was in general agreement with him on the need for institutional change.

Kadivar's first major book, *Nazariye-haye Dowlat dar Fiqh-e Shii* (Theories of State in Shii Jurisprudence), was not a direct critique of the institution of the *velayat-e faqih* but a comparative study of nine distinct Shii theories of state. They ranged from the absolute rule of the divinely designated *faqih*, a theoretical view held by Ayatollah Khomeini, to a state where religious texts dictated nothing about politics and the *faqih* had no claim to power, a theory most associated with Ayatollah Mehdi Haeri Yazdi.[44] Even though the book was more descriptive than critical, it contained ingredients for constructing an argument against the theory of the *velayat-e faqih* by pointing at the dearth of supporting references in Shii juridical opinions.

If opposition to the idea of *velayat-e faqih* was subtle in this first installment of Kadivar's three volumes on Islamic political thought, it was naked enough in the second one, the *Hokumat-e Velayi* (The Theocratic State), to land its author in jail. The book was a thorough and careful jurisprudential look at the subject. It started with the etymology of *velayat* (guardianship) in the multiple fields of theology, gnosticism, and jurisprudence. Even though the etymological approach of the first part of the book cast suspicions on the recent political usage of guardianship, it did not criticize it. Soon after, however, in the chapter on "Guardianship of the Jurist and Republicanism," Kadivar set the stage for a critique of the theocratic concept. Pointing out ten areas he considered zones of incompatibility between the two types of governing, Kadivar concluded that republican rule could never be reconciled with the rule of the *faqih*. The divide between the two was evident in the insurmountable gaps between the model of *velayat* (guardianship) vs. *vekalat* (representative); between rule for life vs. term limits; and between the view of people as immature entities requiring guardianship vs. people as mature individuals in charge of their destiny.[45] Relying on his jurisprudential expertise and the authoritative sources of the Quran, the *hadith* of the Prophet and the Infallible Imams, and reason, Kadivar, in the second part of the book, directly undermined the rule of the *faqih*.[46] It was his knowledge and use of jurisprudential method that worried the state most.

Mehdi Haeri Yazdi[47]
Haeri shared Shabestari's interest in philosophy and its branches, particularly epistemology.[48] Unlike Shabestari, though, he focused not on hermeneutics, but on human capacity for reason, volition, and knowledge; he concluded that reason had made humans masters of their own worldly dominions.[49] Haeri, who in many respects saw eye to eye with the established clergy in its interpretation of humans and their capacities, drifted away from them when he considered humans and human

reason in the domain of politics. In *Hekmat va Hokumat*, the book on his theory of state, Haeri contended that state–society relations belonged exclusively to *'aql amali* (practical reason) and were therefore completely out of the realm of metaphysics.

Haeri distinguished practical reason from *'aql nazari* (theoretical reason) according to their different applications. Religious matters, such as knowledge of God and His attributes, fall within the realm of theoretical reason, while managing the affairs of a city or creating a secure environment for commerce is the purview of practical reason. For Haeri, the conduct of government was nothing more than the management of domestic relations (relations among the citizens) and international relations (relations among the nations).[50] These practical functions of government did not belong to the metaphysical domain, and hence did not require the expertise of religious doctors.

But refuting the claim of religious jurists to rule on the basis of Islamic religious knowledge was one thing; undercutting the general basis for an authoritarian form of government was another. Haeri tackled the latter by introducing the concept of "joint private ownership," a concept derived from Islamic jurisprudence. Human ownership of one's body and one's capability is at the basis of private and exclusive ownership of things, including the land on which one lives. In the communal life of a society, the area under one's exclusive private ownership adjoins that of another person and creates spaces for joint private ownership of larger magnitude (*mosha'*). This practical common ownership is in essence individual ownership without an explicit separation of shares. Haeri viewed the territory of a nation-state as common private property whose owners constitute its citizens.

The inherent ambiguity of joint private ownership, however, can lead to conflict among the members of a community. To prevent tension and violation of property rights, a government must be constituted as an agent to preserve those rights and provide for order.[51] For Haeri, the primary reason for establishing government was no different from that of John Locke, the founding father of the liberal state in the West. Locke asserts that the chief end of "men's uniting into commonwealths, and putting themselves under government" is "the preservation of their [private] property."[52] In Haeri's view, too, the function of government is to provide for public welfare by protecting citizens' joint private property. Citizens are the true political sovereign of the country, and hence have the right to choose or dismiss whoever they wish as their agents. Anything else, particularly a guardianship of the jurist, would amount to treating citizens as incompetent, like children or the insane.[53]

By conceptualizing the citizens of a country primarily as individuals and autonomous private owners, Haeri sided again with liberals in their disagreement with communitarians, who viewed society as an organic entity in which each individual was an incomplete and inseparable part of a whole.[54] Not surprisingly, Haeri's ideas on politics were rejected by the authorities of the Islamic Republic, and his book was banned in Iran.

Shabestari, Kadivar, and Haeri, all of them clerics, took different approaches in making their respective cases against the institution of *velayat-e faqih*, but their reformist discourse had a strong common theme: the need to shift the balance of power from the state to the people. This point was received with indignation by many adherents of the *vali faqih*, whose rebuttal presented a strongly opposing view of government.

The Authoritarian/Conservative Discourse

The authoritarians based their arguments on God's omnipotence, His plans for human felicity and eternal salvation, and the concomitant necessity for human obedience. Though unanimous in their agreement on rule by the *faqih*, there were some variations in how strongly they distanced themselves from the reformists. Among the conservative authoritarian clergy, Ayatollah Abdollah Javadi Amoli (1933–) and Ayatollah Mohammad Taqi Mesbah Yazdi (1934–) exemplify such differences.

Abdollah Javadi Amoli[55]
Amoli was not a central figure of the revolution, but became a part of the political elite when Khomeini selected him as a member of the High Judiciary Council. He was also a member of the AFRC, and served in the next two sessions of the newly formed Assembly of Experts. For close to thirty years, he held the position of leader of the Qom Friday Prayers.

On November 27, 2009, Amoli resigned from the post of Qom's Friday Prayer leadership, reportedly due to his disapproval of the violent tactics used against the participants in the Green Movement.

Earlier, during the 2005 presidential elections, he had voted for the pragmatic Rafsanjani rather than for Mahmud Ahmadinejad, the favorite of the conservatives. Yet no one could accuse Amoli of crossing the line that divided the conservatives from the reformists. What explained these seemingly friendly gestures to the other side was the increasing gap between two groups within the conservative camp itself. The first term of Ahmadinejad's presidency brought with it a new type of populist authoritarianism that concerned some of the traditional conservatives – an uneasiness that intensified with the violent start of Ahmadinejad's second term. Amoli belonged to this group of traditional conservatives. Despite his firm belief in an elitist approach to governing, he preferred a more patronizing and benevolent method of control.

His support for the rule of jurist was based on the same philosophical and ontological foundation used by Montazeri.[56] He defended the rule of the religious jurist on these grounds and argued that the responsibility should be placed in the hands of a divinely designated, wise, and knowledgeable *faqih*. Designation meant that this *faqih* did not require people's sanction to be the legitimate ruler because "the status, positions, and rights that religion has given the qualified jurists are established independently of lay judgment."[57] Still, Amoli did recognize the pragmatic importance of obtaining popular consent for a political system controlled by the religious jurist.

Political disputes in the mid 1990's revealed the tension between the supporters of popular sovereignty on the one hand and of total obedience to the dictates of the *faqih* on the other. This prompted a renewed justification for the rule of the *faqih*, which Amoli undertook to provide. He attacked the reformists for their philosophical and epistemological views about a plural interpretation of religious rules, and argued that there was only one correct path (*sarat-e mostaqim*) in religion.[58] Even though he did not advocate the suppression of opposing opinions, he rejected the idea that each side could have valid points. Tolerance did not entail endorsement of multiple paths.[59]

He also objected to the reformists' charge that the guardianship of the *faqih* was comparable to caring for children. He had gotten his hands on a copy of Haeri's banned book, published in 1995 in London, and had decided that its characterization of guardianship as rule over incompetents must be challenged. To do so, he drew a sharp distinction between the guardian of *hasbieh* affairs (guardianship of children and the infirm) and the *faqih* as a political leader. The former was not subject to the laws and rules that he applied on the people under his guardianship. The latter, even though he possessed authority to make laws, was like other citizens subject to the same laws.

Amoli also claimed that absolute guardianship of the *faqih* was not incompatible with republicanism, which for him meant that people would participate in politics by performing their *duty* through giving their consent to the divinely endorsed political system. Not surprisingly, Amoli's attempt to stretch the definition of republicanism was challenged by the reformers.[60]

Mohammad Taqi Mesbah Yazdi[61]

After the revolution, Ayatollah Mesbah Yazdi (whose pre-revolutionary activities were mostly cultural) secured the supervisory position in the High Council of Cultural Revolution and played a central role in designing a new but ultimately unsuccessful Islamic curriculum for universities. He was a member of the Assembly of Experts and a director of the financially well-endowed Imam Khomeini Educational and Research Institute in Qom. Mesbah was a prolific author with a clear and accessible style of writing, and his control over several journals and weeklies brought his message to *howzeh* students and laity alike. His interest in certain strands of Western philosophical traditions also separated him from most other traditionally trained *howzeh* teachers and added to his attraction for some of the faithful of the younger generation.[62]

Mesbah's support for authoritarian rule of the *faqih* was based on traditional assumptions about the physical and intellectual frailty of people and their dependence on divine rules for eternal felicity. But the language that he used to attack the reformist discourse included some conceptual tools used in modern Western philosophy. For example, he wrote of the rise of relativism and associated it with the development of modern empiricism and the separation of the domains of "ought" and "is." Despite his respect for Emmanuel Kant, he blamed him for creating the possibility of this chasm.[63] He then argued that the most damaging aspect of the rise of empiricism was the elevation of the sensory and experiential (or scientific) domain of "is" to the position of true knowledge and the relegation of the moral knowledge to the category of "relative," where no universal standard applied. To him, this development could result only in moral nihilism and the irrelevancy of

God and His laws. He saw religious reformers in Iran as being afflicted with the same problem.[64] Resorting to the traditional language of the clergy, Mesbah called for a literal reading of religious texts as a way of accessing the one and only eternal truth. With this epistemological approach, he then made his case for an authoritarian and theocratic state as part of the eternal divine laws, a position that put him at the lead among the most uncompromising voices against reformists.

In traditional jurisprudence, one way to classify laws is to divide them into *tassisi* (constitutional, originated from God Himself) and *emzai* (pre-Islamic laws, endorsed by God, with or without minor modifications). *Tassisi* laws are, for the most part, unchanging, while *emzai* laws are in general contextual, and thus can be modified through *ejtehad*. The reformist narrative clearly either placed politics and the political system, particularly in terms of its form, within the mutable and contextual category of Islamic laws (as Kadivar did) or else sought to remove them from the domain of religious concerns (as Haeri did). Conversely, Mesbah insisted that the form of the Islamic government – the rule of the *faqih* – was one of the *tassisi* laws of God and that suggestions for its modification were therefore forbidden.[65]

Along with his fierce defense of the rule of jurist as an unchanging law came his dismissal of the role of the people. For Mesbah, like Amoli, the legitimacy of this divinely commanded state came from God and not from the people; their endorsement of the ruler was only a *practical* necessity and not a *moral* one. His dismissal of the concept of a republic was, however, more naked than Amoli's. Mesbah viewed the republican aspects of the constitution as incidental rather than as an integral part of the religious system. In principle, people should behave as obedient subjects of the ruler and of Islamic values and laws.[66] In reducing the importance of the republican aspects of the constitution, he claimed that the popular election of the president was nothing more than the people's *suggestion* to the leader, implying that the leader was entitled to ignore the people's vote.[67] To further show his contempt for republicanism, he supported the call from some authoritarian quarters to eliminate the word "republic" from the official name of the state. Mesbah did acknowledge the practical necessity of a degree of continual popular support for sustaining the rule of the rightful *faqih*.[68] Still, if such a support was lacking, his position was clear: "If we could not secure Islamic goals through peaceful means then the use of violence to achieve those goals is permitted."[69]

Mesbah strongly opposed one of the reformists' central goals: a limitation of the state's control over the individual. Rather, he advocated an expansion of state authority, and argued that the increasing complexities of the modern world required tighter control – all the more so for an Islamic state that bore responsibility for the moral well-being of the people. As demands on the responsible state increased, so would its right to interfere in the affairs of the community.[70] His vision of the ideal state combined a traditional patronizing relationship between the ruler and his subject with sophisticated modern means of control, making the state as authoritarian as possible.

In the late 1990's and 2000's, the debate between the reformists and the authoritarians/conservatives reached its peak. Aware of the central points of the debate, and still under house arrest, Montazeri rethought his own position on state–society relations. He was open to some of the reformist positions but never agreed with the extent of Shabestari's hermeneutical argument nor sided with Haeri's total separation of politics from the metaphysical domain or his liberalist view of citizens. Nor did he fully agree with Kadivar's thesis about the incompatibility of the rule of jurist with the republican form of governing. Conversely, despite his general affinity with the conservatives on theological and ontological matters, he fought them hard on their vision of an ideal state.

Montazeri: Political Thought since the 1990's

The context that led to Montazeri's reevaluation of his political positions also occasioned his reflection on the nature of human reason and its application, all for the sake of creating a more just society.

Human Reason

The victory of the rationalist jurisprudential school of *Usuli* over its rival, the literalist *Akhbari*, in the late eighteenth century allowed the incorporation of reason (*aql*) into Shii legal theories. What that meant was that along with the Quran, *hadith*, and consensus, independent rationality (*mostaqelat aqliyeh*) would now constitute an authoritative source for the derivation of religious precepts. The rationale for inclusion of reason as one of the four sources has its roots in the *Mo'tazeleh* argument that God has endowed humans with the faculty of reason so that they can distinguish the morally good from its opposite, and do so without the aid of revelation. For example, reason is capable of making the moral judgment that justice is praiseworthy and that oppression is blameworthy.

The history of lawmaking, however, shows that Shii jurists, despite their acceptance of the theological argument about reason and its ability to make moral judgment, have ignored its role as an independent source for making concrete and specific laws.[71] Their rejection is the result of the impossible demands they put on reason. For one thing, when there is a conflict between reason and textual evidence in deciding a case, the only way that reason can compete with the text is when it can secure "unanimity of opinion" about the praiseworthiness/blameworthiness of an action. For example, to successfully argue that "equal right to inheritance for men and women" is just and is therefore in accordance with God's judgment requires "unanimity of opinion," or the proof that there is no rationally based disagreement about gender equality in the case of inheritance.

Another difficulty that reason confronts is embodied in the principle of epistemic certainty (*qat'*). Where there is tension between textual validation and rational judgment, anything less than complete certitude in the latter will tip the scale in favor of the former.[72] Even in the absence of textual evidence, Shii jurists (except for a few of their number, and then only recently) have not made it easy for reason to be considered an authoritative source of precepts. Montazeri follows the same pattern when, in his *Eslam Din-e Fetrat*, he argues:

Since the divine laws are bound by [the moral principle of] benefits and harms [*masaleh va mafased*] and since reason can recognize them – in a specific case for which there is no revelatory rules, if reason reaches knowledge with certitude then it can be the source of religious precept.[73]

But he also recognizes and wishes to address the tension between the lofty position of reason as the judge of the highest principle of morality and the humble place to which it has been relegated within the concrete domain of law making.[74] He resolves this tension by sacrificing the first notion at the altar of the second, through focusing on the vulnerabilities of reason. Starting with human nature, he reminds us of the multiple forces that comingle with and contaminate this lofty human faculty. Alongside our natural/essential shortcomigs is the way that we are nurtured. Bad education and customs reduce rationality's access to truth. For Montazeri, the combination of these natural and environmental conditions makes unanimity and certitude a requirement in order for reason to supersede textual evidence.

In the midst of these rationalizations for making reason impotent, however, Montazeri does something curious and divides human reason into two categories: modern and traditional/classical. Classical reason is what he has already described: a natural faculty cohabiting with lust and anger within each individual human. Modern reason, on the other hand, is collective, critical, independent, and realized by means of discussion and dialogue.[75]

Even though the sequence of his argument on rationality in *Eslam Din-e Fetrat* seems to suggest that when he addresses the weaknesses of human reason, he has both its traditional and its modern versions in mind, his acceptance of the latter as a collective and critical entity – a product of deliberation – undermines, whether he means it to or not, his earlier argument on the inferiority of reason. The vulnerability of reason to desires and emotions rests on its description as an isolated faculty easily entrapped by other forces within the nature of humans as individuals. That seems to apply only to traditional reason and not to its modern counterpart. Moreover, vulnerability to stale customs or bad education does not quite fit a deliberative, critical, and collective rationality, as Montazeri sees modern reason to be. The practical consequences of his gradual trust in human rationality appear in his changing views regarding the political system and human rights.

Justice

Montazeri's approach to rationality is linked to his increasing emphasis on justice as the ultimate goal of religion: religion is there to serve justice, and not the other way around.[76] Again, this position has its roots in the *Mo'tazeleh* argument that God would reveal only laws that are inherently good and that goodness comes before law. Since justice belongs to the category of good, it too comes before religion. This line of reasoning was muffled in Montazeri's writings and statements until a few years after the revolution. Throughout those earlier years, his maxim had been that Islamic laws, implemented by the wise men of religion in all areas, including the political, would automatically bring about justice. It was after his realization that the use – or, to him,

the misuse – of Islamic laws by the custodians of the Islamic Republic
had led to horrific injustices that he started to emphasize the priority
of justice over all else. His change in emphasis does not mean that he
doubted the justness of Islamic laws, only that he had lost trust in the
ability/willingness of the Islamic Republic to be true to the genuine
spirit of these laws. The most dramatic example of this loss of trust
can be seen in his reaction to Khomeini's ruling on *ahkam-e hokumati*. In his statement, Khomeini linked the interest of the state to the
long-term interest of Islam and allowed governmental laws to abrogate
religious laws if expediency demanded it (see Chapter 4). Even though
Montazeri was in favor of the utilitarian principle of expediency, experience taught him that what was done in the name of this principle was
not always just. Along the same lines, he found the practical and official
conflation of the interests of the state (an entity he no longer trusted)
and of Islam quite alarming. To rescue religion and its moral status
from manipulation by the elite of the Islamic Republic, he began to
emphasize justice as the standard of religion. Significant also was his
denial of the exclusive right of religious doctors to decide what is just or
unjust in the domain of social and political activities. He now believed
experts in a variety of fields of knowledge were required to decipher
the just course of law making, paving the way to finding democracy a
rational system for managing public life.[77]

Democratic Rule and the Constitution

Written more than a decade after his major book on *The Jurisprudential Foundation of Islamic State*, Montazeri's 2000 essay "Hokumat-e
Mardomi va Qanoun-e Asassi" (Democratic Rule and the Constitution) was different in both style and substance. The earlier work was
a technical and detailed jurisprudential investigation in support of the
rule of *vali faqih*. In its comprehensiveness, it aspired to be a long-
lasting model for all Islamic Shii communities. "Hokumat Mardomi
va Qanoun-e Asassi" was a peculiar mix of moral advice, institutional
analysis, and criticism directed at specific actions of those who controlled state institutions, as well as practical and time-bound procedu-
ral suggestions.

One of the fundamental and potentially far-reaching differences between Montazeri's earlier writings on politics and "Hokumat Mardomi va Qanoun-e Asassi" was his move away from a

backward-looking approach, leaving behind the Prophet's rule as an immutable model for managing the polity. He agreed with reformists that the complexity of the modern world necessitated a rethinking of politics and institutions of the state.[78] Now favoring a shift in power from state to society, he likewise advocated reducing the power of the *faqih*. This particular suggestion had already appeared in his earlier essay, "Velayat-e Faqih va Qanoun-e Asassi" (The Rule of Jurist and the Constitution), written in the summer of 1998. There, he had explained why the unrestrained use of power by the *faqih* was against the principles of a just Islamic rule and the spirit of the constitution.

The impetus for writing the 1998 essay was to help the fulfilment of the reform promises of the new Khatami administration by opposing the forces seeking to expand the power of an already powerful *vali faqih*. At that time, the supporters of authoritarian rule, such as Mesbah Yazdi, had begun to revive the idea that *velayat-e faqih* was a God-designated office and that the role of the people, through the Assembly of Experts, was to discover rather than elect the *faqih*. As mentioned earlier, Mesbah had gone even farther in reducing the republican aspect of the constitution by emptying the popular election of the president of any meaning. Montazeri realized that he needed to address the question of election vs. designation more forcefully than he had done in his *Jurisprudential Foundation*. Still, the terms in which he defined the matter in "Velayat-e Faqih va Qanoun-e Assasi" rendered the choice of the people quite restricted. There, he said:

> If the eight requirements for rulership exist in several jurists ... then it is the *duty* [my emphasis] of the people to elect one from among them. And since such an election is by the order of God and by observing Islamic conditions and standards, then the rule of the elected person is legitimate and binding.[79]

Yet, in the same essay, Montazeri proposed limits to be put on the ruler, which distanced his current thinking not only from that of the conservative supporters of the rule of the *faqih* but also from his own earlier positions. Such are his thoughts in 1998:

> Since, based on the constitution, the *faqih* is elected by the Assembly of Experts, would it be wrong if his election, similar to that of a president, have a time limit, for example six or ten years? This time limit will emphasize the popular nature of the regime and will increase people's trust in the system ... electing a fallible person to be a leader for life and with absolute power is unwise ... Based on this same logic the unaccountability of the

faqih has to be addressed. He should be accountable to both the Assembly of Experts and the people; his rights should be accompanied with responsibilities.[80]

At this point, he did not go so far as to ask for an official separation of powers in the political system – a subject to which he turned in "Hokumat Mardomi va Qanoun-e Asassi" two years later. If Mesbah took the complexity of modern life as a reason for increasing the state's control over society, Montazeri saw in the same circumstances a reason for diluting the power of *vali faqih*. He would require the leader to consult with a wide variety of experts and even delegate certain decisions to them. Furthermore, he now argued for three distinct and separate branches.[81] He was particularly insistent that religious jurists, whose proper role had historically been the dispensation of justice and interpretation of laws, should leave to the president and the rest of the executive branch the implementation of state policies, particularly foreign policy, where these jurists had no expertise.[82]

Montazeri's call for the reduction of the power of *vali faqih* was accompanied by his change of heart about both the depth and the breadth of popular participation in politics. Previously, he had been skeptical about people's judgment due to their lack of adequate knowledge, especially religious knowledge. By the end of the 1990's, in clear disagreement with men like Mesbah Yazdi, he was demanding a greater and more meaningful popular participation in politics through the formation of political parties and greater freedom of expression.[83] The reformists' focus on epistemology as the foundation for their support of democracy did not go unnoticed by Montazeri as he, too, linked his support for the expansion of popular participation to his analysis of knowledge.

Montazeri did not waver in his view that true wisdom came from religious knowledge and that such knowledge could be acquired only by years of study and reflection on divine laws. But from experience with too many influential leaders in the Islamic Republic, he began to think that the possession of religious knowledge did not necessarily result in the wise and just exercise of *political* power. He realized that knowledgeable clergy could be seduced by power and act immorally, and also that religious knowledge alone was insufficient to run a modern state in a globalized world. This convinced him that the power of the *vali faqih* should be decreased and the power of an increasingly more educated and more cosmopolitan populace, equipped with modern reason, should be expanded.

In addition to the deepening of people's participation in politics, Montazeri addressed the matter of the inclusiveness of the political system. He lamented the exclusion of many of the participants in the revolution from the polity, a practice that he himself had pursued in an earlier time but now saw as both unjust and unwise:

Even though people are different in their understanding and interpretation of Islam and in the strength of their faith, their social and political rights are not dependent upon their understanding of Islam or the degree of their faith. Rather, all citizens of this country are equal in their human, political, and social rights because they were and still are the children of the revolution and the country . . . When we give, and rightly so, to the religious minority proportional representation and the right to be elected, how could we deny that right to that third or half of the population which are Muslim but are labeled [pejoratively] by you [the officials of the state] as "intellectuals" or "the other." These people belong here, they love their country, they have the skills the country needs, but they do not believe in what we believe. If, we are really imaginative we should convince them by the force of our argument rather than by denial of their right. [What we do now] is against social justice. It is also a cause for perpetual political tension.[84]

In addition to his general observations about state–society relations, Montazeri recognized in this essay the shortcomings in the constitution. Concerned about the inherent tension between the authoritarian power of the *faqih* and the democratic and republican articles in the 1979 constitution, he considered that the reviewing assembly, with none other than himself as its head, had used poor judgment. He cited the inexperience of most members of the assembly, their fear of dictatorship (which they associated only with the power of the presidency and not with the office of *vali faqih*), and their trust in Khomeini as factors that had blinded them to the problems that lay ahead.[85] He also believed it a mistake to have created an Assembly of Experts for the selection of the future leader and now argued in favor of the direct election of the *vali faqih* by popular vote.[86]

The evolution of Montazeri's views on state–society relations did not end with the essay in 2000, written during Khatami's presidency. Even though that presidency ended in disappointment for Montazeri, his negative attitude toward the Khatami administration paled in comparison to his alarm at the oppressive trend under Ahmadinejad's presidency (2005–13.) The greater the state oppression and violation of people's rights after 2005, the more he objected to and distanced himself from his earlier authoritarian position. Evidence of this shift, already outlined in the "Hokumat-e Mardomi va Qanoun-e Asassi" (Democratic Rule and the Constitution) of 2000, was more systematically elaborated in 2008, with the publication of *Hokumat-e Dini va Huqquq Ensan* (Islamic Government and Human Rights), a semi-*estedlali* treatise.[87]

Islamic Government and Human Rights

The new treatise on government was not a complete break with the past. There was much that connected it to the earlier *The Jurisprudential Foundation of Islamic State*, such as the philosophical reasons Montazeri used to explain the need for government. Moreover, he continued to stress the importance of keeping the government Islamic. Nor did he reject the idea of a *vali faqih*, even though he now assigned the office only a supervisory role. Another well-preserved position of Montazeri's 2008 treatise was a firm belief that even though people had the right to elect the leader, they still should *ideally* do it within the divinely set framework.

However, there were some significant changes in the *Hokumat-e Dini va Huqquq Ensan* that testified to the distance Montazeri had traveled. Already, he had moved away from insisting that for a government to be truly Islamic it required a qualified *faqih* at its helm, and now he was willing to concede that Islamic values and principles alone were sufficient guarantors of a good government.[88] He would further reduce the independent authority of the *faqih* by advancing two arguments that extended the rights of the electorate. One was that no one and no institution could rightfully force the people to choose the "divinely qualified" jurist (thereby unburdening people from the practical, if not moral, duty to elect the "right" candidate). The other was that both the actualization (a pragmatic concern) and the legitimacy (a moral concern) of rule derived from people's consent.[89] Enacting these ideas would indeed mark a revolutionary step:

Yes, if people chose a religious state and wished for social implementation of religious orders then the doctors of religion should be involved in implementing those rules. If however, at some point the majority of people turned against religion, or the Islamic government, or if they demanded that some of the rules of Islam become inactive, then the clergy would have no other responsibility than to advise people and to propagate religion. They have no right to continue their rule or insist on carrying out the above mentioned order through the use of force.[90]

Should such a situation come about, the only recourse Montazeri left for the clergy and the minority followers of Islamic rules (whom he called the Muslim minority) was to seek the support of the majority by legitimate means, in the same way that minority political parties functioned in a democratic society. Yet even here he was able to draw upon traditional jurisprudence by arguing that those *ravayat* that alluded to the use of force in support of the "right" ruler were either not authentic or applied only to the political leadership of the infallible Prophet and Imams. Furthermore, he once again hinted at the possibility of the principle of *tazahom* (choosing the most beneficial or least costly options among conflicting rules), which allowed for discontinuation of such rules for the sake of a greater benefit.

In his earlier thought about the centrality of the *faqih* to an Islamic government, Montazeri had concluded that majority support for the officeholder was not essential. But once the legitimacy of government, and therefore its moral standing, was understood to be dependent on the consent of the people, as he asserted in the treatise of 2008, the question of majority vs. minority appeared in a new light. He deemed majority rule imperative on pragmatic as well as rational and moral grounds. How else to provide for the stability of a well-functioning state?[91]

As for the right of the minority, even though he supported its protection, he did not address how or through what mechanisms this protection could be guaranteed, except by good will on the part of the powerful. Still, by contracting the reach of the state, he expanded the domain of privacy for the individual as members of the minority and got closer to the reformers' demand for a less intrusive government.[92] He insisted on the protection of the civil and political rights of citizens and favored a competitive republic in which political parties would form governments and, if they lost the election, work as watchdogs over the majority.

Most of the institutions Montazeri now favored had their origins in the West, and that fact alone shows how far he had departed from his views at the time of the Revolution in 1979. A less adversarial attitude toward the West also emerged in his positions on foreign policy.

A Note on State–State Relations

In general, Montazeri did not give up on his earlier ideas about colonialism and the unjust global power structure and its oppressive rules. He also remained committed to liberation movements and was particularly and continuously moved by the plight of the Palestinians, and therefore never wavered in his critique of Israel as an "usurper regime." But gradually a significant change occurred in his approach to the West, and especially to the United States. For years, Montazeri was steadfast in his unwavering criticism of American policies. In a fiery Friday Prayer sermon on November 23, 1979, at the outbreak of the hostage crisis, he called the United States a hostile power, not only toward Iran, but to the whole Muslim world. At the heart of his stand was America's unconditional support for Israel despite the latter's oppressive treatment of the Palestinians.[93]

Away from the public eye, however, Montazeri's approach to the United States was more nuanced. According to his memoirs, he tried to convince Khomeini, without success, to bring the hostage crisis to an end before the US presidential elections in November, 1980, arguing that a failure to do so would hurt the chances of the Democrats, who were somewhat less hostile than the Republicans toward the Islamic Republic.[94] And as for the hostages themselves, even though in public he joined the chorus of those who threatened to put them on trial should ongoing negotiations with the United States fail, in private he showed sympathies toward them and gave them hope for their release during a visit to the US Embassy compound.[95]

On balance, however, Montazeri remained convinced that the United States was an oppressive global force. There was one episode in particular that assured him of American "malfeasance": the downing of an Iranian civilian airplane over the Persian Gulf by a US Navy vessel in 1988. The images of the more than 300 men, women, and children floating in the water off the gulf affected him deeply, and he called for a response. Wanting justice for the victims, he appealed to Khomeini, asking that millions of Muslims be mobilized with every material and spiritual resource made available to fight the United States, the "real enemy" of the Islamic Republic. He then addressed the American people, naïvely thinking that if they knew what their government had done, they too would protest. At this point Khomeini decided otherwise and asked Montazeri to lend his support to Rafsanjani's policies, which were to avoid further confrontation with the powerful United States.[96]

Figure 5.1 Towering portraits of Khomeini and his heir, Montazeri, at an anti-United States demonstration following the downing of a civilian airliner by the US Navy, July 1, 1988. Photo by Barry Iverson/The LIFE Images Collection/ Getty

Montazeri's later change in foreign policy outlook paralleled that of leftist radicals toward the second half of the 1990's. For the most part, in interviews with foreign correspondents, he expressed as a practical matter an interest in resuming relations with the United States, and refrained from speaking of it as a colonial power. He acknowledged that the world had become like a small village, in which nations, if they wished to survive, had to find ways to get along with one another. Hence, the lack of any relationship between the United States and Iran should not last forever. With this generally pragmatic view, he also suggested that even though the United States had done wrong, Iran and Iranian officials could also be blamed for missing certain opportunities in the gestures made by some American officials, such as Secretary of State Madeleine Albright, who expressed regret for the US role in the 1953 coup.[97]

He also changed his opinion about the invasion of the US Embassy in November 1979. In an interview with a Japanese reporter, he repudiated the act and compared it to invading a foreign country. But he did not skip the opportunity in the same interview to point out that

US support for Israel, "the invader of Palestinian lands," was worse by far. Still, he regretted the cutting of relations with the United States and wished for their restoration based on a "mutual recognition of independence."[98] What he meant by this particular phrase was revealed a few years later when he spoke of the matter of nuclear energy. He insisted that the United States and the rest of the world recognize Iran's right to peaceful nuclear technology, as it was an inalienable right of an independent country.[99]

In harmony with his changing views on state–state relations, he retreated from tough earlier positions on countries of the region and suggested cordial relations with all – with the exception of Israel – based on mutual respect, cooperation, and non-interference in internal affairs. Notably, his more accommodating attitude on foreign affairs became most evident at a time when Iran, under Ahmadinejad, moved toward an earlier, more radical approach to foreign policy.

The Last Stand

The treatise on *Hokumat-e Dini va Huqquq Ensan* was the culmination of Montazeri's evolution on theories of state–society relations; he died within a year and a half after its publication. But shortly before his passing, and moved by the violent suppression of the Green Movement in the 2009 presidential elections, he, as a source of emulation, took a last dramatic stand, offering legal rulings in response to questions posed by his follower Mohsen Kadivar (see Chapter 4). Most of these rulings – on the qualifications of rulers, the legitimacy of the state, the rights of the people, and the people's duty to participate in politics – had appeared in one or another of his previous writings. But it was in his juridical responses to Kadivar's questions that Montazeri presented his most forceful and specific case against unjust rulers and in favor of the rights of the people to dismiss them, discussing the process of adjudication in case a ruler refused the popular verdict. It was also in these legal rulings that Montazeri, more emphatically than ever, emphasized the right to resist an unjust system or ruler. Once people lost their trust in their political leaders, they – without the requirement to explain themselves before an arbiter – had the right to dismiss them. In effect, the leader had automatically lost their right to govern. This provison situates the contract between people and leaders closer to the confines of *'aqd-e jayez* (a contract that can be nullified) than *'aqd-e lazem* (a contract that is irrevocable). Did this mean that Montazeri had turned revolutionary on the Islamic Republic?

Some argue that the most foundational change in Montazeri's writing on politics was presented in *The Jurisprudential Foundation of Islamic State*, where he switched from designation to election as the method for choosing the *vali faqih*. Everything else, significant as it might be, is not fundamental in itself but a by-product of that earlier sea change.[100] I disagree. As already discussed, elections by themselves do not guarantee either a democratic form of government or genuine popular sovereignty. These latter are contingent upon many other factors, some of which Montazeri addressed only later in life. Two are of prime importance.

One is the idea that reason, at least what Montazeri called "modern reason," can play a more meaningful role in judging and thus be a source for making rules. It was his openness to this idea that prepared the stage for a significant departure from *The Jurisprudential Foundation of Islamic State*. In that book, even though the leader required a contract with the people, for all intents and purposes he was accountable to them only in name. In actuality, his right to remain leader, which was contingent on his following the laws of Islam, depended not upon the judgment of the ordinary people, who did not have adequate knowledge of Islamic laws, but on that of an elite few (other knowledgeable clergy). As we have seen, in Montazeri's later writings, ordinary people – the citizenry – replaced the elite few as the trustors of the system. And this transference of actual right is indeed foundational.

The other factor is an emphasis on justice and its application in a modern context. It was this emphasis that led Montazeri to shift his gaze from the duties of humans to their rights. Such a shift has consequences, one of which is a move away from a view of government as master ruling over a duty-bound populace to one of it as a servant of citizens with rights.

Conclusion

The overarching belief that God has total dominion over all His creatures always hovered over Montazeri's approach to politics; he never gave up on the metaphysical foundation for constructing an ideal polity. But belief in such a foundation, which at the dawn of the Islamic Republic had made him a strong proponent of a divinely designated jurist as the uncontested leader of the community, did not prevent him from changing his mind later about the structure of his ideal polity. The change came gradually, as he went from an idealist revolutionary to having experience of actual political processes. The first stage was his move away from the theory of divine designation to belief in the popular election of the *vali faqih*.

Several new assumptions about reason and knowledge encouraged the later moves. Realizing that concentration of power in the hands of one person could have corrupting influence, he submitted to the view that knowledge was not a guarantee for moral acts and that religious knowledge was sorely deficient in dealing with the complexities of the contemporary world. More importantly, particularly in its implication for the future of jurisprudence, he came to believe that human reason in modern times was much more capable of discerning rules for living on earth than the reason of previous times, and thus must be more trusted.

Montazeri became an advocate of the separation of powers and a supporter of institutional safeguards that would keep the leader accountable to the rule of law. His next step, one that closed the gap between his ideas and those of one of the most celebrated religious thinkers of the constitutional era of the early 1900s, Ayatollah Mohammad Hossein Naini, was his shift from insisting on the rule of the person of the *faqih* to preferring the rule of Islamic laws.

The realities of the early twenty-first century pushed Montazeri toward further change and beyond what Naini had envisioned a hundred years earlier. He entrusted the legitimacy of the political system, unconditionally, to the people, even if that meant that they might go against the laws of Islam. He recognized that accepting the right of the people to decide on their political system also meant that, instead of being shielded by an authority, the people were free to make "mistakes" (by becoming autonomous agents), and thus struck a hard blow against the patriarchal view of government: the rule of a father over his sons. Montazeri did not wish for changes that might lead to taking religion out of the realm of the public. For him, politics must be informed by morality, and for that to happen religion must have a prominent presence in the public sphere. At the same time, his lived experience with the Islamic Republic allowed him to gradually accept and promote a form of public religion that was in harmony with modern sensibilities.

Notes

1 For a detailed analysis of the doctrine of Imamate and its relations to the modern concept of *velayat-e faqih*, see Hamid Mavani, *Religious Authority and Political Thought in Twelver Shi'ism: From Ali to Khomeini* (London: Routledge, 2013).

2 For a pioneering book on the development of Shii political thought in Persian, see Mohsen Kadivar, *Nazariye-haye Dowlat dar Fiqh-e Shii* [Theories of State in Shii Jurisprudence] (Tehran: Nay Publications, 1997).

3 'Allameh Mohammad Baqer Majlesi, the influential jurist of the Safavid era, was one of the advocates of such a division of domains of responsibilities.

4 On this point, see Hamid Algar, "The Oppositional Role of the Ulama in 20th-Century Iran," in *Scholars, Saints, and Sufis*, Nikki Keddie, ed. (Berkeley, CA: University of California Press, 1972), 231–56. For a more detailed exposition of Naini's overall political approach, see Masoud Kuhestani Nejad, *Chalesh-e Mazhab va Modernism: Sayr-e Andishe-ye Siasi-Mazhabi dar Iran, Nimey-eh Aval-e Qarn-e Bistom* [The Battle of Religion and Modernism: The History of Political Religious Thought in Iran, The First Half of Twentieth Century] (Tehran: Nay Publications, 2002), 24–33.

5 For an elaboration of all these points, see Kadivar, *Nazariye-haye Dowlat*, 119–26.

6 These lessons, which contained a section on the rule of the *faqih*, were collected, edited, and published in *Ketab'ol Bay'*, and later the section on the rule of jurist appeared in Persian in Ruhollah Khomeini, *Velayat-e Faqih: Hokumat Eslami* [The Rule of Jurist: The Islamic Government] (Tehran: Amir Kabir Press, 1981).

7 Ruhollah Khomeini, *Kashfol Asrar* [Unveiling of Secrets], n.d., 179–84.

8 Ibid., 184–6.

9 Ibid., 6–7.

10 Ibid., 62–6.

11 Ibid., 121–2, 142.

12 See, for example, the Iraqi Sayyed Mohammad Baqer al-Sadr, *The Emergence of Shi'ism and the Shi'ites*, trans. Asaad F. Shaker (Montreal: Imam Ali Foundation, 2006) and the Lebanese Mohammad Javad Moghni-ye, *Al-Imam al-Khomeini wa-l-Dowlat al-Islamiyya* (Lebanon: Moassesseh dar al-Ketab al-Islami, 2006).

13 Montazeri, *Eslam Din-e Fetrat*, 586.

14 Montazeri, *Az Aghaz ta Anjam*, 62–94.

15 Montazeri, *Eslam Din-e Fetrat*, 316–19.

16 In explaining human nature, Muslim scholars speak of two separate natures: (1) the material nature that humans share with other living beings (plants and animals); and (2) the real essence of humans (*fetrat*), which separates them from other living beings.

17 This explanation of the human soul, which has its origin in Plato's theory of the soul and its powers, elaborated in both *Republic* and *Phaedrus*, was and still is a standard approach in traditional Islamic ontological and ethical writings. Khomeini, in particular, approached the human soul using Plato's unforgettable parable in *Phaedrus* of the charioteer and the two horses of opposite characters. But Muslim thinkers go beyond Plato to develop categories of the powers of the soul, as we just saw in Montazeri's elaboration.

18 Montazeri, *Eslam Din-e Fetrat*, 172–3.

19 Montazeri, *Memoirs*, 98–9.

20 Borujerdi's views on the rule of an Imam-designated *faqih*, as articuted in the book *Al-Badr-ol Zaher*, were meant to be only a theoretical argument, as he himself was never involved in undermining the Pahlavi monarch.

21 See the text of several of these sermons in Izadi, *Faqih-e Aliqadr*, 1:114–27.

22 See Montazeri, *Memoirs*, 491.

23 Hossein Ali Montazeri, *The Jurisprudential Foundation of Islamic State* (Tehran: Sarayi Press, 2000), 1:93–6. Most of these categories were in fact used by other traditional jurists, such as Khomeini, with the exception of party rule as a distinct form. Its addition was due to the discourse of the left.

24 Ibid., 1:94–5.

25 Ibid., 3:30.

26 Ibid., 1:97.

27 Ibid., 2:5–180.

28 Ibid., 2:23–140.

29 Ibid., 2:177.

30 Ibid., 2:295–301.

31 Ibid., 2:190.

32 Ibid., 3:334–5.

33 See Morteza Motahhari's definition of the two terms at http://mortezam otahari.com/fa/bookview.html?BookId=398&BookArticleID=129427.

34 Ibid., 2:193.

35 For a comparative study of Mojtahed Shabestari and Mohsen Kadivar, see the two-part article by Farzin Vahdat, "Post-revolutionary Discourses of Mohammad Mojtahed Shabestari and Mohsen Kadivar:

Reconciling the Terms of Mediated Subjectivity" *Critique* 16 (2000): 31–54 and 17 (2000): 13–57.

36 Shabestari studied jurisprudence, philosophy, and exegesis with prominent mentors, such as Khomeini and Allameh Tabataba'i, for sixteen years in Qom's *howzeh*. He left Qom for Tehran in 1966, and within two years had moved to Germany to replace Ayatollah Beheshti as the director of the Islamic Center in Hamburg. Living in Germany was a significant experience for Shabestari's intellectual development; there he learned to read and speak German, and studied Continental philosophy, including the work of Hans Georg Gadamer, whose book on hermeneutics, *Truth and Method*, had the greatest impact on his developing ideas about religious knowledge. In 1978, he returned to Iran and, excited by the prospect of an Islamic revolution, threw himself wholeheartedly into the movement. After the revolution, he won a seat in the parliament, but soon became disillusioned with the Islamic Republic and withdrew from official politics, at which point he directed all his energy into writing.

37 Mohammad Mojtahed Shabestari, *Hermeneutic, Ketab va Sonnat* [Hermeneutics, the Book and the Tradition], 2nd ed. (Tehran: Tarh-e Nou Press, 1998), 17–25.

38 In later years, Shabestari moved even further from this position (i.e., from the problem associated with the understanding of a text to the problem of the nature of the text). By doing so, and by focusing on the impact of human language on text, he now argues that the language of Quran is a human language (the Prophet's language) and therefore it shows the human world and not the divine world. See Shabestari, "Prophetic Interpretation of the Universe (14): The Humanness of the Language of Quran and the Truth of Mohammad's Experience," at http://mohammadmojtahedshabestari.com/%D9%82%D8%B1%D8%A7%D8%A6%D8%AA-%D9%86%D8%A8%D9%88%DB%8C-%D8%A7%D8%B2-%D8%AC%D9%87%D8%A7%D9%86-14-%D8%A7%D9%86%D8%B3%D8%A7%D9%86%DB%8C%D9%91%D8%AA-%DA%A9%D9%84%D8%A7%D9%85-%D9%82%D8%B1%D8%A2%D9%86/.

39 Shabestari, *Hermeneutic*, 29–30.

40 For Shabestari's elaboration on this point, see *Naqdi bar Qaraat Rasmi az Din: Bohranha, Chaleshha, Rahehalha* [A Critique of Official Interpretation of Religion: Crises, Battles, Solutions] (Tehran: Tarh-e Nou, 2002), 94–8.

41 Shabestari, *Hermeneutic*, 67–75.

42 Shabestari, *Naqdi bar Qaraat Rasmi*, 108–12.

43 Kadivar was born in Fasa in the province of Fars in a non-clerical family. After receiving his high school diploma from a state-run school, he was admitted to Shiraz/Pahlavi University. But his secular studies came to a sudden halt in 1980 when the universities were temporarily shut down. He then left Shiraz and entered the Qom *howzeh*, where, for the next sixteen years, he studied jurisprudence, theology, gnosticism, and Quranic exegeses. In 1987, he received permission from his mentor, Ayatollah Montazeri, to be an interpreter of Islamic laws. For Kadivar's brief biography, see http://kadivar.com/?page_id=3802.

44 Kadivar, *Nazariye-haye Dowlat*, 58–188.

45 Mohsen Kadivar, *Hokumat-e Velayi* [The Theocratic State], 4th ed. (Tehran: Nay Publications, 2000), 204–19.

46 Ibid., 246–395.

47 Mehdi Haeri was the son of the founder of the Qom *Howzeh*, Abdolkarim Haeri. After he finished his *howzeh* studies, he moved to the capital to begin teaching theology at Tehran University. In the late 1950's, Haeri, as the representative of Ayatollah Borujerdi, left Iran for the United States to propagate Islam in the West. Realizing that to do so he first needed to learn about Western philosophy, he entered Georgetown University in Washington, DC, then went to the University of Michigan in Ann Arbor, and concluded his studies in analytical philosophy with a doctorate from the University of Toronto. He taught philosophy at Georgetown, Yale, and Oxford, and died in Tehran in 1999. For more on Haeri, see *Memoirs of Doctor Mehdi Haeri Yazdi* (Tehran: Nader Ketab Publications, 2003).

48 For an analysis of Haeri's philosophy, particularly his ontological views, see Farzin Vahdat, "Mehdi Haeri Yazdi and the Discourse of Modernity," in *Iran: Between Tradition and Modernity*, Ramin Jahanbegloo, ed. (Oxford: Lexington Books, 2004), 51–70.

49 Ibid., 53.

50 Mehdi Haeri Yazdi, *Hekmat va Hokumat* [Knowledge and Government] (London: Shadi Press, 1995), 64–79.

51 Ibid., 85.

52 John Locke, *Second Treatise of Government*, ed. C. B. Macpherson (Indianapolis, IN: Hackett Publishing, 1980), 66.

53 Haeri Yazdi, *Hekmat va Hokumat*, 107–19.

54 Ibid., 381.

55 Javadi Amoli was born into a family of clerics. After finishing a six-year elementary secular curriculum, he started his religious education, first in his hometown, later in Tehran, and finally in Qom. His main interest was Islamic philosophy, which he studied with Allameh Tabataba'i.

56 Abdollah Javadi Amoli, "Sayri dar Mabani-ye Velayat-e Faqih" [A Look at the Foundation of Rule of Jurist], *Hokumat-e Eslami* 1 (Fall 1996): 50.

57 Abdollah Javadi Amoli, *Piramoun-e Vahy va Rahbari* [On the Subject of Revelation and Leadership] (Qom: al-Zahra Press, 2001), 75–8.

58 Here the primary target of attack was Abdolkarim Soroush, the lay religious reformist, whose argument on the relative nature of knowledge, including religious knowledge, was the most serious challenge to the traditional epistemology.

59 Abdollah Javadi Amoli, "Ayatollah Allameh Javadi Amoli va Pluralism-e Dini," *Ketab-e Naqd* 4 (Fall 1997): 352–3.

60 Specifically, Mohsen Kadivar took Ayatollah Javadi Amoli to task by arguing that Amoli's conceptualization of the role of the people in the constitution as evidence that the system was both Islamic and republican was misleading. Amoli, Kadivar argued, had stretched the meaning of "republic" to the extent that even the rule of the Prophet could be construed as republican, and thus had rendered the concept meaningless. See Kadivar, *Hokumat-e Velayi*, 212–14.

61 Mesbah Yazdi was born in the city of Yazd in 1934. He had six years of elementary education in a secular school, and then entered Yazd's *howzeh* in 1947. After four years in Yazd and a brief sojourn to Najaf, he went to Qom, where he studied under the mentorship of Ayatollahs Khomeini, Behjat, and Tabatabai. His primary interest, like Amoli's, was Islamic philosophy.

62 See Sussan Siavoshi, "Ayatollah Misbah-Yazdi: A Voice of Authoritarian Islam," *Muslim World* 100, no. 1 (2010): 124–44.

63 Mohammad Taqi Mesbah Yazdi, *Amuzesh-e Falsafeh* [Teaching Philosophy], vol. 1 (Tehran: Sazman-e Tablighat-e Eslami, 1987), 42–3.

64 Mesbah targeted in particular the lay religious intellectual Abodolkarim Soroush and his controversial series of essays on "Qabz va Bast-e Teorik-e Shari'at" (The Theoretical Contraction and Expansion of Islamic Law). See Mohammad Taqi Mesbah Yazdi, *Nazariy-e Siasi-e Eslam*, ed. Karim Sobhani (Qom: Imam Khomeini Educational and Research Institute, 2009), 2:257–61.

65 Ibid., 2:129–41.

66 Mohammad Taqi Mesbah Yazdi, "Mashru'iyat va Maqbuliyat," in *Porseshha va Pasokhha* [Questions and Answers], 8th ed. (Qom: Imam Khomeini Publication, 2012), 1:35–6.

67 See *Hamshahri*, December 6, 1998.

68 Mohammad Taqi Mesbah Yazdi, "Rabeteh Moteqabel-e Mardom va Hokumat," in *Kavoshha va Chaleshha* [Searches and Battles] (Qom: Imam Khomeini Educational and Research Institute, 2003), 4:109.

69 *Sobh-e Emruz*, June 7, 1999.

70 Mesbah Yazdi, *Nazariy-e Siasi-e Eslam*, 2:99–100. For a much longer elaboration of the concepts of right and responsibility, and a comparison of the liberal and the Islamic state, see Mesbah Yazdi, "Rabeteh Moteqabel-e Mardom va Hokumat," 1:9–38. Most of these essays were written at the end of the 1990's, and thus were part of a raging debate.

71 For an analysis of the sources of the incongruity between the place of reason in moral principle and its absence in juristic practices, see Ali-Reza Bhojani, *Moral Rationalism and Shari'a: Independent Rationality in Modern Shi'i Usul al-Fiqh* (Oxon: Routledge, 2015).

72 For an elaboration of these obstacles, see Bhojani, *Moral Rationalism*, 143–57.

73 Montazeri, *Eslam Din-e Fetrat*, 430.

74 Ibid., 53.

75 Ibid., 51–5.

76 Montazeri, *Didgahha*, 1:474–5.

77 Montazeri, *Didgahha*, 1:476–7.

78 Hossein Ali Montazeri, "Hokumat-e Mardomi va Qanoun-e Asassi" [Democratic Rule and the Constitution], in *Didgahha*, 1:186.

79 Hossein Ali Montazeri, "Velayat-e Faqih va Qanoun-e Asassi" [The Rule of Jurist and the Constitution], in *Didgahha*, 1:35.

80 Montazeri, "Velayat-e Faqih," 56.

81 Hossein Ali Montazeri, "Hokumat Mardomi va Qanoun-e Asassi," in *Didgahha*, 1:196.

82 At that time, the reformist president Khatami, who wished to reduce tensions with the outside world, particularly the West, had confronted stiff resistance by conservative clergy.

83 Montazeri elaborated this point more fully in an earlier essay, "Khoshunat, ya Tasahol va Tasamoh" [Violence or Tolerance], in *Didgahha*, 1:143–4.

84 Montazeri, "Hokumat-e Mardomi," 228–9.

85 Ibid., 190–1. See also his response to questions asked by his son Sa'id in Montazeri, *Enteqad az Khod*, 26–32.

86 In a written correspondence with two journalists of the UK *Guardian*, which was published shortly before this essay, Montazeri, in his critique of the institution of the Assembly of Experts, mentioned several factors that made the assembly less than a suitable body for the election and supervision of the *faqih*. Chief among these was the *faqih*'s influence in choosing the candidates for the assembly through his appointment of the members of the Guardian Council who would vet them. Another was the assembly's narrow range of qualifications. See the entire text of the interview in Montazeri, *Didgahha*, 1:151–67.

87 Semi-*estedlali* treatises are in Persian and fall somewhere between treatises written only for specialists in the field and those written for the wider non-specialist audience. They have argumentation, but are simplified so that a lay reader can understand them.

88 Montazeri, *Hokumat-e Dini va Huqquq Ensan*, 23.

89 Ibid., 13.

90 Ibid., 36.

91 Ibid., 20–1.

92 Ibid., 142–5.

93 See Montazeri's Friday Prayer sermon in *Kayhan*, November 24, 1979, 5.

94 Montazeri, *Memoirs*, 258.

95 Personal interview with John Limbert (one of the American diplomats held hostage in Tehran), August 19, 2013. According to Limbert, in that visit Montazeri talked about his own prison experiences and told the hostages that he understood their feelings, and added that despite the hardship of jail, there would be an end to it. He then wished them patience.

96 Montazeri, *Memoirs*, apps. 139 and 140, 576–8.

97 Montazeri, *Didgahha*, 2:131–2 and 2:248–9.

98 Ibid., 2:162.

99 Montazeri, *Didgahha*, 3:58.

100 This view has been expressed by some of Montazeri's own students, such as Mohammad Hassan Movahedi Savoji. See http://dinonline .com/doc/news/fa/4355/.

6 | *Human Rights*

I call you father because I learned from you how to defend the oppressed without using violence against the oppressor. I learned from you that being silent means helping the oppressor. Father, I learned much from you, although I never showed my appreciation for being your child and student. Father, forgive us. You are the father of Human Rights in Iran and I and millions of others are your children and disciples.

With these words, Shirin Ebadi, the 2003 Noble Peace Prize winner, mourned the passing of Montazeri.[1] Ebadi was not alone in paying homage to the deceased ayatollah for his attention to the plight of the vulnerable. In 2009, shortly before his death, Montazeri received an award from the Center of Defenders of Human Rights, a reformist and non-governmental body. Scores of admirers wrote on his website and saluted him for his attention to human rights. What, we might ask, accounts for all these accolades? What were his actual stands on human rights? And to what extent was traditional Islamic jurisprudence, to which Montazeri was deeply committed, compatible with the underlying principles of the UDHR?

The Universal Declaration of Human Rights: The Contour of the Debate

As its title suggests, the UDHR was drafted with the expectation that its principles would apply universally. But one of the long-standing questions in the global debate on human rights has been whether the envisioned human (and by extension his/her rights) in the UDHR is indeed a universal being or belongs only to the categories of "secular" and "liberal."[2] Some contend that if one has to accept a universal code,

A version of this chapter first appeared as "Human Rights and the Dissident Grand Ayatollah Hussain Ali Montazeri," *Journal of Muslim People*, 106 (July 2016): 605–25.

there must first be agreement on a set of moral philosophical foundations, such as natural rights or divine justice.[3] Others argue that such emphasis only delays putting a code that they believe is reasonable into practice, and they therefore prefer to focus on the legal obligation of nation-states to live up to the commitment made to the UDHR. This has been the position of a large number of supporters of the UDHR in the West. Their criticism of violators of the UDHR, including the Islamic Republic, has been primarily on the basis of concrete, documentarian, and legal arguments.[4] In Iran, however, the debate over human rights has revolved around a set of philosophical, theological, and epistemological questions. Complicating the debate are perspectives that connect the UDHR with the global political structure.

Human Rights and the Islamic Republic

Iran was one of the signatories of the UDHR in 1948.[5] The Pahlavi state also committed itself to the other two declarations of human rights that, together with the UDHR, constitute the International Bill of Human Rights (IBHR).[6] Yet, having signed these documents, the authoritarian Pahlavi state did not feel compelled to adhere to its commitments, and, particularly after the 1953 coup d'etat, became increasingly oppressive. Judging by the slogans of the revolution, the regime's violation of human rights clearly fueled revolutionary sentiment. In a speech to a group of Iranians soon after his move from Najaf to Paris, Khomeini criticized the use of force against people and appealed to the UDHR: "Each nation wants its fate to be in its own hands, that is part of the Universal Declaration of Human Rights."[7] His appeal was selective, however, and he frequently condemned the UDHR on political grounds.

After the victory of the revolution, even though Iran did not formally withdraw from its commitment to human rights, the Islamic Republic quickly ceased to follow the provisions of the UDHR. During the constitutional debate, Articles 2 and 18 of the UDHR were particularly contentious, and they were ultimately ignored in the final draft of the constitution. Article 2 states, "Everyone is entitled to all the rights and freedoms set forth in this Declaration, without distinction of any kind, such as race, colour, sex, language, religion, political or other opinion, national or social origin, property, birth or other status." And Article 18 provides that, "Everyone has the right to freedom of thought, conscience and religion; this right includes freedom to change his religion or belief, and freedom, either alone or in community with others and in public or private, to manifest his religion or belief in teaching, practice, worship and observance." These articles clashed with some of the rules of the traditional Islamic jurisprudence by putting women and men, as well as Muslims and non-Muslims, on equal legal footing; and by also undermining other rules, such as the law on apostasy.

The adopted constitution acknowledged a citizen's rights and freedoms only when those things did not contradict Islamic precepts. Article 19 of the constitution stated that all Iranians were equal before the law on the basis of ethnicity, tribal affiliation, race, color, and language but left out gender and religious affiliation. These omissions worried some Iranians, who took them as the harbinger of further discriminatory or harsh laws. Their worries were justified, as rule after rule was passed that took the legal system of the Islamic Republic further and further away from the principles of the UDHR.

After the suppression of the liberal seculars who were the primary force behind the UDHR, disagreements over the question of human rights appeared within religious circles. Religious reformists supported the UDHR and argued that the declaration was in harmony with the spirit of Islam. Conversely, the traditional religious establishment criticized the declaration for its secular approach, pointed at its incompatibility with Islamic laws, and asked for a new human rights code that was in harmony with Islam. For them, that alternative was embodied in the Cairo Declaration of Human Rights in Islam (CDHRI), to which the Islamic Republic was a signatory, and which acknowledged the centrality of Islamic law. Article 24 of the CDHRI stated, "All the rights and freedoms stipulated in this Declaration are subject to the Islamic Shari'ah," and Article 25 declared, "The Islamic Shari'ah is the only source of reference for the explanation or clarification of any of the articles of this Declaration."[8] Religious conservatives applauded the unequivocal departure of the CDHRI from the secular nature of the UDHR, but the International Commission of Jurists condemned it.

No one in Iran publicly criticized the CDHRI, but the reformers intensified their support for the UDHR, and the theme of human rights played a key part in the increasingly public contest between the conservatives and reformists over state–society relations. The mounting international criticism of the Islamic Republic's violation of human rights, particularly after the mass executions of political prisoners in the late 1980's, gave a special significance to these internal debates.

Religious Discourses on Human Rights in Iran

As discussed in Chapter 5, reformists distanced themselves from the conservatives in how they understood such concepts as human nature and human reason. Briefly put, the conservatives saw human nature as bifurcated and conflicted and human reason as weak and imperfect, incapable of creating true order within the self. The religious reformists generally did not focus on the duality and tension within the human self and treated it as a coherent whole. And even though they acknowledged the mysteries of existence and the power of revelation in the journey of the spirit, they saw human reason as capable of making proper judgments in the area of human interrelationships, a domain to which human rights belong. The position of Montazeri on the debate over human rights was a complicated one. He had deep attachment to his tradition but at the same time made moves that distanced him from it. A brief look at the general debate helps us understand his position more fully.

The Conservative Approach to the UDHR

The conservatives criticize the UDHR on two grounds: political and ideological/religious. The fraught relationship between the Islamic Republic and the West and the fierce adherence of the revolutionaries to Iran's independence provided the impetus for challenging the UDHR on political grounds. Soon after the establishment of the Islamic Republic, and in response to criticisms of the executions of former members of the Pahlavi regime, Ayatollah Khomeini made the following statement:

Where were the human rights specialists when the dissidents' feet were cut off in Iranian torture chambers? . . . Those who play the human rights game strategize, and their call for human rights serves the interest of big capitalist countries to the detriment of small ones.[9]

More than three decades later, deep suspicion of the West still plays a significant role in the Islamic Republic's approach to the UDHR. The first of two major complaints about the UDHR is that the West uses two standards in enforcing compliance: one, quite lax, is reserved for countries whose leaders are subservient to the West, and the other, a strict one, is applied on countries that resist submission. The second complaint concerns the "hypocritical behavior" of the West, its "do as I say, not as I do" attitude. Many critics consider the West a major violator of its own UDHR rules, particularly through what they see as its suppression of the rights of the Third World's nations. From this perspective, they emphasize the virtues of the CDHRI, which draws attention to the global power disparity and acknowledges the right of oppressed people to resist colonialism.[10]

The heart of the substantive critique of the UDHR, however, is grounded in philosophy. Three ayatollahs, Javadi Amoli, Mesbah Yazdi, and Mohammad Taqi Ja'fari, have been the most influential representatives of conservative interpretations of these foundations. Despite some differences in tone, particularly in the more dialogical approach of Ja'fari as opposed to the more confrontational one of Mesbah, all three share certain fundamental principles.

They argue that a doctrine of universal human rights depends on a prior and accepted definition of a "universally true" human being with a well-articulated essence.[11] The UDHR has failed to present or recognize such a being; therefore, its claim to universal rights cannot be taken seriously.[12] Within this general criticism, the detractors question the UDHR's implied description of human dignity as a universally shared attribute. The preamble of the UDHR begins with this: "Whereas recognition of the inherent dignity and of the equal and inalienable rights of all members of the human family is the foundation of freedom, justice and peace in the world." For the conservatives, innate or natural dignity is not the correct standard for determining the rights of humans because, they argue, people can lose that dignity through their actions. Instead, a true foundation of human rights must be based on a higher and more meaningful notion of dignity, one that has been *acquired*. Since one's share of acquired dignity depends on one's success in following the laws of God, each person's portion of rights should follow accordingly.[13]

Needless to say, the conservatives' epistemological argument about the inability of independent human reason to recognize the truth provides them with yet another means to criticize the UDHR, whose articles are the product of human reason. But, for these critics, the final and central fault of the UDHR is its failure to acknowledge *haqq-ollah*(the right of God), the source of all rights.[14] In relation to God, humans only have duty. For all these reasons, the conservatives see fundamental incompatibilities between the UDHR on the one hand and Islamic principles and laws on the other.

The Reformist Approach to the UDHR

Despite a shared belief that the UDHR is compatible with Islam, the reformists differ in their judgment of the place of jurisprudence in connection to human rights. For the lay philosopher Abdolkarim Soroush, Islamic jurisprudence presents a serious problem in making the case for the compatibility of Islam with the UDHR, while for the traditionally trained jurist Ayatollah Yousef San'ei, his discipline is not where the challenge lies. Somewhere in the middle, younger clergy, such as Mohsen Kadivar, criticize the traditional jurisprudence but see the heart of the problem not in the essence of Islamic law but only in the traditional approach to it.

Abdolkarim Soroush

Soroush's primary contribution to the discourse of religious reformism is in the area of epistemology, where he questions and undermines the stability and certitude of knowledge. Contending that religious knowledge is comparable to other kinds of knowledge, he argues that even though the sacred word of God is immutable, human understanding of it remains contextual.[15] No one, not even clerics, can ever claim access to the absolute truth of religion. Soroush's approach to reform is grounded on this epistemological view.

For the most part, Soroush refrains from using a religious language in his arguments for sociopolitical reforms and the promotion of human rights. On occasion, however, he has defended human rights by resorting to a metaphysical argument. His lecture on *"Haqq va Taklif va Khoda"* (Right and Duty and God) is one such instance where he appeals to Quranic exegesis to undermine the religious conservatives' demand for the total and unconditional submission of humans to God.[16] Choosing "claim" from among several meanings of the concept of "right" (*haqq*) as the most relevant to a discussion of human rights, Soroush asserts that "right as claim" is always logically conjoined with duties, and whoever is entitled to a right can legitimately expect its fulfillment/protection to be the duty of another. He then uses the Quran to make a case for human claims against God.

Soroush confesses that the human of the Quran, particularly in the jurisprudential verses of the text, is rarely a creature with rights, and therefore one should search in other verses to find support for the rights of humans. For him, the support comes in a verse from the chapter on women, where God says, "We send prophets with two main responsibilities: to *tabshir* [give hope to people of God's rewards], and to *anzar* [install fear of God's punishment]." Soroush interprets the sending of prophets in this verse as God's attempt to not only reassure people of future rewards, but to shield Himself from people's potential complaints against Him. Soroush takes this verse as a proof that humans have "claims" over God, and that God in turn has a "duty" to fulfill them. To fortify this contention, Soroush lists examples from Islamic gnostic writings and highlights the famous quarrel of Abraham with God, an event that is mentioned not only in the Hebrew Bible but also in the Quran. Through this interpretation, Soroush hopes to create a hole in the conservative argument from an intra-religious discourse. But for the most part he is reluctant to use the traditional authoritative sources such as the Quran in promoting human rights. For that, one can turn to Mohsen Kadivar.

Mohsen Kadivar

Where Soroush finds tension and quarrel in the way the rights of God relate to those of humans, Kadivar sees harmony. Appealing to authoritative sources, Kadivar contends that the fulfilment of the rights of God begins with respecting the rights of His creatures. He also rejects the idea that the UDHR is irreconcilable with Islam and argues that one can be both a devout Muslim and a supporter of the universal principles of human rights. He makes his case in his collected volume on *Haqq-ol Nas* (The Right of Humans).[17]

Kadivar recognizes that some aspects of Islamic jurisprudence are hardly reconcilable with UDHR. His solution is to isolate those aspects without giving up jurisprudence on the whole. Hence, he divides Islam into two categories: "historical" and "spiritual". The first is an outmoded version of religion whose adherents take the social, cultural, and political conditions of the seventh century as the determinant and the rule of the Prophet as a sacred model for all times. The second is an Islam that focuses on the knowledge of and search for spirituality, and on the ultimate purpose of human existence.[18] A firm supporter of the UDHR, Kadivar argues that the "historical Islam" – particularly in such areas as the penal code and the treatment of women and minorities – is in conflict with some of the key articles of the declaration. However, the "spiritual Islam" accepts human reason as the ultimate authority in all interrelational and temporal rulings.[19] He concludes that it is time for the "historical Islam" to relinquish to the "spiritual Islam" its position as the true religion. For Kadivar, a new jurisprudential approach, one that addresses all the needs of modern Muslims, including their demands for observance of the UDHR, can indeed be built on this second view of religion.

It should be mentioned that Kadivar, despite believing in the irrelevance of many of the traditional rulings, only advocates their *naskh* (discontinuation), rather than their *hazf* (complete elimination). The reason for his caution is his view that human reason is not infallible and hence the sound judgment of people in one era might be found erroneous in another.

Ayatollah Yousef San'ei

San'ei, another advocate of the UDHR, does not address the problems of traditional jurisprudence as Kadivar does, but in practice he defies some of its fundamentals through issuing several rulings in favor of the UDHR. As a student of both Borujerdi and Khomeini, Yousef San'ei (1936–) became a teacher and received permission for *ejtehad* at an early age. He was only moderately involved in the revolution, until its final stages brought him and other members of the *howzeh* community into the streets. After the establishment of the Islamic Republic and the passage of the constitution, San'ei became a part of the political elite as a member of the Guardian Council and the Assembly of Experts, and also as the general prosecutor. He joined the critics of the regime years after Montazeri had done so. Yet, once he had become a critic, he too was outspoken, and, like Montazeri, he was seen as a serious threat to the state. In 2009, San'ei condemned in the strongest terms the suppression of the protest movement, and for that, he was attacked. Vigilante groups vandalized his office in Qom, and the state denied permission for reprinting his books and filtered his website. Above all, the influential and conservative SQSS declared him to be unsuited to be a *marja'*, a status that he had held for years.

Even though San'ei's theological, ontological, and epistemological convictions are traditional, his judgment on social and political matters distances him from his conservative peers. His support for the UDHR is clearly stated in the following:

On the basis of Shii religion I do believe that human dignity is a foundational principle, and a day will come when the world will be filled with justice . . . The direction of the global movement particularly after WWII and the adoption of the Universal Declaration of Human Rights and International laws are signs of such a claim.[20]

One area in which San'ei can fairly claim to be a pioneer among the high clergy is that of gender.[21] He asserts that women are eligible not only to become judges and sources of emulation but also to occupy the highest office in the Islamic Republic, the office of *vali faqih*. Adressing a few of the several problems embedded in family laws, he speaks for stricter conditions on polygamy, a greater role for mothers in guardianship of their children, and more equitable divorce and inheritance laws in the interest of women.[22] He also suggests the reform of penal codes so that women and men are treated equally. Even though San'ei's suggestions are modest, they reduce the considerable gap between the traditional family laws of Islam and the principle of gender equality in the UDHR. But, as already mentioned, San'ei has yet to use these reformist rulings as opportunities to seek systematic reforms to traditional jurisprudence.

Changes in Islamic jurisprudence require the negotiation of a complex set of precepts, whose legal status varies by category. Islamic jurists divide religious precepts in several ways, always with an eye to their degree of longevity or flexibility. Which rules are forever and which are contextual depends on the category to which they belong. Of particular relevance for the discussion of human rights is whether the laws are worship-related, or whether they deal with interrelational matters. As explained in Chapter 5, interrelational rules are themselves of two kinds: constitutional (originated directly from God) and endorsed (made by the pre-Islamic reason of the sages but endorsed by God).

For the most part, worship rules fall outside the parameters of the debate on human rights. The key conflict thus revolves around interrelational rules and whether they are constant or contextual. In general, the traditional clergy consider almost all interrelational laws, constitutional or endorsed, unchanging and eternal, and demand unwavering obedience to them.[23] Their logic therefore requires the retreat of reason when reason finds itself in conflict with these laws.

The reformists, on the other hand, refute the idea of inviolability where interrelational laws are concerned, particularly those of the endorsed kind. They argue that new circumstances and sensibilities demand innovative rational judgment and thus reject many of the old interrelational laws as irrelevant. To them, God's acceptance of some of the judgment of the collective reason of several centuries ago should also provide the justification and the precedent for His endorsement of contemporary human reason. If they are in conflict with modern requirements, interrelational laws should either be eliminated forever, as Soroush has argued, or discontinued, as Kadivar would have it. Where did Montazeri stand on this and other questions related to human rights?

Montazeri and Human Rights

In the *Resaleh Huqquq* (Treatise on Rights), Montazeri declared:

The principal and fundamental rights of humans are not the products of exigencies or necessities of a particular social milieu or of the temporal and spatial circumstances. These rights – such as the right to decide one's fate, right to life, right to work and to a healthy living, the right to freedom of thought and expression, and the right to personal and social security – are first and foremost natural rights and thus are constant, inalienable, and essential. Humans, due to their humanness and their dignity, should enjoy these rights. Such rights are not dependent on any legislation or governmental will, but have roots in nature ... Even the Shari'a's approach to these rights is advisory and not compulsory.[24]

It took Montazeri many years and many painful experiences to arrive at this position. Previously, he had been actively involved in suppressing the religious minority of Baha'is and was an outspoken supporter of the most elitist version of the *velayat-e faqih*. He had also been in favor of more extensive restrictions on the rights of the people than the preliminary draft of the constitution allowed.[25] At the same time, though, he showed some concern about the dangers of an overcontrolling state and defended certain civil freedoms to guarantee a safe public space for citizens. In one of the sessions of the AFRC, during a debate on an article that would allow room for peaceful demonstrations and gatherings, a great many members of the assembly were in favor of adopting strict conditions on the right to demonstrate. Montazeri spoke against them:

Sometimes when we try to improve upon certain articles we make them worse. In other words in our attempt to fix the eyebrow we blind the eye... Tomorrow, if a few people wish to have a gathering, a policeman would have the right to accuse them of conspiring against national security. The consequence [of such a restriction on the right to demonstrate] will be sanctioning the power of the government to prevent any gathering, religious or secular.[26]

Moreover, he rose in defense of the rights of political prisoners and against the abuses of state. He wrote letters, made statements, and gave speeches. On the whole, however, it was not until 2004 that his sporadic writings on human rights appeared in one focused volume, called *Resaleh Huqquq*. He was prompted, as explained in the treatise's preface, by his profound dismay about the widespread portrayal of Islam as a violent and anti-human rights faith. For him, Islam was the embodiment of generosity and kindness.

The treatise is a curious mixture of pronouncements on a person's traditional duties along with concerns for individual rights. Montazeri began *Resaleh Huqquq* with an elaboration on human nature, the purpose of human life, and the means to reach that purpose. He reminded his readers of the ultimate goal of human life, which can be achieved only by performance of duty.[27] Moreover, like other conservatives, he emphasized God's rights and human obligation to fulfill those rights. But then he started a move away from the conservatives by asserting that most such obligations fall in the domain of faith and rituals of worship. With respect to the interrelational laws, his position was complex, as he showed more flexibility than the conservatives by adopting an ambiguous approach to human reason.

As mentioned in the previous chapter, Montazeri viewed human reason as both dependent on and inferior to divine laws in discovering the truth and the path to eternal salvation. In a 1999 interview, in reaction to the establishment of the Expediency Council as a permanent article of the amended constitution, he stated:

On many occasions humans can recognize [through the use of reason] the benefit and harm of issues at hand and thus make rules accordingly. But there are circumstances when such a recognition can only be made through an appeal to the language of divine laws. Most of the worship rules and their derived benefits and harms are outside the domain of human understanding while the situation is reversed when it comes to the interrelational rules. Still, even in the latter domain there are certain divine conditions that human reason might fail to understand.[28]

Thus, when human reason finds itself in conflict with Islamic laws, even in the case of some of the interrelational precepts, reason should bow to the divine rule. The only exception that Montazeri allowed is when the judgment of reason is accepted universally and across time. This puts such a burden on reason as to make its authority over revelation/*hadith* virtually a moot point. Here, Montazeri was in good company, agreeing with such conservatives as Mesbah Yazdi.[29]

But he also signaled some changes in his view, again as discussed in Chapter 5, by differentiating modern from traditional reason and by praising the former over the latter. This approach to reason, along with his relentless emphasis on the priority of justice over religion and his increasing attention to the sensibilities of the contemporary world, allowed Montazeri to distance himself from many of his conservative colleagues in his attitude toward interrealtional precepts. His last stand on these laws, as expressed in *Resaleh Huqquq*, was this: since God is just, His laws must always be just as well, and if modern reason and new circumstances call for new laws or new interpretation of the old laws for justice to prevail, then some of the earlier interrelational laws can and should be shelved.[30]

From the Rights of God to the Rights of Humans

Despite his belief in the importance of God's divine right, Montazeri gave a temporal priority to the fulfillment of the rights of humans over the rights of God. Like Kadivar, his invocation of human rights in relation to God's rights was different from Soroush's. If Soroush made his case for human rights by arguing that humans have a claim in relation to God, Montazeri did it by insisting on the affinity and harmony between the two sets of rights. Through his appeal to the words of the first Shii Imam, Montazeri argued that the realization of the rights of a person is a gateway to the fulfillment of the rights of God.[31]

Montazeri's different prioritization of divine vs. human rights was not the only indication of his evolving distance from the authoritarian narrative; he also shifted his position on the extent of rights and duties by expanding the former and contracting the latter. In response to his son's last question in *Enteqad az Khod*, he stated:

> One of our most serious mistakes in the area of Islamic knowledge was that we ignored the rights of humans as humans in our studies and limited ourselves to the rulings of our predecessors, and therefore rejected discourses that emphasized the innate dignity and rights of humans as a Western import. As a matter of fact many of these rights have been extracted from Islamic precepts and have the support of both the Quranic verses and the sayings of the Prophets and the Imams. And, there are of course others which [can be discovered] through further study and reflection.[32]

Montazeri rectified his earlier mistakes as much as he was able in his *Resaleh Huqquq* by recognizing a group of inalienable and essential rights for people. He concluded that there are several categories of rights (domestic and international, human and animal) whose observances are demanded by Islamic justice. Among them are the right to self-determination, the right to supervise the performance of state leaders, the right to personal security, and the right to change one's religion.[33] He also paid attention to the right of the accused and the right to defense and fair trial. In addition to these civil and political rights, he held the government responsible for social and economic rights, such as the right to a retirement pension (without discrimination against non-Muslims) and the right to a decent life for the poor. Government is duty-bound to uphold these rights, and in return, based on the social contract, the people owe the government the observance of justly made laws and regulations.[34]

In dealing with the international rights of nations, Montazeri determined that Muslim and non-Muslim countries are entitled to the same rights and that the fulfillment of international obligations is mandatory for all. Among internationally related rights, he emphasized the rights of prisoners of war, the rights of refugees, immunity for the diplomatic corps, and the rights of all nations to be free from aggression and from outside interference in their internal affairs. In the case of the right to be free of outside interference, he allowed for two vaguely defined exceptions: (1) when the people in such countries ask for outside help in facing an oppressive regime; and (2) when internal matters have international repercussions, such as narcotic trafficking or the acquisition of weapons of mass destruction.[35]

In addition to the rights of human beings, Montazeri briefly addressed the duty of humans to protect the rights of nature and of animals. People are forbidden to engage in undue deforestation and in overextraction of mineral and other natural resources. They are also forbidden to pollute air, water, or soil with industrial and nuclear waste or through overconsumption. Humans should be mindful of the rights of animals and refrain from overexploiting or abusing them. They are obligated to feed animals well and treat them humanely.[36]

In the same treatise, he approached the UDHR in a dialogical rather than a confrontational manner, not through the invention of a new approach to jurisprudence but by emphasizing those Islamic precepts that reconcile the two narratives most effectively. The most important point of conversion rests in his recognition of the innate and universal rights of all humans. Beyond this general principle, he endorsed many specific articles of the UDHR, while disagreeing with others. Then he made a significant concession and asserted that the Islamic Republic, as a signatory to the human rights declaration, should do its best to uphold its legal commitment. Overall, however, he saw the UDHR as a product of human reason in a specific time and place, and as such believed that it could legitimately be challenged by later generations.

Through actions and words, Montazeri left his mark on several areas of human rights, while remaining within the tradition in others. The rest of this chapter focuses on his approach to a few specific themes in the human rights debate, including the Islamic penal code, the rights of political prisoners, the right to privacy, the position of religious minority, and the status of women.

Penal Code

The penal code of the Islamic Republic stipulates several categories of punishment: (1) *hadd*, fixed punishment clearly set by religious precepts; (2) *ghesas*, punishment that equals the crime (an eye for an eye); (3) *diyeh*, monetary punishment (compensation for injury or death); and (4) *ta'zir*, punishment decided by the judge. According to Islamic principles, the ceiling for *ta'zir* should always be lower than the lowest punishment in *hadd*. This principle was the source of Montazeri's earliest criticism of the judicial system, where some judges arbitrary passed heavy sentences on prisoners beyond the limit set by *hadd*. In those early days, Montazeri never insisted on more than correcting the wrongful application of the penalty and remained faithful to the idea of the immutability of Islamic penal code. In some areas of the penal code, he even took a harsher line than Khomeini did. One of

Khomeini's *ehtiatat*, which he referred to Montazeri, was on the question of the fate of *mofsed-e fel arz* (one who spreads corruption on earth). Khomeini was hesitant to rule on the death penalty as the appropriate punishment, while Montazeri believed that the essence of the act might be sufficient for condemning a person to death.[37] Montazeri's ruling became part of the penal code of the revolutionary Iran. However, the use of the code for the indiscriminate executions of thousands, particularly the killings of political prisoners in 1988, disturbed Montazeri and prompted him to define strict conditions – all of which entailed waging war against the fabric of the Islamic community – that had to be met before a "corrupter on earth" could be justly sentenced to death.[38]

Montazeri raised his voice not only about abuses related to the specific matter of *mofsed-e fel arz* but against the misapplication of the general code. It is worth mentioning that as early as the first half of the 1980's, he had called for a more restricted use of corporal punishment, imprisonment, and exile by advocating the use of alternatives such as verbal reprimand and monetary fines.[39] His distancing from the harsh penal code was best shown in his treatment of apostasy cases. Three famous cases of apostasy led Montazeri to think of safeguards against undue punishment.[40] One was that of Salman Rushdie, whose *Satanic Verses* led to protests in the streets in London, Karachi, and many other cities around the world. Offended Muslims accused Rushdie of not only insulting the Prophet but questioning the Quran as the authentic Word of God. Eventually, Khomeini, in his position as the Supreme Source of Emulation of the Shiis, pronounced Rushdie an apostate deserving of a death sentence. The ruling, strongly criticized particularly in the West, put the Islamic penal code in general and apostasy in particular in the limelight. At first, Montazeri supported the verdict, but he then came to view it as unjust and unwise.

Closer to his heart were the charges of apostasy against two Iranian religious reformists: Yusef Eshkevari and Hashem Aghajari, in 2000 and 2002, respectively.[41] The accusations and the threat of death sentences for the two men resulted in international condemnation and raised serious protests from reformists at home, including President Khatami. Montazeri, the jurist, criticized the behavior of the judiciary not just because of the political nature of its charges against the two reformists but also because of its harsh and inflexible interpretation of the code.[42] Not everyone, of course, agreed with him.

Apostasy and its due penalty are contentious matters, partly due to the different approaches of the Quran on the one hand and the *ravayat* on the other.[43] The Quran does not specify a corporal punishment for apostasy, but some *ravayat* (specifically the ones attributed to the Fifth and Sixth Imams) unequivocally demand it. These sayings assign apostasy not only the status of a sin, with its associated eternal damnation, but also that of a capital crime. Since the conservatives consider the *ravayat* authoritative along with the Quran, the severity of the penalty for apostasy is obligatory.[44]

There remain, however, certain differences among the conservatives in their approach to apostasy. According to some, this offense pertains to the denial of one of two basic principles of faith: the unity of God and the prophethood of Mohammad. Others expand the definition to include also the denial of other and lesser principles. These conservatives differ from one another in one other respect. Some argue that an apostate is any Muslim who relinquishes the religion; others argue that the charge should be reserved only for those who not only leave Islam as their religion but actively try to lure others away from it.

The reformers take the Quran as the only relevant source of judgment in this matter and argue that since the Holy Book does not assign any temporal punishment for relinquishing Islam, apostasy cannot be treated as a crime, and thus there should be no legal prosecution of those accused of it.[45] They also reject the assertion that renouncing Islam as one's personal faith is in itself sufficient to make one an apostate. Only acting with ill intention against Islam and Muslims justifies that charge.

Montazeri's view did not fit either of these categories comfortably. In 1999, he wrote a piece, "*Dar Bab-e Tazahom*" (On the Matter of Conflict), to argue pragmatically against punishing people accused of apostasy by using the principle of *tazahom*. In the same essay, however, and in tune with the conservative view on apostasy, he wrote: "If a long standing Muslim becomes an apostate and publicly questions the holy articles of faith then s/he would be like a cancerous tumor who will gradually contaminate the healthy body of the society."[46] He also believed that the law against apostasy, with its associated corporal punishment, is God's law and thus irrefutable, irrevocable, and eternal.[47] But after Aghajari and Eshkevari were accused as such, he started to rethink his view about the nature of apostasy. In 2008, he contended that simply changing one's religion does not make one an apostate; to be guilty of that offense, one must purposefully act against Islam or the Islamic community.[48] This opinion was based on an argument he had made a couple of years earlier in his *Eslam Din-e Fetrat*. There he had argued that "the standard of apostasy is not the change of heart because the choice of faith is a function of certain preliminaries and therefore is out of one's control."[49] As such, a genuine change of faith cannot be subject to punishment. But even in the case of a true apostate, one who intentionally leaves Islam for the sole purpose of corrupting others and weakening Islam, assigning punishment is not easy. The reason, he argued, is the difficulty of proving a person's intention, even if the accused has confessed. Considering his disdain for state-extracted confessions, few would have been surprised at his reservation about taking them as clear proof. For him, the smallest doubt about the actual intention of the accused was reason enough to withhold a judgment that imposed punishment.[50]

Yet his eventual crossing of the line from a traditional to a reformist stance in this area of jurisprudence came through a pragmatic turn, one that mitigated strictly moral judgment. Here, he contextualized the criminality of apostasy. He didn't deny that apostasy was a crime, but recognized a vast difference between the status of Islam at its dawn and its power in the contemporary world. During the early days of Islam, competing religious beliefs threatened to discredit and destroy the new faith, and with it the small community of the faithful.[51] But now, he declared, Islam is no longer a young and vulnerable religion, and therefore the necessity to carry out certain religiously sanctioned punishments has ceased.

Using a utilitarian argument, Montazeri concluded that the benefit of these practices at this time has been outweighed by their cost, and for the overall well-being of Islam and Muslims these practices should be shelved. In response to a jurisprudential question posed to him about the possibility of stopping the use of certain Islamic punishments, even if ordered by God, Montazeri stated:

The principal goal of the Islamic penal code is protection of life, property, and dignity of each individual and their community through punishment and education of the criminals...The achievement of this goal in the radically changed circumstances might require different tools. Some of these codes due to their incompatibility with the character of a particular society, or their mistaken application, or the inability of explaining them correctly [to those who do not believe in these laws], can result in suspicion toward the principle of the law itself. In such a situation the application of these laws should be halted until a later time when their philosophy is both well-articulated and accepted by the society.[52]

Montazeri's jurisprudential approach to reform of the penal code can therefore be summed up in a few points. First, in the areas in which he seems to have been unable or unwilling to go against the law, he made serious efforts to focus on aspects of the law that might create severe limitations on the exercise of the punishment. Second, he argued that the primary goal of punishment is not to exact revenge but to bestow repentance and rehabilitation. He supported a new interpretation of the punishment and its application that fit new circumstances and new sensibilities, and asked for other methods and mechanisms to achieve the goal of rehabilitation.[53] Finally, he used the jurisprudential principle of *tazahom* (conflict) to argue that if the implementation of certain punishments creates more harm than good – in this case, the creation of a negative image of Islam among the global community – then those punishments should be discontinued.[54]

Still, reformers, including some of his own students, do not consider these steps sufficient. The earliest criticism, related to his emphasis on *tahazom* and expediency as methods to get around punishment, was voiced in an essay by Abdolkarim Soroush. There, he argues that such methods, without a revolution in the jurisprudential foundation of religious law, will lead only to "chaotic pragmatism."[55] Following Soroush, Kadivar argues that his mentor's argument for stopping the punishment is not juridically binding, and thus leaves the decision to punish or not to individual judges.[56] More importantly, he faults his teacher for not unequivocally ruling against worldly punishment of apostates, since neither the Quran nor the Prophet has condemned anyone to death for their loss of faith in Islam.[57] A more hopeful interpretation of Montazeri's approach to apostasy and whether it allows for contemplation of fundamental changes in the principles of *fiqh* comes from Emaddedin Baghi, one of Montazeri's close followers. Baghi urges a holistic approach toward Montazeri's positions and argues that his specific statements on the problematic of apostasy must be connected to his ruling on the fundamental and inalienable rights of humans as humans, independent of their creed. Such a connection, Baghi insists, will provide the juridical basis for meaningful changes in the principles of religious laws.[58]

Rights of Prisoners

From the early days of the Islamic Republic, Montazeri took a progressive position on the rights of prisoners. In his lessons on the Islamic state in the early 1980's, he wrote: "[I]t is incumbent [upon the authorities] to provide for the material and spiritual needs of the prisoners, to make their lives comfortable and to do what they can to release them from prison provided that the purpose of the prison sentence was not undermined."[59] During the constitutional debate, Montazeri challenged those who did not oppose the use of torture and argued that the harm torture causes always outweighs any resulting benefit.[60] For this reason, he supported a ban on any and all forms of torture. Doubtless, his and his son's personal experiences during the Pahlavi regime influenced his approach. Also, later, particularly in 1988, his encounters with the families of political prisoners, who crowded his office in Qom day after day, moved him deeply. It is worth repeating that his insistence on challenging the treatment of prisoners by the judiciary system and the Ministry of Information played a central role in his eventual downfall.

Montazeri elaborated on his views on prisoners and their rights in his *Resaleh Huqquq*, and to some extent in *Mojazatha-ye Eslami va Huqquq-e Bashar*. His position hinted at his sensitivities to the well-being of the accused from the moment of arrest to the end of the assigned sentence. He insisted on the principle of *esalat-e baraat* (innocent until proven guilty), and argued that no one should be detained without a cause or a clear legal reason, nor for a long period of time without a trial. As for the arrest of people for political activities, he contended that since at the time of the Prophet there was no arrest, imprisonment, or maltreatment of non-violent political opponents, no state can find justification in Islam for incarcerating people on political grounds, especially for non-violent political activities.[61]

In addition to his opposition to torture, Montazeri insisted that confession under duress is worthless as evidence against the accused. He pressed for the observance of legal equality of prisoners by the court, and insisted that each and every prisoner is entitled to a fair trial and legal counsel regardless of the alleged crime. For the sake of the mental well-being of prisoners, he demanded that the state recognize and observe the rights of the incarcerated to have regular visitations with their families, as well as access to educational and communication facilities. If the state failed to meet these obligations, or if it maltreated prisoners, then the latter had the right to take the state or the prison officers to court.[62]

These are no mean requirements that Montazeri spelled out for the reduction of the possibility of abuse of prisoners. His traditional and jurisprudential approach added special weight to his position and made for a powerful discursive weapon against those who in the name of Islam would mistreat prisoners in the Islamic Republic.

Right to Privacy

The right to a private and secure space is a foundational aspect of both liberalism and modern conceptions of human rights, as has been emphasized in several human rights-related treaties. Article 8 in the 1950 European Convention for the Protection of Human Rights and Fundamental Freedom, for instance, states that:

(1) Everyone has the right to respect for his private and family life, his home and his correspondence; and (2) There shall be no interference by a public authority with the exercise of this right except such as is in accordance with the law and is necessary in a democratic society in the interests of national security, public safety or the economic well-being of the country, for the prevention of disorder or crime, for the protection of health of morals, or for the protection of the rights and freedoms of others.[63]

The clause "protection of health of morals" is vague enough to allow for intrusive interference in the area of privacy, yet in practice it is the first part of the article – the protection of the domain of privacy along with the provision for concrete and adequate guarantees – that has informed the approach of advocates of human rights. Their criticisms of religious traditions and ideologies, which emphasize the rights of the community over those of the individual or of minority groups, is partially based on the lack of adequate attention to privacy: the space where individuals and minorities are free from external/communal interference.[64]

Islam's challenge to the right to privacy appears most clearly in the principle of "commanding the good and prohibiting the bad" (CGPB). It is incumbent on individuals, families, groups, the community, and the state to push others toward "good deeds" and to pull them away from "bad behavior" for the sake of the health and security of the community and/or for the sake of their eternal salvation. In the Islamic Republic, the prohibition of alcohol, sexual relationships between unmarried people, and certain kinds of entertainment exists in the name of this principle. Conservative members of the political elite support the use of the principle to reduce what they perceive as the harmful consequences of liberal individualism. For instance, Mohammad Javad Larijani, the conservative Director of the Human Rights Committee of the Islamic Republic Judiciary, agrees that CGPB is in conflict with the liberal notion of the right to privacy. He argues that the right to privacy artificially separates the private and public domains and forces competition and conflict between the rights of the community and those of the individuals. He then lauds the Islamic Republic for having solved the problem inherent in the Western approach to the "rights of the citizens" by introducing an alternative: the "experience of citizenship." Larijani defines the "experience of citizenship" to be a relationship between the individual and the community, as well as between people and the government, based on negotiation and harmonious understanding rather than on confrontation and conflict. He sees the principle of CGPB as the ideal tool in the hands of the community/state to strengthen the "experience of citizenship."[65]

Montazeri, who watched the misuse of this principle by the state and its agents, would be suspicious of Larijani's intention. Yet he himself was a firm believer in CGPB. In his *Ma'aref va Ahkam-e Banovan* he wrote:

In Islam, the people's supervision over acts that occur within the community is a natural right that originates from the ties that connect the fates of members of the community to each other. The harmful consequences of any bad deed can spill over into the lives of others and each sin or bad behavior has the potential to become a social ill... therefore as the Holy Quran has indicated, faithful men and women should guard each other, help each other, and command each other to do good deeds and prohibit each other from the bad ones.[66]

Montazeri repeated this theme in many of his other writings and sermons, and particularly highlighted the right of the community over that of the individual when the two clashed. For this reason, he has been criticized by liberal reformers, who find his attention to the oppressive tendencies of the community inadequate.[67] He did not, however, meld individual persons completely into the community, but conceded to them a certain amount of privacy. He insisted that everyone had a right to feel secure in their private life, and added that "no one should be fearful about the exposure of their private secrets...The Holy Quran has explicitly forbidden probing into an individual's life."[68]

Montazeri had in mind two particular Quranic Suras (49:12 and 24:19) as endorsing the principle of a secure domain of privacy. In Sura 49, the Quran provides humans with the right to conceal; and in Sura 24, it forbids the faithful to pry into other people's personal lives.[69] To add strength to the Quranic verses, he also appealed to *ravayat* such as the one attributed to the Sixth Imam: "whoever listens to people's conversation without their consent will be severely punished in the Day of Judgment." He relied on these authoritative rulings and declared that neither searching people's houses nor making their private sin public is permissible. He made these arguments for the protection of individual privacy with the state in mind as the probable violator.

Beside specific suggestions, Montazeri's general advice to the state was that the long-term interest of Islam as a prosperous religion could be assured only when the religious state adopted a more tolerant and hands-off attitude. This does not mean that he forgot the principle of CGPB in the context of state–society relations. But, unlike the conservatives, who give the exclusive right of interpreting and using the principle to the government and its affiliated vigilante groups, he employed it as a tool to check the state's dictatorial tendencies.[70] The principle of CGPB gives people not only the right but the duty to hold the government accountable and requires that it behave in a just and lawful manner.

Montazeri's treatment of privacy within the triad of individual, community, and state was not straightforward. His awareness of the state's ability to suppress individuals led him to argue in support of protection of the individual, including the right to privacy. The community and the individuals who comprise it were therefore allies in confronting the state's potential assault on their rights to private/communal acts by pushing for a true democratic and open system, with all its checks and balances. His view of the relationship between the community and the individual, however, made for a more problematic case for the latter's right to privacy.

In *On Liberty*, John Stuart Mill explains this problem succinctly by distinguishing between two kinds of suppression, one governmental and the other societal. If government suppresses through the threat or actual use of force, society does it through its demand for conformity to its mores, beliefs, and traditions. For Mill, liberation from the first kind of suppression requires democracy: people's active participation in politics in pursuit of self-government. Freedom from the second kind of suppression demands liberalism: non-interference by others in one's private domain. Mill, of course, does not ignore the principle of "prevention of harm to others," which puts certain limitations on individual freedom, but he is insistent on the principle of non-interference when it comes to acts that affect or even harm only the individual self.[71]

Montazeri committed himself to democracy but not to liberalism. He remained strict in his warning to the state and its vigilante associates against abusing the rights of the people and demanded that they leave people alone.[72] But, for him, the rights and interests of the community always trump those of the individual, and hence one's right to privacy and non-interference by others is limited by the principle of "prevention of harm to the community."

The Civil Status of Baha'is

Toward the end of his life, and despite his disdain for Baha'ism as a religion, Montazeri argued for protection of the citizenship rights of the Baha'is. When, in 2008, he was asked about the status of the Baha'is, he wrote in response:

Not having the heavenly book like those of Jews, Christians, and Zoroastrians in the constitution, Baha'is are not considered one of the religious minorities. However, since they are the citizens of this country, they have the rights of citizenship. Furthermore, they must benefit from Islamic compassion which is stressed in Quran and by the religious authorities.[73]

This was prompted by an earlier event. In 2007, Shirin Ebadi, the Nobel laureate and human rights activist, became the defense lawyer for a group of Baha'i leaders accused of spying for Israel. She was then targeted by the conservative media and was accused of many unsavory acts, including apostasy. Knowing the possible dire consequences of such a charge, she asked for a religious ruling from Ayatollah Montazeri about whether a Muslim lawyer can defend an accused Baha'i.

In response, Montazeri issued a *fatwa* permitting Muslims to defend Baha'is in court.[74]

Montazeri's second *fatwa*, in 2008, was the first of its kind from a prominent member of the clergy and was noteworthy for its contrast to his own earlier and strong anti-Baha'i attitude.

As a religious minority, the Baha'is have always been a vulnerable community, frequently subjected to persecution since the founding of the religion in the nineteenth century.[75] Unlike Jews, Christians, and Zoroastrians, Baha'is were never recognized by the clerical establishment as a religious minority with rights or protection. The root cause of the perilous existence of Baha'is is theological. The belief that God intended for Mohammad to be his last prophet would automatically delegitimize in the eyes of the faithful any claim for recognition by future religions. What intensified this theological view was the political conspiracy theory (believed by many Muslim Iranians) that Baha'ism was the work of British colonialists, created for the specific purpose of dividing and conquering the Islamic community. These theological and political views were strong enough that the Baha'i community became subject to perpetual persecution. During the reign of Reza Shah, the harassment of Baha'is subsided, but it soon reemerged as a powerful current in the 1940's and 50's. In this period, a number of organizations and groups were formed to confront Baha'is suspected by the religious establishment of pursuing large-scale conversion of Muslim youth. Montazeri was involved in this effort.

In 1951, Montazeri wrote a twenty-four-page pamphlet, *Monazereh Mosalman va Baha'i* (The Debate of a Muslim and a Baha'i), to expose "the falsity" of Baha'ism.[76] In addition to preventing Muslim youth from converting, he was also hoping, as he asserted in the introduction to the book, to "awaken the Baha'is" from their "stupor" so that they would have a chance for eternal felicity.

Montazeri was also the representative of the strongly anti-Baha'i Ayatollah Borujerdi in Najafabad, home to a thriving Baha'i community. Around the same time that he wrote the booklet on Baha'ism, he inquired of Borujerdi about what tactics were permissible in confronting the Baha'is in Najafabad. In response, his mentor made the following statement: "It is incumbent upon Muslims to disengage with this sect socially and economically. My only request from Muslims is to not disturb the order and peace of the state."[77] Montazeri abided by Borujerdi's directive and invited preachers, guild members, and the members of other social classes to boycott trade by Muslims with Baha'is.[78] According to Montazeri himself, the pressure on Baha'is was intense enough to force many to leave Najafabad, and for others to hide their religious identity.

Montazeri's involvement in boycotting Baha'is caused his first and, for a long time, only brush with the state authorities. A confidential memo from the intelligence section of the Pahlavi regime's military recounts Montazeri's anti-Baha'i activities and expresses the need to put an end to them.[79] The prospect of a revolution against the Pahlavi state, however, was the real reason behind Montazeri's decision to end his anti-Baha'i activities. Similar to Khomeini, Montazeri believed that the first priority of the clerical establishment now was opposing the Pahlavi regime; everything else had to wait. As a consequence, Montazeri not only refused to become a member of the Hojjatieh Association, a group formed in the early 1950's with the primary goal of eradicating Baha'ism from Iran, but joined Khomeini in criticizing it.[80]

With the triumph of the revolution, the anti-Baha'i forces could now seek the active support of the Islamic state in uprooting the community. The intensity of anti-Baha'i activities in post-revolutionary Iran has varied from period to period, but the denial of citizenship and its associated rights has been from the very beginning the official policy of the state. However, whether in a position of power or after his dismissal, Montazeri never again took an active role in persecuting the Baha'is. Instead, his changed approach toward state–society relations and his statement on the innate dignity of all humans regardless of their creed ultimately led him to make his ruling on the civil rights of Baha'is. This *fatwa* is probably the most important demonstration of the tension between his loyalty to his faith and education and his lived experience. In this case, when he was convinced that the Baha'is were treated unjustly by the Islamic Republic, his belief that justice is prior to religion prompted him to speak on their behalf.

Montazeri's theological position on Baha'is remained unchanged, however. He never accepted Baha'ism as a legitimate religion. Neither did he change in any profound way his views on the unequal legal status of the other religious minorities that Islam recognizes as legitimate People of the Book. Standing on Islamic jurisprudence, he did not submit to Article 2 of the UDHR, where it states that religion should not be a source of discrimination.

Gender

In his *Treatise on Rights*, Montazeri did not address discriminatory laws against women, but only the mutual rights and duties of men and women toward each other and their children. Yet, his silence on gender inequality was not to conceal his disapproval of it. Rather, he continued to hold the centuries-old positions on the legal status of women, within the family as well as in the social and economic domains. Many of these positions became over time part of the legal system of the Islamic Republic.

The Pahlavi regime, in the last twenty years of its rule, took some modest but still significant steps to address the discriminatory laws on gender. Through the Family Protection Act of 1967 and its 1975 amended version, the state modified laws – in favor of women – on polygamy, marriage, divorce, and child custody. But soon after the establishment of the Islamic Republic, these reforms were rolled back and the Family Protection Act was suspended. Instead, the traditional Islamic laws on family were adopted and enforced. Moreover, the state took measures to restrict the extent of women's public participation. It barred women from becoming judges, closed some educational fields to women, and encouraged women to enroll in programs regarded as fitting for them, such as teaching and nursing.

From the beginning, women voiced their objection to these policies, first through a predominantly secular discourse, and eventually through the language of religion. In the 1990's and continuing into the twenty-first century, Iran witnessed the emergence of a feminist discourse that was consciously rooted in Islam but which demanded gender equality through the abrogation of discriminatory laws against women. Meanwhile, the state (which, from the outset, had relied on women as voters) retreated from some of its most hardline laws and policies, especially in the area of education. During Khatami's presidency, a modified version of the Pahlavi family protection laws resurfaced. Women also scored a victory in their struggle to reverse the ban on judgeship, and female judges could now issue verdicts on legal cases, though in a de facto manner. The overall reformist policies of the Khatami era contributed to the flourishing of the Islamic feminist movement. But the movement did not create much of a ripple within the circle of conservative jurisprudents, and their views on women remained as conservative as ever. On the gender question, Montazeri was in their camp.

Montazeri said what he thought about the matter of women in several of his writings, including *The Jurisprudential Foundation of Islamic State*, his responses to questions posed by his followers, and his *resaleh 'amalieh* (practical treatise) on *Ma'aref va Ahkam-e Banovan* (Knowledge and Rulings for Ladies). In the latter, he addressed the responsibility of a female from the age of *taklif* (duty-maturity) to the time of death.

Though Montazeri recognized that the style and institutions of the early period of Islam were no longer practical, he did not apply this to the question of gender. He gave his approval to almost all the original rules of Islam, frequently stating how progressive Islamic laws on gender were compared to their pre-Islamic counterparts. His defense of laws on polygamy, divorce, and inheritance followed the wisdom and justice of the seventh-century model. For example, he defended laws that determine a woman's share of inheritance to be half that of a man, noting a parallel inequality against men when it comes to dowry or alimony, so that the two inequalities cancel each other out. More importantly, men – unlike women – have the responsibility for providing for the family. Thus, it is only just that men should inherit twice as much as women.[81] He followed a similar line in almost all other gender-related areas, including public participation.

He maintained that with the exception of certain public activities, which according to Islam are exclusive to men, women can participate in all such activities providing that they meet certain conditions. One of these conditions is that the public activity not interfere with the women's responsibilities at home, and another is the observance of all rules of chastity and modesty, including wearing the proper *hejab*. Among the offices not open to women, he counted the top office of supreme leadership as well as the presidency and, of course, judgeships. But if his argument on discriminatory laws of inheritance was based on practical/legal grounds, his promotion of rules for excluding women from judgeships and high political positions was clearly constructed on his beliefs about the nature of women.

Montazeri grounded his case for gender discrimination in the biological distinctions between men and women, as he understood them.

Rejecting the idea that these differences make one morally superior to the other, he nonetheless argued that men and women are suited for different and distinct roles in the family and society. Women are delicate creatures in need of physical protection: a need that only a man, with his rougher and stronger constitution, can provide.[82] But this is not all that disqualifies them from being equal public participants, especially at the highest level of decision-making. Along with physical differences are intellectual and psychological ones. He believed that women allow their emotions to rule over them, while men are more successful at letting reason determine their behavior. In his 1979 pamphlet, "Collection of Two Messages," he wrote:

The president must be a man. Some of our intellectuals might disagree and some of our saintly sisters might be offended by this statement, but the truth has to be told, because the veiling of the truth is a big sin. According to Islamic laws, ruling and judging are not for ladies. But this should not be construed as either disrespecting the saintly sisters or ignoring their rights. Ruling and judging are not rights but heavy duties, and the individuals who are committed to carry them faithfully would be crushed under their heavy weight. Therefore, the generous and kind God who does not wish for sisters with their delicate souls and loving emotions to be contaminated and entangled, has put them in charge of the emotional aspects of family and society. There is no doubt that the faculty of reason and problem-solving is more present in men, and love and emotions in women. Of course it is possible that a woman would be ahead of a man in reason and intellect, but this is not the norm. No matter how well educated and experienced, women are naturally sensitive and emotional, and are more vulnerable to being manipulated. But the person of the ruler or the judge has to be patient, strong, and objective.[83]

It is not difficult to trace Montazeri's tripartite ontological order of human nature in this description of the attributes of men and women. Men and women both share the lowest level, the material common to all living beings. They also share the level that is the domain of emotions, though women have a larger portion of the gentler emotions of love and kindness than do men. Yet, at the highest level, the seat of reason and intellect, women are handicapped, while men excel. And, therefore, as in the case of the human self, where reason should reign over emotions and prepare the individual to achieve eternal salvation, the "rational man" should be in charge of the "emotional woman" for the sake of temporal social order.

Considering Montazeri's responsiveness to the sensibilities of the modern world, his unchanging approach to gender might seem puzzling, especially when compared to the more progressive positions of another ayatollah, Yousef San'ei. San'ei adopted a critical tone against the harsh policies and authoritarian attitudes of the Islamic Republic much later than Montazeri did; he also lagged behind him in developing a new attitude toward state–society relations. When Montazeri raised his voice against the treatment of prisoners, San'ei was silent. When Montazeri spoke of the civil rights of Baha'is, one didn't hear from San'ei. So what could explain Montazeri's reluctance to make any meaningful gesture in support of changing the discriminatory laws against women when San'ei was already doing so?

One clue to this puzzle might be found in the circumstances of Montazeri's life around the time when the Islamic feminist movement was reaching its peak under Mohammad Khatami's presidency. For most of that period, Montazeri was under house arrest and isolated from the feminist movement and its demands. His distance from people involved in that movement was in sharp contrast to his personal involvement in the case of prisoners in 1988. Then, he was in close contact with the prisoners' families and was affected deeply by their daily visits. Those contacts played a crucial role in strengthening his resolve to support the prisoners. As is evident in his response to Golbarg Bashi, who interviewed him soon after the lifting of his house arrest, Montazeri either did not know or had not thought through the implications of the socioeconomic changes in post-revolutionary Iran that affected the status of women. He was not aware of their surpassing men in institutions of higher education. Had he known, he might have reconsidered his assumptions about women's innate lack of ability to excel or about men being the natural breadwinners.[84] He had stated earlier, in regard to the penal code, that he allowed for the shelving of Islamic rules if they went against the sensibilities of the times and the prevalent understanding of justice. And in the case of the Baha'is, he permitted his belief in justice to prevail over his deep-rooted dislike of Baha'ism. It is possible that he would have used the same reasoning and the same sentiments with regard to family laws had he become aware that gender inequality was now recognized by a large numbers of people, including many Muslims, as unjust. But this is only a conjecture.

As Montazeri traveled from advocating an elitist political system controlled by a father figure – the designated *faqih* – to embracing popular sovereignty based on a social contract, he left out women as equal citizens in both private and public spheres. A contract based on equality of the sexes in areas of marriage, divorce, inheritance, and employment was never part of Montazeri's concern. While he fought against those who wished to retain the dominance of "fathers" over "sons," he stood firmly by the side of the fathers in their insistence on keeping the dominance of men over women.[85]

A Final Reflection

When the members of the Center of Defenders of Human Rights chose Montazeri as the recipient of their Person of the Year Award in 2009–10, they focused on his concrete support of the civil rights of all citizens.[86] An argument of human rights theorists and activists has been that the principles of human rights are not just values but a particular kind of social practice against the oppressive forces of state or society.[87] Even though Montazeri's record is mixed, where he embraced human rights, he indeed became their ardent practitioner.

Notes

1 For the complete text of Ebadi's statement, see http://www.rahesabz.net/story/5812/.
2 One of the most important books that raises this question and challenges the universality claim of the UDHR is Asad, *Formations of the Secular.* See in particular 148–58.
3 As we will see, the critique of a number of Iranian clergy of the UDHR is related to this matter.
4 For a sample of the critical literature on Islam in general and the Islamic Republic in particular regarding the areas of the penal code, women's rights, and Baha'i religious minority, see Ann Elizabeth Mayer, *Islam and Human Rights* (Boulder, CO: Westview Press, 1995); Afshari, *Human Rights in Iran*; and Nazila Ghanea Hercock, *Human Rights, the UN and the Baha'is in Iran* (Oxford: George Ronald, 2002). For a more recent collection of short articles on human rights debates related to cultural relativism, the penal code, and women's rights, see http://www.iranrights.org/english/library-86.php.
5 Fereydoun Hoveyda, the brother of a Pahlavi-era prime minister, Amir Abbas Hoveyda, was a member of its drafting committee. See Mayer, *Islam and Human Rights*, 10. For Hoveyda's own recollection of his participation in the Third Committee, which drafted the declaration, see

"Signed, Sealed & Delivered: Casting the Affirmative Vote for Iran in Approving the Universal Declaration of Human Rights in 1948," *Iranian.com* (2005), at http://www.iranian.com/FereydounHoveyda/2005/August/UDHR/index.html.

6 The IBHR has been accepted by a significant portion of the international community as the embodiment of the standards of human rights. It consists of a few declarations, starting with the UDHR of 1948, the International Covenant on Civil and Political Rights (ICCPR) of 1966, and the International Covenant on Economics, Social, and Cultural Rights (ICESCR) of 1966.

7 See Khomeini, *Sahifeh Imam Khomeini*, vol. 3, October 11, 1978.

8 The text of the CDHRI can be found at http://www1.umn.edu/humanrts/instree/cairodeclaration.html.

9 *Ettela'at*, May 16, 1979, 2.

10 See, for example, Ali Bagheri, "E'lamieh-e Jahani-e Huqquq-e Bashar va E'lamieh Huqquq-e Bashar-e Eslami: Tazadha va Eshterakat" [Universal Declaration of Human Rights and the Islamic Declaration of Human Rights: Incompatibilities and Similarities], at http://adlpub.com/%D8%B9%D9%84%D9%8A-%D8%A8%D8%A7%D9%82%D8%B1%D9%8A-%D8%A7%D8%B9%D9%84%D8%A7%D9%85%D9%8A%D9%87-%D8%AC%D9%87%D8%A7%D9%86%D9%8A-%D8%AD%D9%82%D9%88%D9%82-%D8%A8%D8%B4%D8%B1-%D9%88-%D8%A7%D8%B9%D9%84%D8%A7/.

11 Abdollah Javadi Amoli, *Falsafeh Huqquq-e Bashar* [Human Rights Philosophy] (Qom: Osara' Publications, 1996), 26–7.

12 For example, Mesbah Yazdi considers neither the "natural law" nor the social contract theories of human rights satisfactory foundations for arriving at a universal code for human rights. For an elaboration of his critiques, see Mohammad Taqi Mesbah Yazdi, *Nazariyeh-e Huqquq-e Eslam* [The Legal Theory of Islam] (Qom: Imam Khomeini Educational and Research Institute, 2012), 1:79–86.

13 Mohammad Taqi Ja'fari, *Moqayeseh E'lamiyeh Huqquq Bashar Eslami va E'lamiyeh Huqquq-e Bashar Gharb* [A Comparison of the Islamic Declaration of Human Rights and Western Declaration of Human Rights] (Tehran: The Parliamentary Center for Research, 2011), 17–21.

14 For an elaboration of the right of God, see Mesbah Yazdi, *Nazariyeh-e Huqquq-e Eslam*, 1:99–110.

15 Soroush elaborates his views on knowledge in *Qabs va Bast Teorik-e Shari'at: Nazariy-e Takamol-e Ma'refat-e Dini* [Theoretical Constriction and Expansion of Shar'ia: The Theory of Evolution of Religious Knowledge] (Tehran: Serat, 1994).

16 See the entire speech at http://drsoroush.com/fa/%D8%AD%D9%82-%D9%88-%D8%AA%DA%A9%D9%84%DB%8C%D9%81-%D9%88-%D8%AE%D8%AF%D8%A7/.

17 Mohsen Kadivar, *Haqq-ol Naas: Eslam va Huqquq-e Bashar* [The Right of Humans: Islam and Human Rights] (Tehran: Kavir Publications, 2007), 8.

18 Ibid., 15–16.

19 Ibid., 160.

20 Yousef San'ei, *Chekide-ye Andisheha* [The Summary of Reflections] (Qom: Maysam Tamar Publications, 2008), 40.

21 There have been high clergy outside Iran, such as Sayyed Mohammad Hossein Fadlallah, the respected Lebanese source of emulation, and Shaykh Mohammad Mehdi Shamsaddin, the Iraqi religious scholar, who have issued edicts to redress some of the traditional and discriminatory rulings against women.

22 These rulings are scattered across several part of San'ei's website, www.saanei.org.

23 For a discussion of "endorsed" laws, old and new reasons, and the desirability of discarding many of these laws by Islamic reformists, or what Kadivar calls "new thinkers of Islam," see Mohsen Kadivar, "Questions and Answers, Human Rights and Religious Intellectualism," in *Haqq Ol-Nas* [Human Rights], at http://kadivar.com/?p=7319.

24 Montzeri, *Resaleh Huqquq*, 15.

25 See Asghar Schirazi, *The Constitution of Iran: Politics and the State in the Islamic Republic* (London: I. B. Tauris, 1997), esp. 33, 37, and 249.

26 *Proceedings of the Assembly*, 1:721.

27 Montazeri, *Resaleh Huqquq*, 16.

28 Montazeri, *Didgahha*, 1:296–8.

29 Kadivar criticized this approach due to its demand for "definite" proof. See http://en.kadivar.com/human-rights-and-intellectual-islam/.

30 Montazeri, *Resaleh Huqquq*, 21.

31 Ibid., 24–32.

32 Montazeri, *Enteqad az Khod*, 164–5.

33 Montazeri argued that governments do not have the right to prosecute anyone for the act of changing one's religion provided that the act is not done with malicious intention. See Montazeri, *Resaleh Huqquq*, 52.

34 Ibid., 79.

35 Ibid., 115–26.

36 Ibid., 129–33.

37 See Khomeini, *Sahifeh Imam Khomeini*, 20:397. It should be mentioned, however, that Montazeri put great restrictions on what make a

corrupter deserving of a death sentence. See Montazeri, *Didgahha*, 1:423 and 1:460.

38 The most extensive elaboration of the *mofsed-e fel arz* by Montazeri was in his response to a question raised by his student and follower, Mohsen Kadivar. See the entire question and answer at http://kadivar.com/?p=3499.

39 See the section on punishment in Montazeri's *The Jurisprudential Foundation*, 3:488–530.

40 See the listing of some of these conditions in Montazeri, *Didgahha*, 3:132–8.

41 Neither of these two men denounced their religion, but they criticized certain practices, particularly the official reading and practices of religion.

42 See Montazeri, *Didgahha*, 3:315–16 and 3:623–7. The cases, particularly the one against Aghajari, backfired and made even some conservatives criticize the judiciary for playing with the idea of apostasy in these specific cases.

43 Reza Alijani, "Barrasi-ye Mafhoum-e Ertedad" [An Analysis of the Concept of Apostasy], at http://talar.shandel.info/pdf/alijani1011.pdf.

44 See, for example, the answer to the question on apostasy and its punishment on the Center for Answers to Religious Questions, an Internet site created by Qom Seminary's Bureau for Islamic Propaganda, at http://www.pasokhgoo.ir/node/63760.

45 For an elaboration of the reformist argument against earthly punishment for apostasy, see Emaddedin Baghi, *Falsafeh Siasi Ejtema'i Ayatollah Montazeri* [Ayatollah Montazeri's Political and Social Philosophy] (Tehran: Sarayi Press, 2015), 103–5.

46 The quote appears in Abdolkarim Soroush's response to Montazeri in the following edition of *Kian*. Abdolkarim Soroush, "Fiqh dar Tarazou" [*Fiqh* on the Scale], *Kian*, no. 46 (1999): 15.

47 See, for example, his 1999 letter to the questions posed to him by Abdolkarim Soroush in Montazeri, *Didgahha*, 1:111–22.

48 Montazeri, *Hokumat-e Dini*, 130.

49 Montazeri, *Eslam Din-e Fetrat*, 696.

50 Montazeri, *Hokumat-e Dini*, 130–1.

51 Ibid., 131.

52 Montazeri, *Mojazatha-ye Eslami*, 35.

53 Ibid., 86–7.

54 Montazeri, *Didgahha*, 1:96–9.

55 Soroush, "Fiqh dar Tarazou," 18.

56 Personal interview with Kadivar, July 2012.

57 See Mohsen Kadivar, *Mojazat-e Ertedad va Azadi-ye Mazhab* [Punishment for Apostasy and Religious Freedom] (2014), 11–29, at http://kadivar.com/wp-content/uploads/2014/07/%D9%85%D8%AC%D8%A7%D8%B2%D8%A7%D8%AA-%D8%A7%D8%B1%D8%AA%D8%AF%D8%A7%D8%AF.pdf.

58 See Baghi, *Falsafeh Siasi Ejtema'i*, 119–42. Here, Baghi is principally responding to the criticism raised by Soroush in his 1999 exchanges with Montazeri on the relevance of traditional *fiqh* in the modern world.

59 Montazeri, *The Jurisprudential Foundation*, 4:124.

60 On his position against torture, see *Proceedings of the Assembly*, 1:777–8.

61 Montazeri, *Resaleh Huqquq*, 86.

62 Ibid., 87.

63 The complete text of the declaration can be found at http://conventions.coe.int/treaty/en/treaties/html/005.htm.

64 Recent pressures on their Muslim citizens to conform to the norm of the majority by some Western secular states, such as France, with its recent attempt to ban the burkini, should also be mentioned as examples of how liberal secular ideology has been used to violate the principles of human rights.

65 See Larijani's speech during the First National Gathering on the Rights of Citizenship at http://peivandweb.blogfa.com/post-1737.aspx.

66 Hossein Ali Montazeri, *Ma'aref va Ahkam-e Banovan* [Knoweldge and Rulings for Ladies] (Isfahan: Mobarak Publication, 2004), 181.

67 See his exchanges with Soroush in Montazeri, *Didgahha*, 1:118.

68 Montazeri, *Resalaeh Huqquq*, 72.

69 Ibid., 72–3.

70 Montazeri, *Didgahha*, 1:91–2.

71 John Stuart Mill, *On Liberty* (Cambridge, MA: Hackett Publishing, 1978).

72 Montazeri, *Ma'aref va Ahkam-e Banovan*, 193.

73 See the statement at http://www.radiofarda.com/a/o2_montazeri_behai/448956.html.

74 Personal correspondence with Shirin Ebadi, August 11, 2015.

75 For a succinct account of anti-Baha'i activities in Iran, see Mohamad Tavakoli-Tarqhi, "Anti-Baha'ism and Islamism in Iran," in *The Baha'is of Iran*, Dominic Parviz Brookshaw and Seena B. Fazel, eds. (Oxon: Routledge, 2008), 200–31.

76 The text of the pamphlet used to be available at http://www.sobhe-emrooz.com/wp-content/uploads/2012/04/montazeri.pdf (last accessed October 2015).

77 Montazeri, *Memoirs*, 87.

78 Ibid., app. 4, 444.

79 Izadi, *Faqih-e Aliqadr*, 1:43.

80 Montazeri, *Memoirs*, 109.

81 Montazeri, *Ma'aref va Ahkam-e Banovan*, 440–5.

82 Montazeri, *Didgahha*, 3:573–4.

83 Montazeri, *Memoirs*, app. 59, 494.

84 Bashi, "The Question of Women."

85 For an interesting analysis of the conflict between a social contract that leads to democracy and a sexual contract that paves the way for gender equality, see Carole Pateman, *The Sexual Contract* (Stanford, CA: Stanford University Press, 1988).

86 See the text at http://www.humanrights-ir.org/php/view_print_version .php?objnr=333.

87 Jack Donnelly, "The Relative Universality of Human Rights," *Human Rights Quarterly* 29, no. 2 (2007): 284.

Conclusion
Legacy of a Grand Ayatollah

Montazeri died in 2009. In his wake, he left a contested personal, political, and religious record. Some remember him as a just, honest, and courageous man, and celebrate his influence on Iranian and Islamic histories. For them, if he had remained in power and succeeded Khomeini as the Supreme Leader, the Islamic Republic would have been in a stronger position at home and abroad. Others, mostly the supporters of the Islamic Republic, recall him as a naïve, parochial, and impressionable man, one whose faulty judgment had already harmed the Islamic Republic. In their view, he would have been a disaster for both Iran and Islam if he had replaced Khomeini. Then there are some ardent seculars who, similar to the theocratic authoritarians, are critical of Montazeri. They come, however, from an opposite angle, and accuse him of having been an enabler of a reviled system and consider his later criticism of the Islamic Republic either trivial or disingenious.

Even though Montazeri's religious record has been less scrutinized than his personal and political character, he still has passionate followers and critics on this score as well. His status as a grand ayatollah and his jurisprudential treatises made him worthy of the position of the Supreme Source of Emulation in the eyes of his followers; whereas some of his detractors wished to strip him of all his religious titles and ignored most of his writings. Such discrepancies reveal the complexity of Montazeri's life and legacy. In addition to his religious record as such, within the established *howzeh* context there is a debate about his impact on the reform of Islam in general and jurisprudence in particular. Was he, as a traditional cleric – a label attached to him by friends and foes – able to contribute meaningfully to the reform of fundamental principles of jurisprudence and thus make his field truly responsive to the needs of modern times? The debate over this question takes us into a larger realm, one where the fight over secularization theories and its mother paradigm have been fought for decades.

Personal Legacy

Born to a pious and poor family in a small rural town, Montazeri's childhood experience shaped his later character and influenced him both as a man of politics and as a religious scholar. Precocious and curious, he was also down to earth, sincere, and faithful. Later in life, when he was a major post-revolutionary figure, some did not take him seriously because of his lack of oratory eloquence, his rural accent, and his disregard for ranks and positions. But the same attributes – his humility, his openness, his unadorned speaking manner, his simple lifestyle, and his identification with the downtrodden – resonated with others and touched the hearts of millions of ordinary people. So, too, did Montazeri's natural inquisitiveness, courage, general disregard for political expediency, stubborn pursuit of what he considered justice, and juridical rulings attract a younger generation of politically aware Iranians. Some became his religious followers, some his political supporters, and some saw in him both a source of emulation and a political role model. These numbered among the earnest revolutionaries who had lost faith in the Islamic Republic and its political elite.

One is hard pressed to find any self-criticism by Iranian leaders, either before or after the revolution. Therefore, Montazeri's ability to criticize himself and ask for forgiveness should be considered a part of his personal legacy. In answer to a series of questions posed to him by his son in *Enteqad az Khod*, Montazeri, while defending most of his own actions, nonetheless acknowledged many of his weaknesses. He pointed to the constitutional debate and his mistake in pushing for an all-powerful and "God-designated" office of *valayat-e faqih*. He regretted his role in supporting Iran's position during the American hostage crisis, and accepted some responsibility for misunderstanding the power configuration within the political elite.

His humility does not, however, hide other aspects of his personality. Montazeri was stubborn and impatient, a man who prided himself for being a contrarian. By his own admission, he made some important decisions without sufficient knowledge or prudence. He was somewhat oblivious to political and social decorum, at times making himself the subject of mockery. Some of his critics have accused him of opportunism and greed for power, qualities that, they insist, caused his downfall. However, they fail to provide credible evidence to support this claim. There is some truth to the charge that he exhibited political naïveté while he was the Successor. His reading of the power configuration, especially of Khomeini and his "House," was simplistic, and so was his belief that if he stuck to his ideals/positions he could prevail. His dogged support for Mehdi Hashemi, best expressed in his harsh letter to Khomeini, was only one indication of imprudence. As we have seen throughout this book, all these personal attributes influenced Montazeri in his role as a political activist, for good or ill.

Political Legacy

Montazeri's revolutionary activities, his resilience and tenacity, his endurance of torture, imprisonment, and the solitude of exile made him a symbol of defiance. He did all he could to elevate Islam as a political ideology in the face of the Pahlavi regime and to inspire many in the fight for a new order. His risky and high-profile support for the book on *Shahid-e Javid* was a vivid testimony for this aspect of his activities. During Khomeini's exile, and as his representative in Iran, Montazeri was a significant revolutionary participant. Yet it was his post-revolutionary political activity in particular that cast him as a historical, and yet controversial figure.

From the beginning, Montazeri played a crucial role in shaping the Islamic Republic. As a religious jurist and the author of the most extensive juridical book on *velayat-e faqih*, he lent legitimacy to the post-revolutionary governing system, and as a preacher he did his utmost to garner support for it in his Friday Prayer speeches. In the process, he did his part to exclude other voices from participating in building the new state. He was eventually chosen as the most suitable revolutionary cleric to succeed Khomeini. In the early months and years of the new order, he effectively bore the elitist conventions of conservative Islam.

If enabling a theocratic authoritarian state is part of Montazeri's record, his defiance of the same state constitutes a larger and longer part of his post-revolutionary political story. The seed was sown in the first few years of the Islamic Republic when he challenged the judiciary and the prison system. The opposition of some among the political elite of the Islamic Republic to his nomination as Successor to Khomeini had its roots in these early signs of defiance, and they suspected more was yet to come. They were not wrong. Once he became the Designated Successor, Montazeri began to contest certain actions of the state, especially the widespread executions of political prisoners in 1988.

Considering the charged political context of the period, his declaration that shedding the blood of the innocents could never be justified and thus should not be tolerated by the faithful was significant and daring. It was then that a serious tension started to stir within him. His belief in the Islamic Republic state and the idea that it would guide people on to the path of eternal salvation came into conflict with his experiences and observations. Violence inflicted on the *earthly body* of men and women in the name of protecting the *celestial felicity* of Muslims was the source of the tension. He faulted the state and found its actions unjust and intolerable. It was then that he started to put more emphasis on justice as the standard of religion and not the other way around.

Outside Iran, it was colonialism in both old and new forms that Montazeri found most contrary to justice. His concern for the well-being of the oppressed masses, particularly Muslims, and his subsequent strong support for liberation movements were manifested in this outlook. His goal of helping liberation movements, however, became entangled with Mehdi Hashemi's affair, Iranian factional politics, and the Iran–Iraq war, and hence was never truly realized. Yet, in his spiritual support, particularly for the cause of the Palestinians, he never wavered.

The fall from official power robbed Montazeri of the means to affect policies directly, yet it also unburdened him of the little constraint he felt in criticizing the government. Once again, particularly after the death of Khomeini, he found himself in a position that came naturally to him: being argumentative and speaking truth to power. Montazeri proved to be more effective at being a dissenter than a man in power. For the rest of his life, through his writing, sermons, and teaching, he progressively challenged the Islamic Republic when it violated the principles upon which he believed it was built. He gradually but steadily moved toward advocating a democratic system where popular sovereignty and accountability of the government were institutionalized. He raised these points every chance he got.

Religious Legacy

Montazeri's reputation as a political actor should obscure neither his religious legacy nor his impact on Shii jurisprudence. He was a prominent and accomplished scholar, a grand ayatollah with learned and influential followers. In his letter of dismissal, Khomeini saluted Montazeri as a religious authority, a jurist who could provide religious guidance to all, even to the state. His standing as an authoritative jurist derived from a prolific stream of writings. These included commentaries on the work of his own teachers and studies on a wide range of subjects, including ethics, Islamic taxation, and Islamic governance. In all these technical writings, he demonstrated great knowledge of traditional authoritative sources and skill in employing them in support of his position. Nowhere was his jurisprudential command more evident to many than in *The Jurisprudential Foundation of Islamic State*, a book that has remained a standard reference for supporters of the rule of jurist. However, his greatest impact on reformed Shii political thought appeared in his final, less technical writings.

In these later treatises, he made a case that would effectively diminish the power of the guardian jurist by calling for term limits and transforming the absolute authority of the office to that of a supervisor and guide. Like other reformist clergy, both within and outside Iran, he asked for governmental accountability, separation of powers, a competitive electoral system, and genuine popular participation. Much has been said about Montazeri's everlasting loyalty to the office of the guardian jurist. It is true that he held fast to the concept, or more accurately to the rule of Islamic principles as the guiding light of the state, but that preference remained in the realm of the ideal rather than the domain of the actual.

In practice, he invested people with the authority to choose their own preferred political system. People were no longer only a "tool" to actualize the rule of the leader at the moment of its inception but the real and continuous source of the legitimacy of the state. A corollary of this ruling was his assertion that if people decided to remove the laws of Islam from the realm of politics, neither the state nor the clergy had the right to impose these laws through force. All that could be done by supporters of a religious state was to use the democratic rules and gain a majority support for bringing religion back into the state arena. What this suggests is that Montazeri accepted the legitimacy of a secular state, if put in place democratically. The basis of this decision – acceptance of people's choice of government, even of a secular government – was not expediency or *tazahom*, which are tools for rationalization of new rulings on pragmatic and unsteady basis; even though Montazeri came to it based on his observations within a specific time and space, he made this ruling on the timeless principle of justice and its priority over religion.

Also significant were his rulings on human rights. By recognizing the innate dignity of all humans, regardless of their station in life or faith, he distanced himself from the conservatives, whose primary focus was on the discriminatory "acquired" dignity. He further enlarged that gap by shifting his focus from the duties of humans to their rights. Humans are not just creatures of duties but are the possessors of rights and, therefore, they can have claims over the state and over each other. This was indeed a significant ruling, one with revolutionary implications. It is true that Montazeri was not a liberal and believed that the interest of society has priority over the rights of individuals, but his emphasis on innate rights could be a springboard for a more nuanced interpretation of the supremacy of societal interest over that of the individual.

Pragmatically important was his frequent appeal to the principle of *tazahom* in favor of gentler rules for circumstances where the necessities of contemporary times and sensibilities require them. Despite the already mentioned problems with pragmatism of this kind, his appeal to expediency in modern times allowed him to change his approach to *ravayat*, a promising development for fundamental reform of the traditional *fiqh*. But in some key areas, such as the status of women, he remained squarely within the old traditions – and never came to comprehend the injustice embedded in some of the Islamic laws. He also did not abandon his belief in the superior status of Muslims, both legally and morally, over non-Muslims.

In his later years, Montazeri raised a fundamental question about the value of reason, finding a distinction between its traditional and modern versions. Modern reason was critical and independent, and its verdict was based on dialogue and consensus. Accordingly, reason involved all the necessary elements for making sound judgments. He came to this conclusion as a consequence of his exposure to the realities of the modern world and people within it. He perceived that modern humans were knowledgeable, cosmopolitan, and equipped with the necessary skills to manage the affairs of the country, and therefore were entitled to be participants in decision-making. Montazeri's reflections on reason created an opening for raising the following question: Since modern reason is separate from and "better" than the traditional one, could it be the final judge in making laws without necessarily requiring the retreat of religion from public space? This is at the heart of the debate on the role of religion in the modern world.

Contemporary Local/Global Debate on Public Religion: The Relevance of Montazeri

The debate has been outlined in Chapter 1 of this book. An important part of it revolves around the question of whether the presence of religion in the public space is incompatible with modernity and retards its progress. Supporters of the classical/traditional paradigm of modernization and secularization thesis believe so. But the expansion of public religion in many parts of the modern world occasioned the emergence of a rival literature. As for the specific case of Iran and Shii Islam, there are also two sides in the debate. On one side, a group of secular intellectuals promotes the incompatibility narrative, and to that extent they find their allies in the authoritarian religionists who also see matters in a binary fashion. The difference between the two is that one hopes to expel religion from the public space, while the other wishes to get rid of secularism and give Islam a hegemonic control over that space. Challenging both these forces is a cluster of thinkers consisting of predominately religious reformers who see modernity and secularity as reconcilable with religion. Montazeri's two most famous students, Ahmad Qabel and Mohsen Kadivar, and his devoted family friend and follower, Emad Baghi, are three important voices in this group. Finding solutions for the thorny issues that have plagued traditional Islam and its jurisprudence, such as gender inequality, the inferior status of religious minorities, and the harsh penal code, is at the forefront of their agenda.

Ahmad Qabel (1957–2011) elevated the role of reason over all other authoritative juridical sources and argued that whenever there is a conflict between reason and these other sources, the judgment of the collective reason should prevail.[1] To him, the supremacy of reason was already in the Shii holy texts, and all that was needed was to reread these texts. He advocated a re-examination of established rules, particularly in the area of gender and family. For example, he deemed marriage between a Muslim woman and a non-Muslim man, even one who does not belong to the "People of the Book," permissible. He also promoted the idea of women's equal rights to inheritance (provided that family economic conditions justify it) and divorce. He asserted women's rights to judgeship, *ejtehad*, and political leadership, and made the wearing of head cover optional. In the area of penal code, he argued for removing apostasy from the list of criminal acts.[2] Qabel's premature death prevented him from further expanding on these changes.

Mohsen Kadivar is already a familiar name for the reader of this book. His ideas on traditional and reformed jurisprudence have been sketched in Chapters 5 and 6. What is left to be said is that he arrived at many of his reformed positions through the training he received from Montazeri, his main mentor. In long and sometimes tense conversations with Montazeri, he received permission and eventually the blessing of his Source of Emulation to go further and break with traditional jurisprudence.[3] Based on his belief that modern reason can legitimately question everything and that "justice is the standard of religion," Kadivar criticizes those traditional Islamic laws that permit the discriminatory treatment of women and members of religious minorities and calls for their abrogation.[4] By the same rationale, he defends the legal rights of religious minorities and their equal standing before the law.

The journalist Emad Baghi, a champion of human rights, came to know the ayatollah, with whom he had many opportunities to meet, through his close friend, Sa'id, Montazeri's youngest son. In response to a question I asked him about the impact of Montazeri in shaping his ideas on human rights, Baghi emphasized less Montazeri's juristic position than his actual treatment of people, his respect for individuals (even children), his constant preoccupation with the fate of those who were treated unjustly, particularly the most vulnerable (i.e., political prisoners).[5] Baghi himself is the founder of the Committee for the Defense of Prisoners and has written extensively on matters related to human rights, including a book on *Haqq-e Hayat* (The Right to Life), an anti-capital punishment work. There, he argues that abolishing capital punishment does not contradict Islam and/or its values and that there are ways to appeal to *Shari'at* in order to get rid of cruel punishment, including execution.[6] By doing so, the Islamic Republic of Iran can come closer to bridging its differences with the modern notion of human rights. Even though Baghi is more concerned about the application of laws than with their epistemic foundation, he does pay attention to the problematic of reason, in both its traditional and modern versions. He does so, however, through elaboration of the arguments of others, including Qabel and Montazeri.[7]

Kadivar, Qabel, and Baghi each try to reconcile secularity with religion and modernity with tradition. They are or were (in the case of the deceased Qabel) ardent critics of the Islamic Republic and its efforts to extend control over Iranian society in the name of religion. They advocate a new interpretation of Islam, abrogation of many of its old laws, and a reduction of its sphere of control, so that it can answer the needs of modern Muslims. At the same time, and like their mentor, they believe that religion provides the body of a community with its soul, conscience, and morality, and therefore is an integral part of the experiences of social beings. And therein lies their reason for why faith cannot be confined to the private space and why Islam plays a positive role in the promotion of democracy.

Such positions have made these followers of Montazeri the targets of multipronged criticism by strict seculars. For example, the secular critics find their suggestions for the reform of jurisprudence and their concrete solutions woefully inadequate, akin to superficial dressings for wounds that require major surgery. But, as explained in Chapter 1, it is at the epistemic level, and with a focus on reason, that the secularists attack most seriously the position of the reformers. Some argue that there is an unbridgeable gap between premodern/religious and modern reason, and some go further and assert that religion is an exclusively faith-related matter, where reason has no place.[8]

Linked to this epistemic approach is the secularists' judgment on the appropriate characteristics of participants in a democratic polity. Able to exercise critical reason, a modern secular person has agency and can therefore build and maintain a democratic state. Shackled by faith, a religious/traditional human remains static and subservient and therefore is at home only within an authoritarian political setting. These are the reasons why public religion will harm a modern and democratic society and polity.

Montazeri's students and followers have responded to these charges,[9] but their mentor's record and lived experiences challenge the seculars' assumptions and assertions in their own unique and powerful manner. Montazeri was a grand ayatollah and his credentials would leave no doubt about his "authenticity" as a religious or what secularists might call "traditional" man. In the abstract, this labelling brings certain expectations regarding his action and thought, which relegate him to a time that has passed. But as we know,

Montazeri's life experience involved multiple currents of tradition, modernity, religiosity, and secularity, which problematizes the seculars' dichotomous and neat model of behavior. There might be a temptation to call his efforts to reformulate the laws of his religion and to come to terms with the modern world a naïve, ineffective, disingenuous, and/or ultimately confused project. This temptation becomes stronger when one looks at his philosophical and epistemological positions, all of which were traditional. There is no denying the significance of a philosophical/epistemological foundation in informing a political and legal system and in formulating policies. But it is also difficult to ignore that the same foundation can result in two conflicting paths of emancipation and oppression.[10] On the one hand, the philosophical and epistemic foundations that informed Montazeri's approach to the world led him to keep women under an oppressive system of law, but on the other, they did not prevent him from supporting democracy or acknowledging the dignity and rights of all humans, including the right of Baha'is to citizenship. Since philosophical and abstract foundations can lead to contradictory paths, their importance in the debate on modernity, secularism, and religion needs to be tempered through the inclusion of people's actual stands and social practices.

Montazeri's praxis allows for a project of reconciliation of secularity with religion, modernity with tradition. And that provides a large number of people who wish to be both "modern subject" and "religious faithful" with a cognitive and practical map for negotiating their way in the world.[11] In this might reside Montazeri's most significant legacy.

Notes

1 Qabel, *Shari'at-e Aqlani*, 48–50.
2 Ibid., 51–5.
3 Personal interview with Mohsen Kadivar, August 2015.
4 Mohsen Kadivar, "Bazkhani-ye Huqquq-e Zanan dar Islam: Edalat-e 'Mosavati' be-Ja-ye Edalat-e 'Estehqaqi'" [The Rereading of Women's Rights] (2010), at http://kadivar.com/?p=8931.
5 In Chapter 1 I recounted a story about one of Baghi's most memorable encounters with Montazeri. Another episode that touched him deeply was when he was in prison and Montazeri was dying. On the last night of his life, Montazeri called to his son Sa'id, who had just come back from his trip to Tehran. According to Sa'id, the last sentences that he

heard from his dying father were inquires about the conditions of Baghi and other prisoners. E-mail correspondence with Baghi, July 25, 2015.

6 Emaddedin Baghi, *Haqq-e Hayat* [The Right to Life] (Tehran: Sarai Press, 2007), 21.

7 See Baghi at http://www.emadbaghi.com/archives/001221.php#more.

8 See Mehdi Khalaji's view on reason and his criticism of Qabel in Qabel, *Shari'at-e Aqlani*, 279–82 and Mostafa Malekian, "Johareh Din Bandegist na 'Aqlaniyat" [The Essence of Religion is Obedience not Rationality], at http://bayanbox.ir/view/5688630601044346468/%D9 %85%D8%B5%D8%B7%D9%81%DB%8C-%D9%85%D9%84 %DA%A9%DB%8C%D8%A7%D9%86-%D8%B9%D9%82%D9 %84-%D9%88-%D8%AF%DB%8C%D9%86.pdf.

9 For example, see Qabel's response to Khalaji in Qabel, *Shari'at-e Aqlani*, 117–72 and Kadivar's to Mohammad Reza Nikfar at http://kadivar .com/?p=3493.

10 For example, Enlightenment ideas liberated European individuals from the yoke of oppressive norms, legal systems, and political structures. At the same time, these same ideas justified a colonial structure that oppressed a large number of people, globally.

11 Many participants of the Green Movement regarded Montazeri as their spiritual leader.

Glossary

Allameh title for a member of the clergy who knows all the Islamic sciences

Ayatollah "sign of God"; the title for a high clergyman

Ayatollah ozma grand ayatollah

Basij "mobilization"; a paramilitary volunteer militia formed after the 1979 revolution

Bed'at an arbitrary revision of the established readings of the Islamic laws

Bay'at from the root "*bay*," meaning to shake hands to seal a deal; in Shii political theory, *bay'at* means to give consent to the rule of a leader

Bayt "house"; the household and administrative office of a prominent member of the clergy

Dars-e kharej "external course"; the third and highest level of the *howzeh* education

Ejtehad independent judgment in interpreting Islamic laws

Estedlal seeking *dalil* (proof) through argumentation

Estefta'at "request for decree"; a treatise consisting of responses to followers by a source of emulation

Faqih religious jurist; expert in Islamic laws (plural: *foqahah*)

Fiqh religious law

Fetrat the true essence of a human being; the part of human nature that guides humans toward God

Hadith a saying or action attributed to the Prophet Mohammad or one of the the twelve Infallible Imams (plural: *ahadith*)

Hojjat-ol Islam "proof of Islam"; a title assigned to students who attend the highest-level classes

Hojjat-ol-Islam ol Moslemin a title assigned to those who have received permission to engage in limited *ejtehad*

Howzeh Elmieh "sphere of learning"; a center of religious education

Kalam "discourse," "word," "speech"; Islamic philosophy

Madreseh school for higher religious education, or a seminary
Maktab a traditional elementary school (plural: *makateb*)
Marja' taqlid source of emulation
Marja' taqlid-e tamm supreme/general source of emulation
Marja'iyat the institution or principle of source of emulation
Mojtahed a person who has the permission to interpret Islamic laws
Naqli traditional method of relying on *ravayat*
Ravayat authoritative interpretations of the Prophet's and the
    Infallible Imams' words and actions
Resaleh 'amalieh "practical treatise"; a book of rules to provide
    guidance for followers – required for becoming a source of
    emulation
Sahm-e emam a form of religious tithe; one half of an annual
    religious income tax, given to one's source of emulation
Shii the second dominant sect of Islam, as well as an adherent to that
    sect
Sunni the first dominant sect of Islam, as well as an adherent to that
    sect
Tazahom the conflict between two religious rulings or two *hadith*
Vali guardian
Vali faqih guardian jurist
Waqf religious endowments (plural: *awqhaf*)

Bibliography

Abdo, Genevieve, "Re-thinking the Islamic Republic: A 'Conversation' with Ayatollah Hossein Ali Montazeri," *Middle East Journal* 55, no. 1 (2001): 9–24

Abrahamian, Ervand, *Iran between Two Revolutions* (Princeton, NJ: Princeton University Press, 1982)

  The Iranian Mojahedin (New Haven, CT: Yale University Press, 1989)

  Khomeinism: Essays on the Islamic Republic (Berkeley, CA: University of California Press, 1993)

  Tortured Confessions: Prisons and Public Recantations in Modern Iran, (Berkeley, CA: University of California Press, 1999)

Afshari, Reza, *Human Rights in Iran: The Abuse of Cultural Relativism* (Philadelphia, PA: University of Pennsylvania Press, 2001)

Ahmad, Ahmad, *Memoirs*, ed. Mohsen Kazemi (Tehran: Sureh Mehr Publications, 2005)

Akhavi, Shahrough, *Religion and Politics in Contemporary Iran* (Albany, NY: SUNY Press, 1980)

  "The Thought and Role of Ayatollah Hossein Ali Montazeri in the Politics of Post-1979 Iran," *Iranian Studies* 41, no. 5 (2008): 645–66

Akhzari, Ali and Ali Akbar Kajbaf, "Structure and Social System of the Clergy in Safavid Era," *Interdisciplinary Journal of Contemporary Research in Business* 4, no. 11 (2013): 216–23

Algar, Hamid, "The Oppositional Role of the Ulama in 20th-Century Iran," in *Scholars, Saints, and Sufis*, Nikki Keddie, ed. (Berkeley, CA: University of California Press, 1972)

  "Borujerdi, Hosayn Tabataba'i," in *Encyclopaedia Iranica*, vol. 4, fasc. 4 (1989), 376–9

Alijani, Reza, "Barrasi-ye Mafhoum-e Ertedad" [An Analysis of the Concept of Apostasy], at http://talar.shandel.info/pdf/alijani1011.pdf

Almond, Gabriel and Genco, Stephen, "Clouds, Clocks, and the Study of Politics, *World Politic*, 29 (1977): 489–522

Amanat, Abbas, "In Between the Madrasa and the Marketplace: The Designation of Clerical Leadership in Modern Shi'ism," in *Authority and*

Political Culture in Shi'ism, Said Amir Arjomand, ed. (Albany, NY: SUNY Press, 1998) 98–132

Amirpur, Katajun, "A Doctrine in the Making? Velayat-e Faqih in Post-revolutionary Iran," in *Speaking for Islam: Religious Authorities in Muslim Societies*, Gudrun Krämer and Sabine Schmidtke, eds. (Leiden: Brill, 2006) 219–40

Arasteh, Reza, *Education and Social Awakening in Iran, 1850–1968* (Leiden: Brill, 1969)

Ardestani, Ahmad Sadeq, *Zendeginameh Hojjat-ol Islam Shahid Mohammad Montazeri* [The Life Story of the Martyr Hojjat-ol Islam Mohammad Montazeri] (Qom: Mohammad, 1982)

Arjomand, Said, "Traditionalism in Twentieth Century Iran," in *From Nationalism to Revolutionary Islam* (New York: SUNY Press, 1984)

The Turban for the Crown (New York: Oxford University Press, 1988)

Arkoun, Mohammad, *The Unthought in Contemporary Islamic Thought* (London: Saqi Press, 2002)

Asad, Talal, *Formations of the Seuclar* (Stanford, CA: Stanford University Press, 2003)

Ayazi, Sayyed Mohammad Ali "Negahi be Maktab-e Ejtehadi Ayatollah Montazeri: Mabani va Raveshha" [A Look at Ayatollah Montazeri's School of Ijtehad: Foundation and Methods], at http://www.rahesabz.net/print/48191

Badamchian, Asadollah, *Khaterat-e Montazeri va Naqd-e An* [Montazeri's Memoirs and Its Critique], 2nd ed. (Tehran: Andisheh Nab, 2007)

Bagheri, Ali, "E'lamieh-e Jahani-e Huqquq-e Bashar va E'lamieh Huqquq-e Bashar-e Eslami: Tazadha va Eshterakat" [Universal Declaration of Human Rights and the Islamic Declaration of Human Rights: Incompatibilities and Similarities], at http://adlpub.com/%D8%B9%D9%84%D9%8A-%D8%A8%D8%A7%D9%82%D8%B1%D9%8A-%D8%A7%D8%B9%D9%84%D8%A7%D9%85%D9%8A%D9%87-%D8%AC%D9%87%D8%A7%D9%86%D9%8A-%D8%AD%D9%82%D9%88%D9%82-%D8%A8%D8%B4%D8%B1-%D9%88-%D8%A7%D8%B9%D9%84%D8%A7/

Bani Sadr, Hassan, *My Turn to Speak*, trans. William Ford (Washington, DC: Brassey's US, 1991)

Baghi, Emaddedin, *Vaqe'iyat-ha va Qezavat-ha* [Truths and Judgments] (1998)

Haqq-e Hayat [The Right to Life] (Tehran: Sarai Press, 2007)

Falsafeh Siasi Ejtema'i Ayatollah Montazeri [Ayatollah Montazeri's Political and Social Philosophy] (Tehran: Sarayi Press, 2015)

Bartlett, Frederic C., *Remembering: A Study in Experimental and Social Psychology* (Cambridge: Cambridge University Press, 1954)

Bashi, Golbarg, "The Question of Women: Interview with Ayatollah Montazeri," *Iranian.com* (2006), at http://iranian.com/Bashi/2006/March/Montazeri/index.html

Bashiriyeh, Hossein, *The State and Social Revolution in Iran* (New York: St. Martin Press, 1983)

Bayat, Asef, *Making Islam Democratic: Social Movements and the Post-Islamist Turn* (Stanford, CA: Stanford University Press, 2007)

Post Islamism: The Changing Faces of Political Islam (New York: Oxford University Press, 2013)

Bazargan, Abdol-Ali, ed., *Moshkelat va Masa'el Avalin Sal-e Enqelab az Zaban-e Mohandes Bazargan* [Challenges and Problems of the First Year of Revolution: The Words of Mohandes Bazargan] (Tehran: Daftar Nezhat Azadi, 1983)

Bazargan, Monhandes Mehdi, *Enqelab Iran dar Do Harekat* [Iranian Revolution in Two Movements] (Tehran: Nehzat Azadi, 1984)

Behbudim, Hedayatollah, *Sharh Esm: Zendeqi-Nameh Ayatollah Sayyed Ali Hosseini Khamenei* [Description of the Name: The Life of Ayatollah Sayyid Ali Hosseini Khamenei] (Tehran: Institution for Political Studies and Research, 2012)

Behi, Kambiz, "The 'Real' in Resistance: Transgression of Law as Ethical Act," *Unbound* 4, no. 30 (2008): 30–50

Behrooz, Maziar, "Factionalism in Iran under Khomeini," *Middle Eastern Studies* 27, no. 4 (1991): 597–614

"Tudeh Factionalism and the 1953 Coup in Iran," *International Journal of Middle East Studies* 33 (2001): 363–82

Berger, Peter, *The Sacred Canopy: Elements of a Sociological Theory of Religion* (New York: Anchor Books, 1990/1967)

Bhojani, Ali-Reza, *Moral Rationalism and Shari'a: Independent Rationality in Modern Shi'i Usul al-Fiqh* (Oxon: Routledge, 2015)

Bielefeldt, Heiner, "'Western' versus 'Islamic' Human Rights Conceptions? A Critique of Cultural Essentialism in the Discussion on Human Rights," *Political Theory* 2, no. 1 (2001): 90–121

Boroujerdi, Mehrzad and Shomali, Alireza, "The Unfolding of Unreason: Javad Tabatabai's Idea of Political Decline in Iran," *Iranian Studies* 48, no. 6 (2015): 949–65

Bourdieu, Pierre, *Outline of a Theory of Practice* (Cambridge: Cambridge University Press, 1977)

Brugsch, Heinrich, *Safari be Darbare-ye Soltan-e Sahebqaran*, trans. Mohammad Hossein Kord-Bacheh (Tehran: Etela'at Press, 2010)

Brumberg, Daniel, *Reinventing Khomeini: The Struggle for Reform in Iran* (Chicago, IL: University of Chicago Press, 2001)

Canfield, Robert L., "New Trends among the Hazaras: From 'The Amity of Wolves' to 'The Practice of Brotherhood,'" *Iranian Studies* 37, no. 2 (2004): 241–62

Casanova, Jose, *Public Religions in the Modern World* (Chicago, IL: Chicago University Press, 1994)

"Public Religions Revisited," in *Religion: Beyond the Concept*, Hent de Vries, ed. (New York: Fordham University Press, 2008)

Chehabi, Houchang, *Iranian Politics and Religious Modernism: Liberation Movement of Iran under Shah and Khomeini* (Ithaca, NY: Cornell University Press, 1990)

Cottam, Richard, *Iran and the United States: A Cold War Case Study* (Pittsburgh, PA: University of Pittsburgh Press, 1988)

Dabashi, Hamid, *The Theology of Discontent* (New York: SUNY Press, 1993)

Damad, Sayyed Mostafa Mohaqqeq, "Tahavolat-e Ejtehad Shii: Sayr-e Tarikhi, Howzeh-ha, Shiveh-ha (2)" [The Evolution of Shii *Ejtehad*: Historical Background, *Howzehs*, Methods (2)], *Tahqigat-e Huqquqi* 46 (2007–08): 7–44

Davani, Ali, *Nehzat-e Do Mahe-ye Ruhanyoun –e Iran* [The Two-Month Movement of the Iranian Clergy], 2nd ed. (Tehran: Markaz Asnad-e Eslami, 1998)

Davari, Mahmood T., *The Political Thought of Ayatullah Murtaza Mutahhari* (Oxon: Routledge, 2005)

Davoudi, Rashid "Bazshenasi Ahkam-e Avalieh, Sanaviyeh va Hokumati az Manzar-e Emam Khomeini" [Reinterpretation of Primary, Secondary, and Governmental Ordinances from Imam Khomeini's Perspective], at http://www.jamaran.ir/fa/NewsContent-id_32243.aspx

Dehnavy, M., *Majmoo'a-yi as Mokatebat va Payamha-ye Ayatollah Kashani* [A Collection of Ayatollah Kashani's Correspondence and Messages] (Tehran: Chapakhsh Publications, 1981)

Dehqani, Ashraf, *Hamaseh-e Moqavemat* [The Epic of Resistance], 2nd ed. (London: Cherikha-ye Fada'i Khalq-e Iran Publications, 2004)

Donnelly, Jack, "The Relative Universality of Human Rights" *Human Rights Quarterly*, 29, no. 2 (2007): 281–306

Doustar, Aramesh, *Emtena'-e Tafakor dar Farhang-e Dini* [Abstention from Reflection in a Religious Culture] (Paris: Khavaran Publication, 2004)

Enayat, Hamid, *Modern Islamic Political Thought* (Austin, TX: University of Texas Press, 1982)

Fischer, Michael, *Iran: From Religious Dispute to Revolution* (Cambridge, MA: Harvard University Press, 1980)

"Portrait of a Molla: The Autobiography and Bildungsroman of Agha Najafi Quchani (1875–1943)" *Persica* (1982): 223–57

Ganji, Akbar, ed., *Naqdi bara-ye Tamam-e Fosul* [A Criticism for All Seasons] (Tehran: Tarh-e Nou Press, 1999)

Ghanea Hercock, Nazila, *Human Rights, the UN and the Baha'is in Iran* (Oxford: George Ronald, 2002)

Ghobadzadeh, Naser, *Religious Secularity* (New York: Oxford University Press, 2014)

Giddens, Anthony, *The Constitution of Society: Outline of a Theory of Structuralism* (Cambridge: Polity Press, 1984)

Golpaygani, Lotfollah. *Shahid-e Agah* (1971), digital version, 13–15, at http://toraath.com/index.php?name=Sections&req=viewarticle&artid=168&page=1

Haeri Yazdi, Mehdi, *Hekmat va Hokumat* [Knowledge and Government] (London: Shadi Press, 1995)

Memoirs of Doctor Mehdi Haeri Yazdi (Tehran: Nader Ketab Publications, 2003)

Handlin, Oscar, *Truth in History* (Cambridge, MA: Belknap Press, 1979)

Hashemi Rafsanjani, 'Ali Akbar, *Karnameh va Khaterat-e Hashemi Rafsanjani, 1357–58: Enqelab va Pirouzi*, ed. Abbas Bashiri (Tehran: Daftar Nashr Ma'aref Eslami, 2004)

Karnameh va Khaterat-e Hashemi Rafsanjani, 1361: Pass az Bohran, ed. Fatemeh Hashemi, (Tehran: Daftar Nashr Ma'aref Eslami, 2007)

Karnameh va Khaterat-e Hashemi Rafsanjani, 1362: Aramesh va Chalesh, ed. Mehdi Hashemi (Tehran: Daftar Nashr Ma'aref Eslami, 2007)

Karnameh va Khaterat-e Hashemi Rafsanjani, 1363: Be Su-ye Sarnevesht, ed. Mohsen Hashemi (Tehran: Daftar Nashr Ma'aref Eslami, 2007)

Karnameh va Khaterat-e Hashemi Rafsanjani, 1364: Omid va Delvapasi, ed. Sara Lahuti (Tehran: Daftar Nashr Ma'aref Eslami, 2008)

Karnameh va Khaterat-e Hashemi Rafsanjani, 1365: Oje Defah, ed. Emad Hashemi (Tehran: Daftar Nashr Ma'aref Eslami, 2009)

Karnameh va Khaterat-e Hashemi Rafsanjani, 1366: Defah va Siasat, ed. Alireza Hashemi (Tehran: Daftar Nashr Ma'aref Eslami, 2010)

Karnameh va Khaterat-e Hashemi Rafsanjani, 1367: Payan-e Defah Aghaz-e Bazsazi, ed. Alireza Hashemi (Tehran: Daftar Nashr Ma'aref Eslami, 2011)

Karnameh va Khaterat-e Hashemi Rafsanjani, 1368: Bazsazi va Sazandegi, ed. Ali Lahuti (Tehran: Daftar Nashr Ma'aref Eslami, 2012)

Hobbes, Thomas, *Leviathan*, ed. Richard Tuck (Cambridge: Cambridge University Press, 1991)

Hoveyda, Fereydoun, "Signed, Sealed & Delivered: Casting the Affirmative Vote for Iran in Approving the Universal Declaration of Human Rights in 1948," *Iranian.com* (2005), at http://www.iranian.com/FereydounHoveyda/2005/August/UDHR/index.html

Huntington, Samuel, *The Third Wave: Democracy in the Late Twentieth Century* (Norman, OK: University of Oklahoma Press, 1993)

The Clash of Civilization and the Remaking of the World Order (New York: Penguin Books, 1996)

Izadi, Mostafa, *Faqih-e Aliqadr* [The Exalted Jurist] (Tehran: Soroush Publications, 1982)

Ja'fari, Mohammad Taqi, *Moqayeseh E'lamiyeh Huqquq Bashar Eslami va E'lamiyeh Huqquq Bashar Gharb* [A Comparison of the Islamic Declaration of Human Rights and Western Declaration of Human Rights] (Tehran: The Parliamentary Center for Research, 2011)

Ja'afarian, Hojjat-ol Islam Rasoul, *Jarianha va Sazmanha-ye Siasi-e Iran dar Faseleh Salha-ye 1320–1357* [Iran's Political Movements and Organizations between 1941–1978] (Tehran: Islamic Revolution Document Center, 2006)

Javadi Amoli, Abdollah, *Falsafeh Huqquq-e Bashar* [Human Rights Philosophy] (Qom: Osara' Publications, 1996)

"Sayri dar Mabani-ye Velayat-e Faqih" [A Look at the Foundation of Rule of Jurist], *Hokumat-e Eslami* 1 (Fall 1996): 50

"Ayatollah Allameh Javadi Amoli va Pluralism-e Dini," *Ketab-e Naqd* 4 (Fall 1997): 352–3

Piramoun-e Vahy va Rahbari [On the Subject of Revelation and Leadership] (Qom: al-Zahra Press, 2001)

Kadivar, Mohsen, *Nazariye-haye Dowlat dar Fiqh-e Shii* [Theories of State in Shii Jurisprudence] (Tehran: Nay Publications, 1997)

Hokumat-e Velayi [The Theocratic State], 4th ed. (Tehran: Nay Publications, 2000)

Haqq-ol Naas: Eslam va Huqquq-e Bashar [The Right of Humans: Islam and Human Rights] (Tehran: Kavir Publications, 2007)

Daftar-e Aql [The Book of Reason], 2nd ed. (Tehran: Ettela'at Publications, 2008)

"Bazkhani-ye Huqquq-e Zanan dar Islam: Edalat-e 'Mosavati' be-Ja-ye Edalat-e 'Estehqaqi'" [The Rereading of Women's Rights] (2010), at http://kadivar.com/?p=8931

Dar Mahzar-e Faqih-e Azadeh: Ostad Ayatollah-ol-Ozma Montazeri [In the Presence of the Liberated Jurist: the Mentor Grand Ayatollah Montazeri] (2014), at http://kadivar.com/wp-content/uploads/2014/02/%D8%AF%D8%B1-%D9%85%D8%AD%D8%B6%D8%B1-%D9%81%D9%82%DB%8C%D9%87-%D8%A2%D8%B2%D8%A7%D8%AF%D9%87.pdf

"Questions and Answers, Human Rights and Religious Intellectualism," in *Haqq Ol-Nas* [Human Rights], at http://kadivar.com/?p=7319

Faraz va Foroud Azari Qomi [The Rise and Fall of Azari Qomi], at http://kadivar.com/?cat=1720

Keddie, Nikki, *Roots of Revolution: An Interpretive History of Modern Iran* (New Haven, CT: Yale University Press, 1981)

Religion and Politics in Iran (New Haven, CT: Yale University Press, 1983)

Modern Iran: Roots and Results of Revolution (New Haven, CT: Yale University Press, 2006)

Khalkahli, Sadeq, *Khaterat-e Ayatollah Khalkhali: Avalin Hakem-e Shar' Dadgaha-ye Enqelab* [The Memoirs of Ayatollah Khalkahli: The First Religious Judge of the Revolutionary Court] (Tehran: Sayeh Press, 2005)

Khamenei, Sayyed Ali, *Gozareshi az Sabeqe-ye Tarikhi va Oza' Konouni-e Howzeh-ye 'Elmieh Mashhad* [A Report of Historical Records and Current Conditions of the Mashahad Howzeh] (Mashhad: Imam Reza Global Congress, 1986)

Khomeini, Ahmad, *Ranjnameh be Hazrat-e Ayatollah Montazeri* [The Book of Sorrow to the Excellency, Ayatollah Montazeri] (Tehran: 1989)

Khomeini, Ruhollah, *Kashfol Asrar* [Unveiling of Secrets] (1944)

Velayat-e Faqih: Hokumat Eslami [The Rule of Jurist: The Islamic Government] (Tehran: Amir Kabir Press, 1981)

Sahifeh Imam Khomeini (Tehran: Moasesseh Tanzim va Nashr-e Asar-e Imam Khomeini, 1999)

Kramer, Martin, ed., *Shi'ism, Resistance and Revolution* (Boulder, CO: Westview Press, 1987)

Kunkler, Miriam, "The Special Court of the Clergy and the Repression of Dissident Clergy in Iran," in *The Rule of Law, Islam, and Constitutional Politics in Egypt and Iran*, Said Arjomand and Nathan Brown, eds. (Albany, NY: SUNY Press, 2013), 57–100

Lerner, Daniel, *The Passing of Traditional Society* (New York: Free Press, 1958)

Locke, John, *Second Treatise of Government*, ed. C. B. Macpherson (Indianapolis, IN: Hackett Publishing, 1980)

Lotfi, Mojtaba, ed., *Faraz va Foroud Nafs: Darsha-yi az Akhlaq* [Ascension and Fall of the Soul: Lessons in Ethics] (2010)

Mahdavi Kani, Mohammad Reza, *Memoirs*, ed. Gholam Reza Khajeh Sarvi (Tehran: Islamic Revolution Document Center, 2006)

Makdisi, George. "Muslim Institutions of Learning in Eleventh Century Baghdad," *Bulletin of the School of Oriental and African Studies*, 24, no. 1 (1961): 1–56

Mala'i Tavani, Alireza, *Zendeginameh Siasi Ayatollah Taleqani* [The Political Biography of Ayatollah Taleqani] (Tehran: Nay Publication, 2010)

Malekian, Mostafa, "Johareh Din Bandegist na 'Aqlaniyat" [The Essence of Religion is Obedience not Rationality], at http://bayanbox.ir/view/5688630601044346468/%D9%85%D8%B5%D8%B7%D9%81%DB%8C-%D9%85%D9%84%DA%A9%DB%8C%D8%A7%D9%86-%D8%B9%D9%82%D9%84-%D9%88-%D8%AF%DB%8C%D9%86.pdf

Mamaqani, Ebrahim Khalil Misaq, "Sayri dar Adab-e Maktabkhaneh" [A View on the Manners of Maktabkhaneh], *Honar va Mardom*, nos. 165–6 (1956): 104–8

Martin, Vanessa, *Creating an Islamic State: Khomeini and the Making of a New Iran* (London: I. B. Tauris, 2000)

Matthee, Rudi, "Transforming Dangerous Nomads into Useful Artisans, Technicians, Agriculturists: Education in the Reza Shah Period," *Iranian Studies*, 26, nos. 3/4 (1993): 313–36

Mavani, Hamid, *Religious Authority and Political Thought in Twelver Shi'ism: From Ali to Khomeini* (London: Routledge, 2013)

Mayer, Ann Elizabeth, *Islam and Human Rights* (Boulder, CO: Westview Press, 1995)

Menashri, David, "Iran," *Middle East Contemporary Survey*, 10 (1986): 333
Education and the Making of Modern Iran (Ithaca, NY: Cornell University Press, 1992)
Post Revolutionary Iran: Religion, Society and Power (London: Frank Cass, 2001)

Mesbah Yazdi, Mohammad Taqi, *Amuzesh-e Falsafeh* [Teaching Philosophy], vol. 1 (Tehran: Sazman-e Tablighat-e Eslami, 1987)
"Rabeteh Moteqabel-e Mardom va Hokumat," in *Kavoshha va Chaleshha* [Searches and Battles] (Qom: Imam Khomeini Educational and Research Institute, 2003)
Nazariy-e Siasi-e Eslam, ed. Karim Sobhani (Qom: Imam Khomeini Educational and Research Institute, 2009)
"Legitimacy and Popularity," in *Porseshha va Pasokhha* [Questions and Answers], 8th ed. (Qom: Imam Khomeini Educational and Research Institute, 2012)
Nazariyeh-e Huqquq-e Eslam [The Legal Theories of Islam] (Qom: Imam Khomeini Educational and Research Institute, 2012)

Milani, Mohsen, *The Making of Iran's Islamic Revolution: From Monarchy to Islamic Republic* (Boulder, CO: Westview Press, 1988)

Mill, John Stuart, *On Liberty* (Cambridge, MA: Hackett Publishing, 1978)

Mirmobini, Hossein, "Written Debates with Shi'i Leader 'Ayatollah' Montazeri," in *Persian Cultural Review* (Sacramento, CA: 2006)

Mirsepassi, Ali, *Political Islam, Iran, and the Enlightenment: Philosophies of Hope and Depair* (New York: Cambridge University Press, 2010)

Moghni-ye, Mohammad Javad, *Al-Imam al-Khomeini wa-l-Dowlat al-Islamiyya* (Lebanon: Moassesseh dar al-Ketab al-Islami, 2006)

Moin, Baqer, *Khomeini: Life of the Ayatollah* (New York: St. Martin Press, 2009)

Montazeri, Hossein Ali, *The Jurisprudential Foundation of Islamic State* (Tehran: Sarayi Press, 2000)

    Dars-ha'i az Nahj-ol Balagheh [Lessons from Nahj-ol Balagheh], ed. Emaddedin Baghi (Tehran and Qom: Sarayi Press, 2001)

    Khaterat [Memoirs] (Los Angeles, CA: Sherkat Ketab Corp, 2001)

    Didgahha [Points of View], 3 volumes (Qom, 2002)

    Az Aghaz ta Anjam: Goftegooye Do Daneshjoo [From Beginning to End: The Conversation of Two University Students] (Tehran: Sarayi Press, 2003)

    Ma'aref va Ahkam-e Banovan [Knoweldge and Rulings for Ladies] (Isfahan: Mobarak Publication, 2004)

    Estefta'at (Tehran: Sayeh Publications, 2005)

    Mo'ud-e Adyan [The Promise of Religions] (Tehran: Kherad Ava Publications, 2005)

    Resaleh Huqquq [Treatise on Rights], 4th ed. (Tehran: Sarayi Publications, 2005)

    Eslam Din-e Fetrat [Islam: The Religion for Human Essence] (Tehran: Sayeh Publication, 2006)

    Hokumat-e Dini va Huqquq Ensan [Islamic Government and Human Rights] (Tehran: Sarayi Press, 2008)

    Mabaniye Nazari-ye Nabovvat [The Theoretical Foundation of Prophecy] (Qom: Arghavan-e Danesh Publications, 2008)

    Mojazatha-ye Eslami va Huqquq-e Bashar [Human Rights and Islamic Penal Code] (Qom: Arghavan-e Danesh, 2008)

    Enteqad az Khod: Ebrat va Vasiyat [Self-Criticism: Lessons and Last Will], ed. Sa'id Montazeri (2009), at https://amontazeri.com/ayatollah/censure/336

    Estefta'at (Tehran: Argavan Danesh Publications, 2009)

    Resaleh-e Estefta'at, vols. 1 and 2 (Tehran: Sayeh Publications), vol. 3 (Tehran: Arghavan-e Danesh, 2009)

Motahhari, Morteza, *Takamol-e Ejtemah* [The Evolution of Society] (Tehran: Tavakol Press, 1993)

Mottahedeh, Roy Parviz, *The Mantle of the Prophet* (New York: Simon and Schuster, 1985)

    "Introduction" in Muhammad Baqir al-Sadr, *Lessons in Jurisprudence* (Oxford: Oneworld, 2003)

    "Afterword," in *Shari'a: Islamic Law in the Contemporary Context*, Abbas Amanat and Frank Griffel, eds. (Stanford, CA: Stanford University Press, 2007) 178–82

"The Quandaries of Emulation: The Theory and Politics of Shi'i Manuals of Practice" (2011), at http://depts.washington.edu/nelc/pdf/event_files/ziadeh_series/Ziadeh2011Booklet_FINAL.pdf

Na'ini, Mohammad Hossein, *Tanbih al-Umma wa Tanzih as-Milla, ya Hokumat az Nazar-e Eslam*, edited with commentary by Mahmud Taleqani (Tehran: 1955)

Nejad, Masoud Kuhestani, *Chalesh-e Mazhab va Modernism: Sayr-e Andishe-ye Siasi-Mazhabi dar Iran, Nimey-eh Aval-e Qarn-e Bistom* [The Battle of Religion and Modernism: The History of Political Religious Thought in Iran, The First Half of Twentieth Century] (Tehran: Nay Publications, 2002)

Nikfar, Mohammad Reza, "Elahiyat-e Shekanjeh" (2009), at http://www.nilgoon.org/archive/mohammadrezanikfar/pdfs/Nikfar_Theology_of_Torture.pdf

Opwis, Felicitas, "Islamic Law and Legal Change: The Concept of Maslaha in Classical and Contemporary Islamic Legal Theory," in *Shari'a: Islamic Law in the Contemporary Context*, Abbas Amanat and Frank Griffel, eds. (Stanford, CA: Stanford University Press, 2007), 62–81

Pateman, Carole, *The Sexual Contract* (Stanford, CA: Stanford University Press, 1988)

Qabel, Ahmad, *Shari'at-e Aqlani* [The Reasoned Islamic Laws] (2013), at www.ghabel.net

Qane'i-Nejad, Erfan, *Dar Damgah-e Hadeseh: Goftegou-yi ba Parviz Sabeti, Modir-e Amniyat Dakheli-ye Savak* [In the Trap of Events: A Conversation with Parviz Sabeti, The Savak Internal Division Director] (Los Angeles, CA: Sherkat Ketab, 2012)

Quchani, Aqa Najafi, *Siahat-e Sharq va Gharb* [Journey to East and West] (Qom: Afarineh Press, 1998)

Rahimi, Babak, "Democratic Authority, Public Islam, and Shi'i Jurisprudence in Iran and Iraq: Hussain Ali Montazeri and Ali Sistani." *International Political Science Review* 33, no. 2 (2012): 193–208

Rahnama, Ali, *An Islamic Utopian: A Political Biography of Ali Shari'ati* (London: I. B. Tauris, 1998)

Nirouha-ye Mazhabi dar Bastar-e Harekat-e Nehzat-e Melli [Religious Forces within the Current of the Nationalist Movement] (Tehran: Game No Press, 2005), 57–9

Rajaee, Farhang, *Islamic Values and World View: Khomeini on Man, the State and International Politics* (Lanham, MD: University Press of America, 1983)

"Post-Revolutionary Historiography in Iran," in *Musaddiq, Iranian Nationalism and Oil*, James Bill and W. Roger Louis, eds. (Austin, TX: University of Texas Press, 1988), 118–40

Randjbar Daemi, Siavush, "Building the Islamic State: The Draft Constitution of 1979 Reconsidered," *Iranian Studies* 46, no. 4 (2013): 641–63

Rayshahri, Mohammad, "Montazeri: az Owj ta Forud" [Montazeri: The Rise and Fall], *Arzeshha* (January–February 1998): 5
Khatereha [Memoirs] (Tehran: Islamic Revolution Document Center, 2004), 4

Reza'i Esfahani, Mohammad Ali, "Shiveha-ye Tahsil va Tadriss dar Howzeha-ye Elmieh" [Methods of Learning and Teaching in Seminaries], *Payam-e Howzeh* 12 (1997): 289–303

Roy, Olivier, "Afghanistan: An Islamic War of Resistance," in *Fundamentalism and the State*, M. Marty and R. S. Appleby, eds. (Chicago, IL: University of Chicago Press, 1993), 490–510

Sadowski, Yahya, "The New Orientalism and the Democracy Debate," *Middle East Report* 183 (July–August 1993): 14–21

al-Sadr, Sayyed Mohammad Baqer, *The Emergence of Shi'ism and the Shi'ites*, trans. Asaad F. Shaker (Montreal: Imam Ali Foundation, 2006)

Sahabi, Ezatollah, *Nagofteh haye Enqelab va Mabahes-e Bonyadi-i Melli* [The Unsaid of the Revolution and the Fundamental National Issues] (Tehran: Gam-e Nou, 2004)

Sajjadipur, Hadi, *The Fourth Session of the Islamic Consultative Assembly* (Tehran: Islamic Revolution Document Center, 2009)

Salehi Najafabadi, Ne'matollah, *Shahid-e Javid* [The Eternal Martyr], 9th ed. (Qom, 1970)

Salimi Namin, Abbas, *Pasdasht-e Haqqiqat* [Guarding the Truth] (Tehran: Daftar Motale'at va Tadvin Tarikh Iran, 2000)

San'ati, Reza, *Gofteman-e Mesbah: Gozareshi az Zendegani-ye Elmi va Siasi Ayatollah Mesbah Yazdi* [Mesbah's Discourse] (Tehran: Entesharat-e Markaz-e Asnad-e Enqelab-e Eslami, 2008)

San'ei, Yousef, *Chekide-ye Andisheha* [The Summary of Reflections] (Qom: Maysam Tamar Publications, 2008)

Sanjabi, Karim, *Omid ha va na-Omidiha* [Hopes and Despairs] (London: Jebheh Melliun Iran, 1989)

Schirazi, Asghar, *The Constitution of Iran: Politics and the State in the Islamic Republic* (London: I. B. Tauris, 1997)

Sewell, William, "A Theory of Structure: Duality, Agency, and Transformation," *American Journal of Sociology* 98 (1992): 1–29

Shabestari, Mohammad Mojtahed, *Hermeneutic, Ketab va Sonnat* [Hermeneutics, the Book and the Tradition], 2nd ed. (Tehran: Tarh-e Nou Press, 1998)
Naqdi bar Qaraat Rasmi az Din: Bohranha, Chaleshha, Rahehalha [A Critique of Official Interpretation of Religion: Crises, Battles, Solutions] (Tehran: Tarh-e Nou, 2002)

Shahram, Mohammad Taqi *Bayanieh Elam-e Mavazeh-e Ideologic Sazman-e Mojahedin-e Khalq-e Iran* [Statement on the Ideological Stands of People's Mojahedin of Iran], at http://www.peykarandeesh.org/PeykarArchive/Mojahedin-ML/bayaniyeh-1354.html

Shari'ati, Ali, "Ma va Iqbal," in *Majmou'eh Asar*, vol. 5 (Tehran: Elham, 1995)

Shirkhani, Ali, *Hamase-ye 17 Khordad 1354-e Madrase-yi Fayziyah* [The Epic of Fayziyah Seminary's Uprising of June 7, 1975] (Tehran: Islamic Revolution Document Center, 1998)

Siavoshi, Sussan, *Liberal Nationalism in Iran: The Failure of a Movement* (Boulder, CO: Westview Press, 1990)

    "Ayatollah Misbah-Yazdi: A Voice of Authoritarian Islam," *Muslim World* 100, no. 1 (2010): 124–44

Siegel, Evan, "The Politics of Shahid-e Jawid," in *The Twelver Shia in Modern Times: Religious Culture and Political History*, Rainer Brunner and Werner Ende, eds. (Leiden: Brill, 2001), 150–77

    "The Case of Mehdi Hashemi," at http://iran.qlineorientalist.com/Articles/MehdiHashemi/MehdiHashemi.html

Soroush, Abdolkarim, *Qabs va Bast Teorik-e Shari'at: Nazariy-e Takamol-e Ma'refat-e Dini* [Theoretical Constriction and Expansion of Shar'ia: The Theory of Evolution of Religious Knowledge] (Tehran: Serat, 1994)

    "Fiqh dar Tarazou" [*Fiqh* on the Scale], *Kian*, 46 (1999): 15

Sultani Najafabadi, Muhammed Ali, *Tazkireh Shu'ara-yi Najafabad* [Biography of Poets of Najababad] (Isfahan: 1975)

Tabatabai, Javad, *Dibacheh-i bar Nazari-ye Enhetat-e Iran* [An Introduction to the Theory of Iran's Decline] (Tehran: Nigah-e Mo'aser, 2002)

Taleqani, Mahmud, *Az Azadi ta Shahadat* [From Freedom to Martyrdom] (Tehran: Abuzar Publication, 1979)

Tavakoli-Tarqhi, Mohamad, "Anti-Baha'ism and Islamism in Iran," in *The Baha'is of Iran*, Dominic Parviz Brookshaw and Seena B. Fazel, eds. (Oxon: Routledge, 2008), 200–31

Tilly, Charles and Tarrow, Sidney, *Contentious Politics* (Boulder, CO: Paradigm Publishers, 2007)

Vahdat, Farzin, "Post-revolutionary Discourses of Mohammad Mojtahed Shabestari and Mohsen Kadivar: Reconciling the Terms of Mediated Subjectivity" *Critique* 16 (2000): 31–54 and 17 (2000): 13–57

    "Mehdi Haeri Yazdi and the Discourse of Modernity,"in *Iran: Between Tradition and Modernity*, Ramin Jahanbegloo, ed. (Oxford: Lexington Books, 2004), 51–70

von Schwerin, Ulrich, *The Dissident Mullah: Ayatollah Montazeri and the Struggle for Reform in Revolutionary Iran* (London: I. B. Tauris, 2015)

Walbridge, Linda S., ed., *The Most Learned of the Shi'a. The Institution of the Marja Taqlid* (New York: Oxford University Press, 2001)

Proceedings

The Proceedings of the Assembly for the Final Review of the Constitution of the Islamic Republic (Tehran: Office of Cultural Affairs and Public Relations of the Islamic Consultative Assembly, 1985), 3 vols

Document Banks

FBIS, *Foreign Broadcast Information Service*
Markaz-e Asnad Enqelab-e Eslami, http://www.irdc.ir/Search.aspx?lang=fa
Markaz-e Barresi-e Asnad-e Tarikhi

Newspapers

Enqelab-e Eslami, daily
Ettela'at, daily
Hamshahri, daily
Jomhuri-e Eslami, daily
Kayhan, daily
Rajanews, daily
Resalat, daily
Sobh-e Emruz, daily

Index

Abdo, Genevieve, 3
Abuzar group, 83
academic life. *See* religious scholar, Montazeri as
ACC (Association of Combatant Clergy or *Majma'eh Rohaniyoun Mobarez*), 161
Afghanistan, post-revolutionary foreign policy regarding, 124, 125–7, 140
AFRC (Assembly for the Final Review of the Constitution), 107–10, 195, 200, 243
Aghajari, Hashem, 248
ahkam-e hokumati, 159, 204, 216
Ahmad Ahmad, 81
Ahmadinejad, Mahmoud
  Amoli and, 210
  Green Movement and 2009 elections, 1, 181–4
  presidency of (2005–2013), 179–81, 219
Akhavi, Shahrough, 3
Akhbari school, 52, 213
Alam, Asadollah, 64
Albright, Madeleine, 223
Ali (successor of Mohammad and first Shii Imam), 48, 195
Alviri, Morteza, 165
American embassy occupation. *See* hostage crisis
Amini, Ali, 62
Amoli, Abdollah Javadi
  on hegemonic control of public space by religion, 8
  on human rights, 238
  on state-society relations, 205, 209–11, 230, 231
Anvari, Mohammad Baqer Mohiyeddin, 77

apostasy, in penal code, 248–51
Arafat, Yasser, 103
Araki, Mohammad Ali, 160, 166, 169, 170, 173
Aristotle, 202
Assembly for the Final Review of the Constitution (AFRC), 107–10, 195, 200, 243
Assembly of Eleven, 72, 73, 74
Assembly of Experts, 110, 119, 136, 159, 160, 162, 201, 219, 232
assembly, freedom of, 244
Association of Combatant Clergy (ACC or *Majma'eh Rohaniyoun Mobarez*), 161
Ayat, Hassan, 107

Badamchian, Asadollah, 92, 191
Baghi, Emaddedin, 11, 40, 133–4, 251, 275, 276, 278
  Vaqe'iyat-ha va Qezavat-ha (1998), 156, 158
Baha'is
  clerical concern with perceived power of, 63, 257
  evolving views of Montazeri on civil status of, 256–9
  Monazereh Mosalman va Baha'i (The Debate of a Muslim and a Baha'i, Montazeri; 1951), 257
  Montazeri's role in suppression of, 243, 257–8
Bakhtiar, Shapur, 88, 89, 92, 100
Bakhtiar, Taymour, 73
band-e jim, 117, 137
Bani Sadr, Hassan
  Khomeini on, 144, 152
  Ahmad Khomeini supporting, 156